CONTENTS

CW01501336

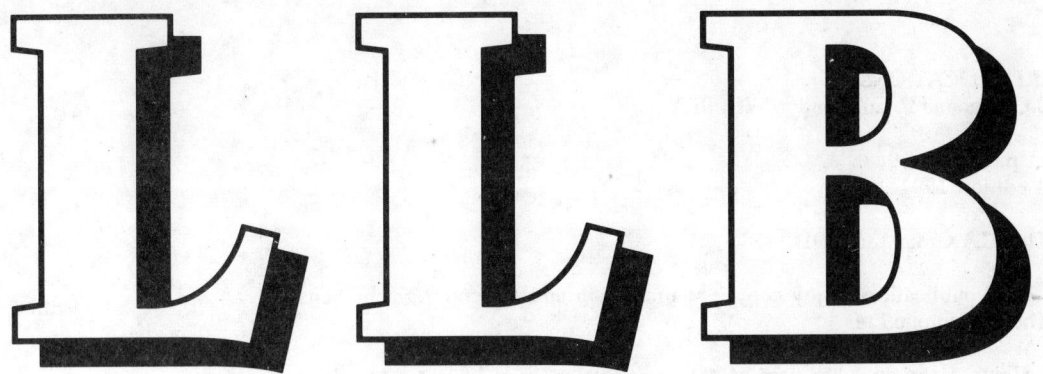

JURISPRUDENCE AND LEGAL THEORY Textbook

2nd edition

Rowel Genn
LLB (QUB), LLM (Lond)

Revised and updated by K P Bampton
LLB

HLT Publications

HLT PUBLICATIONS
200 Greyhound Road, London W14 9RY

First published 1988
2nd edition 1991

ISBN 1 85352 389 5

ACKNOWLEDGEMENT
The publishers and author would like to thank The Incorporated Council of
Law Reporting for England and Wales for kind permission to reproduce
extracts from the Weekly Law Reports.

British Library Cataloguing-in-Publication.

A CIP Catalogue record for this book is available from the British Library.

Printed and bound in Great Britain

PREFACE

HLT Textbooks are written specifically for students. Whatever their course, they will find our books clear and concise, providing comprehensive and up-to-date coverage. Written by specialists in their field, our textbooks are reviewed and updated on an annual basis.

This Jurisprudence textbook is designed for use by undergraduates who have jurisprudence within their syllabus.

The contents of different syllabuses in this subject vary considerably, so that emphasis in this text is inclined towards the London University LLB. However, it should be of equal interest to any student of jurisprudence.

Due to the nature of the subject the student is encouraged to challenge the evaluations of the writers. Any Jurisprudence textbook should be regarded as essays on, rather than simply representing, the views of the jurists examined.

This edition includes: a re-evaluation of the relevance of Marxism in the light of recent developments; a section introducing and examining linguistic and semiotic approaches; an expansion on the influential views of Dworkin as well as other additions. However, a considerable amount of the text (Chapters 9-12, and 20) is as in the previous edition and other sections (Chapters 8, 15 and 18) stand, with minor amendments, as written by Rowel Genn.

The developments represent the jurisprudential debate as at 1 May 1991.

TABLE OF CASES

1 THE NATURE OF JURISPRUDENCE

1.1   The relevance of jurisprudence

You are probably opening this book with some trepidation. Jurisprudence and Legal Theory never was the most popular of subjects taken at the LLB degree course. Perhaps this is because it is compulsory when all other topics at part two are optional. Perhaps it is because of a received prejudice; however, whatever the reason there is much value in a jurisprudence course. This book should be read as an introduction to the subject and not as an alternative to core material.

a) *The relevance of jurisprudence*

   i) *The attitude of Common Law lawyers*

   There is in the English tradition a scepticism for anything theoretical in connection with the law. This is in marked contrast to the position in Europe where theoretical perspectives are welcomed. In English law schools most of the lecturers are also practitioners in the law and have little time for what they perceive to be 'waffle'. Those who profess a leaning towards the practice of law argue that if a client came through the door of their office seeking legal advice on, say, being charged with theft, only to find the lawyer explain the law of theft in terms of societal protection of the fundamentally moral institution of property he would doubtless seek the advice of another lawyer, to the loss of a criminally aided case for the jurisprudentially minded lawyer. Put in such a manner it is clear that jurisprudence is of no assistance to the practitioner of law. Yet in their practice lawyers continually apply much from jurisprudence. Their attitudes display a type of approach to the subject of law that would legitimately be the scope of inquiry of a jurisprudence course. If law students were to avoid the study of jurisprudence they would in effect be accepting other people's views on the issues within the jurisprudence course without question. If the lecturer told the student X then the student would accept X without necessarily knowing why or how. Jurisprudence shows the student what questions need to be asked and gives guidance on how others have sought to answer these questions.

   ii) *The arguments*

   Lenin once wrote that 'theory without practice is pointless and practice without theory is mindless.' He was espousing a Marxist notion that the point was not so much to interpret the world as to change it. Without necessarily adopting a Marxist analysis in the context of jurisprudence it could be argued that practice without a theoretical matrix would indeed be mindless, whilst acknowledging at the same time that theory without practice would be pointless. With this in mind and in spite of the heavy leaning towards a practical training in English law schools and of the practitioners's scepticism of the subject, it is proposed in this book to demonstrate the relevance of the subject to the practitioner. In doing so one is constrained by the scope of the syllabus as laid down by the University of London for their external LLB degree course. Students taking other courses should check whether the content of this book is adequate to cover the extent and scope of their syllabi.

b) *What to expect*

Jurisprudence is not like the other topics that one studies for the LLB degree. It calls for and expects a student to develop a capacity for critical thought rather than the dogmatic acceptance of legal rules as part of the natural order and the learning by rote of the course material. It is essentially an interdisciplinary study. As Dias has written in his *Jurisprudence* the course is designed to show the student ... 'How to think profitably and for yourself as well as educate and equip you to be an efficient lawyer.' This is an admirable goal. It can be likened to the construction of a matrix for the substantive law information absorbed in the other eleven substantive law subjects studied for the University of London external LLB degree which contain the detailed rules of law. Students become practised at applying those rules of law to hypothetical problem situations under examination conditions, yet there is almost no understanding of the role of those rules in society; why those rules were developed in the way they were; and indeed underlying this exercise is an unquestioning acceptance of the method of identification of these rules. Jurisprudence seeks to challenge this. The examiners in this subject write that '... A law student, if he is to have a real understanding of his subject, must not be content with mastering the different branches of the law. He must also try to find answers to some fundamental questions about the nature of law, its place in society and how a legal system operates both as a system of rules and as a social institution. He must examine the relationship between law and morality and law and justice. It is the object of a course in jurisprudence to examine these issues critically...'

c) *The technique of jurisprudence*

By its nature the course is rather like a jigsaw puzzle where the whole picture can only be ascertained upon completion of the whole course. The student is therefore advised to continue to put each piece of the course into its place. Experience shows that later in the course the pieces start falling into place. The course is also far too wide for any student practically to cover all the material required given that this is only one of four topics being taken by those on the full time course. Hence there will be a need to develop a critical evaluative approach to the topics being studied. It is suggested that the student should read the theories in an effort to understand what they are saying as opposed to what has occasionally wrongly been attributed to them and then to place that within an historical and political perspective. It is a theme of this book that these theories were not developed under conditions of inspiration such as Newton enjoyed for the law of gravity, sitting (as the legend goes) under an apple tree. They are a product of their time and of their circumstance and are heavily tinted with the political outlook of their authors. This is more clear with regard to some of the theories within this course and more obscure with regard to others. As Finch rightly observes, a jurist cannot conceal his education, social philosophy or ideology for ever. These are what the distinguished American Justice of the Supreme Court, Oliver Wendell Holmes, called 'the inarticulate major premises'of any thesis. The student should be concerned to identify these during the course of his reading.

The student should then examine the criticisms that have been made of the theory, reflect on these and evaluate their validity in the light of his own legal knowledge. In this way the student will develop his own understanding of law and the legal system. Essentially the student should enter into a dialogue with the texts being read. Imagine the person who wrote the text was beside you. You do not try to learn what the other person in a conversation is saying. Rather one engages them in the conversation and either agrees or disagrees with what they are saying. Once again the personal views of the student become important. In your other courses you have been told by your lecturers (and I am as 'guilty'as other lecturers in this regard) to leave your personal views at the entrance to the seminars because therein we are interested in the law as it is laid down – a strict logical application of the legal rules to the hypothetical factual situation in hand. Over time I imagine that students forget they have any personal views. Well, now is the time to find them again.

Professor Twinning has identified three levels on which to read a jurisprudence text:

i) The historical level – placing the text in its historical perspective – what were the issues of the day on which the text was written? Today many of those issues may be wholly irrelevant. In examining a text on its historical level it should be borne in mind what was available to that author. Who was he replying to? What was the problem at that time? Whose work was available at that time?

ii) On the analytical level – where it would be appropriate to examine the questions raised, scrutinise the answers given and then evaluate the reasons provided for those answers. On this level it is important that the student clarifies the nature of the question before accepting the author's answer. Some questions do contain false assumptions and it would be necessary to identify these.

iii) On the applied level – here the student examines the implications of accepting the position outlined by the author. I suppose the question really is 'so what?'in reading the text. It is on this level that one can decide why the author wrote what he did when he did particularly with regard to the political implications of the text.

This is what will be required from the student of jurisprudence. The technique required for 'doing jurisprudence' is to engage in such a critical and evaluative discussion. This requires the student to develop his own understanding and illustrates that there is no right answer to a question in jurisprudence – although there are plenty of wrong answers!

1.2 The scope of jurisprudence

By its very nature this is a topic whose province has been determined and redetermined from time to time. It is not thought helpful to set out a delimitation to the topic at the outset. Different authors set their own task for jurisprudence. Mention has been made of the views of Dias who thinks that jurisprudence is all about developing into a good lawyer. Finch, on the other hand, in his *Introduction to Legal Theory*, takes the view that the task of legal theory is to examine the characteristic features essential to law and common to legal systems. There is some debate about whether the course is one of jurisprudence or of legal theory or indeed whether it contains elements of legal philosophy. I cannot see the value in examining these labels. This course covers some schools of thought; some individual theorists; addresses some particular questions and even some general questions. The best description of this course is as an introduction to the area of jurisprudence and legal theory.

a) *Classifications*

There are different classifications of jurisprudence. General jurisprudence is concerned with speculations about law as distinct from speculations about a specific law. There are many ways to arrange the questions that are posed in general jurisprudence. One will not find any agreed list from the literature. Questions such as the following seem to be common to most:

What is 'law'?

What is a legal system?

Should law enforce morality?

How does the nature of society affect law?

What role does law play in society?

What is the purpose of law?

Is law just?

These are a few of the relevant questions that are the concern of general jurisprudence. They demonstrate that general jurisprudence is the area where the work of the legal scientist overlaps with other disciplines such as morality, anthropology, politics and economics. These questions make up a substantial portion of the course covered in this manual. The student ought to be thinking about some of these questions throughout the course. Experience shows that if an attempt is made to answer these at an early stage in the course, and in my view that should be encouraged, these answers will undergo a substantial change towards the latter part of the course when the questions may be re-asked.

General jurisprudence is, according to Harris in *Legal Philosophies*, of little value in instilling the technical skills of legal reasoning and argumentation. He believes that these skills come as he puts it from 'immersing oneself in substantive legal studies'. On the other hand he sees some value in particular jurisprudence which involves speculations about particular legal concepts such as rights and duties.

In raising these questions answers are not always provided. The theorists are studied, it is suggested, because they throw light on these rather difficult topics. The perception remains that of the onlooker. In a study by King entitled *The Concept, the Idea and the Morality of Law* (1966) the author asks whether it is possible to define the object of inquiry without anticipating the result. Take the work of John Rawls (see infra). His theory of justice arrives at the conclusion that might be expected from a democratic liberal viewing justice as fairness yet subjecting economic inequality to political equality. Did he only arrive at that view after writing his book or did he have in mind his conclusion before he set pen to paper? The argument that King makes out is that the law concept, being the basic concept about law, has a considerable influence on subsequent exposition. By reflecting on this point at an early stage the student will equip himself to deal with the plethora of literature that he is required to deal with on this course.

b) *Course content*

By way of a general introduction to the content of this course one would point out that this manual will be covering topics connected with the nature and working of law by examining the nature of laws and of the legal system, by examining the relationship, if any, between law and justice and morality, and then examining the social nature of law. Also considered will be questions concerning rights and the rudiments of moral argument, the nature of legal authority and the question of why laws are obeyed and finally the justifications/reasons that are given for the decisions in cases through an examination of legal reasoning.

1.3   A word about words

a) *Words*

The tools of the lawyer's trade are words. These tools are not expressible in terms of mathematical precision, yet they are the only tools available with which the lawyer will perform his function. This can be seen as the cause of many of the problems of the law. The majority of appellate court cases concern the construction of words and phrases used in statutes. As Oliver Wendell Holmes observed, 'words are not crystals', they are not clear. They are capable of different meanings. Jurisprudence according to Holmes should be concerned with the reality of the legal experience. To that extent definitions are useful if they correspond to the way in which lawyers actually behave and think. Otherwise a definition is of no value. Pollock reinforces this by stipulating that '... a definition would have no business to prejudge how far that is the case ...'

There is much in jurisprudence concerned with definitions. Indeed one of the earlier writers on this course, John Austin, sought by definition to determine the limits of the course of study in his *Province of Jurisprudence Determined*. The problems with definitions are that they are derived from inadequate prior knowledge and that they involve misconceptions formed at the outset which further burden the definition, and thirdly that they impose artificial limits on the area of study. Professor Hart has attacked the usefulness of building a theory on the back of definition and shown that it is preferable to engage in an essay in 'descriptive sociology'- descriptive at least of concepts.

Professor HLA Hart has identified in words a core of settled meanings around which there will be no dispute and a penumbral area of doubt in which disputes will arise. Say a hypothetical law provided that all vehicles were to be taxed at £100 per annum. Within that core meaning would come cars and lorries, but what about a skateboard? Or a spaceship? Or a chariot? The issue would become important when a person in control of a chariot was charged with failing to tax his 'vehicle'. He would not argue that the law was unjust, rather he would argue that it did not apply to chariots. The whole issue will be determined on the basis of the interpretation given to the words.

The same problem is faced in jurisprudence where many problems can be reduced to one of semantics. Indeed the work of WN Hohfeld (infra) attempted to clarify some of the linguistic problems surrounding the use of the word 'right'. Wittgenstein observed that the meaning of the word depends on the context in which it is used; 'the meaning of a word is its use in the language.' The context will require an explanation for the whole sentence or phrase. Hence the phrase that X owns Y will require an explanation of the concept of ownership. Would it include the control over Y exercised by a thief? Would it include the right of a tenant to enjoy for the present exclusive possession of the property? In many instances this approach will be satisfactory; however, even then, it will not be sufficient in all cases.

Since language is dynamic the meaning of words can shift. An example would be the use of the word 'gay'which has changed in time to have a meaning not that with which it was originally used.

b) *Language*

There are three distinct purposes for which language can be used. They are all connected with communication. These are to cause the listener to act either by command (get up!) or by the giving of information or by persuasion. It is in the realm of persuasion that the jurists are writing.

I do not propose to give attention to the first two of these categories. With regard to persuasion it can be observed that some statements are capable of being proved while others are not. Those that cannot be proved are matters of opinion. They can neither be proved nor verified. Are Chelsea FC the best football team in the world? Statements which refer to facts should be distinguished from statements of facts. They differ in that they can be expressed at different levels of generality. Dias observes that an inference or matter of opinion, whilst it cannot be verified, may however still be checked in order to see whether it is an admissible statement of fact based on that occurrence.

When reading texts in jurisprudence it is crucial to bear in mind that different authors use the same term to describe different things. This leads to no end of confusion unless the student is prepared to identify exactly what the author is trying to say. It would not be appropriate for example to criticise someone for saying something they did not actually say. Terms are the most difficult in this regard. For example the term 'natural law'is used by many authors yet they all mean something different. They are not talking about the same phenomenon.

A word of warning – some words carry an emotive element which according to Dias lends illegitimate weight to a statement. It will be the task of the jurisprudence student to cut through that emotive use of language. Emotion is no substitute for rational argument.

c) *The is/ought distinction*

The student should remain ever vigilant for what David Hume terms the 'illicit transition' from the ought to the is. In his *Treatise on Human Nature* he criticises an example of argumentation that seems logical because of the ambiguity of language, but results in illogical propositions. There are two aspects to this mistake.

i) *Confusing factual propositions with normative ones*

If I step out of a twentieth floor window into thin air, there is a strong possibility, one might say a certainty, that I might fall. This is because objects that are denser than air usually are susceptible to the law of gravity. Without more information one cannot say for sure that I will fall – I might be suspended by a wire. Therefore the proper expression of the situation is:

'A person who steps out of a twentieth floor window into thin air *ought to* fall.'

This is a statement of probability on the basis of past experience. It is not necessarily a fact, since, as I have pointed out, there may be some other force exerted upon me. However, let us look at a different situation.

Most people in England consume alcohol, especially in pubs. If I went into a pub, there is a probability that I will consume alcohol. One might alternatively say:

'A person in a pub *ought* to consume alcohol.'

This would be a correct statement of probability, but in a badly expressed form. It sounds as if I am suggesting that I would prefer people in pubs to drink – that they are obliged to do so. There is thus a difference between a statement that is descriptive of factual probability and a normative statement that expresses the desire that something should be so. However, it is perfectly easy, by using normal language to cross from a descriptive statement about people's drinking habits to a normative statement about what those habits should be.

There is thus a difference between factual 'oughts' and normative 'oughts'. Legal statements are of the second kind. They do not describe what people actually do, they prescribe what people ought to do.

However, another problem arises. The law says that we should pay our taxes (a normative or prescriptive statement). People generally pay their taxes because of the law. As such, the statement that people ought to pay their taxes also coincides with the factual truth. People ought (are likely) to pay their taxes.

But this in no way explains why a person is obliged to pay taxes, other than because the law wants people to. We should not confuse a descriptive statement of probability with the reason for obeying a prescriptive statement. Thus, there is a fundamental difference between a factual ought and a normative or prescriptive ought.

ii) *The truth of normative propositions*

That factual statements are true or false is a question of looking at facts. A descriptive ought statement can be proven true or false with reference to facts. For example:

Fred jumps out of the window so he ought to fall. Whether he does is a question of fact. In fact, Fred was tied to a helium balloon and floated off, never to be seen again. The statement that Fred ought to have fallen, was, in that instance false, although generally it is a correct statement of probability.

Normative statements do not depend for their validity on statements of fact. That a person ought to do something (in the normative sense) depends on whether there is a normative reason for doing it, which is ultimately reducible to someone's wishes. Consider the following:

Normative statement: 'Do not kill'.

Reason why it is a valid statement: 'Because it is against the law' (the law wants me not to kill or I want to obey the law).

Reason why I should do what the law says: 'I will be punished if I do not'. (The law says I ought to be punished and I think there is a probability that I will be punished which I do not want to happen.)

The reason for me to comply with a normative statement is usually another normative statement from which it derives its authority. Reasons for obeying normative statements are

(a) because I choose to obey them or (b) because I recognise that the norm has been issued by an authority that I do not wish to disobey. For example, I might stop at a traffic light, even though I do not want to, because I want to obey the highway code. The reason why I want to obey the highway code is none other than the fact that I do not want to commit a traffic offence. It is a traffic offence because the law says I should not break this aspect of the highway code. And so on perhaps ad infinitum. Norms (normative propositions) are deducible from other norms.

The student may ask what the relevance of all of this is. Simply put, most issues in jurisprudence are about the reasons for norms, their effect on behaviour and how they are related to other norms.

iii) *Summary*

- Factual statements are fundamentally different from normative ones.

- The validity of a descriptive ought is verified by reference to objective facts.

- The validity of a normative ought is verified by reference to either:

  - another normative 'ought' that one regards as authorising it

  - our acceptance of the norm itself as being valid

  - our acceptance that the maker of the norm has authority to tell us what to do;

- Thus, a norm derives from another norm or a will. That we abide by it indicates that it is effective. The nature of validity is a matter of controversy, but it seems likely that validity is a normative judgment of sorts.

1.4 The case of the Speluncean Explorers

Seeking to introduce a course in jurisprudence, Professor Lon Fuller used among others the hypothetical example of a case involving a situation very similar to the facts of the case of *R* v *Dudley & Stephens* in which survivors have to cannibalise one of their number in order to survive. The judgments which Fuller outlines in this hypothetical case are supposed to outline the area of study for a jurisprudence course. However, the judgments are of themselves a product of their own time. There is no Marxist judgment given nor a feminist judge and so there are limits to the value of this as an introductory text. Students can find an extract in Lloyd and Freeman's *Introduction to Jurisprudence* and are strongly recommended to read this in detail.

Fuller was attempting to examine the relationship between law and morality and the use of moral and legal excuses and justifications in a particularly hard case. He also examines the role of the judge in a hard case, the technique of legal reasoning and the perennial question of the fidelity to law – under what circumstances if any may the citizen disobey the law? Dworkin has taken the view that this is the full list of relevant questions for a jurisprudence course, concentrating as they do on the development of a theory of adjudication. Professor Twining thinks that the introduction is fair as far as it goes but it does not tackle enough questions and he has cited as an example the failure to take account of Marxism.

In the judgments Fuller focuses on certain divergent philosophies of law and government. Handy J examines the question in terms of practical wisdom. He wants to know what should be done with the defendants and expresses concern that the judiciary will lose touch with reality. He seems less concerned with the letter of law and more concerned with public perception. He states that public opinion is relevant in the criminal law. The judges may take account of public opinion in the sentencing of offenders yet in this case the sentence is mandatory. Given that sentence is mandatory, Handy J seeks to take account of the personality of the chief executive, being the elected official in whose hands the question of clemency would constitutionally rest. This rather appears to be somewhat of an abdication of the role of the judge although it does look at factors that may well actually influence a real life judge. Handy J states that he is becoming more perplexed at the refusal of the judiciary to apply a common sense approach to problems. Quite what the connection between common sense and the letter of the law is remains the unanswered question in this judgment.

Staying true to the literal interpretation tradition that was prevalent in the common law, Truepenny CJ approaches the problem from the point of the strict letter application of the law, regardless of the potential injustice of the outcome. He demarcates the role of the judge in the application of the law from the role of the legislature in the making of law. According to the constitutional arrangements in this hypothetical country the executive branch have the power to grant clemency. Truepenny CJ says that it is no part of the role of the judge in the case and indeed in doing so the judge would be usurping the role of the executive branch if the judge granted what would in effect be clemency.

Foster J outlines two alternative approaches to the answer to the problem. It is not difficult to detect that Fuller himself identifies with and supports the second of these approaches. Foster firstly postulates that the premise on which the positive law is based is that of the possibility of men's coexistence. He maintains that where that coexistence is impossible then the condition that underlies all positive law ceases to exist. Therefore what the defendants did was not a crime because the law which said it was a crime did not exist. Foster J then continued that if that line of reasoning was not acceptable then he suggested the line favoured by Fuller himself, namely that positive law should be interpreted reasonably in the light of its evident purpose, and gives as an example the law on self defence. He states that the 'correction of obvious error is not to supplant the legislative will, but to make that will effective'. This is the purposive approach to the role of the judges in the interpretation of statutes.

We now turn to a rather unusual judge. Tatting J approaches the case and becomes confused. He is worried about the implications of his decision but is also mindful of the strict letter of the law. He asks '... by what authority do we resolve ourselves into a court of nature?...' He is unable to resolve the doubts that so trouble his mind about this case and therefore seeks to withdraw from the decision. I have categorised this as unusual because the very suggestion that the judge can decide not to decide the case in so blatant a manner raises eyebrows. As Dias has observed, the judge not only has a power to decide a case, he is also under a duty to decide and to do so in the light of applicable standards. Tatting is not fulfilling that duty by withdrawing. He seeks to shift blame on to the prosecuting authority whom he suggests ought to have exercised their discretion and not prosecuted these defendants. Had they done so that would have absolved the court (including Tatting) from having to reach a decision. Tatting insists on that withdrawal even when it is made clear to him that his failure to participate will lead in the end result to the death penalty being imposed on the defendants. He seems simply to wash his hands of the whole affair. Can a judge actually do this?

Finally, Keen J states that it is not the proper role of the court to instruct the executive on the exercise of clemency. He maintains that the court is not in session in order to apply conceptions of morality, rather it should apply the law. He cannot take the speech of Foster seriously since in his opinion Foster J has failed to distinguish the legal from the moral aspects of the case. As to the purpose of the argument, Keen maintains that due to the supremacy of the legislature it is not always possible to know what the purpose was that it had in mind and it would not therefore be possible to fill the gaps. He would affirm the convictions of the defendants on the grounds that '... judicial dispensation does more harm in the long run than hard decisions ...' Nonetheless he seems to go on to say how the matter should be approached from the point of view of an ordinary citizen. Why does he do this? Do you agree that judicial dispensation does more harm? Do these defendants have to be executed? What is the social role of the law? Has law got anything to do with justice? These are some of the questions that Fuller would want to tackle in a jurisprudence course. Hopefully, by the end of this course you too will have addressed these questions and will have developed your own reasoned response to these questions.

2 THE RELATIONSHIP BETWEEN LAW AND MORALITY

2.1   Introduction

Perhaps because of the language of law, with its references to crimes, wrong-doings and rights, there has been a long association between morality and law. Traditionally, law has been associated with religions, customs and divinity. In the West, the revealed laws of God in the form of the Bible have dominated legal concepts. Similar relationships with other religions have attributed the origin of law to the spiritual rather than the rational.

Equally, most legal systems appropriate to themselves the enforcement of contemporary moral and ethical values. The purpose of law can sometimes be confused with morality. Olivecrona suggests that morality is the product of law and certainly developed social morality would probably be impossible if it were not for legal enforcement. However, there are moral elements which would seem to stem primarily from human nature such as love and consideration. On the other hand, there are certain legal rules that could be termed as 'morally indifferent' such as which side of the road to drive on. To this extent there is quite evidently a difference in content between law and morality. Morality may inform the legislator, but must law be morally valid in order to be legally valid?

2.2   The nature of morality

a) *Concepts*

Before we try to address some of the issues raised here it might be helpful to define some closely related concepts of morality. If I say something is moral or immoral, I might mean a variety of things, but issues of morality are normally decided by conscience or instinct. It is not our place at this moment to ask whether conscience and instinct are learned responses or 'pre-programmed'. It suffices to say that there is no requirement to look to outside information or reason in order to find an answer to some moral dilemmas. Often moral feelings run against the grain of other people's views and even our own reasoning.

As such, morals defined in this way are capable of producing infinite disagreement, since different people's consciences dictate different things.

b) *Social morality*

Where, however, a society shares certain moral values on such matters as adultery, prostitution or abortion, we might say that these are social mores. This could also be termed 'morality'. But, social mores are to a certain extent a matter of faith. Even in the age of opinion polls we cannot be sure whether contemporary people actually feel prostitution is morally wrong since they might have been persuaded by arguments rather than conscience. Propaganda and indoctrination have a powerful effect on so-called 'shared morality'. Not just in Nazi Germany, but in thirties America and many other societies, public morality has been manipulated by subtle propaganda about 'racial hygiene'. In Germany the desire for healthy beautiful babies led rapidly to the sterilisation of the disabled and the eradication of undesirable populations.

Thus, relying on what people's 'revealed preferences' are may succeed in producing moral norms that offend against many people's consciences. This problem has plagued moralists and lawyers for centuries. The obvious response was to find a way in which moral imperatives can be translated into practical imperatives, without perverting the original moral intentions. This is the task that ethics has set itself.

c) *Ethics and practical reason*

The language of ethics and the language of law are very similar, centring around questions of obligation, duty and so forth. Much jurisprudence such as that of Finnis is inspired by ethical studies, however the differences between these disciplines are wide.

If an ethical scholar says I should follow a certain code, I may ask why, and I will obey only if I am convinced by his reasoning. But I cannot avoid the binding effect of a law, simply because I do not agree with the reasoning behind it. Ethics change according to improvements in practical reasoning. But although jurists, such as Raz, concede that practical reasoning is not entirely excluded from the law, they also insist that part of the process of law becoming law is the exclusion of further debate.

This may be illustrated by simple analogy. Parliament may debate a Bill on the basis of practical reasoning, ethics, social mores or individual consciences. However, once the Bill is made into law such debate is largely excluded. Cases such as *Cheney* v *Conn* illustrate the finality of debate, even when norms of international morality are invoked. The law to this extent differs from ethics. This closed-minded system of legal reasoning often leads people to say that law is 'formalistic', pedantic or simply unjust.

However, it may be argued that this merely separates law from ethics, not morality. We have seen, however that social mores are difficult to ascertain and not necessarily related to personal morality. (We shall look at the debate relating to the enforcement of morality by the law later on in this chapter.) Law is shy of taking account of personal conscience simply because one cannot necessarily look into a person's mind to tell whether it is a genuinely held conviction and because of the vast differences between people's attitudes.

The view taken so far would suggest that law and morality are condemned to separate paths.

However, the debate on the relationship between law and morality is far from over. In this chapter we will consider the relationship in general. In subsequent chapters we will return to it in different contexts.

2.3   A historical background

It is difficult for the law student to gain an objective perspective of the debate on law and morality since issues of morality are largely excluded from the study of substantive English law. This may be as a direct result of the tradition of classical English positivism in legal studies. Duncan Kennedy in *The Ideological Content of Legal Education* (cited Chapter 8, Lloyd and Freeman) posits an interesting insight into this situation. Discussing the education techniques employed in law schools, which he views as 'liberal' in their ideological approach, rather than being pluralistic, he states: 'if one thinks about law in this way, one is inescapably dependent on the very techniques of legal reasoning that are being marshalled in defense of the status quo.'

Thus, some jurists' insistence that there is a necessary separation between law and morality may be a self-perpetuating myth.

a) *A moral perspective*

As a starting point we might consider the understanding of the nature of law in times past when such a view was perhaps less prevalent. The case of John Lilburne, though it might be taken as exceptional, illustrates the wide gulf between the law's own definition of itself in the mid-seventeenth century and the modern view.

During the English Commonwealth, Lilburne was subject to an Act of Parliament banishing him on pain of death. Lilburne fought the case on the authority of Coke's *Institutes* which stated: 'Where reason ceaseth, the law ceaseth ... All customs and prescriptions (Acts of Parliament, laws and judgments) that be against reason are void and null in themselves.' The court was persuaded by this argument even to the extent of deciding that the jury was the judge of law as well as fact. That such arguments were entertained and indeed prevailed was no mere anomaly of the Commonwealth. Coke's laws and cases are taken to be accurate statements of the law to the present day, even though it has been shown persuasively that at least in *Slade's* case Coke reports contain more of his opinions than the judge's.

This seems strange to the modern eye, but very much in keeping with the legacy of early English jurisprudence. Perhaps the most 'positivist' and 'modern' of sixteenth century juristic writings was Smith's *De Republica Anglorum*, in which, while conceding the absolute power of the King in Parliament, Smith takes a very non-committal position on the question of immoral laws. To Smith the question of whether a law's validity is linked to morality depends, in hindsight, on whether civil disobedience results in political success.

If, on the one hand, there was an assertion that reason and common sense governed the application of new law, there was also a deep-seated belief that law was a heritage stronger than governments or kings, a guarantee of rights in itself. The Elizabethan lawyer, Maynard, contends that the king is subject to law 'because the law doth make him king'. Therefore, if he sought to change the law to something immoral or irrational he could not.

The view that law was immutable and fixed was implicit in the common usage of the word 'law' itself and adherence to law was partly due to the 'wisdom of antiquity' which had been tried and tested over the ages. Moreover, in the early sixteenth century, law enforcement was scarcely in the hands of the government, being more dependent on the practice and teachings of the Church.

The Church contributed two great factors to the law and morality issue. Firstly, until the English reformation, it represented a supra-national entity with real political and theological sanctions at its disposal, in an age when, although its power was on the decline, the fear of excommunication could still keep an unruly prince in check. In theory the Church was itself accountable, not politically, but morally to God.

Secondly, it had a monopoly on the truth of moral determinations. If the Church said something was wrong – it was wrong! There was therefore no problem in the law determining what moral standards it must conform to. In essence England was a place where there was the Church's law, the people's law and the King's law in Parliament.

c) *The enlightenment*

Across Europe similar situations prevailed, but also the same problems arose. Kings and Parliaments became wealthier and consequently more efficient at government. Science was eroding superstition and religion. The moral and religious authority of the Church was being challenged, because of the growing feeling that the Church was a mere number cipher for national powers and riddled with moral corruption.

With apologies to historians, these factors may be seen as accounting for some of the jurisprudential developments that urged law and morality to part company in the minds of lawyers, legislators and jurists alike.

d) *Absolutism*

With the increasing strength of national kings and the declining fortune of the Church, James I, Richelieu and Louis XIV amongst others denied any legal or religious fetters on monarchic authority. Law became simply what the sovereign willed law to be and matters such as morality or religion were solely in their keeping. England had an edge on the rest of Europe, since the English Reformation had unified Church and State in the person of the monarch.

Not surprisingly, since the absolute monarch was no longer necessarily king by virtue of the law and custom of the land, another reason was needed. Conveniently, therefore, the monarch became the monarch by Divine Right, requiring moral and religious obedience, and the link with morality was thereby maintained. In this also the seeds of the imperative theory are to be found – law is the will of the sovereign, irrespective of subjective moral or other considerations.

Europe was rapidly realising that the rest of the world had moralities of a different kind: 'Every nation has its own type of wisdom. Mahomet symbolises the wisdom of the Arabs. Christ symbolises the wisdom of the Jews.' 'Moral truths did not seem to be so certainly the exclusive monopoly of any particular Church', wrote one Elizabethan jurist.

e) *Secular morality*

The secularisation of morality and its application to law at the hands of Grotius and others is largely relevant to the Natural Law issues of the next chapter. Instead of relying on religion, the secular Natural Lawyers sought to superimpose moral standards on law by the application of Reason. Bayle philosophically separated religion from morality, but in doing so contributed to the theoretical separation of the law from morality, which was quite opposite to his desire.

The eighteenth century saw scientific development, which engendered an absolute faith in observation and reasoning to solve all problems. If Mr Newton could make a law true for all falling objects, then Locke could find the key to law that would explain the science of legislation. His *Essay Concerning Human Understanding* was widely read and influential, especially his emphasis on observable facts and inductive knowledge as the preferred methodology for jurisprudence. As to the question of morality – that was simply a matter of human sensations of pleasure and pain, backed by the power of desire. Others of his conclusions, although influential, are manifestly contradictory to his espoused methodology being more the result of his political opinions rather than empirical observation. However, his influence is very evident in the writing of Hume and others, the American Constitution, the 'Glorious Revolution', while his account of morality is to be found in the writings of Bentham, amongst others.

If we combine Locke's psychology with Hobbes' pessimism – he thought that men's desires were naturally brutish – we not only come to Hobbes' conclusion that all power should reside in an absolute sovereign, but may also come to feel that popular morality is not necessarily a good thing. Thus Voltaire, although advocating a humane legal system, dismissed ordinary people as the 'rabble', following Lockean logic.

Locke's infectious ideas reached even the priesthood in the shape of Condillac. He viewed man as being born morally neutral with the capacity to develop morally only by learning. It was, for Condillac, the environment and education that made man good or bad – he rejected determinism altogether. Thus, by improving the environment, man could become perfect. Following in this mould Helvetius concluded that man was simply sensitive matter to be motivated simply by pleasure and pain. On this account morality was simply what is good, ie pleasure, so that the object of morality could simply be seen to be obtaining the greatest pleasure for the greatest amount of sensitive matter. A rather similar verbal formulation is at the crux of utilitarianism, which is the foundation of a positivist ethical theory of law.

Helvetius does state that people who are less educated and in a worse environment are obviously less competent to understand how this should be achieved, but it should be achieved through legislation and education. As a result Helvetius is as much a charter for privileged paternalism as for equality.

2.4   The effect of philosophy

It will be noted that all this development was simply theoretical, mere discussion about the nature of things and how things should be. The significant effect of the Enlightenment was that parts of Europe adopted these philosophies into their way of making and perceiving law, but the adoption was on the basis of convenience of ascendent interests rather than the 'truth' or morality of the propositions. For example, in England, where the Divine Right had lost one king his head and another his Crown, Locke was closely associated with the 'elected' William of Orange, who kindly acceded to Parliamentary sovereignty and the obligations of a constitutional monarch.

In England, therefore, the King was not king by virtue of God; the Church dogma was to be settled by King and Parliament; law was what the sovereign power said it was; the sovereign power was nominally the King's, but actually Parliament's, and no law or morality could constrain the sovereign.

All of these changes in the way in which law was conceived successfully excluded the language of morality from understandings of the law. Thus, between Lilburne's trial in 1653 and the Bill of Rights 1689, the concepts of law could not have seemed more at variance. It was believed that morality and practical reason could overturn the law, even of Parliament, in the sixteenth century. But this is at a time where law was seen not simply a tool of government, as it had become by the later seventeenth century.

2.5   The contemporary debate

It is evident that the law and morality debate produced critiques on the way law was practised and perceived. The insistence of Locke and others on a scientific method was based on a belief that since science could open the mysteries of the physical world, the same methods could explain the nature of human institutions and human behaviour. Certainly, this 'positivist' methodology has been indispensable in certain of the human sciences, but has been applied with somewhat less success to what we term arts.

Positivism dominates jurisprudence because of its certainty and apparent similarity with the legal systems we are familiar with. The constant criticism made by positivists particularly of Natural Lawyers is that law is not what we want it to be, but what it is, meaning that law is not morality. Certainly, many positivists insist that law must be judged by moral standards and immoral law should not be obeyed. Nonetheless, they maintain that since law is law, then there remains a legal obligation to obey, and anything that fits positivist criteria is law, irrespective of content. This simplifies the situation, but marks the problem that has led to positivists being labelled 'moral cripples'.

Ideally, legal systems would have a failsafe so that immoral and unreasonable law need not be applied. In this respect it would be desirable that a jurist could identify in the nature of law a legal or moral duty, necessitating an adherence to certain standards of morality, which constrain the legislator and/or the judge.

As we have already seen, however, absolute moral obligations are not easily arrived at. In the multi-cultural society moral variance is the norm. Furthermore, the empirical method accepted by some of those who advocate a link between law and morality seems to have resulted in dilution of the 'moral nature' of morality. Thus, the debate may be couched in terms of the moral cripples versus the hopeless idealists.

a) *The positivist objections of Bentham and Kelsen*

Bentham was exceedingly condemnatory of theories that equated the nature of law with static moral norms. Speaking of natural rights theories, he dubbed their view as 'the pestilential breath of fiction'. Instead, he made a distinction between what law actually is, which must be viewed without moral norms superimposed upon it, and how law should be reformed, which he saw as a fundamentally ethical or moral problem. Bentham arrived at this, he claimed, through logic and reasoning. If we analyse this reasoning we may find some errors in Bentham's logic.

When we look at history, we do not say that because Adolf Hitler was morally reprehensible he was not the leader of Nazi Germany. Similarly, we do not say that because the pass laws in South Africa are not morally agreeable, they did not have the effect and were not regarded as law.

The difference between these two examples is subtle, but significant. An historical fact is a statement which is based on as much empirical evidence as is available and claims nothing more. However, to say that something is law, is to say that people are responding to legal rules or persons in a certain way. South African pass-laws were law because the legal system enforced them. Alternatively, we might narrow the definition by saying that law is what lawyers say it is, which is probably what Bentham envisages. The problem remains that if the rest of society disregard what the legal caste say is law, then is it still law? The lawyer's idea of law might be the same as the clergy's idea of morality, and often definitive in a given society, but not necessarily right. Objectively the Benthamite view sees the author of all laws as the sovereign. All legal systems are viewed as hierarchical, with the sovereign as the authority for law. The sovereign is essentially, within Bentham's analysis, a political entity. Although Bentham merely states that the sovereign is the person or persons who are supposed to be in disposition to obey, this seems open to being construed differently. The sovereign's authority might stem from the sanction of a given society's current political morality.

To Kelsen, moral perspectives distort the accurate perception of law as a normative science. Raz effectively criticises the logical justification for this proposition. Kelsen excludes any link between morality and law, because subjective value judgments do not lend themselves to the scientific method that he wishes to use. Raz puts the problem simply: 'If an object cannot be studied "scientifically" then its study should not strive to be scientific.'

If we contrast the two positivist thinkers discussed so far we find the following:

i) *Bentham asserts that law is the will of the sovereign, whatever that will may be (the imperative theory of law).* The authority of the sovereign stems from the fact that in a political society people are supposed to be of a disposition to obey a person or body and that person or body is the sovereign. People's judgment of the morality of the acts of that sovereign will not affect whether it is law or not law. As long as the sovereign wills something to be law it will be law and morality is therefore is not linked to validity of the law.

This is not only unhelpful to his definition of law, but also amounts to a truism. Essentially, law is the will of the person who is for whatever reason regarded as the lawmaker, providing that people are thought likely to obey him. The difference between lawmaker and sovereign in this analysis is non-existent since, in Bentham's analysis, only the expressed will of a sovereign is law, and law is the will of the person you are disposed to obey (ie the sovereign).

Many Natural Lawyers used to point out that tyrants and other thoroughly immoral 'sovereigns' have not been tremendously successful in holding on to power. Lon Fuller suggests that immoral legal orders tend to be transitory. No matter how many purchased favours, it is generally the political morality of the day that maintains the author of laws in power. However much we might dislike Nazi laws, the political morality of the Nazis was widely accepted – albeit because of propaganda. It is sustainable, I believe, to assert that one cannot assume that people will be disposed to obey a sovereign who does not satisfy the standards of contemporary political morality. In such circumstances, the subtle normative qualities of law normally give way to repressive strong-arm tactics on the part of the sovereign. The law is not obeyed – instead force is feared. To Bentham, of course, arbitrary detention without trial and torture, would equally be attributed to law if it had the tacit or overt approval of the sovereign. However, this would to most people be the antithesis of law, because arbitrary executive action, without published approval, contradicts our view of law as being differentiated from arbitrary power.

Bentham's wide definition of law might thus insulate his theory from these factors, but I do not think he excludes them completely. A definition of law that is based upon the political aspect of society will almost certainly be moulded by the political morality of that society. A law may be immoral, but a legal system founded on immorality, in the light of contemporary political morality, is unlikely to remain in force. Thus, the relationship between law and morality may exist even in the imperative thesis. Whether a particular law is immoral or not might not be directly relevant – this is a question of the content of law, rather than nature. Rather, if the nature of law is rooted in political society, then the legal system is liable to be torpedoed by political morality.

ii) Kelsen sought to avoid these problems by relating the nature of law not to the political attributes of a person, but to superior norms. Raz notes that Kelsen firmly believes that there is no necessary connection between law and morality and that there is no need to revert to moral arguments to identify the existence of law. But his separation is not entirely convincing. Again Raz identifies some problems.

Kelsen sees moral values as relative rather than absolute. Different societies have different moral values and therefore, Kelsen believes, there is no content common to all moralities that is also respected by all legal systems. Raz submits that if there is no absolute morality, the issue becomes whether Kelsen's own morality is respected to some extent in every legal system.

I think that Raz himself is slightly in error here. He does not draw a distinction between personal morality and social morality. Personal morality seldom is organised into articulated rules; we either morally approve or disapprove of a given subject, often without being able to say what rule it contravenes. The articulation of moral norms is a feature of collective moralities – a search for a communicable form for a feeling and as a way of giving others advice.

To illustrate this, imagine if we ask: 'Is apartheid wrong?' Firstly not everybody would agree it is wrong – since apartheid stems from a religio-moralistic theory. Most people would say it is unfair, but to fit it into a broad moral norm (such as it is wrong to discriminate on the basis of race) is only of use as an explanation rather than a reason. If I think something is morally wrong, it is because I feel it is wrong, I do not need to recall a specific norm to make that judgment. Raz recommends the application of one personal morality, Kelsen's own morality, as the focus of the question. I would suggest that the proper question that should be addressed is whether the predominant morality in a given society is respected by the law of that society.

b) *Relativism*

i) The moment we concede that morality is relative, we must treat it as such. To say that morality is relative is to say that its contents vary from person to person and society to society. To the positivist, anything can be law, but positivists often seem committed to the view that there are absolute moral values. Certainly Kelsen does not deal with morality in a relative way, but instead tries and fails to find elements that are common to all moralities and to all legal systems. Hart's minimum content of natural law is an attempt to do this and is not entirely unsuccessful. However, Kelsen and Hart's views both betray an insistence that any connection between law and morality must be between a morality with an absolute and common content and a definition of law that is content neutral. This is logically bound to find little success. In the absence of a generally acceptable definition of a content neutral morality it is essentially a comparison of chalk with cheese! If one were to compare common morality with a content neutral religion, ie where religious rules are excluded from the definition of a religion, one might equally find that there is no necessary connection between religion and morality. This has, indeed, been used as a critique of religions, but it is not exactly a logical proposition.

There is a perfectly laudable reason for such an attitude. The concession that morality is not absolute, is also a concession that our own moral judgments are not absolute. In effect we cannot use morality as a method of censuring someone else who is being true to his own morality. We cannot say that apartheid is objectively immoral, because some believe that it is inherently moral. Thus, a society is limited to saying whether or not it is being true to its own morality, and a person can judge only himself by his own personal morality. If one reads Hart's *Positivism and the Separation of Law from Morals* we do not feel that Hart is a moral cripple, for by advocating the separation of law from morality he echoes many religious views. Morality should be kept independent and virginal as the objective judge of law. This argument is almost a moral argument in itself, a possibility which Hart does concede.

ii) The second issue is one that we will consider further. There is the lurking question: what is the nature of legal obligation? A reliance on coercive forces does not sufficiently explain how a relatively small amount of forces of law and order maintain comparative legal order. Hart is closer than Kelsen to an appreciation of the voluntary nature of adherence to rules. Hart gives the example of a smoker alone in an underground carriage, who nonetheless refrains from smoking. It must be a personal reason rather than an external threat or reward that compels him to obey the rule. Hart would stress that moral values are only one of many possible reasons why someone might want to obey rules, irrespective of his natural desires. Kelsen does not allow for such inferences, because these are importations from psychology and sociology. Kelsen excludes these and looks only at legal statements, a problem that haunts him through many critiques.

iii) Thirdly, Raz notes that Kelsen like other positivists assumes that the link between morality and the law necessitates the view that an unjust law is not a law at all. This view is not shared by all people who advocate a link between law and morality. Fuller, who we shall consider at length, advocates a very interesting aspect of the law-morality relationship that does not require the disappearance of a law because it fails to meet moral criteria.

2.6 Hart and the separation of law from morals

a) Hart has done much to bridge the gap between the positivists and the advocates of a link between law and morality, but he sturdily defends the middle ground. Hart goes straight to the problem when he discusses the Nazi law problem.

A fundamental concern of those who insist on a linkage between law and morality is that history shows the frightening testament of inhumane laws. Hart cites Radbruch, who blamed the predominance of positivism with its rejection of the nullity of immoral laws, for the dilemmas faced by German jurists during the Nazi era. Hart's riposte is a wise one: 'law is law ... but that does not conclude the question. Law is not morality; do not let it supplant morality.' He advocates that in moral terms, an immoral law ought not to be obeyed and indicates 'an enormous overvaluation of the importance of the bare fact that a rule may be said to be a valid rule of law.'

He further cites the problem the post-war German courts faced with punishing those who had perpetrated immoral acts under the protection of Nazi law. He suggests that there are three choices. Firstly, they might be allowed to go unpunished. Secondly, Nazi laws could be declared void on the grounds of immorality. Thirdly, retrospective legislation be passed to criminalise the immoral behaviour. The third alternative is approved of by Hart on the grounds that it is morally right to honestly address this moral dilemma.

Before we consider Fuller's response to Hart there are certain aspects of the issue that might be noted. Hart seems to believe that there are fundamental and consistent principles of morality. Most people would agree with him. Such a reaction is not based on empirical truth but common consent and wishful thinking.

b) When we look at the Nurenberg trials of jurists, we get an interesting insight into this dilemma. One senior jurist maintained his abhorrence of the Nazi system, but said in his defence that remaining a judge within the system would mean that there would be less chance of a zealous Nazi taking his place. By remaining a part of the system he could at least ensure fair trails and perhaps save lives. On the other hand the chief prosecutor of the Nazi regime maintained that Nazi law was based on sound principles of 'scientific morality'. A major issue was the authorisation of involuntary sterilisation of the mentally ill by the judiciary, which was held to be morally reprehensible at that time. The Nazi was able to cite the writings of contemporary American jurists such as O W Holmes who were, during the thirties, widely interested in the achievement of 'racial hygiene' through such methods. Both of these individuals were sentenced to execution by the Nurenberg court.

Now, the problem that Hart fails to address is not what do you do in hindsight, but what do you do at the time? The first jurist was faced with a moral dilemma – he did not wish to apply Nazi law, but knew it would be enforced in any case. In this situation, one might see it as a morally brave act to engage in a loathsome pursuit in order that its effect might be a little less ruthless. Certainly, Pappe notes that Nazi statutes were often manipulated and misunderstood by the judiciary, which is a recipe for wide judicial discretion, if not towards moderation, then towards fanaticism. The jurist would have been better on his own account had he pretended not to see the dilemma.

The latter jurist was a committed Nazi. If morality is learned rather than in-born there is ample evidence to illustrate that the Germans had been heavily influenced since before the Nazis by some very odd moral values. One merely needs to read Odon Von Horvath's *Age of the Fish*, written decades earlier, to see a picture of German youth not dissimilar to the children of the Hitler Jugend.

The problem that Hart should identify in his separation of law and morality, is that while his advice is of use to the subject of the law, the judge is still faced with valid law in front of him and thus must enforce and perpetuate an odious law. The choice of resignation may be the worse of two evils. As long as there are judges and policemen to enforce it, the law will remain efficacious, but may be applied without even consideration of procedural propriety.

In the alternative, the judge who may be guided by his conscience may be a moral deviant and may invalidate the most humane of laws because of a conflict with his personal morality. The personal morality of the judge is a matter that is of concern to the issue of adjudication. Detmold argues that although a judge's authority can be referred to higher authorities or norms, he cannot evade the moral consequences of his decisions. His moral responsibility, lies not only with him as an individual, but qua judge, reflecting on his response to a case. However, his view is not typical, and depends on a logic that requires further elucidation in a later chapter.

The dilemma if it is framed in this way is unanswerable. Fuller's response to Hart's more general view may well not be an answer, since it is concerned with different questions, but gives us an insight that is worth quoting. 'As we seek order, we can meaningfully remind ourselves that order itself will do us no good unless it is good for something. As we seek to make our order good, we can remind ourselves that justice itself is impossible without good order, and that we must not lose order itself in the attempt to make it good.' Since fascism is a ideological obsession with order, this seems a good evaluation of the problem, although it does not solve it.

2.7 Fuller and the inner morality of law

a) *Law and purpose*

Fuller identifies a dichotomy of views as to the proper purpose of legal study. On the one hand there is the positivist contention that law must be treated as a manifested fact of social authority to be studied for what it is and does. Such a position is certainly proper for the study of substantive law, for a law student would learn precious little unless he treated individual legal materials as categorical. However, this does not mean that the method is apt to the study of law as a general phenomenon.

On the other hand, Fuller's argument is that the theoretical concept of law cannot be understood without attributing to it the purpose 'of subjecting human conduct to the guidance and control of general rules'. Such a view cannot be faulted and would probably be accepted by all. However, he goes on to assert that without this idea of purpose one cannot judge the degree to which a legal system has succeeded in meeting its goals. Fuller considers that one might term the goal of all legal systems 'the ideal of legality'. When positivists like Kelsen set down a criterion such as efficaciousness as a required element in the definition of law, they are thus stating that if law fails to achieve its purpose then it is not law. There is a qualitative difference between Kelsen's view and Fuller's. Kelsen suggests an all or nothing view of law, begging the question 'how many people need to disobey a legal system before it ceases to be 'efficacious' and hence ceases to become law?' On the other hand Fuller sees the legality of a system of rules as a question of degree. His criteria for legality we will explore in a moment.

b) *A critique of positivism*

He claims to identify two falsifications in positivism. The first is that some aspects taken as legal facts are merely achievements of legal aspirations. For example, we say Parliament is supreme, but this is not 'a datum of nature', it is a manifestation of a tradition of agreement that it legally should be regarded as such. This 'should' is not in itself a moral evaluation, but a result of the success of a rule. To state the nature of a legal system in terms of 'is' statements is to endorse that a legal system is what it says it is, which creates a problem if a society rejects a legal system. For example, when Parliament passed the Southern Rhodesia Act 1965, it considered that it was the supreme legal authority for that country. However, the country declared independence and simply ignored Parliament.

A legal fact is a matter of truth or falsity within the legal system, eg English law is a system of binding rules. However, a legal fact is a question of degree in reality. Law can only be said to be binding if people believe or act as if it is. Some people certainly do not feel that law is binding upon them; they may disregard the rules, fail to observe them and many evade punishment for breaking them. One could not say that such a person is actually 'bound' by the law. When a legal system asserts that it is binding, that is itself a legal rule. If it can be said that the laws of a particular system are binding, that is an appraisal of the success or adherence to the rule. Therefore, I think that Fuller's contention is that when a person seeks to describe a legal system as it is, he is actually evaluating the degree of success it has achieved in pursuing its purpose. To summarise our example; law is not a binding set of rules, but something that aspires with some degree of success to be binding.

A second interesting contribution is the recognition that a working legal system cannot be understood merely by looking at the rules consciously created by law-makers. Fuller cites as an example the fact that the American constitution, from which all American legal authority flows, never mentions a requirement to legislate. This has not stopped Americans from making laws, because this is activity implicit in the pursuit of legality. Thus, a statute made in 1700 may still be enforceable in 1991. To Fuller the judiciary seem to be charged with an implicit duty to be the curators of statutes, so that if those plants regarded as weeds change over the decades, the judge invests the Statute of Weeds with the new, more appropriate meaning. Such implicit rules of legality serve as a bridge between the legal world and the social world.

This is an insightful proposition that is the basis for his very original view of the relationship between law and morality.

2.8 Procedural morality

a) *Moralities of aspiration*

Whilst this critique of positivist methodology is very interesting, the student might find it somewhat remote from the issue of law and morality. But, Fuller does not seek to prove that substantive morality is bound up with law. As I have mentioned earlier, there are perils in seeking to prove a relationship between a relativist, content-based concept of morality and a content-neutral, universal conception of law.

Fuller seems to base his view of this relationship on the following logic. If morality must be seen as being relative rather than absolute, then if we seek to relate morality to law, that morality must be one specific to the nature of law. Therefore legal morality is a particular type of morality to be found in the nature of law itself, rather than being abstracted from other moral norms.

Now, Fuller's conception of law is that of a purposive activity which aspires towards the ideal of legality. As such it is not surprising that Fuller's concept of morality is founded on practical criteria which are goals to be aspired to. For example, one of his legal-moral criteria is legal clarity. This 'morality of aspiration' is thus largely a question of degree; obviously, things are usually more or less clear, although occasionally we may say something is completely incomprehensible. However, Fuller's morality is not a morality of duty, which is normally expressed in terms of the rules of a substantive morality. An example of a morality of duty is illustrated by the rule 'thou shalt not kill'.

The difference between moralities of aspiration and of duty is largely one of formulation. We might employ a rule 'do not kill', but this can be equally expressed as expounding respect for human life. The former gives us the ability to judge individual acts individually, the latter allows us to give a judgment of degree. If a legal system does not completely prohibit killing then it has broken the spirit of the rule, but it may be shown that to a greater or lesser extent it accords with the principle.

The second aspect of moralities of aspiration is that they do allow for complete censure, if there is no satisfaction of the criteria. Rules of substantive morality carry with them absolute obligations, while Fuller's morality of aspiration is founded on the desire of the legal system to achieve an ideal of legality.

b) *The internal morality of law*

The only problem is that Fuller is concerned to relate a morality that is linked to his content-neutral concept of law rather than following the conventional approach of asserting that law respects certain substantive moral values. As such, the content of the 'internal morality of law' looks remarkably like common sense rules of good craftsmanship. Indeed, Fuller's contention is that there is an inherent logic to the subjugation of human conduct to legal rules, which if ignored will lead to failure.

Fuller asserts that:

i) A legal system must be based on or reveal some kind of regular trends. As such law should be founded on generalisations of conduct such as rules, rather than simply allowing arbitrary adjudication.

ii) Laws must be publicised so that subjects know how they are supposed to behave.

iii) Rules will not have the desired effect if it is likely that your present actions will not be judged by them in future. As such, retrospective legislation should not be abused.

iv) Laws should be comprehensible, even if it is just lawyers who understand them.

v) Laws should not be contradictory.

vi) Law should not expect the subject to perform the impossible.

vii) Law should not change so frequently that the subject cannot 'orient his action' to it.

viii) There should not be a significant difference between the actual administration of the law and what the written rule says.

Now, I have stated these criteria in the form of rules that are in the form of morality of obligation. Fuller deliberately avoids this, instead expressing them as principles or goals; generality of laws; promulgation of laws; minimising the use of retrospective laws; clarity; lack of contradiction; possibility of obedience; constancy through time; consistency between the word and the practice of law.

I think Fuller's evaluation speaks for itself: 'Though these natural laws touch one of the most vital of human activities they obviously do not exhaust the whole of man's moral life. They have nothing to say on such topics as polygamy, the study of Marx, the worship of God, the progressive income tax, or the subjugation of women. If the question be raised whether any of these subjects, or others like them, should be taken as objects of legislation, that question relates to what I have called the external morality of the law.'

That these principles amount to a morality depends on Fuller's rather tenuous construction of the word. He demonstrates that the Nazi regime had a progressive decline in its adherence to these principles of legality. Furthermore he concedes that even if these standards are adhered to, this does not guarantee that they will prevent law being the instrument of oppression. Even disregard of these principles does not necessarily make a system 'not law', just further away from the ideal of legality. In essence, Fuller states that the internal morality of law is neutral towards the law's substantive aims.

There are, however, aspects of the internal morality of law that he claims are not so neutral. The urge for legal clarity fights against laws that direct themselves against 'alleged evils that cannot be defined' such as discrimination on the basis of race. He cites the 1948 decision in *Perez* v *Sharp* where a statute preventing the marriage of white persons to any 'Negro, mulatto, Mongolian or member of the Malay race' was held unconstitutional on the basis that the constitution requires clarity.

I find the gist of this argument a little transparent. It is more or less certain that a statute formulated with the same categories, but to prevent societal discrimination, would not meet such a fate. But I will leave this to the reader's judgment.

c) *The legal approach to human nature*

More interestingly, Fuller asserts that the very purpose of law embodies an inalienable view of humanity. 'To embark on an enterprise of subjecting human conduct to the governance of rules involves of necessity a commitment to the view that man is, or can become, a responsible agent, capable of understanding and following rules, and answerable for his defaults.' If we revisit Fuller's inner morality of law in this light we probably get a better perspective of why he considers it appropriate to term these criteria as being moral in nature.

By making laws general and predictable, a choice is given to the subject – the opportunity to predict when he will be punished, for example. By making laws known people may know on what basis they will be judged and how they must act so as not to fall foul. A purpose that is furthered by the relative absence of retrospective legislation, the pursuit of clarity and the other principles. By this, Fuller is stressing that law is, to a certain extent, a partnership between the legislator and the subject. An illustration of this might be the principle of taxation law that although a person may not evade his tax obligations, he has the right to act so that he can minimise the amount of tax that the law requires him to pay.

From a libertarian perspective, the inner morality of law's view of human nature is one committed to a rather limited notion of humanity. The ability to learn to respond to rules and commands and avoid falling foul of the wrath of a master is little more than one would expect of a dog!

d) *Evaluation*

What Fuller succeeds in doing is setting up what amounts to an 'optional morality' that has very little to do with questions of right or wrong. One wonders whether he has actually made any contribution to asserting there is a link between law and morality. Certainly, one has to view law itself as a morally acceptable thing, rather than a necessary evil, as Nozick might view it, or an instrument of class oppression, which is Marxist attitude.

However, one of the more unfair criticisms of Fuller is based on his assertion that beyond the satisfaction of a very minimal standard the legality of a system is a matter of degree. The criticism is put like this; who talks about a legal system existing more or less? A legal system either exists or it does not, it cannot half-exist. The second element of the criticism is that if a legal system can exist to a lesser degree, how can we decide when we do or do not have an obligation to obey it?

I think that this argument is illusory and ignores Fuller's identification of the positivist 'falsifications'. When we talk of the 'existence' of a legal system it is not like talking about the existence of a piece of steel. It is either steel or not steel. A legal system is a social fact which depends on the degree of co-operation achieved between its members and its subjects. The advocates of the 'all-or-nothing' point of view have never answered the question – how many people need to obey a legal system for it to cease to be a legal system? The assertion that a legal system either exists or it does not stems from the lawyerly desire to have clear yes-or-no answers. I think this has a little more to do with the very human need to know when one must obey a legal system and when one no longer has a legal obligation. As a result, many positivists seek to find a rule that is the criterion for the existence of a law. Most notable amongst these has been Kelsen, yet still he has to relate the legal system to the principle of 'efficaciousness', which is a matter of degree – some systems are more effective than others. Fuller seems to offer us a recipe for achieving efficaciousness, and perhaps even a formula for when a legal system might cease to be, ie where none of the eight principles are achieved at all. However, he does not, at least in Hart's eyes, give us an explanatory link between law and morality.

Fuller and Hart, in the opinions of many observers such as Dias, never really meet conceptually when they discuss morality. Fuller describes a morality which has two distinct facets: (1) It is procedural, rather than sustantive, relating to the nature of legal endeavour rather than to any specific purpose to which it is put. (2) It is a morality of aspiration, rather than duty. In contrast, Hart founds his conception of morality on facts of the human condition that are important enough to require some kind of reflection in human institutions without necessarily requiring a particular response.

Hart's minimum content of Natural Law does not imply a necessary link between law and morality, and for this reason we shall consider it in the next section.

2.9 The nature of legal obligation (see also Chapter 5)

a) *A claim to moral authority*

If the nature of law itself does not easily lend itself to inherent logical links with morality, we might seek to find out whether the obligation to obey the law is to any extent a moral one.

It is a manifest fact of legal systems that in the 'marketing' of laws, legal systems virtually always claim to have moral authority. Even the most reprehensible of laws made by the most reprehensible regimes are couched in a pseudo-morality. In South Africa the illegality of inter-racial marriages was based on the premise that it would be immoral for a white to be in union with a 'lesser species'. Even where there is obvious brutality that cannot itself be justified, the moral rectitude of the political order may be invoked. If a government in England were to pass a law that was regarded as 'immoral', it could still point to the moral legitimation of being electorally accountable. The tradition of moral 'marketing' in England is well illustrated in Douglas Hay's account of the ideology of Force, Justice and Mercy in *Albion's Fatal Tree*. It is hard to understand the genuine paternalism of generations past that enshrined the belief that the ruling classes had a moral duty to rule. Still harder to understand is the widespread acceptance, by the ruled, of the repressive legal system as being not only naturally but morally right. Speaking of the arbitrary nature of eighteenth century criminal law, Hay puts this well. 'Englishmen ... tended to think of justice in personal terms, and were more struck by understanding of individual cases than by the delights of abstract schemes. Where authority is embodied in direct personal relationships, men will often accept power, even enormous despotic power, when it comes to the 'good King', the father of his people, who tempers justice with mercy. A form of this powerful psychic configuration was ... the law's greatest strength as an ideological system, especially amongst the poor, and in the countryside.'

Certainly, in the static and personal world of the eighteenth century, patterns of authority and obligation had more in common with the feudal morality of loyalty to one's lord than to an allegiance to a social idea such as law. However, the same cannot be said of the modern situation in England, leading to a particular mystique about the nature of legal obligation.

The fact that law is still packaged as being 'in the interest of society' can be seen in the judgments of most criminal cases. To this extent, Detmold in *The Unity of Law and Morality* claims that all legal judgments seek to refer themselves to corresponding moral norms. This may well be an insincere attempt to gain moral approval on the part of the law-giver. Even if it seems that a law does not accord with the consensus or individual morality, but this does not mean that there is no appeal to morality. In dramatic terms, the judge who regrets having to apply a law, because it seems to be unfair, but stresses that it is nonetheless his duty to do so, reinforces the feeling that there is a higher moral duty binding the judge.

There is considerable evidence to suggest that moral reasoning is learned, rather than innate (see Kohlberg *Moral Development and Behaviour*). It may be that our response to legal obligations is learned in a related way. When we are children we are told that certain things are wrong because they are not (morally) nice and others are wrong because they are against the law. The difference between the obligation to obey the law and the obligation to obey moral laws is obscure, but the dichotomy is defined by the differences between practical and legal solutions to moral problems. As such, if faced with the choice of breaking the law and betraying moral principles, the language of legal 'marketing' often encourages us to see it as a moral dilemma. When a judge criticises a person for seeking to set himself above the law, this implies a moral argument; everyone else surrenders their problems to the law because it is socially right and prevents anarchy, so why should the individual be the exception?

b) *Is the moral obligation to obey law simply 'propaganda'?*

To suggest that there is no moral element to legal obligation would be to contradict this 'marketing approach', but then who believes packaging? However, this brings us no nearer to understanding the nature of legal obligation. Asserting that law is to be obeyed because it is binding is a tautology – it is simply saying that it ought to be obeyed, while asserting that law is to be obeyed because it is law would seem to be deriving an ought from an is, which for reasons explained previously is not a very acceptable viewpoint. We might take the Kelsenite view that law is obeyed because it is validated by an unwritten rule or grundnorm. This is an ultimate rule or norm that requires the legal system to be obeyed. Such a norm in Kelsen's eyes is a 'presupposition of juristic thinking' which amounts to a lawyerly assumption.

From a moral standpoint this is, perhaps the least satisfactory solution. It amounts to a suggestion that the obligation to obey law stems from lawyers saying that it should be obeyed. This seems unsatisfactory, because it provides us with no firm rationale. It is rather like a child asking his parent why he must go to bed at bedtime and being answered 'because I say so'.

However, although this might seem unacceptable, it can easily be maintained that such an approach is true. In modern civilisation, few aspects of life are not impinged upon or dependent on the legal system. As such, the citizen might feel he has little alternative but to play along with the rules of the game. However, this passive attitude would not seem to completely explain what ethical scholars would term the 'pro-attitude' towards law that is manifest among the ordinary population. Harris, in *Legal Philosophies*, notes that although most people will participate in law breaking activities themselves, they are still critical of others' illegal activities.

Now this might be easily explained. Certainly, some legal prohibitions accord with the common view of what is morally unacceptable, while other minor laws seem simply an administrative nuisance. Thus, one could easily envisage even a petty thief criticising a rapist. This is not necessarily a moral endorsement of the obligation to obey law, but an endorsement of the obligation to obey what are subjectively felt to be morally correct laws.

c) *The positivist view*

That one need not obey an immoral law has always been conceded by positivists, although their tones are resonant of Anglicanism; one need not obey an immoral law, but one cannot evade the legal consequences of so doing. For this reason, it is the consequences of disobedience to the law to which its binding effect is largely credited. The positivists see respect for law in consequentialist terms. For most positivists law is obeyed, to a certain extent, because some benefit may be accrued from doing so, and to a greater extent because of the apprehension that a sanction might be imposed.

This formulation is a convincing one. However, the nature of benefits anticipated by the upright citizen is viewed by writers such as Bentham as being more in the nature of a bribe. If part of the recognition of an obligation to obey is the acceptance that a law might be of benefit to oneself or to others, then this might explain some of the 'moral' element of legal obligation.

Such an explanation is not so difficult to accept when one considers that society is very much a submission of freedom and acceptance of obligations on the premise that such sacrifices contribute to the good of the whole. This explanation remains conditional on a law being *seen* to be morally justified by the common good; the law in question need not actually be advanced for moral reasons by the legislator, it needs only to have the appearance of being morally right. Thus, social security reforms in the eighties which made life significantly harder for many people at the lower end of society, were seen by many as being morally right because such people were presented as lazy parasites.

d) *Social contractarian theories*

A particular version of the theory that law is obligatory because it satisfies social needs is to be found in the so-called 'social-contract' theories. We have already noted that Hobbes viewed humans, in their natural state, as nasty and brutish. To Hobbes the legal system is the instrument by which order is achieved, and, in fact, he considered it the only means of maintaining social cohesion. Law is therefore obeyed in return for the maintenance of order.

In contrast, Locke considered that although humans had certain unalienable rights, they surrendered their freedom for the purpose of channelling their efforts in the collective enterprise of society. As such, the law-maker holds their interests on trust, directing society through the agency of the law. However, if this trust is betrayed, then the law-maker cannot command obedience.

These theories are dubbed social contract theories because they see the relationship between legal authority and civil obedience resting on unspoken mutual promises. To Hobbes, the brutes obey, but in return the law-maker must maintain order. Locke's premise is that the partial surrender of freedom is in return for good order. It is thus as if the parties had entered into a contract. The major difficulty with these theories is that they fail to adequately explain how such promises were obtained. Do I, by being born into a society, automatically consent to be ruled? It may be argued that by my presence within the territory I have given my consent, but there is hardly an inch of the world now where law does not claim to exist. Alternatively, it might be said that by being born, I have already taken the benefit of society and as such have 'accepted' my obligation to obey. This would seem very unsatisfactory as an explanation.

The broad, political morality of the social contract theory is, thus, not very convincing. When we consider justice we will consider Rawls, who postulates a theory not dissimilar to the social contract theory, which proposes a calculus of fairness suggesting what laws should be obeyed and when there is no longer an obligation to do so.

e) *Utilitarian theory*

The utilitarian ethic is based on the promotion of the greatest happiness for the greatest number. Not surprisingly, their belief is that the obligation to obey the law is based on the promotion of the collective good. Certain actions might be prohibited by the law, such as the sale of liquor in 1920s America. The evil that the law seeks to prevent might not be viewed in itself as being important; however, the consequences of disobedience might be wider than the perpetration of the offence. The infectious effects of law-breaking are well illustrated by the effect of breaking prohibition or of the narcotic trade, with the associated gangland activities. In the 'felicific calculus' of the utilitarians, the benefit of the few who gain their happiness or make money from the sale and consumption of drugs and alcohol would be outweighed by the harm to the collective good. However, such examples are perhaps sui generis. Moreover, to judge the obligation to obey the law in terms of potential consequences is a little difficult. Such a view seems to be a complex way of expressing the dictum 'what would happen if everyone were to do that?' Furthermore there is an assumption implicit in this principle of 'act-utilitarianism' that the individual believes that if he breaks the law others will too. There is little evidence of the imitative nature of law breaking, except where collective law-breaking is used as a weapon against an unpopular law.

A subtly different utilitarian principle is based upon the consequences of observing a rule. 'Act-utilitarianism' asks whether a particular person's disobedience or the hanging of one man is in the interests of the collective good. 'Rule-utilitarianism' asks whether a particular practice required by a rule is, on the whole, more beneficial than harmful to the collective good. For example, if the law required the top 15% of wage-earners to be compelled to give half their salary to hospitals, more people would benefit than would lose.

However, as a representation of reasons why people obey the law the utilitarian point of view seems a little unconvincing. Popular notions of the collective good are tempered by our feelings that certain things such as human rights are of fundamental importance. The utilitarian view has often been criticised on the basis that the greatest happiness for the greatest number could mean the greatest misery for the few. Not surprisingly this brings us back to the problem of moral safeguards against the binding effect of an immoral law.

f) *Finnis*

In response, Finnis postulates a view of legal obligation based upon natural and self-evident principles of good and practical reasonableness. While law is whatever is legally valid, the obligation that accrues to law is obviously greater, the more respect a legal system has for these principles. Legal systems are seen as carrying with them a general moral obligation if they carry with them moral approval. Without such approval Finnis would not dispute that a law is a law, but would assert that there is no obligation to obey it. Such a conclusion seems to be almost too obvious, but the strength of Finnis' argument is based on his derivation of absolute moral values. We shall give him due consideration in the next chapter.

g) *Conclusion*

That there is the possibility and even likelihood of a link between the strength of the obligation to obey the law and general moral obligations cannot be denied. However, I do not feel that anyone has shown that law necessarily relies on moral feelings to any great extent in order to ensure obedience.

As to the ultimate question of whether there is a necessary link between law and morality, perhaps the last word deserves to go to Raz. He seems to have managed to marry practical and moral reasoning with positivism in a way that has gained him widespread respect. When addressing the question as to whether law is value free, he identifies the process of law creation as being a process of gradual purification. The debates that precede the creation of statutes are ultimately based on practical and political reasoning, including moral consideration. Once a Bill becomes law, part of the broader debate is excluded; however, there may remain executive decisions. It may be necessary for executive action to be taken in the form of delegated legislation. Even when a court is faced with a 'complete' statute, there are clearly still issues to be addressed in the form of the correct principles to apply. Court decisions are influenced by the participants, and to this extent even the subject to the law can affect legal values by pursuing legal arguments. However, law is for Raz a matter concerned with the executive stage of institutional decisions and, as such, what has been decided by Parliament or a Ministry or a court excludes further discussion. However, the deliberative stages that continue until the final decision of the final court of appeal of a particular case 'reflect our moral and intellectual interests and concerns'.

2.10 The enforcement of morality

a) *Introduction*

The extent to which courts and legislators should reflect our moral and intellectual interests is a matter of considerable debate. Certainly, we feel that in a democratic society, law should be sensitive to social attitudes. However, one must address the issue as to how far the law should go to protect us from ourselves. The law is, of its very nature, an instrument of restraint frequently associated with the enforcement of more 'enlightened' morality, such as the prohibition of sexual and racial prejudice.

We have, to a certain extent, relied heavily on the critique of morality favoured by Hume. The empiricist view of morality seems to be one that offers us no absolute moral facts. However, when we approach the question of how people should act, there seems to be a convergence of views. Professor Isiah Berlin suggests that the fact that people do react consistently when they communicate matters of morality would seem to suggest a relative stability in moral values. Moral values may thus be found in the consistency of attitudes, rather than resulting from some empirical or logical process.

The modern view of ethical philosophers shies away from the relativist concept of moral norms. Singer, a notable ethical philosopher, observes 'Human nature has its constants and there are only a limited number of ways in which human beings can live together and flourish.' Now, how ethics has arrived at this view is hard to understand and still harder to explain, but it suggests that it is morally acceptable to make moral judgments about the behaviour of others. If we go further and accept Kantian ethics, which are based on equally difficult reasoning, but are largely regarded as being the 'right' approach, we are bound to enforce moral propositions which would prevent harm to another. This is, of course, all theory.

The enforcement of morality debate is essentially a moral or ethical one; whether we prohibit homosexual activity is not a legal issue. Law either prohibits it or it does not.

Unlike murder, which has a clear formula of evil intent and destruction of human life, not all moral issues easily provide pragmatic reasons for censure. Even if life had no value, the malicious killing of a slave, as property of economic value, would be wrong. Most 'settled' issues of morality that English law enforces can be reduced to attitudes to property, especially if you reduce people to being 'mere chattels'. Rape becomes as easily accounted for as trespass, even to the extent of the former fiction that marriage provided a sort of 'easement' over a wife's body and therefore excluded the concept of 'marital rape'. Thus simplified issues of enforced morality can be easily if not satisfactorily accommodated by the law.

However, the process of modern development confuses society and the State. Social cohesion is built up on moral institutions and values. The things that make it work are factors such as reliability, trustworthiness, affection, loyalty etc and most human endeavours are founded on these aspects of mutuality and consistency. Equally, it carries with it taboos, which do not fit easily into the legal framework. Law seeks to superimpose rules of behaviour on this matrix and to tinker with it, without destroying the links that make society work. Law is a social fact, but if society breaks down so does law. John Stuart Mill was concerned with social progress, but with a formula for legislation that did not allow the destruction or substitution of these fundamental social values with theoretical ones.

Mill was much influenced by Bentham, but like our contemporary ethical philosophers he was a believer in the synthesis of the seemingly irreconcilable doctrines of utilitarianism and Conservative idealism. He presents the dilemma of democracy in his essays contrasting Bentham and Coleridge. On the one hand '[he] is deeply impressed with the mischief done to the uneducated and uncultivated by weaning them of all habits of reverence, appealing to them as a competent tribunal to decide the most intricate question, and making them thinking themselves capable, not only of being a light to themselves, but of giving the law to their superiors in culture.' On the other hand the pursuit of self-interest by the ruling elite has been 'generally to a ruinous extent ... and ... the only possible remedy is pure democracy, in which people are their own governors ...'. Having seen the latter achieved (after a manner) by the passing of the Reform Bill in 1832, he turned his attention to the former problem, that of the tyranny of the self-serving interests of the numerical majority. In *On Liberty* he addresses himself to the protection of individual rights and minority interests from the popular opinion in a democratic state. However, his concept of individual rights is often seen as a charter for 'the permissive society'. This is to take his views out of historical context. The Reform Act enfranchised the industrial middle and artisan classes, so that the 'interests' Mill saw as a threat were largely those of the rampant capitalists. Linked to his concern is his detestation of utilitarianism as a substitute for societal values. 'A philosophy like Bentham's ... can teach the means of organizing and regulating the merely business part of social arrangements ... it will do nothing (except sometimes as an instrument in the hands of a higher doctrine) for the spiritual interests of society; nor does it suffice even of itself even for the material interests ... All he can do is but to indicate means by which, in any given state of national mind, the material interests of society can be protected; saving the question, of which others must judge, whether the use of those means would have, on the national character, any injurious influence.' This reflects Coleridge's concern that 'we shall ... be governed ... by a contemptible democratic oligarchy of glib economists.' Mill saw a distinction between the public realm of morality and the private realm, employing the 'harm principle' as the acid test. 'The only purpose for which power can be rightfully exercised over any member of a civilised community, against his will, is to prevent harm to others. His own good, either physical or moral, is not sufficient warrant.' This is an insurance against the danger of cultural and societal decay which he fears is the result of throwing out societal values. 'Bentham's idea of the world is that of a collection of persons pursuing each his separate interest and pleasure.' To Mill an alternative institution should protect societal mores because he was unsure of what sort of guardian of morality the electorate would make. This judgment has been criticised by Dias as being primarily one based on his own elitist moral values.

c) *Critique of Mill*

The formula therefore becomes more complicated in a democratic society. Law has an educative and regulatory role; however, true democracy requires that laws be made by the people who are subject to them. Law made by the wishes of the numerical majority may result in misery for the minority. Mill, in his later work, advocates the dualism of political self-determination through the instrument of law, but elite determination of moral and cultural values. Not surprisingly, Marx criticises Mill for trying to reconcile the irreconcilable.

Other critics of Mill, such as Stephen J, in *Liberty, Equality and Fraternity* (1873) doubt that a distinction can be truly made between acts that harm others and acts that harm oneself. Individuals are, to a certain extent, what St Exupery called 'knots' in the web of society. Society must be free to judge what is harmful to itself. In the present democratic system this would mean the will of the majority, which returns us to the tyranny of the electorate.

Fortunately, or unfortunately, we do not really exist in the sort of pure democracy where the electorate makes moral decisions. Parliament reserves the right to vote paternalistically on matters of conscience, such as hanging or the preservation of Sunday trading laws. Equally the courts consider 'There is in the courts as custodes morum of the people a residual power, where no statute has yet intervened to supersede the common law, to superintend those offences that are prejudicial to public welfare ...' (Viscount Simmonds *Shaw* v *DPP* [1962]).

However, even if we grant that institutions exist that might enforce and retain a static content of morality, the problem is far from solved. The credibility, or 'efficaciousness' of a legal system in a democratic society depends on it treading a tightrope. On the one hand the legal system should not be seen as over-paternalistic and interfering, while on the other, it must retain a relativity to society. A legal system cannot take for granted that because it tolerates something, society will as well, for forces in society that see unrestrained 'deviance' may be prompted to take action independent of the law. The law is placed in the situation of a schoolmaster who cannot use corporal violence, but must nonetheless maintain discipline. Law cannot dictate, but neither would it be acceptable for it to ignore society's maladies. The problem, therefore takes on a legal dimension.

d) *Reasonableness as a test*

One attempt at solving this equation was the Wolfenden Committee *Report on Homosexual Offences and Prostitution* (1957). The committee deployed the arguments of the harm principle and a proposition similar to that of Mills: 'there must remain a realm of private morality and immorality which is not the law's business'. Both prostitution and private homosexual acts were determined to be unharmful to non-participants and, as such, outside the 'proper' ambit of legal restriction. That the findings were correct, in the historical framework of societal mores, is not widely disputed. However, the employment of the harm principle was seen by some, such as Devlin in *The Enforcement of Morals*, as being unduly restrictive. Instead he appeals to the widely employed legal fiction of the 'reasonable man'. Devlin, in the true spirit of democracy, supports the view that law should not tolerate that which the reasonable man finds disgusting. Society needs a moral identity, because it is the moral values of society that make it cohere. For Devlin, even private acts of immorality can weaken the fabric of society if they are sufficiently grave.

The balance that Devlin seeks to achieve is placed in the context of the political morality of contemporary society, where toleration is itself a prime moral principle. Thus, '(there) ... must be toleration of the maximum individual freedom that is consistent with the integrity of society'. I am unsure of the consistency of Devlin's argument. His justification for the legal enforcement of morality is an extension of the 'harm principle' to a perceived threat to society, rather than harm to other individuals. This seems quite a reasonable proposition. However, his test is one that masquerades as (1) a relevant test for the principle, and (2) an objective test. Devlin's reasonable man is not asked in sociological terms what immorality is threatening to society's fabric – this would surely be the appropriate test for his argument. He is asked instead, what he feels disgust at. Most Englishmen feel that eating frogs' legs is disgusting; that does not mean that they consider it 'harmful food'. An appeal to aesthetic sense, is to rely on preferences to answer what should surely be a rational question. Furthermore, while the 'reasonable man' test is employed as a way of alienating a courtroom issue from the subjective opinions of parties to a particular legal issue, it does not necessarily have the same effect in this situation. Devlin employs the term 'reasonable man' to give the impression of objectivity. However, it is a fiction to suggest that there is a 'reasonable man' when it comes to more difficult moral issues. The reasonable man of legal fiction is one who employs practical reason and due consideration when acting. However, all the practical reason and due consideration in the world will not change the preferences and prejudices that embody disgust. On the issue of homosexuality, many people intellectually feel that people's sexual orientation is not a matter for legal intervention, but they nonetheless find homosexual acts to be repellent. The reasonable man test is thus a spurious validation for prevailing societal aesthetics, rather than a test of what society feels to be threatening.

Devlin's fundamental thesis is one of conservatism. He advocates maximum privacy, freedom and toleration, subject to the overriding principles of societal harm and public outrage. Law should be slow to change since it protects the institutions that are the fabric of society. To subvert the morality of a democratic society by attacking these institutions is, to Devlin, tantamount to treason.

For a Liberal, such as Dworkin in *Taking Rights Seriously,* Devlin is seeking the legislation of a sort of 'moral majority' that can veto change to the moral environment, when it opposes that change. This simply highlights the fact that the welfare of society is not something that encourages a good deal of agreement. To Dworkin a healthy society is one that diversifies and reflects an innovative pluralism, because the individual, in his own affairs, has an absolute right against society. For Devlin, the individual in the eyes of the law is ultimately a part of society, and, as such, is morally accountable if he is, in himself, grievously deviant.

e) *Liberalism*

Devlin proposes in justification of this view, that many moral judgments can be identified with harm, on the basis of an argument not dissimilar to 'act-utilitarianism'. He cites the example of drunkenness. If everyone got drunk every night then this could seriously undermine the fabric of society. Consequentialism of this kind can justify the prohibition of practically everything. If everyone drove their cars at the same time, all traffic would come to a stop!

It is not difficult to emotionally agree with Devlin's conservatism, which is reluctant to derogate from moral consistency, but his appeal to public outrage cannot help being an appeal to traditional prejudice. His requirement that the reasonable man arrives at his disgust 'in good faith' is a nonsense. Most people have moral prejudices, as they will freely admit, and this is almost an inalienable part of their reasoning. Dworkin's liberality on the other hand is intellectually attractive, but I think it is less sustainable. Morality is largely something that is learned. The 'anything goes so long as it is not harmful to others' school of thought seems usually to be the demoralising agent that is the prelude to extreme moral backlashes. This is possibly a very subjective view of history, but it is one that might be sustainable. The excesses of the Weimar Republic in Germany, followed by the Nazi 'moral purges', or the current censorship backlash in America might illustrate this. Popular disgust may be prejudice, but it seems that a moderate content of prejudice may be as necessary to national identity, as it is to personal identity. Moderate conservatism may thus be preferable to tides of moral permissiveness followed by suppression.

However, the 'conservative morality' that Devlin perceives people as holding is not necessarily one of their own making. If morality is learned, then the morality we have is probably the one disseminated by the dominant educational interests in our lives. Shared morality may well be the ideology of the cultural elite that we have been brainwashed into accepting. The enforcement of morality by the law would thus become the perpetuation of interest. Now that religion is on the decline, the major influences on our moral judgments are the media, the market and the education system. However, our view of a shared morality is represented as being expressed through these organisations. It may be that 'shared morality' is a self-creating phenomenon.

f) *Paternalism*

This rather casts us back on the same sea of conflicting moralities that we have been navigating. Fortunately, Hart is willing to take us in tow in *Law, Liberty and Morality.* He recognises the point that I have been trying to make; that (1) there does not seem to be any real widely shared morality, and (2) there can be no freedom if we are compelled to accept only those things that others approve of.

Hart notes that there are certain constants of the human condition, which he terms 'the minimum content of Natural Law', such as the vulnerability of human beings. If we disregard these sociological facts it would be tantamount to suicide. But beyond these facts, society is faced with a choice of what rules to adopt in order to protect us from the frailties of the human condition. Hart seems to assert that since the development of a society is a collective odyssey, the values that a society has adopted for its preservation and progress constitute a shared morality of sorts. This does not mean that the norms that a society has accepted and retained are ones that are logically necessary for the achievement of social preservation. However, they are instrumental in the maintenance of social cohesion. For this reason he would not accept Devlin's analogy of deviation from moral norms with treason against society. It may be that a change in morality can result in friction, but it need not result in the collapse of society.

Hart also adopts the harm principle, but denies that consent can be used as mitigating factor. In the case of a minor, for example, the fact that the child consents to something does not necessarily mean that the law should not protect it from harm. Equally, immoral acts in public may be harmful to others and, as such, open to legal censure, whereas acts in private should not be a matter for the law. His justification is that while the first is the legitimate prevention of harm, the latter is the enforcement of societal will over the individual. Hart finds paternalism justified, but not enforced morality, per se.

Such a differentiation seems rationally justifiable; however, Hart's application of the principle seems to be a distortion of it. Thus, he supports the age restriction on homosexual acts, because of the danger of 'corruption'. As Dias correctly points out, this is a moral distinction, couched in the terminology of harm. He criticises Hart's view that there is a public and private sphere of morality, since acts in private may have an effect in public. For example, the act of prostitution usually occurs in private. However it is inconceivable that prostitution could occur without solicitation either on the part of the prostitute or the client. Such solicitation is deemed to be in the public realm. The illegality of this public act relates to the private act of immorality. If I were to add an edge to Dias' example, one could compare asking a woman for sexual favours, which would be illegal, with paying a female doctor for sexual therapy, which is quite legitimate. Indeed, the custom of a dowried marriage could easily be recast in terms of the paying of consideration in return for, inter alia, a sexual relationship.

Although Dias is pointing out justifiably the fact that acts are differentiated on the basis of their moral end, this does not necessarily negate Hart's argument. Hart's insistence on the harm principle can be reargued in the case of prostitution. One of the great public criticisms of brothels and ladies of the street is not, as Dias would suggest, that people fear being accosted by a woman, but that groups of individuals meeting in front of houses, or pulling up in cars in the small hours of the morning, is a nuisance. Nuisance is not a moral proposition, but an infringement of proprietary rights recognised by the law.

Hart's argument against bigamy is somewhat more flawed. He asserts that bigamy confuses the contractual obligations between parties. This is somewhat fallacious. The law of marriage is orientated towards the Christian norm of monogamy. He does not demonstrate actual harm, for the law of marriage could equally accommodate polygamy with a registration system like the system of registration for property. One could find out whether there are any other parties involved in a marriage contract.

Hart's employment of the arguments for paternalism to prevent 'harm' does not satisfy the liberals, who regard the nannying of people as insulting and a licence for elitist morality. Neither does it satisfy moralists. Adultery is more empirically harmful than some other moral norms that would be justifiable on the basis of the harm principle; to make it illegal would prevent the expense and potential harm caused by marital break-ups, reduce the possibility of unwanted pregnancies, abortions and one-parent families, and would be justifiable even from the perspective of AIDS. But then so would the outlawing of 'fornication'.

The use of rationalistic theories to justify the enforcement of morality is somewhat undermined by the arbitrary application of those principles. Most sports are not subject to moral censure, yet there are many sports harmful to participants and non-participants alike. Arbitrariness of this nature betrays the fact that the legal enforcement of morality is a matter more settled by tradition than reason. Perhaps it may be more honest to approach the problem from an alternative perspective that the law should enforce those moral norms that it has traditionally enforced, unless it cannot be morally or rationally justified.

The danger of this is well illustrated by the situation occasioned by the offences of blasphemy, which the law still prohibits within the context of the Christian religion. The Law Commission report on *Offences Against Religion* (1985) (No 145) recommended the complete abolition of blasphemy offences, a recommendation that has not been acted upon.

This non-rationalist and non-moralist approach is hardly a recipe for successful prescriptive law reform. Dias proposes a more complex equation that does not help us justify the existing moral codes, but gives us a sense of priorities that can be taken into account. In his equation, reference must be made to the following considerations:

  i)   The danger of the activities to others.

  ii) The danger to the actor himself.

  iii) Economy of forces needed for detection and pursuit.

  iv) Equality of treatment.

  v)   The nature of the sanction.

  vi) Possibility of hardship caused by the sanction.

  vii) Possible side effects.

Dias is however, concerned that the criminal law should not be used to enforce morality, since its associations with punishment and retribution are not appropriate, particularly when there is harm caused only to the actor. Instead, immorality should be deterred by rules and 'cured' and thus it is proper in Dias's eyes for the law to concern itself with moral issues.

2.11 A practical problem

a) *Introduction*

It may well help the student, in his search for a meaningful evaluation of the law and morality debate, to consider a problem issue. Much has been written on the issue of the prohibition/rights of homosexuals. I think the problem is a useful one, since its paradigm is the clash between judeo-christian and liberal moralities. The debate seems to be hottest in America, where the lack of explicit constitutional safeguards and the federal system of legislatures has placed the courts in the invidious position of making what is, essentially, a moral choice.

In *Bowkers* v *Hardwick* the American Supreme Court was faced with the question of the constitutionality of Georgia's anti-sodomy laws. It was argued that the broad provisions of the American constitution should be read as being applicable to gay men. The majority of the court found the Georgian state laws to be constitutionally valid.

Bowkers presents an interesting situation. On the one hand, since *Brown* it has been clear that the courts may apply the constitution as if it were higher law. The 'gay' case was that, by reasonable implication, the constitutional protection of private life applied equally to homosexual men as to any other minority group. The 'state' case was that the explicit legislation was designed to prevent acts, that of their nature took themselves outside the normal protection of constitutional rights. In legal terms the choice was between implicit higher law and explicit lower law. Thus, legally speaking, the court was faced with six of one and half a dozen of the other.

The moral problem may be formulated in many ways, depending on one's attitude towards the issue. Whichever way the court had decided, one could argue with equal vigour that the law was seen to be settled on moral grounds or pragmatic grounds. The situation is thus an interesting one, for it presents us with what is essentially a moral dilemma. The dilemma is one of construction of a concept that is a moral rather than factual issue. In his consideration of the case, Mohr in *Gays/Justice*, posits the idea that the notion of homosexuality as a phenomenon is sociological judgment, rather than a biological fact, one that is derived from the stereotypation of sexual roles. Certainly there are those who do not agree with him on this, such as Moran. However, the law is asked to consider gays at the same time as a special case and not a special case. The criminalisation of sodomy itself is not the issue in *Bowkers*. It is the restriction on the freedom of sexual expression and privacy of gay relationships that is being criticised. As such, to a certain extent, the argument is that gays are a special case. On the other hand, there is an appeal to broad constitutional provisions, that gays are equally entitled to privacy in their private lives as heterosexuals. The vital question becomes what the nature of being gay is.

b) *A theoretical solution?*

The Georgian laws do not seek to prevent a homosexual disposition, for this would be almost impossible. The effect of the law is to label homosexual activity as aberrant. By the same token, to deny equal constitutional treatment of homosexual men, is to either deny homosexuality as a 'normal' practice, to judge it to be aberrant, or simply to ignore it altogether.

Now, we might seek to apply some of the theoretical knowledge to this practical problem. The positivist view of this issue would certainly be that the law is what the law is. The only problem with this approach is that before *Bowkers,* and even after *Bowkers*, what the law is seems very hard to tell. The tradition of constitutional construction is one that derives fairly complex decisions from very static norms. There is no real guarantee that a differently constituted court would not make a different decision in the same circumstances. Traditional positivism, such as that of Kelsen, has a narrow view of law, based on the assumption of validity of legal statements. Thus, if Georgian law states that sodomy is illegal, then it is illegal. However, to state that law prohibits such and such is to say what legal statements have been made in the past and then to presuppose that such statements will be valid in the future. But law is something more than the history of legal statements. The vital elements in a living legal system involve advocates and advisers evaluating the probability of certain legal arguments being successful. In addition personnel of legal institutions are not only required to decide what the law requires them to decide in terms of posited norms, but also to make rational judgments in the light of these norms in detailed factual circumstances that are unlikely to have been exactly determined by existing legal norms. In such terms, Raz's reformulation of positivism, accommodating practical reasoning, seems to be more satisfactory. However, practical reasoning is seldom free of moral considerations, whether it be of a personal, political or societal nature.

This view would certainly be endorsed by Fuller, who appreciated the implicit nature of law as a human activity. However, Fuller's procedural morality of the law would have little to say about the problem faced by the court in *Bowkers*.

In contrast there seems to be a tension between Hart's view of what law is and what he believes its role should be. Hart justifies the positivist separation of law and morality, not just on empirical grounds, but also on moral grounds. He reminds us that law is not morality and should not supplant it. He also recommends that law should be paternalistic in the prevention of harm. His concept of harm principle would censure certain classes of homosexual activities on the ground of 'corruption'. This seems to be at issue with his advocacy of the separation of law and morality.

On the other hand Devlin's 'disgust' test would be of critical difficulty for the judge. The judge would have to decide whether the reasonable man can only be a heterosexual. To assume this would be to almost certainly to preclude any answer other than the legitimation of state censure of homosexuality. Since the majority in America are taken to be heterosexual, this is the validation of moral standards on the basis of numbers. In the past, slavery and segregation have been regarded by the majority as morally right at the expense of the minority.

Mill's harm principle, coupled with his moral libertarianism, would isolate the problem from the danger of the 'moral majority', but would require an empirical and/or sociological justification for legal prohibition. This remains the subject of controversy since most empirical and sociological studies of the subject evoke emotionally charged criticisms of 'homophobic' premises.

Still more controversial would be the application of Dias' principle that moral deviance should be 'cured'. Previously in England, before the relaxation of controls on homosexual activity, a harsh regime of 'aversion and diversion' therapies had been employed to 'cure' homosexuals. The results were mixed. It seems from the body of scientific research that there is an element of 'conditioned' rather than innate homosexuality. But to justify 'curing' conditioned homosexuals would be to justify sexual conditioning to fit in with a perceived sexual normality. The premise would once again seem to require a pre-judgment on moral grounds.

c) *Conclusion*

Ultimately, the application of the enforcement of morality debate is of little help to the solution of practical problems, since the theories do not provide a sure method of determination, free of moral considerations. What the arguments do provide is rational justifications for preconceived moral attitudes. Conversely, the fact that such a debate exists, and the nature of the problem faced in *Bowkers*, emphasises that moral judgments cannot be excluded from legal discourse, since legal discourse is simply a specialised form of human discourse. What it does reinforce, is that although no firm moral content to law, the nature of the legal pursuit is to regulate human behaviour. Some of the most important areas of human activity involve moral issues. A legal system that does not address the moral facet of human behaviour is one that inadequately comprehends human nature and therefore is almost certainly doomed to failure. This is not to say that the legal system's morality needs be convergent with that of its subjects, but it requires the legislators and judiciary to be aware of the moral impulses that propel individuals.

If a country had a criminal code entirely based on strict liabilities it would be unable to differentiate between fraud and salesmanship, between murder and self-defence. Even in the absence of a criminal code, which is itself a judgment of what is good or bad for the State and society, many civil concepts such as contract, negligence and even property stem from a particular view of the constancy of certain moral relationships in society. However much a legal system might distort morality, it is founded on the reality of social behaviour which is flavoured with moral concepts.

These are personal conclusions that the student need not accept. Hopefully the problem of law's actual and proper relationships with morality will spur the student on to reading deeper into the authors who have examined this problem in greater depth.

The picture of morality that has been examined in this chapter has been one of a relative and uncertain morality. Empiricism spurs us on to accept this conclusion when we look at peripheral issues. There are, however, those who see that there is a natural, rational and to some extent morally good system of laws that is nascent either in human nature, or indeed the natural world. This natural law is what legal systems must be judged by and what legal systems aspire to. The advantage of such a view, if it can be rationally justified, is that it gives a structural and rational solution to the question of what laws we should morally obey. Moreover it is asserted that a Natural Law theory holds true, not only for one individual, or indeed, one society; it is of universal application. Although law and morality issues are the concern of natural law theories, the methodology is slightly different. Instead of asking whether we can see in human laws a reflection of human values, natural law theorists tend to ask whether we can look at sociological and cosmological facts in order that we can derive a pattern of order that represents 'natural behaviour'. Of these natural laws, we can select those laws we see to be for the good of humanity.

3   NATURAL LAW

3.1   Introduction

Despite a recent revival, Natural Law theories have been frequently scorned by jurists, for a mixture of methodological and philosophical reasons. There seem to be three major areas of criticism of Natural Law theories;

a) The method used to derive rules of Natural Law makes an illogical jump from questions of fact (what is) to questions of obligation (what we ought to do). This will be explained later.

b) Natural Law theories have frequently been employed to justify the status quo and to validate what would seem to us to be unjust regimes.

c) Natural Lawyers have failed to satisfactorily explain what effect a difference between Natural Law and human law has.

These three criticisms are not necessarily applicable to all Natural Law theories, as we shall see. But they should be borne in mind by the student.

3.2   What is Natural Law?

Professor D'Entreves, whose *Natural Law* is a considerable survey on the subject, points out that 'many of the ambiguities of the concept of Natural Law must be ascribed to the ambiguity of the concept of nature that underlies it.' This is hardly surprising, since the search for a coherent system of Natural Law spans two and a half millennia. As a result the content and the role of Natural Law is varied. However, the core assertion of Natural Law is that rather than all moral rules being a product of reason, there are some moral rules that exist independently of reason, but may be understood by it. The way in which man should live is 'locked up' in his nature and/or the nature of his universe.

Now, this may sound a little crazy to the non-religious student. Indeed many Natural Law theories have relied on the will of God to justify the theorem, but this is not necessary for the theory to work. There are essentially three questions that need to be satisfied by the Natural Lawyer in order to logically justify his position:

a) Are there pre-determined patterns of behaviour in nature and in human nature? For a while, under the influence of thinkers such as Condillac, the idea that humans were born with any pre-determined ends was denied. However, it is clear from, for example genetic theory, as well as ecological theories, that human behaviour and the human race have certain innate characteristics, impulses as well as a place 'in the order of things'. Thus, a human is born with the urge for sexual reproduction, with social instincts such as the protection of offspring. This leads us onto the next question.

b) Why should a human follow the pattern of behaviour he has been programmed with? Since human beings have free choice, a human might easily decide to be celibate or not to have children. The fact that people usually do have children does not mean that an individual should. It is therefore a matter for his or her own choice, and, as such, pragmatism and self-interest or personal preference would temper such a decision. The only justification above the rational, is the moral. We say a person should follow a pattern of behaviour, in moral terms, because it is good. This leads to the problem of whether (a) there is a difference between what is good and what is expedient in the light of desires or enlightened self-interest (b) we can ascertain a criterion for determining what is good that is of universal application.

c) How do we know that it is good to follow the natural patterns of behaviour and, even if it is, might it not sometimes be better to go against it? For me, this is the hardest of the questions that Natural Law has to answer. A logically independent concept of good has to stem from some person's non-rational preference. There are two alternatives. (i) If we can show that all men think that a particular thing is good, then we might say that Natural Law is self-evidently good and needs no rational justification. (ii) There is a superior entity who requires us to do what is good and has ordained these laws.

The latter proposition usually is not employed to stand by itself. We obey God, rather than the Devil, because God is good. Thus we are reflected back to the question of how we get to this proposition of 'good'. The former proposition of the self-evidence of good denies that there is basis of the concept in normal reasoning. Finnis explains it thus:

'When discerning what is good ... intelligence is operating in a different way, yielding to a different logic, from when it is discerning what is the case (historically, scientifically, or metaphysically); but there is no good reason for asserting that the latter operations of intelligence are more rational than the former ...'

The three questions – of what the content of Natural Law is, what the nature of the obligation is and why it is a moral obligation – are necessary to overcome the criticism of the empiricists. The empiricist criticisms of Natural Law follow the pattern of these problems.

a) The content of Natural Law theories is varied and sometimes contradictory. Thus, while the Greeks thought that slavery was a naturally justified institution, modern moralists would disagree. There is an ongoing struggle to nail down the content of Natural Law. Most thinkers prefer to assert the existence of principles from which a variety of rules can be derived, rather than asserting the rules themselves. On this basis, thinkers such as Stammler can safely assert that while the principle of justice is universal, its application is varied. While this overcomes the problem of moral variance, this also limits the usefulness of the concept. Natural Law thus becomes reduced to universal platitudes.

b) Empiricists criticise the fact that even if universal patterns can be demonstrated, this does not show that there is an obligation to follow them. Just because people do something, does not mean they ought to do this. There are alternative answers to the question:

   i) People and things have a purpose and are part of a definite order, established by a benevolent creator;

   ii) The universal principles are motivations, rather than patterns of behaviour and as such they are automatic preferences. This then requires that bad motivations be separated from good motivations.

   iii) The principles are sociological and psychological facts which practical reason dictate we should obey. When faced with the fact that a road is peppered with land mines we do not need to ask why we should not go over it. Similarly, Hart would assert that human vulnerability means that it is self-evident that we should not hurt or injure some human beings. However, this approach provides us with reasons for doing something rather than principles for action that are to be followed for moral reasons.

c) Empiricists find it hard to understand why there is a need to subjugate individual morality to a universal morality, since in the absence of objectively provable moral norms one can only know one's own conscience. It would seem to be a moral contradiction if one were to ignore one's own conscience in order to obey some 'universal moral law'.

3.3 The relevance of Natural Law to Jurisprudence students

The student of law might question why he should be concerned with people's attempts to say what the law should be. In the previous chapter we discussed legal statements. Describing law in conditional statements does not commit one to saying what makes law valid, it simply describes what law is, if it is valid. An example of this might be taken to be Hart's concept of law, which describes what law is if it is effective. Such an attitude begs the question of why, logically, law should be effective. Alternatively, we might describe law in terms of detached statements, which assume that law should be obeyed, because it is assumed to be valid. This leads to an uncritical formula which does not necessarily place law in any social context and leads to the mindless formalism that distances law from practical and moral considerations. Finally we might use committed statements which assert that law is valid, but this requires an acceptable reason. (A further discussion of this is to be found in 6.6(c).)

All three types of statements are descriptive, but uncritical. If a scientist were to describe scientific phenomena in terms of the accepted theories, without necessarily testing whether those theories are valid in the light of facts, science would not have progressed from the 'flat earth' of the Middle Ages. Similarly, the advocate, judge and legislator are embarked on a practical course of controlling human behaviour. The lawyer is likely to be more successful in this pursuit if he can not only say what someone should do, but give reasons that will encourage a person to obey. Merely threatening the use of sanctions and employing bribery is not enough to ensure adherence to the law.

What the Natural Lawyer is seeking to offer us is an authoritative guide to what human nature thinks it ought to do. Thus, although positivism insists on what lawyers actually do and say in order to define the concept of law, Legal Naturalism seeks to understand what the unifying idea and ideal of law is.

3.4 The origins of Natural Law

a) *Introduction*

The origins of Natural Law are obscure; however, clearly the human concern to understand an apparently arbitrary world in terms of order would be a starting point. Clearly, although certain natural phenomena seemed to obey definite patterns, human nature did not always, the difference being that humans seemed to have free choice. While natural things seemed to conform to a regularity, as if they were ordained to do so, man did not. Without the complex faith that we have in cause and effect, the idea of some inscrutable purpose of a mysterious creator seemed the obvious way in which things could be accounted for. However man, with his free choice, was not behaving in a clear and uncomplicated way. Man had obviously gone wrong somewhere, since he did not seem to always fit into the order of things.

This is mere speculation, but it seems to fit in with the tenet of a lot of ancient theological theories that form the premise for some Natural Law theories. The appeal of such theories is an appeal to an order that is above the order that can be attained by individual human cognisance. Plato advocated that society should be ruled by contemplative philosopher-kings, whose inward reflection would allow them to comprehend the divine truths locked in their own hearts. But this did not mean that there was, for early Greek philosophers, a necessarily consistent truth for all peoples, or one that was for the common man, rather than merely the wise ruler. As such Natural Law was an ideal, which in no way had a true practical value.

b) *The Romans*

It was left to the ever pragmatic Romans to utilise the concept of Natural Law. Greek stoic philosophers speculated that a man who lived naturally was a man who lived by reason. Since reason is common to all men, then there are universal laws that can be derived by reason, that man could live by. The Romans employed this concept in implementing their laws within the empire, while Cicero employed Natural Law as a legal argument for striking down laws that did not favour his case. The dedication of the Romans to the idea of Natural Law was a matter of expediency, since it was an ideology that justified the homogeneity that Roman imperialism entailed. Thus, while some insist that the Romans were guilty of a 'naturalistic fallacy' of confusing what they applied universally with what is universally valid, I prefer to see it as the shrewd use of a useful ideology.

c) *Thomas Aquinas*

Aquinas, a thirteenth century theologian and philosopher, made probably the most rationally compelling justification of the Natural Law theory. His followers in the Middle Ages are termed Scholastics or Thomists. However, Aquinas still influences modern Natural Law theories.

i) Aquinas sees law as being binding on people's actions. However, people act according to their reason therefore ' ... will, if it is to have the authority of law, must be regulated by reason when it commands.' The compulsion of law, though it might be backed by sanctions, relies on reason for it to have an effect on the will. What must compel humans' reason is, for Aquinas, the promotion of the collective good. The power of the legislator therefore stems from a duty to promote the collective good. It is because the legislator is under such a duty that the subject has a duty to obey the law. Aquinas's emphasis is on society subjugating individual interests to the good of the whole, the force of law being that it is a superior institution to other institutions where rules may be made. Thus, although the head of a family may lay down prescriptions for its members, for the good of the whole, this gives way to the good of a whole community. In conclusion law '... is nothing else than the ordering of things which concern the common good; promulgated by whoever is charged with the care of the community.'

ii) Aquinas divides law into four categories. Eternal law is the reason of the creator of all things and is revealed, in part, in the scriptures as Divine law. Natural Law represents the attribute of humans that allows them to make choices and follow their inclinations towards good. As such a man may use his reason to help himself progress. As a result of speculations about what is good, people seek to reason practically as to how to attain this. The sum of practical reasoning is Human Law.

iii) Consequently Aquinas sees temporal law as a dual order. The precepts of Natural Law are speculations about the truth of how humans should behave. Primarily, there is an inclination towards the 'good', which to Aquinas, is the fulfilment of the divine purpose.

However, the inclinations of man are towards the preservation of human life, and other instincts that he shares with other animals, such as sexual relationships and the rearing of offspring. However, there is a category of Natural Law that is specific to humans alone, such as the social nature of man and his urge for truth, which Aquinas views as stemming from religion and God. The 'reason' employed in coming to know the precepts of Natural Law is distinct from practical reason employed for the attaining of specific rules. While the former is the pursuit of absolute truth, the latter is concerned with the facts of human behaviour, but is subject to the perversions of human reason, motivated by the evil desires of some.

Natural Law is not something that is perfectly comprehended by all, but something that can be comprehended, if it is not obscured by certain contingencies of human behaviour. Natural Law can be added to as man progresses, but may not be subtracted from.

Human Law is justified as providing order, which is itself simply justified in that '… man, unlike all animals, has the weapon of reason with which to exploit his base desires and cruelty.' In addition to human law that is inspired by precepts of Natural Law, such as the prohibition of murder, laws contain things that are practical derivations of how to enforce Natural Law. Thus, although, to take a modern example, Natural Law does not require the wearing of seat-belts, but such a law serves as a way of protecting human life, which is a precept of Natural Law. Since Human Law is thus partly a question of how best to achieve the enforcement of Natural Law principles, the content of human laws may change from time to time and place to place.

Aquinas believes that Human Laws that does not correspond to Natural Law are corruptions of law. These are human laws that lack the character of law that binds moral conscience. Because of the imperfections of individual reason and the need for order, disobedience to law is not however necessarily justified, even if Human Law contradicts Natural Law.

The student will note that the paradigm of Aquinas' theory is the existence of God's universal purpose as the foundation of all truth about how people should act. Thus, ultimately, Aquinas is stating that we must obey Natural Law because God so wills it. However, the major contribution of his theory is that Aquinas attributes to humans the ability to determine truth from falsehood by speculative reasoning. Furthermore he asserts that there are absolute moral values, but the fact that we do not always see them does not eliminate their truth, since they cannot be detracted from. Moreover, Natural Law precepts are inclinations, rather than the result of practical reasoning. This final distinction is one that Finnis develops.

However, the Thomists and subsequent adherents of the Natural Law theory employed the concept as a justification for the less than moral regimes of the Middle Ages. Efforts were made to distance the concept of absolute justice that Natural Law entailed from the dictates of monarchs and the stranglehold of the Catholic Church. Additionally, thinkers, such as the Dutch protestant, Grotius, advocated the logical independence of Natural Law from Divine will. Because man could reason, he could discover principles that are absolutely proper for all people. To this end Grotius created a theory of international law, built upon the cornerstone of peaceful co-existence between sovereign states. Grotius viewed law as necessarily binding because subjects of the law surrender their freedom in return for security. Grotius thus advocates that obedience to the law is a natural facet of social organisation, validated by a 'social contract' between the citizen and the ruler. Once again the Natural Law element is the ideology that allows Grotius to universalise his concepts of international law, rather than the impetus for doing so. The importance attributed to Grotius, justly or unjustly, is the secularisation of Natural Law – the assertion that irrespective of the existence of God Natural Law held good.

Philosophers such as Locke, Rousseau and to a lesser extent Hobbes looked to the concept of Natural Law as a way of justifying minimum principles of rights in their social contract theories. The student should read about these theories; however, their contribution to Natural Law thinking is minimal.

3.5 Hume

Hume's contribution to Natural Law theories may be likened to the contribution of Attila the Hun to Roman civilisation. Hume's empirical attack against Natural Law theories was two-fold:

a) Hume asserted that Natural Law theories were bedevilled with the cardinal sin of deriving normative statements ('oughts') from factual ones ('is statements'). The critical method of Hume has been discussed in the introductory chapter (1.3(c)). Whether this criticism is justified, and Finnis asserts that it is not, the stigma has stuck.

b) 'Having found that natural as well as civil justice derives from human conventions, we shall quickly perceive, how fruitless it is to resolve the one to the other, and seek, in the laws of nature, a stronger foundation for our political duties than interest, and human conventions; while the laws themselves are built on the very same foundation.' Effectively, Hume denies that there is any difference between moral judgments and other judgments. He denies the existence of God. He does not deny the existence of Natural Law, but his view is a strongly empirical one. Natural Law is simply the consistent values that are the spontaneous product of societal life and as such the 'invention of a naturally inventive species'. This sociological and psychological approach, founded on an assumption about the nature in which human reason functions, signalled a change in the way law was to be considered.

The fruit of Hume's empiricism is the broad spread of theories labelled positivist. Most positivists are more concerned with the first of the criticisms of Natural Law, which has been labelled the 'naturalistic fallacy'. However, perhaps due to the growing search for a foundation for justice and rights in the twentieth century, Natural Law has been revisited, not only by the 'idealists', but even by positivism. In the last chapter, we extensively reviewed the ideas of Lon Fuller, whose theory, even if does not truly amount to a morality in a substantive sense, have much in common with the Natural Law tradition. Equally, we mentioned Hart's minimum content of Natural Law, which seems to naturally flow from Hume's conception. Indeed, McCormick sees very close analogies between Hume and Hart.

3.6   Hart

Although Hart denies any implicit link between law and morality and he recognises a broad category of legal rules of moral derivation, and recognises that the human condition requires certain protections. As such Hart posits the one indisputable goal of human society, that of survival. Social institutions must therefore accommodate a realisation of certain criteria which have an effect on survival. He cites the following 'sociological/psychological facts':

a) Humans are vulnerable;

b) Humans are approximately equal;

c) Humans have limited altruism;

d) Humans are subject to limited resources;

e) Humans have limited understanding and strength of will.

Hart concedes that even if these facts were accepted by a legal system, then they would not necessarily make a legal system more just and fair. Moreover, he acknowledges that many legal systems do not necessarily even take cognisance of any of these. Nor are these themselves the rules of natural justice, but simply the considerations that must be taken into account as a basis of an ideal legal system. What Hart does is to posit an indisputable factual end that most societies will aspire to – survival – and remind us of the obstacles to achieving that goal, in the form of his five human weaknesses. He takes it as self-evident that in order to circumvent these weaknesses there is a necessity that there be some protection of property, persons and promises.

Hart's thesis is worthy of consideration. Hart's starting point of the assumption of the validity of survival has been criticised by Fuller. That people need to survive in order to do any other thing seems acceptable. However, even this is disputable. Take, for example, the 'Jonestown' community which committed mass suicide on the basis of religious belief, or the Jewish community of Masada, which extinguished itself rather than submit to the Roman Empire. But these extreme cases are the exception rather than the rule. Survival thus becomes a generally accepted aspiration, rather than a necessary premise for a society.

Hart says instead that 'an overwhelming majority of men do wish to live, even at the cost of hideous misery'. Hart's assertion that individual survival underlies all moral and teleogical thinking is manifestly wrong, as Fuller points out. He paraphrases Aquinas, 'if the highest aim of a captain were to preserve his ship, he would keep it in port forever.' In essence, there is a contradiction even in terms of Hart's own acknowledged facts. Human altruism may be limited, but as demonstrated by research into ants, as well as humans, individual and even mass self-sacrifice in the name of society's protection or even a core ideology, is a widespread feature.

I find Fuller's contention that a more consistent theme in morality and Natural Law theories, as well as a more indisputable object of human striving, is the communication and aggregation of information.

Moreover, societies are willing to sacrifice very large numbers of individuals in the name of survival and as such protection of the individual lives becomes secondary. Hart might assert that we do not participate in a suicide club, but this also means that the *R* v *Dudley & Stevens* principle of cannibalism for survival is not excluded, nor indeed the maxim 'dulce et decorum est pro patriam mori' which exalts the virtue of the soldier's ultimate sacrifice.

What makes it unacceptable for the wanton sacrifice of individual lives seems to be bolstered by the second 'weakness' that asserts the equality of people. This is clearly a value judgment, rather than a factual statement. People vary in physical, mental and sexual characteristics, rendering them more or less useful to society. There is no factual basis for saying that they are all equal. All we can genuinely say is that humans are of the same species, are born in the same way and die in the same way (though not with any great uniformity even in these aspects).

Lloyd points out that the limited altruism and the limited resources of human beings are inextricably bound together. Altruism is in contradiction with the drive for personal survival, and is rather a social virtue. However, altruism varies according to resources available and also from person to person. The limits to resources are always relative to the desires of the individual.

Furthermore, Hart's society is unlikely to survive longer than eighty years, since he ignores the urge for sex and parenthood, which are the strongest natural manifestations of the need for survival, but are nonetheless also weakening in their effect on immediate societal resources.

His derivation of the requirement to protect persons, property and promises from these facts of existence may even open itself up to the criticism that he is deriving an ought from an is. This is possibly unfair, since Hart's argument is that human activity is purposive, towards survival, and these are the things that we need to do in order to avoid the obstacles to survival.

What we may criticise about Hart's formulation is its confusion of the survival of the individual and the survival of society. Hart does not bring out adequately the tensions between the needs of societies and the needs of individuals who comprise it. The concern of Natural Law is to produce not only guarantees for individuals, but to find the morally correct balance for society. By ignoring this he ignores the collective aspect of the human condition. One could posit additional considerations that are necessary for the survival of society; the need to sacrifice or punish the individual for the good of the whole; the need to allow individuals to profit from their contribution to society as a recognition of their usefulness to society; the allocation of status to those with particular abilities.

D'Entreves is more concerned with the extreme noncommittal nature of Hart's Natural Law principles. For all their evasive sociological premises they are practically useless, because Hart will not commit himself to any moral or factual interaction with law-making.

3.7 Finnis

Hart says of Finnis' restatement of Natural Law that it is of 'very great merit'. By delving into the works of Natural Lawyers such as Aquinas and Aristotle, Finnis attempts to dispose of what he regards as two cardinal misconceptions about the theory:

a) Finnis denies that Natural Law derives from objectively determinable patterns of behaviour, but instead asserts it is ascertainable from inward knowledge of innate motivations.

b) Natural Law does not entail the view that law is not law if it contradicts one of the precepts of Natural Law.

In *Natural Law and Natural Rights* (1980) Finnis seeks to distance his own position and that of his philosophical predecessors from these much-vaunted criticisms. Natural Law may be 'the set of principles of practical reasonableness in ordering human life and human community', but he asserts that they are pre-moral. By this he means that they are not the product of logical deduction, nor are they merely 'passions' verified with reference to something objectively regarded as good. The latter position represents the view of the empiricists, which states that all moral values are subjective 'whims' that have the extra force of validity because others accept them as being good (this is a simplification of Hume's position).

To the extent that the empiricist criticism of some Natural Lawyers might be right, he states that 'there is no inference from fact to value'. Therefore the 'goods' that Finnis speaks of are not moral goods, but they are necessary objects of human striving. The peculiar nature of this view is that these goods are subjective insofar as they require no justification from the outside world, but are really objective since all humans must assent to their value. Finnis is therefore suggesting that these are the result of innate knowledge.

There is a strong affinity between Finnis' view of Natural Law and that of Aquinas. However, the major difference is that, for Finnis, the existence of God is only a possible explanation for the comparative order that he seeks to project on human values, not the necessary reason. Finnis instead states that his 'goods' are self-evident. This is demonstrated by, though not inferred from, the consistency of values that are identified throughout all human societies, such as, inter alia, the respect for human life.

Finnis' process of reasoning is to address any individual with the question 'X is good, don't you think?' He maintains that it is because of the consistency of these basic values of human nature that 'one gets one's ability to sympathetically (though not uncritically) see the point of actions, life-styles, characters and cultures that one would not choose for oneself.' Now, although Finnis does not mean this as evidence for his theory, I find it a compelling reason. The consistency of human nature over the millennia is one of the strongest justifications for the Natural Law position. One can read, with total understanding, the recorded life of a tax-gatherer in ancient Egypt or a mediaeval monk with the freshness of a report in a modern magazine because in fundamental human strivings, in human nature there is an undoubted consistency. Often we refer to the writings of Shakespeare whose observations of humanity are as relevant today as they were when he was writing. I think Finnis can certainly say with justification, that, as a speculative truth, human nature seems remarkably constant.

a) Finnis' seven basic goods are:

   i) Life

   Finnis is well worth reading, if only because of the poet in him, which sets him above most other jurists because he writes as a human, rather than a tired old machine. To Finnis, life is not bare material existence, but is a matter of quality, so that mental and physical health and comfort are necessary aspects of living. The striving and lust for life are brought out in his example: '... the crafty struggle and prayer of a man overboard seeking to stay afloat until his ship turns back to him; the team-work of surgeons ...' and even to 'watching out as one steps off the kerb ...'

   Allied to life as a basic good is its promulgation. As most schoolboys know, life, like death, is a sexually transmitted disease. However, Finnis separates the good of procreation from the more complex sexual and paternal/maternal urges. Such urges can be diverted to other goods. Thus, sex can be a recreational activity (play) or a cementation of relationships (sociability, friendship). As Hume might put it, the diversion of the urge for copulation to these other ends may be another invention of a naturally inventive species.

   ii) Knowledge

   Finnis sees curiosity and the quest for truth in itself as a manifest human good. He hastens to add that 'it is knowledge, considered as desirable for its own sake, not merely instrumentally'.

   iii) Play

   Everyone, asserts Finnis, engages to a greater or lesser extent in activities that are pointless except for their own sake, from sports and games, on the one hand, to mischiefs and diversions such as toying with one's pen as one writes. 'An element of play can enter into any human activity, even the drafting of enactments.'

iv) Aesthetic experience

Although linked to play, and indeed to life and knowledge, the appreciation of forms and spirits of beauty is, Finnis asserts, equally a common and self-evident human good.

v) Sociability (friendship)

'To be in a relationship of friendship with at least one other person is a fundamental form of good, is it not?' The bonds of human community, even at the level of pure self-interest, are involved with this good, but Finnis obviously views friendship as its flourishing.

vi) Practical reasonableness

The ability to reason provides a level of personal autonomy, since it is the measure of active choice and free will as well as providing the potential of self improvement by ordering one's thoughts. Through reason comes therefore, in Finnis' view, 'peace of mind' as well as 'self-determination'.

vii) Religion

Finnis seems reluctant to use this word, but employs it 'summarily and lamely' for want of a better choice. Finnis suggests that all humans are concerned to know: (a) how things came to exist as they do; and (b) whether there is not something greater and more powerful than human intellect, to which humans are subject. Finnis' explanation is obviously contaminated with his own faith, but these questions are fairly universal concerns and in the absence of explanations that are proof positive that God does not exist or that Big Bang actually happened, we choose theories to cling to, or at least search for them, and our adherence to them is a matter of faith.

b) Finnis makes two further relevant points.

i) These are not the only goods, but simply all other goods may be reduced to being means by which these basic goods are attained. Nor are they the only common urges or inclinations. He does not deny that some people, perhaps all, have an urge for gratuitous cruelty; however, these are not self-evidently good.

ii) None of these goods can be reduced to a mere extract of another, since they are ultimate ends in themselves of equal value and importance when one focuses on them individually.

It may be seen that Finnis' list, although it has some peculiarity, is not radically different from the lists of others, such as Aquinas. However, the difference Finnis asserts, is that these goods are not the result of speculative reason; they are not good because of anything, they are just good. The problem is that they are, according to Finnis, 'primary, indemonstrable and self-evident'.

The student may be tempted to view life as a necessary material pre-condition to all of the others. You cannot play cricket or study law if you are a corpse. However, Finnis, with his emphasis on life as being a 'good' rather than an empirical necessity, prevents this criticism. By saying that these goods have equal value, he seems to be asserting that they are all mutually dependent. The value of life is nothing without the other goods in some measure. If one reads *A Day in the Life of Ivan Denisovitch*, it is stark what Finnis is trying to get at. Simply the student must ask himself 'do you believe (any of the seven goods) is intrinsically good?'

It is almost impossible to argue with Finnis' derivation of the seven goods and would be foolish to argue with them, since he offers no logical proof of them and indeed says they are not demonstrable. I am, however, surprised that Finnis excludes love from his list, since I find it hard to see that it is necessarily a derivation from any of the seven goods he posits here; love need not even manifest itself in a relationship, and is not necessarily intense friendship. Love is certainly regarded as more than an urge, and if anything was self evidently held to be good, irrespective of reason, I would have thought love would be.

Much fruitless pursuit of logical criticism has been expended on Finnis' goods, the most obvious being based on the principle that since Finnis offers a logical justification of knowledge, he is defective in not providing logical justifications for his other goods.

Finnis states, quite rightly, that even a man who denies knowledge, relies on his knowledge to deny its value. As McCormick puts it, 'why should ... anyone ... care to know that knowledge is not worth having unless, after all, at least that knowledge is worth having?' It is a neat argument, but is divorced from the premise of Finnis' argument. Finnis may provide empirical explanations, say from anthropology, to illustrate the prevalence of these values, but he does not employ them as proof.

c) The student may find all of these quaint philosophical burblings quite irrelevant to the study of jurisprudence. However on these poetic foundations, Finnis seeks to rebuild the edifice of Natural Law.

Finnis suggests that the concept of law has a focal content that is based upon the convergence of legal systems with the various facets of a central definition of law. These facets are concepts that law is: made, determinate, effective, communal, sanctioned, rule-guided, reasonable, non-discriminatory and reciprocal. However, to Finnis, as to Hart, the Concept of Law is a common sense category that is applied to varied institutions that have roughly, though by no means exactly, the same function in society. As such a conceptual definition of law is a fool's errand. It is rather like, to resort to my old favourite, giving a substantive definition of weeds.

> '[T]he intention has been not to explain a concept, but to develop a concept which would explain the various phenomena referred to (in an unfocussed way) by "ordinary" talk about law – and explain them by showing how they answer (fully or partially) to the standing requirements of practical reasonableness relevant to the broad area of human concern and interaction.'

Finnis accepts that lawyers are concerned with categorical statements about what is valid law. This varies from society to society and from time to time. His theory '... cannot be assumed to be applicable to the quite different problems of describing and explaining the role of legal process within the ordering of human life in society, and the place of legal thought in practical reason's effort to understand and effect real human good.'

What Finnis is suggesting is that the moral success or failure of a law is not the test of whether it is law. His concern is not to posit what he wants law to be, but rather to evaluate what expectations there are of law in order to critically evaluate law itself. To Finnis, the focal meaning of his concept of law is not intended to explain what law is, but what moral expectations are made of it. As such the purpose of law is to work for the common good, but this does not mean that laws that work against the common good are not laws and should be 'relegated to some other discipline'. What such laws amount to is 'an imperfect or fringe meaning of law in its focal meaning.'

An example of this might be the man who walks into a restaurant and orders 'Bombay Duck' (curiously, a fish dish). When the waiter brings his dinner he might say 'I ordered the Bombay Duck, but this is not a duck'. The waiter is not deceiving him, but his own expectations are not satisfied. Similarly, Fuller would not deny the appellation of law to what a legal system claims to be law, but his focal meaning is concerned with expectations rather than classifications.

The legal system must thus, to some extent, satisfy the common requirements of human good, although 'there are no very precise yardsticks for assessing this.'

d) Equipped with the knowledge that Finnis has shown us what he thinks the natural absolute values are, as well as his conception of law, we might seek to understand how these two relate to each other.

The objects of human striving are the seven basic goods, but they are best and perhaps only achieved through communal enterprise. This is the result of the application of one of the goods themselves, practical reasonableness, to the question of how to best attain the others. However, it is not just necessary for life, play, etc, that people act collectively, but they should do so in an organised manner. This requires that the individual works for the collective good. Now Finnis does not deny that there might be varying conceptions of what the collective good is, but these are simply aspects of the ongoing process of reasoning to find the best way to promote the collective good. Certainly, organised communal activity for the collective good can be well-organised by the employment of law.

However, practical reasonableness must also be applied to ensure that the individuals within society can attain the basic goods that they seek. Finnis articulates nine methodological principles for practical reasoning. These include the need for a coherent plan in life, no arbitrary preferences amongst values or people, detachment and commitment, an evaluation of the relevance of consequences, the requirements of the common good, and following one's own conscience.

This is the foundation of justice and rights. Justice and rights represent a tension between the common good and human goods.

However, our present concern is the link between Positive Law and Natural Law. Finnis cites the easy case of murder. The law of murder is derived from the general 'good' of the value of human life, interpreted by another good, that of practical reason. The force of the law against murder thus doubly derives from Natural Law. The process of doing this is, however, a complex one. Finnis' explanation of the nine requirements of practical reasonableness and their interaction with legal reasoning is very sophisticated to the extent that it cannot be justly described here. But the application of practical reasonableness is the determinant factor of law. Obviously reason allows the choice of a multitude of means to be thought up in order to achieve ends. But Finnis' conclusions are of interest to us:

i) Natural Law is concerned to prove that the act of positing law is an act that can and should be guided by moral principles.

ii) Moral principles are derived by practical reasonableness from objective principles, not from subjective whim or custom.

iii) Law itself, its structure and the institutions that it creates, such as contract etc, is justified by moral norms.

Finnis is not satisfied to say that history shows that law normally reflects contemporary morality, but seeks to determine what the requirements of practical reasonableness really are in order to have coherent standards for legislation.

3.8   Evaluation of Finnis

Finnis has to be applauded on what can either be viewed as an explanation of the inexplicable or a philosophical sleight of hand. By employing the principle that goods are self-evident, rather than derived from objectively observable facts, Finnis not only avoids being accused of deriving an ought from an is, but also deprives us of any attack on his methodology. Since we cannot show precisely where values come from, we are reduced to attacking the paucity of analogous arguments. However, this reduces us to shadow-boxing and is in no way dispositive of his method. All we are left to do is face Finnis on his own grounds, answering whether we agree with him or not. However, we can ask whether we agree because of our learned instincts, our reason, rather than because they are self-evident. I would imagine that the Humian criticism would be to grant that these are aspects of passions and urges that we all recognise; however, that they are good is the result of learned experience and pleasure, and our agreement is to be qualified by an appreciation of the different ways in which individuals perceive them. This would be tantamount to saying that humans participate in broadly similar activities from which they gain pleasure. As such it is the form and experience of what games we enjoy that enjoins us to agree with Finnis, but we pursue our goods in different ways.

Finnis' concept of play, for example, could cover any human activity from pulling wings off insects to watching a person being burnt to death. It is the direction of his methods of practical reasoning that essentially make these good look good.

His second sleight of hand is his inclusion of practical reasonableness as a good. Obviously, it is expedient and useful to reason, and it has beneficial side-effects that Finnis notes. However, the whole essence of practical reasoning is that it is concerned with moving to practical solutions from general inclinations or urges. His methods of practical reasoning are laden with value considerations, that unlike the broad propositions of the seven goods are not necessarily the self-evident methods of practical reasoning. He asserts that practical reasonableness dictates that the promotion of the common good and justice are necessary factors of life. This view only works if an element of practical reasonableness is taken to be the liberal/moral conceptions of equality and of following one's conscience.

This leads him to focus on law from the point of view of what he terms practical reasonableness, tinged with moral priorities. Though, perhaps, this can safely be overlooked, since his criteria of practical reasonableness still allow a vast diversity of systems to be justified. However, Finnis' focus is on a concept of law that is assumed to be differentiated from other normative social orders because there is a prima facie moral obligation to obey it. The reason why there is such an obligation is because legislators are assumed to be acting in the interests of the common good. The reason why legislators are so assumed to act is because it is a necessary dictate of Finnis' norms of practical reasonableness.

Now, Finnis is honest, he is not attempting a definition of law, but of what are, fundamentally, legislative and judicial ethics. He criticises Hart's focal concept of law, centred on the internal aspect of rules, on the basis that it does not focus on the main reason for the adherence to legal rules – the promotion of the common good. However, Hart is not seeking to go further than a functional/descriptive concept of law. Finnis is self-avowedly seeking to define what the requirements are for a practically reasonable legal system.

This does not help us understand what is essential to law and is arguable as a definition of what morally good law is, since there are many morally doubtful assertions in Finnis' book. Moreover, although it establishes that law might be instrumental in the maintenance of societal values, it is only the inclusion of practical reason as a good that forges any link between these natural goods and the law.

One significant problem is that Finnis advocates what is essentially a materialist/capitalist society, which may have its virtues as a political institution, but it need not promote these ultimate goods. The by-product of this kind of society is the reliance on materialism for the achievement of goods. However, it is arguable that the wise man chooses not to be diverted by maximisation of material, but seeks these goods in a simple life. Indeed this is the assertion of many idealists, who regard political society as an aberration (Rousseau) and law as a diversion from the human achievement of good (Marx).

Finnis thus shows that law has an instrumental value, but not that it is necessarily morally superior to other methods of social regulation. Furthermore, his conclusions are far too vague to give adequate guidance about whether a system is practically reasonable.

What Finnis does achieve is a distinct method of asserting that there are constant aspects of human nature.

3.9   Natural Law – some conclusions

In most human activities the urge for the best leads to critical processes that seek to exclude the worst practices by theoretical justification, in order thereafter to eradicate the practice. For example, nineteenth century medicine sought to demonstrate with 'scientific theory' that traditional herbal medicines lacked scientific basis. The concern was to demonstrate that doctors should use methods that could be scientifically explained. This was perhaps the best way of removing quackery from medicine, although it did not mean that herbs did not have medicinal effects, as has been accepted in modern times. Equally, natural law seeks to find a coherent theory that will purge us of unjust legal systems. Just as quack medicine lacks scientific justification, unjust law lacks moral justification; this does not mean that neither necessarily work.

The problem with employing Natural Law theories is that they can denounce legal 'heresies' in the same way as medicine denounced medical 'heresies'. This confirms a tendency towards being conservative or even reactionary. If we had adhered to the Greek concept of Natural Law we would probably still retain slaves. Moreover, most moral reforms in law have stemmed from individuals acting against the contemporary societal mores.

The positivist assertion that you cannot derive what you ought to do from the way things are is to a great extent a philosophy that rejects conservatism and retains for each individual the sovereignty of his own conscience. This is not to say that the assertion is not independently without a logical foundation.

The value of Natural Law is, however, to remind us of two things. Firstly, law cannot be conceived purely from the point of view of what lawyers say is law, but from the broader perspective of collective human endeavour. Secondly, a point that positivism very seldom pays attention to is that most humans consider that there is something ineffably unique about humans that requires them to be treated in a certain way. This is somewhat deeper that the 'weaknesses' of humanity demonstrated by Hart. That this belief in the special nature of human beings is true, is immaterial, it is simply that most humans think that at least they, or their race, is uniquely valuable.

Natural Law theories that emphasise the uniqueness of only a portion of a population, be it on the basis of colour, racial lineage or creed normally achieve notoriety. As a result Alf Ross dubs natural law as a 'harlot' at the disposal of any political theory.

The other contribution of Natural Law (found in Fuller as well as Finnis) is that it reminds us that law is a social endeavour, rather than a static fact. Most law students take law to be simply posited legal statements, but what is also critical to law is that people read and/or act on legal norms, or else it is not a legal system. Posited norms may seem more or less static, but the diversity of human behaviour when acting on legal norms is in a constant state of flux. It is thus closer to the truth to say that the law seeks to do such and such than to say that the law is such and such. Positivism has always been concerned with the neutrality of the content of legal rules, but there seems to be something intrinsic in the nature of the legal enforcement of will that itself seems to be purposive.

Stalin demonstrated more than adequately that the employment of terror and punishment secures cheaper, quicker and more absolute compliance to will. Law actually pre-warns the subject, risking that a person will take measures so as to avoid being caught doing a wrongful act. Whereas a political regime could quite easily force people to comply, why should it endeavour that people should choose to behave in a certain way and accept the validity of a requirement? Natural Law theory at least attempts to explain this problem; as we shall see this is not necessarily true of positivism.

3.10 Positivism as a reaction to the 'naturalistic fallacy'

The term positivism has acquired two features: (a) it covers a multitude of various theories with a limited amount in common; (b) it carries with it almost the same pejorative sense as the 'naturalistic fallacy'. However, based around Hart's Harvard Law Report (1958), we might identify five facets that indicate the unhappy family of positivists:

a) Positivists view laws as the expression of the wills of human people, as opposed to the manifestation of any greater purpose, such as divine will.

b) There is, for positivists, no necessary link between law and morality. This does not mean that positivism denies that law should be moral. This, in part, is due to their adherence to the accepted separation between what things are and what they should be (the is/ought) distinction.

c) The analysis of legal concepts is deemed by positivism as an end in itself. Equally, this is to be distinguished from other disciplines such as sociology, anthropology and history. As such the evaluation of law on the basis of morality, social aims and functions is not an aspect of true positivist analysis. The effect of this is to assert that the validity of law is an internal feature of a legal system.

d) As a result of the previous point, some positivists assert that law is a closed system of logic and therefore all legal decisions are deductible from posited legal rules and require no external justifications of a moral or social nature.

e) Positivism often claims that moral judgments cannot be objectively verified by indicating demonstrable facts. Often it follows that positivists deny that there are objective moral values.

It is clear that the radical difference between positivism and Natural Law is that while positivism states that the concept of law is simply what the legal system in a given society recognises as law, Naturalism considers law to be an ideal, commonly shared by human societies. The ideal of law is order, preferably good order, irrespective of the variance of moral values. Positivism cannot ignore the normative nature of law, but does not regard this as a moral premise; rather it is viewed as a social technique.

There are two aspects, therefore, that highlight the contrast between positivism in its 'caricatured form'. Firstly, law is exclusively the premise of the legal caste (including legislators). This deprives law of any spurious claims of intrinsic morality and ensures the individual's right to his own conscience, while reserving the legal system's right to punish him for transgressing. Secondly, it allows for precise statements about the nature of valid law which approximate to the lawyer's experience. This final point might, for the student, be the clinching factor.

4 POSITIVISM 1: IMPERATIVE THEORY

4.1 Sovereignty

The core proposition of the imperative theory is sovereignty, which finds its origin in the rise and independence of the nation-state. The logical sequitur of the self-determining state was that there must be a supreme authority exclusive to that state. A separate, but equally important, development was the logical rejection of the view that law was custom and that legislation was merely a way of declaring the existence of new custom (Blackstone's declaratory theory). The decline in the acceptance of Natural Law doctrines led to the dissociation between any moral or divine authority invested in the sovereign.

The combination of absolute authority and the dethronement of the idea that law was the restatement of the customs of people, in favour of the idea of law as an instrument of government led to the view that law was the will of the sovereign. The imperative theory enshrines this belief.

The fact that the positivists who professed the imperative theory denied the existence of natural rights (which had been used to justify social iniquity) and rejected any necessary connection between legal and ethical standards allowed them to be freely critical of existing law. Bentham made the distinction between expository jurisprudence, which describes what law is, and censorial jurisprudence which is the study of legislative reform – a sort of empirical ethics. We shall examine the expository jurisprudence of the imperative thinkers first.

4.2 Bentham – an introduction

a) Reading the expository jurisprudence of Jeremy Bentham gives all the thrills of perusing a statutory instrument. Hart, in his somewhat understated style, says that he lacks the technical expertise to unravel Bentham's deontic logic. Yet it is precisely this closed system of language and pedantic definition that makes his writing so informative. It is fair to say that he anticipated many of the insights made by later jurists. However, much of his expository work, aimed at defining the nature of law, was unpublished and is currently being sifted through for publication. The manuscripts were discovered at University College London, where Austin, the first purveyor of jurisprudence to law undergraduates, lectured. Austin's theory of law is a somewhat simplified version of Bentham's, perhaps because his lectures were directed at first year students. Thus, the teacher, Bentham, is often tarred with the same brush as the disciple, Austin.

Sadly for law students, Austin's tradition has left a legacy that cannot be ignored – much of our constitutional theory stems from Austinian perceptions. Jolowicz says that Austin's theory needs to be set up simply in order that we can throw bricks at it!

We will, however, examine Bentham first since his insights are illuminating as a starting point. Following the empirical tradition he rejected the notion of Natural Law and an internal moral aspect to law. When addressing the Natural Law fathers of the French revolution, with its written constitution, he described it as 'nonsense – nonsense on stilts' and 'bawling on paper'. We shall analyse some of his definitions to give a little introduction into his expository theory as well as to arm the student with some knowledge that might help him cope with Bentham.

b) In *Of Laws in General* Bentham seeks by demarcation to distinguish law from other activity. His method relies on the linguistic associations of the word law, while appreciating that language can be misleading. Surprisingly, perhaps, Bentham has a little in common with the Natural Law tradition of thinkers such as Aquinas. Aquinas' concept of law is any 'rule or measure of action in virtue of which one is led to perform certain actions and refrain from the performance of others'. This is, of course, so long as it accords with the eternal law – the will of God. Thus, laws are not only the prescriptions of those who are employed specifically for legal purposes, but any prescription that accords with God's sovereign will. Bentham has the same wide definition except the will of the sovereign is substituted for divine will. The form that law is defined to take has the following elements:

    i)   It is an assemblage of signs;

    ii) Expressive of subjective will;

    iii) That will can be directly or indirectly attributable to the sovereign in one of three ways;

        • the author of the law is the sovereign himself;

        • the sovereign has allowed a previous sovereign's law to continue in existence;

        • the law has been made by a person on behalf of the sovereign who is authorised to so do.

    iv) Relating to conduct in a given situation;

    v)   By persons who are supposed (ie presumed) to be subject to his power;

c) It is important at this point to mention that Bentham's concept of a sovereign does not mean to carry with it any 'Natural Law baggage'. It is simply the people or persons who a political community are supposed to be in disposition to be obeyed. This itself requires elucidation!

Bentham talks of a political community as being one in which the members are supposed (that word again!) to be in the habit of obedience to a person or body of persons of known and certain description. A community is a fictitious body composed of individual persons who are considered (it might as well be supposed) to be its members.

Thus, to quote Bentham, we can 'use the same word sovereignty in two different senses; at one time in its strict and proper sense; at another in its popular and improper sense ... Till men are sufficiently aware of the ambiguity of words, political discussions may be carried out without profit and without end'.

To Bentham therefore the term does not carry with it any associations such as 'King by divine right' or even personal supremacy. Nor is it a factual statement that the sovereign is the person who is habitually obeyed; it is the habit of obedience together with the feeling of collective identity that earmarks a political community. With Bentham's careful expression we should not ignore the words 'supposed' and 'disposition'.

The sovereign is the person who it is presumed a society has the inclination to obey. The presumptive or 'suppositive' element of the definition emphasises that sovereignty is not a matter of fact, but a morally-neutral 'ought' statement. (See introduction). Furthermore the sovereign is supposed to be the person to whom people have a disposition to obey, rather than who is habitually obeyed. The distinction is a fine, but important one. If one is disposed to do something, it is not just the doing of the action, but the willing inclination to do it that must be appreciated.

d) The supposition is that society (which Bentham says is a fictional body) is disposed to obey the sovereign. Or one might say that it is supposed that a fictive will deems that the ascertainable sovereign should be obeyed. The student might think, 'so what?' but this strange combination of words is remarkably similar to the theory of the grundnorm, which is the foundation stone of Kelsen's Pure Theory of Law, but rather more credibly expressed.

In addition to the communicative form of law, it has attached to it the motives that are intended to influence subjects to act in accordance with that will.

4.3 'A law can be considered in eight different respects'

Bentham is useful to the student at least insofar as he points out several material focuses for enquiry into the nature of law:

a) *Source*

As has already been mentioned, the source of law, ultimately, is a sovereign. However, Bentham is aware that power is delegated in the name of the sovereign and exercised in the sovereign's name by subsidiary law-makers.

b) *Subjects*

Obviously, a law either applies to a person, or, in the case of, for example, English property law, to a thing.

c) *Objects*

The object of a law is the act, in the appropriate circumstances, which it seeks to regulate.

d) *Extent*

Obviously, a law must specify how widely it is to be applied, as well as to whom. The extent of the criminal law is its applicability to all but the legally immune, for example.

e) *Aspects*

Laws may take various forms of commanding, permitting etc, in order to achieve a given purpose.

f) *Force*

Laws usually rely on motives (sanctions/rewards) to give force to them. Additional laws may be required to bring these motives into play, which Bentham terms *corroborative appendages*.

g) *Expression*

There is a variety of ways in which laws can be expressed – one only needs to think of the variety of English law forms.

h) *Remedial appendages*

If a principal law outlaws an act, a corroborative law directs someone to punish that act; there still might need to be a requirement for another law to remedy the effect of that act. Although the example I am using is not exactly what Bentham meant, it might give the student some idea. The law says that an employee must be paid in accordance with his contract and it will enforce that contract if he is not so paid. This is the principal law and the motive for obeying it is the threat that payment will be forced by the law. However, someone has to adjudge whether the employer has not paid his employee and if so, that person must order payment. That person might be a judge, but he has to be empowered by law to perform this. Therefore, a corroborative law directs the judge to judge and enforce. However, imagine that payment has not been made for a period of time. In such a case, the value of the money owed under the contract to the employer might have decreased in real terms. Therefore the remedial effect of additional interest under the Supreme Court Act may come into play. This might be an example of a remedial appendage. Obviously, not all principal laws required such extra 'help'.

4.4   Sources of law

Bentham employs the concept of sovereign will to demarcate legal mandates from illegal ones, such as that of a mafia boss. The unifying feature that lies behind all laws is, for him, that it accords with the will of the sovereign. However, not all laws emanate from the sovereign. Bentham accommodates this reality with a duality of ideas.

a) As already mentioned, Bentham regards all commands that accord with the will of the sovereign as legal mandates. Thus, a parent's order to a child, an employer's order to a servant, a magisterial, military or judicial order, each of these is a legal mandate, providing that it accords with the will of the sovereign. Bentham concedes that we are not accustomed to viewing such things as acts of legislation, but all legal mandates are law.

There is something that is appealing about this concept, although it is somewhat strange, particularly to the lawyers' mind. The fact that, by convention, lawyers look to limited sources and enforce and recognise only those sources, does not mean that law does not have a force outside them. The student is used to being told that this is law (meaning, this is the proper source for you to act on in practice and in an exam) and this is not law (meaning, irrelevant to the study of substantive law). Bentham succeeds in emphasising that law is enforced and reiterated outside the purely formal context of legal practice.

b) The problem with such a wide definition is that the responsibility for making law is spread, while the authority for law stems from the sovereign. How can we logically relate the source of a law to the authority that gives it its legal character? Bentham points out that we have to consider how any person can have a mandate attributed to him:

   i) A person decides, himself, that something is to be done, making the mandate his by conception.

   ii) Someone else thinks something should be done and a person adopts that other person's thought, so that the mandate is his by adoption. This process is obviously somewhat more complex than the former, and since the bulk of law making in modern systems is not directly the conception of the sovereign, Bentham investigates it further.

If we imagine a simple idea of King Rex and his two advisers, his wife and his Prime Minister. Rex is not intelligent, but his wife suggests ideas for laws to him, which he subsequently declares to be his own. The mandate has already been conceived, but he endorses it and it becomes his by *susception*. Rex is not greatly interested in the business of government, so he declares that everyone should do whatever the Prime Minister tells them to do until further notice. Thus, he *pre-adopts* the mandates that the Prime Minister is going to make in the future. He has thus invested in the Prime Minister a power to make law in his own right, and this is a power of *imperation*.

Susception may equally apply to the adoption by a new monarch of the laws of his predecessor and pre-adoption to the mandates of all those who are authorised to issue mandates on behalf of the sovereign.

c) One interesting aspect of Bentham's view is that if a person issues a mandate and has no authority to do so, it is illegal and the issuing of it is an offence. Now, Hart criticises Bentham for failing to take into account the concept of invalid, but not illegal, mandates. This may well be a valid criticism, but it may also stem from the attitude that the 'Englishman is born free and may do anything that he is not prevented from doing'. It is likely that Bentham does not conceive of things in this way. Bentham clearly envisages that the sovereign will is a seamless web. 'Take any mandate whatsoever, either it is of the number of those which he allows or it is not; there is no medium: if it is, it is his; by adoption at least, if not by original conception: if not, it is illegal, and the issuing of it is an offence.' Thus, an invalid command is one that is permitted to be made, but which the lawyer is not permitted to enforce or act upon. This highlights the curious problem of Bentham's view, that seems to suggest that the sovereign can know all mandates that are issued, and either permits them or prevents them.

d) To understand such a viewpoint fully one needs to understand the logic of the legislator's will or Bentham's 'deontic logic'. Since even Hart confesses that he does not understand all the details of it, the student will forgive me if I present a simplified model.

In our normal use of language, we often camouflage our real meaning, by using different expressions, in order to achieve a given effect:

If we ask a person whether to follow a certain course of action there are four possible aspects of their consent, depending on what their attitude is:

'You must not!'   'You need not!'   'You may!'   'You must!'
(prohibition)   (non-command)   (non-prohibition)   (command)

i) Both 'you must not' and 'you must' are imperative and when applied to the same action cannot both be obeyed.

ii) 'You need not' is a non-command because it points to the fact that there is nothing to say 'you must'. As such it would be a logical contradiction to say 'you need not' and then 'you must'.

iii) By the same token when one says 'you may', it points to the absence of anything to say 'you must not', and as such it is a non-prohibition. It would be equally contradictory to say 'you may' but 'you must not'.

iv) Finally, one might say, 'you may' but 'you need not'. This is not an expression of will at all, it is the same as saying it is up to you or you may do what you like.

It is clear from this model that expressions of will can be imperative, such as commands or prohibitions which require adherence, or permissive, such as a non-command or non-prohibition, which allows action.

Laws can therefore be expressed in any of these ways, but only as logical combinations of these expressions. Thus, expressions of legal will can have a variety of effects. However, the student will have noted that Bentham's is an imperative theory – how is it then that law can be permissive?

One must remember that a legal permission is one that is guaranteed by the sovereign and, as such, may be equally expressed as a prohibition against people forcing someone to do what he does not legally need to do or a command to people to allow him to do what he legally can do;

Thus, with respect to a court, if a person has a legal permission to act in a certain way this has the effect of prohibiting it from enforcing any previous law that would interfere with this action.

With respect to other subjects of the law, if a person is given legal permission to graze his sheep on the common, it might equally be stated that 'let no man stop him!'

4.5   Law is 'broken into shares'

Although all law may be ultimately attributed to a sovereign, as we have seen, not all law-making is that of the sovereign. Bentham thus explains how such power is shared.

a) A legislator may make a law requiring that an act be done or be abstained from – this element is the *directive* element of law. Normally this will be accompanied by the motive for obeying – this is the *predictive* part. However, it unlikely that the legislator can verify that the law has been broken and order that the particular law-breaker be punished. This general law is the primary law.

b) In order that breaches of law be verified and punished the legislator will have issued a law directing that someone such as a judge should do so. This might be termed a *subsidiary law*.

c) Equally, the judge might need to have the help of the police for verification, or the prison service, for punishment, thereby requiring further *subsidiary laws*. These are *remote laws*, whereas type (b) would be *proximate laws*.

In fact subsidiary laws are themselves backed with even more subsidiary laws requiring witnesses etc to contribute their part to the aim of the principal law.

With all these laws flying about it is not surprising that Bentham's view of laws is a complex one. However, he does advocate the concept of a *complete law*. A complete law is the sum of all of the subsidiary and principal laws needed to give complete meaning to a more general principle.

Bentham's example is the general prohibition against meddling with property that is not one's own. This might be categorised in two deontic terms: (1) a prohibition against occupying property, which is imperative; (2) a permission for anyone who has good title to that property, allowing them to occupy it. However, this simple concept requires that there be procedures for the transfer of property, form for valid title and all the verifications, mandates and penalties in order to achieve the enforcement of this complete law. Bentham concedes that such laws are not written down in this complete form.

It will be noted that the title-holder of land in English law has two different types of power. He has the legal permission to use his land, which others may not (without his permission). This power to do that which other people may not is a power of *contrectation*. Such powers stem primarily from permissive laws. However, the title-holder may also rent his land to another, who, if he agrees, must accept duties and obligations. This power to confer on others duties and obligations is, as we have already mentioned, a power of *imperation*.

4.6 Motives

It must be remembered that Bentham does not believe that there is any link between law and morality, and indeed has distinct doubts about morality in general. Therefore, the reason why people obey laws is that there must be some motive provided by the law that would encourage the subject to obey. In Bentham's psychology these are primarily the coercion of punishment and allurement of reward. Now such motives may be provided by politics, religion or morality, although normally the legal system relies on rewards and punishments of its own creation.

Praemary or *invitative* laws rely on the motive of reward, but as Bentham observes these are less than often used. It is a lot easier and more economical for the legal system to implement pain and more likely to have the desired effect! As such *sanctional* or *comminative* laws are far more popular.

The critical problem with this view of the force of law is that, as Summers remarks, there are other educative, supervisory and controlling factors that may be applied to law.

We saw earlier that such motives are not necessarily attached to particular laws that permit or prohibit a particular act and thus there may be a mandate without an obvious sanction being attached. For example, an agent may have a power of imperation to impose obligations on another under a contract, but the power to sanction a breach of contract may lie with another, such as a court. Power, including the power to sanction, is, in Bentham's model, frequently broken into shares. One reason for this is that frequently a law is directed at someone; for example, 'do not steal', but it can hardly be expected that the mandate should say also 'if you do steal, punish yourself'. Likewise, with a contract, although the parties are permitted to mandate each other to do certain things, both are under the broader obligation of not breaking the legal obligations the other party has put on them, so that neither can be expected to punish himself at the mandate of the other (although there might be penalty clauses in the contract).

4.7   Bentham on sovereignty

a) *Introduction*

> 'Now by a sovereign I mean any person or assemblage of persons to whose will a whole political community are (no matter on what account) supposed to be in disposition to pay obedience: and that in preference to the will of any other person.'

Bentham's concept of sovereignty is not one that is greatly elaborated upon. However, it is important to give it some consideration here, since it is often dismissed as being the same as Austin's concept of sovereignty and as such dismissed as being over-simplistic. Harris argues that the sovereign will is a constructive metaphor that provides a consistent logic to law.

b) As a positivist Bentham believes that all 'ought' statements can only be the product of a subjective will. Therefore, law, being comprised of imperatives (oughts), must be attributable to some person or some body. The sovereign is simply the ultimate authority in a legal jurisdiction. Bentham does not necessarily mean a single person – an undivided sovereign. He is not employing the common usage that tends to view the concept of sovereignty as the body that exercises ultimate governmental power in a given jurisdiction. Bentham allows that powers may be separated infinitely and distributed through the law to numerous persons or bodies. Each would be sovereign in exercise of a given power, so long as they are the highest and only power in their particular branch of government. If we look at the British constitution and disregard the constitutional rote that we have learned, we can say that the Crown, Parliament, Courts (in matters of common and European law), European Institutions and electorate all comprise the sovereign, for each in their own role in government have inalienable powers. Parliament can no more create common law than the courts make a statute, nor can the government elect itself or the electorate make European law. Thus, with respect to Bentham's definition of sovereignty, the sovereign will is the will of this corporate venture, which involves much of the country. These bodies are sovereign because with respect to their particular branches of power it is supposed that society is in disposition to obey them.

Bentham does not require that the sovereign be determinate and does not stipulate that it cannot have a superior allegiance. His definition is not based on the empirical fact that people are in the habit of obedience to the sovereign, but on the supposition (for whatever reason) that society is disposed to obey one person or body of persons in preference to any other.

Bentham's sovereign may bind himself in law and may be bound by predecessors, even though this might sound like a logical contradiction, since we normally take a sovereign to be all powerful.

c) Olivecrona suggests that Bentham has overlooked the fact that the concept of 'will' is a fiction. Certainly, if Bentham allows for a divisible sovereign, how can two people have a will? Or indeed, does Parliament have a will? Parliament's will is seldom the will of all, but instead the fiction that a collection of people can speak as one. That Bentham would think this way is evident from the fact that he views a community as a fiction, a legal personality as a fiction. Therefore how is a sovereign to be real, especially since it is merely something that is to be identified by its 'supposed' authority? It may be therefore, that Bentham is fully aware that the sovereign will is not an empirical fact in the same way as he is aware that a 'political community' is a fiction.

Whether or not this is so, there is one considerable problem that Bentham evades. The positivists maintain that oughts cannot be derived from an is. Therefore, one cannot say as Austin does that one must obey the sovereign's will because people do obey him. This would be to imply that a sociological fact (actual obedience) creates an obligation. There is no reason why I should obey someone simply because someone else does.

In contrast to Austin, Bentham does not say this. He defines the sovereign as the person who the whole of the political community are supposed to be in a disposition to obey. Now, the emphasis on whole would, if a factual test, mean that there would never be a sovereign (a whole community would very seldom be disposed to obey the same person), but it is merely the 'supposition' of a disposition (an inclination or desire) to obey. Thus, he is saying that one supposes that everyone thinks they 'ought to' (not necessarily morally) or need to or must obey. A supposition is not a matter of fact, but an assumption. The validity of the law is based therefore on the existence of an assumption that everyone is either willing or feels they ought to or feels they must obey. Whose assumption this is, and on what basis this supposition is made, is not Bentham's concern. The power, as opposed to the authority, of a sovereign or a law is, however, based on the actual obedience to that law.

d) Thus, in my view, Bentham is seeking to achieve what Harris terms a basic legal fiat, by which he means a supposition of the following kind:

> 'Legal duties exist only if imposed by rules originating from the following sources ... or by rules subsumable under such rules. Providing that any contradiction between rules originating in different sources shall be resolved according to the following hierarching among sources ... and providing that no other contradiction shall be admitted to exist.'

In essence therefore, stating that the whole political community is supposed to be in disposition to obey a sovereign is not an assumption of fact or probability, but a means whereby other sources of non-legal mandates can be excluded. Bentham's theory posits the mechanics of the hierarchy of sources, as well as the way in which contradictions are resolved.

As I have maintained before, this analysis (which is by no means uncontroversial) bears a remarkable similarity to Kelsen's grundnorm.

4.8 Austin

While Bentham's theory is hard to understand, Austin's, I cannot help thinking, is hard to accept. However, Austin's jurisprudence has moulded itself into the form of the British constitution as well as into the brains of several generations of lawyers.

Austin's theory is also imperative, but built upon a less complex edifice of sovereignty on the one hand and on the demarcation of laws from other things wrongly called law. Austin's process of demarcation of law from other things is an interesting one, however.

a) *Demarcation*

Austin starts from a broad definition of law:

> 'A law, if the most general and comprehensive acceptation of the term, in its literal meaning, is employed, may be said to be a rule laid down for the guidance of an intelligent being by an intelligent being having power over him. In this the largest meaning which it has, without extension by metaphor or analogy, the term law embraces the following objects – laws set by God to his human creatures, and laws set by men to men.'

Thus, he starts from the empiricist premise that a law is the product of a subjective will. The law of God is to Austin the only real Natural Law, but in order not to confuse the issue with theories that go by the same name, the rules of God to man are termed *Divine Law*.

Laws may be imposed by men in two ways:

i) An indeterminate body of men may feel that certain rules or patterns govern human conduct in the manner of custom, conventions, the law of honour, fashion and etiquette. These are not properly to be regarded as laws, because they are not posited by virtue of political authority, but are opinions, and, as such, he terms these as aspects of morality. To differentiate this from God's edict, he terms it *positive morality*. These are analogous to laws in that they seem as if they have been commanded by a human will, but since they are laid down by indeterminate people, they are not truly laws. Thus, to distinguish these from proper laws, he further terms them as *laws of political morality by analogy*.

ii) Within the realms of positive morality also reside those rules or codes prescribed by men, not in the context of a political relationship, but in another. Thus, the rules of cricket, although they are rules set by one man to another, are not legal rules. The absence of a political character means that for the sake of distinguishing them from legal rules he terms them *laws of positive morality properly so-called.*

iii) Other things conform to regularity and patterns as if they were ordered or ordained to behave in a certain way. Thus, there is the law of gravity, Boyle's law or even Murphy's law. Since there is no determinate or indeterminate will ordering these, then they are only very slightly analogous, these are *laws by metaphor.* Notably, Austin denies that a proper law can act on an inanimate or non-rational object.

iv) Finally, having distilled out all of the non-laws or non-political laws, Austin determines that rules laid down by political superiors are the proper subject matter of jurisprudence. In summary, we might use Austin's tabular expression.

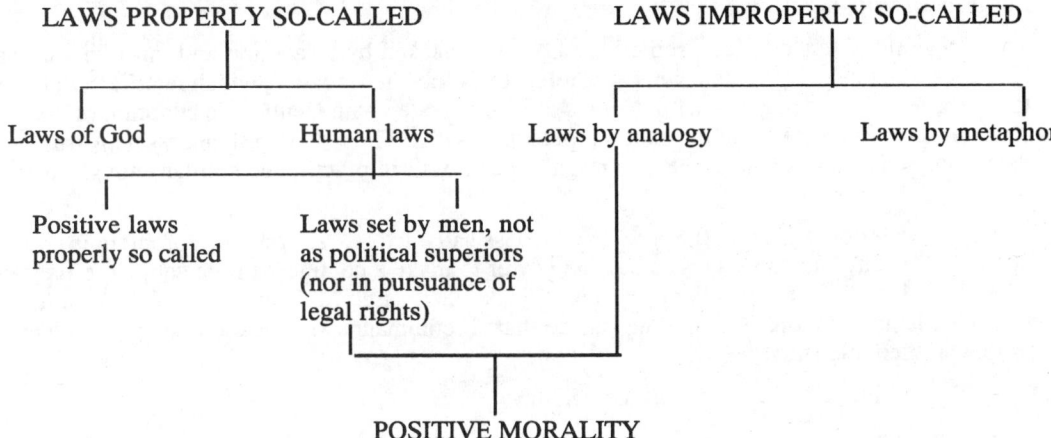

LAWS PROPERLY SO-CALLED   **LAWS IMPROPERLY SO-CALLED**

Laws of God   Human laws   Laws by analogy   Laws by metaphor

Positive laws properly so called

Laws set by men, not as political superiors (nor in pursuance of legal rights)

POSITIVE MORALITY

b) *Law as a command*

Austin states 'Every law or rule ... is a command'. His definition of a command is not based on the way in which it is expressed (ie it need not be in grammatical terms in the imperative mood), but because it is an expression of will of a political superior backed by a sanction. The imposition of a command creates a binding *duty* by virtue of the sanction that will be otherwise imposed.

Law is thus an aggregate of rules made by political superiors, backed by sanctions, therefore being commands of political superiors. In addition, this aggregation of individual commands amounts to the expression of a wish that prohibits or commands a class of acts. Thus, laws are general statements. We can identify four aspects of Austin's definition of a law (or command):

i) a wish of a determinate political superior;

ii) backed by the force of a sanction that will be imposed;

iii) that is expressed; and

iv) is directed generally at a class of acts or forbearances.

c) *Sovereignty*

Obviously, in order to determine what a law 'properly so-called' actually is, we need to understand the concept of political superiority.

'If a determinate human superior, not in the habit of obedience to a like superior, receive habitual obedience from the bulk of a given society, that determinate superior is sovereign of that society, and the society (including the superior) is a society political and independent.'

It may be noted that Austin's definition has the following facets:

i)   The criterion is a factual one, that of habitual obedience to one determinate person or body.

ii) In recognition that all the members of society are very seldom in the habit of obeying one or any body, Austin requires only that the bulk of the people in a society obey. As such, Austin must logically believe that society is an identifiable group, pre-existing law. Austin defines society as being humans in the state of mutual intercourse.

iii) There is a negative condition that the superior does not owe habitual obedience to another, thus being independent.

iv) Since law, properly so-called, is the will of a determinate political superior, backed by a sanction, a genuine sovereign cannot be bound by laws, since he has no superior. Hence constitutional law is an aspect of positive morality, since it is simply the opinion of indeterminate people (subjects, usually) that certain rules need to be respected.

d) *Power-conferring rules*

To achieve the status of a law, something has to be backed by a sanction and must be a command. However, Austin does postulate what Raz refers to as 'obedience laws', which require certain persons to be obeyed. This delegation of powers is to be contrasted with Bentham's adoption of will theory. This requires subjects to obey another person's will. Thus, it is not necessarily true that the delegate's will is the same as the sovereign's, but it will in practice be similar enough to make no difference.

Austin's resolution of some other problems is less satisfactory. A particular problem is contractual powers. He states that a party who has the power to make a contract will be subject to the sanction of nullity of the contract if it is not properly made. But surely, this is a way of disguising the fact that there is no sanction. Austin's insistence that all commands are backed by sanctions leaves him in this problematic situation.

4.9   The value of the imperative theory

a) *Law as a command*

i)   The undeniable contribution of imperative thinking is the view that law is a result not just of a vague collective undertaking, but must be ascribed to a will. Thus, custom, which emerges out of practice, may be differentiated from law, which is posited. The precise relation between custom and law is not clear. But certainly, it serves the modern western lawyers' sense of reality to view law as being created, rather than being the declaration of existing customs. The latter view, associated with Blackstone's declaratory theory, is certainly insupportable. But the recognition of the normative and rule-creating aspects of law does not justify the requirement of a determinable author.

ii) Thus, relative to the real values of the societies in which Bentham and Austin were living, such an account was valuable. However, as Finnis points out, law is a collective enterprise, and much of what Finnis terms 'implicit law' is law that emerges out of practice and is indistinguishable from custom. There is an interpretative function, which is not so much the issuing of another command as giving meaning to a general rule. Bentham seems more aware of this than Austin.

iii) Bentham's appreciation that human laws are imperatives that are interwoven and broken into shares is a more realistic format than that of Austin. The complexities of deontic logic reveal that laws may be permissive as well as commanding.

iv) The underlying view that law is based upon a will is somewhat less easy to justify. Certainly, Austin's sovereign is a very real person or body. However, the legislative will is not something that is that easily understood. One may only determine what the law is, by reference to the interpretation that we put on expressions of will. These need not coincide with what the author actually intended us to understand. Thus, while Magna Carta is regarded as the original authority for 'habeas corpus' there is palpable historical evidence that this was only intended to accord rights to a privileged feudal caste. Kelsen, whose theory of authorised norms is not dissimilar in its hierarchical structure to the present imperative theories, insists that the personal and psychological aspects of the term command must be ignored.

v) Both Bentham and Austin do not see laws as having a responsive element. They both fail, Austin more seriously than Bentham, to go far enough in their consideration of law as rules. A rule stands independent of the identity of its particular author, providing that it is in the acknowledged form that a legal system prescribes. Furthermore, at least Austin, if not Bentham as well, has no room to accommodate principles, which Dworkin would assert are a necessary aspect of the legal enterprise.

The notion of command also makes it logically difficult for rules to bind the sovereign. A man may lay down a rule by which he lives. Although Bentham accepts that a sovereign may bind himself, he still relies on the backing of a sanction or reward. However, the duty to obey a rule may not only be self-imposed, but that duty or responsibility may personally arise even though it cannot be properly framed or defined in an imperative. However, we will return to the issue of duty later on.

vi) It is unclear whether Bentham views the will behind the imperative as a fact or fiction, but he at least seems to intend that the will should be objectivised by supposing that the whole of the political community is disposed to obey it. Austin sees the will of the sovereign as a very real feature. Both beg the question of how such a will may be attributable to mandates issued under it, which the sovereign cannot know. This emphasises that the concept of will presupposes knowledge on the part of a person doing the willing. Hence Raz finds it hard to understand how various responsibilities within a legal system are actually interlinked in the context of imperative theories.

vii) A further problem must be noted in the limitation of which wills count as law. Austin requires that a law be an aggregate of commands formed to command the performance or forbearance of acts. This idea of generality, although convenient for a legal system, is not necessary for laws, since they may address a specific person and a specific act (eg the Abdication Act). Moreover, the demarcation of laws on the basis of superior political wills, in Austin, limits the application of the term law. This works in some respects, but surely we would not see the edict of Conservative Central Office to various constitutuency associations as a law. Bentham does not bother with demarcations, which has the advantage that his theory is not fettered by law-school conventions, but leads also to a lack of distinction between mandates with legal effect and mandates that are coincidental to the law. A father may say 'go to bed' to his son. This is legal, since the law does not prohibit it, but it has no legal effect within any real meaning of the word. Bentham's seamless web of deontic logic does not include any criterion of exclusion, without which no legal system could meaningfully identify relevant sources of law. However, this highlights the potential distinction between a legal system and law. The latter, we might accept is explained by Bentham, but the criteria for a legal system remain hopelessly vague on both accounts.

b) *Sovereigns*

i) The fact that Austin requires an indivisible, determinate, unfettered sovereign that is continuous through time seems to be more a matter of convenience for the superimposition of a utilitarian system than fact. The criticisms of Austin are so numerous on this account that the student must be referred to another text, of which there are many, for a detailed evaluation. Suffice it to say that the United States has a divided, perhaps indeterminate sovereign that is bound by a constitution, where sovereignty has been succeded from and extended over its history.

The Austinian concept of sovereignty would certainly be unable to meaningfully accommodate the development and effect of the European Communities.

ii) Possibly the greatest criticism that can be levelled at Austin is his basing of legal validity on a fact. The problem is that, in simple terms, anyone who the bulk of people habitually obey is the authority for law. We will have to consider the problem of deriving an ought from an is in more detail in the chapter on Kelsen. Austin, however, has simply committed this unpardonable sin, that is practically a moral taboo for a positivist.

iii) Whether Bentham is equally guilty depends on whether he is saying the same thing. I prefer to give him the benefit of the doubt, but I think the jury is still out on the matter. Morison among others would support me in the proposition that Austin's sovereign is closer to being what Austin would like to see in a legal system, for convenience, than any experience of reality.

c) *Motives*

i) Both Bentham and Austin rely entirely on motives external to the subject of laws in order that laws may be enforced. Bentham does not limit himself to sanctions alone and it is evident in Austin's *Lectures* that he does accept that some laws do not in themselves require the direct backing of coercion. Both are agreed that, ultimately, all complete laws require some kind of external motivation.

ii) However, there is a strong argument to suggest that education and persuasive argument, or indeed indoctrinated sympathy for a law, have equal effects. Milgram has sought to prove, in various somewhat spurious experiments, that people will go to extraordinary lengths to obey authority. *Obedience to Authority* demonstrated that students were willing to act out (theatrically) requirements of authority figures. While this demonstration by Milgram may be of dubious merit, it seems clear that enthusiastic obedience and loyalty to authority is a fundamental part of our learning experience. In the complex modern society, the assumption that people in authority should be obeyed and indeed usually have good reasons for being obeyed, is a necessary one. We may well be employed in a complex undertaking, such as a production process, where the relevance of our actions as an employee is obscure. However, we perform to our function without necessarily having the brooding omnipresent fear of sanction. The assumption that authority is to be obeyed is more than one of habit, but possibly one of conditioning at an early age.

iii) The obscurity in Bentham's account of illegality and the insistence of coercion may partially be rescued if we substitute the question 'what is law?' with 'what is illegal behaviour?', as Foley suggests.

Illegal behaviour might be termed 'behaviour that we are disposed to punish'. This would lead to an easier recognition of rules, while giving a real understanding of what the law is seeking to do, which reading rules does not necessarily furnish us with. How far such a view can rescue the crude psychology of imperative theory is unclear, though.

iv) A final observation may be made about imperative theory and sanctions. It is essential that the subject of the law knows the law and believes it to be true in its prediction of a sanction. If these do not apply, then the law will simply not be obeyed in imperative theory, but this is manifestly not so. People are aware that very few burglaries are cleared up in England, yet is everyone a burglar? One must conclude that a sanction is a useful last resort; the sanction is not the force of law, but its last resort.

d) *Power conferring laws*

When Austin says that the force of the power to enter into a contract is the threat of the nullity of the contract as a sanction, this is not only logically inadequate, but contradicts the whole purpose of encouraging people to engage in formal contractual relations.

Bentham may be criticised, on the other hand, in that the exercise of legal powers by persons who are not explicitly authorised is somewhat incredible. That a law may be adopted by a sovereign without him knowing of it is only sustainable if sovereign will is an aspect of fiction. In such a case attribution of a law to a sovereign is merely an artificiality designed to add logical consistency to legal theory. It might be easier to simply attribute a law to the will of the Law. The Law is often attributed with a will of its own in courtroom and common parlance. In this respect law becomes a system of 'independent imperatives', as Olivercrona terms them, which do not need to be ascribable to any will, fictional or not.

However, the breaking of powers into shares is, according to Hart, a valuable contribution to jurisprudence.

4.10   Rees and the restatement of sovereignty

Anyone who listens to the outbursts of the Bruges group or the United Nations' reluctance to intervene in intra-national issues will be well aware that the question of sovereignty has not left the legal or political arena. Rees and others have concerned themselves with the question of what sovereignty is and what the authority of sovereign laws might be. Rees identifies six possible ways in which to envisage sovereignty (although there are possibly more ways):

a) Sovereignty in its *legal sense* is not concerned with the influence or power of the sovereign, other than in its legal sense. In a *political sense*, a body may be sovereign by conquest and the eradication of the previous sovereign structure. However, the fact that a people has been conquered need have no importance in terms of the legal structure. If we think of the Glorious Revolution, the fact that William took over from Charles was immaterial, in itself. This aspect of political sovereignty is not the concern of the lawyer. Instead the lawyer is concerned to determine what the ultimate authority of the law is, rather than what power lies behind the ultimate authority of the law.

b) Early concepts of sovereignty, as well as the Idealist concept of sovereignty, determine that the sovereign had supreme legal authority only insofar as it also had moral authority. This is sovereignty in its *moral sense* in that the requirement of sovereign authority can only be satisfied by moral authority.

c) A sovereign may instead be the person or body that holds the monopoly of coercive power in a state. The sovereign is the person who may guarantee or enforce any law, irrespective of whether it be made by the sovereign or some other body. Thus, in England the sovereign power would be that of the Crown in the form of the courts, police and military (among others). Rees would term this *sovereignty in the institutionally coercive sense.*

d) In strict contrast there may be envisaged the sovereignty of the majority or all of the people in the society, which could be viewed as the *sovereignty of social coercion.* Such a concept of sovereignty is obviously of limited application and must be viewed in terms that pre-date government. Such a sovereignty of collective coercion would be applicable to a tribal or 'primitive' society where law is in the form of custom and is enforced communally. Alternatively, if sovereign power is based on a social contract theory, such a view of sovereignty may be applicable.

e) It seems clear that in a given society more than one of these criteria may apply, so that logically another definition of sovereignty is 'the body with the *strongest political influence*'. Such a view creates a political rather than legal judgment.

f) A final category of sovereignty is that which differentiates between a body that has authority purely on the basis of force and the permanence of a sovereign that rules by authority. Sovereignty in the *permanent sense* differentiates between the ruler who is constantly mobilised in a quasi-military sense, and the sovereign who has stamped his authority on a society and can rule by law as opposed to force.

Rees employs these differing concepts of sovereign power in order to seek answers to four important questions. The first of these needs to be answered in the affirmative if the imperative theories considered here are to be considered as logically sustainable. The imperative theory is built on the assumption that law is the will of the sovereign. If it can be shown that there need be no sovereign in a state, then this definition is logically defective. Therefore the first question must be 'is sovereignty a necessary feature of a state?' Rees analyses this question in some considerable depth, but for the present purposes a more simple analysis must suffice.

i) A sovereign in the legal sense is causally necessary in any given state, though not necessary by definition. In order to govern properly, laws are desirable, though perhaps not logically necessary. In order for laws to be of any effect there must be some ultimate authority: '[in] the absence of such a final legal authority no legal issue could ever be certainly decided, and government would be impossible.'

ii) Equally, it is causally necessary that there should exist a sovereign in the coercive sense, though not logically necessary. Laws can only be enforced either by a supreme coercive power or by social solidarity which punishes transgressions. It would be unreasonable to assume that law can exist without social or institutional coercion.

iii) It is not logically or causally necessary that (as in the fifth definition) there should be one body that can be said to be more supreme than any other body that could be described as sovereign. For example, the electorate is sovereign in the sense of its social coercion, Parliament is sovereign in the legal sense and the executive is sovereign in an ultimate coercive sense. They are, in England, mutually dependent and it would be impossible to ascribe to one more supreme power than the others, since they hold their power by virtue of the others.

Therefore, while it is not logically necessary for a state to have a sovereign, it seems causally necessary for a legal system to work well. What makes sovereignty of logical necessity for Rees, is when there is a requirement to define ultimate legal authority. Without ultimate legal authority, there can be no ultimate determination of legal decisions, nor can rules be married to the coercive force that is necessary to enforce law. Rees makes a useful analysis of different kinds of authority, but then concludes that the authority of law lies in the danger of sanction by a supreme coercive authority.

However, if law is to be regarded as more than simply conventions of the exercise of power, then law must have some logical independence from power. Rules must in themselves be valid. Such a question is a question of validity.

4.11 Some conclusions about sovereignty

Lawyers are ever concerned to differentiate law from other orders, such as that of the robber gang. Suppose a gangster were to take over an island. He populates it with the assorted 'molls and stooges' that he has brought with him. Whatever the gangster says cannot be contradicted and there are standing rules, requiring the sort of things that a gangster might require. He is therefore the supreme coercive authority, but is he making law? The answer surely must be contingent on whether the rules that he makes have some feature that differentiate them from any other mandate that he might give. It would surely be a perversion of the word law if it could apply equally to 'bring me another beer!' and 'only kill those people who I say you can!' Both might be mandates of a gangster, but the latter seems to accord more naturally with our concept of law.

Austin seems to escape from this problem by limiting the legal mandates of a sovereign to those that he makes by virtue of being a political superior. However, this is a mere disguise for the fact that Austin is seeking to limit the term 'law' to things that have a specific purpose, termed as political, as opposed to domestic. It is this element that demarcates law from the dictates of a robber leader. However, as an exclusionary criterion, it is less than successful, because of the ambiguity of the concept of 'political'. The sovereign in Austin's theory provides the power and in the sense that he is the political superior, provides the exclusionary criterion. To this extent it is logically necessary to Austin's concept of law.

In the light of these observations we might draw three conclusions that may be made about the imperative theory:

a) A sovereign is not logically necessary, in itself, for a concept of law. Sovereignty might equally be replaced by the requirement that legal mandates are efficacious.

b) It is not enough that mandates are efficacious, they must also be coherent with each other. Sovereignty provides for the coherence of mandates, since they emane and are attributable to one will. However, the notion of a corporate will is simply a fictional way of saying that mandates are non-contradictory and mutually complementary. What seems unsatisfactory in Bentham is that his seamless web of deontic logic does not allow domestic mandates to be differentiated from mandates with legal effect. Austin, although his demarcation is not entirely successful, does provide an exclusionary criterion. For lawyers, as well as to satisfy our common expectations of law, some exclusionary criterion is needed.

c) We shall see in Chapters 6 and 7 that addressing the three issues of efficaciousness, validity (ie the exclusion of non-relevant mandates) and coherence are questions that should ideally be addressed individually. Sovereignty seems merely a way of merging potential answers for convenience's sake.

5 POSITIVISM 2: UTILITARIANISM

5.1   Bentham on utilitarianism

The imperative theory is, it is to be remembered, merely an analytical framework of law as it is, in order that law reform may be more efficiently achieved. Thus, Bentham must be seen not only as a fairly insightful jurist, but, as has long been acknowledged, an energetic law reformer. The same cannot be said of Austin, whose conservatism is noted to the surprise of many.

Bentham's view of legislative ethics is termed utilitarianism. We have already seen that Bentham was not enamoured of the lack of empirical foundation for Natural Law and moral theories, being simply used to criticise the inexpedient and buttress the expedient. Additionally, a Natural Law theory that stemmed from any other but the ruling class could only be enforced against a legal system by force of arms rather than reasoned argument. Certainly, this is not a very useful concept for stable government and a peaceful society. Nonetheless, it is vital that there is in existence some bench-mark which can be applied objectively in criticism of legislation and by which future legislation could more justly be made.

Bentham proceeds from the assumption that legislation is aimed at securing the good of the community. However, the community is a fictitious body, made up of individuals, so the question becomes 'what laws are good for the individual?'

The second issue is a slightly different one, being directed in the opposite direction – what ought the citizen to do?

Ultimately, the question is one and the same, since the formula of human behaviour is to Bentham a universal truth. People are governed by two forces, pleasure and pain – this view had been expounded by Hume and, as we have seen in Chapter 2, developed by philosophers from Helvetius through to Beccaria. Obviously, therefore, when a person asks 'what should I do?', the answer must be 'do what gives you most pleasure' and 'avoid pain'.

Thus, the question of how the general good might be served was founded on the multiplication of this basic principle in the form of the pursuit of the greatest happiness for the greatest number. This provided a platform whereby laws might be passed, not in accordance with arbitrary moral prejudice, but on the basis of social utility. Moreover, the principle of utility was one that was best expressed by democracy. Only the individual knows what he thinks will make him happy. Thus, if the majority of people vote for a policy, both the question of moral and utilitarian considerations are immediately resolved.

Bentham was not unaware that different things were of varying importance to a man, so he sought also to give weight to different considerations. Bentham's model seeks to reduce issues of morality to easily measured statistics, or what he terms the calculus of felicity.

The Utilitarian calculus is viewed by Bentham as one that needs no proof or justification in terms of 'rightness'; he simply regards it as a 'sacred truth'. This might be hard to accept, but then Bentham seems to see the principle of utility as just the same as any other scientific law that may be observed. However, Bentham was not blind to the problem that (a) too much legal intervention was likely in itself to diminish the degree to which individuals could pursue happiness; (b) in times of increasing misery in the form of unemployment and poverty, legal intervention is needed (see Stone *Human Law and Human Justice*).

However, the inescapable conclusion of the calculus of felicity was that utilitarian law must be backed by an appropriate degree of pain for it to be effective. The defective insistence on pleasure and pain as the force of law, led Bentham to some fairly grave ideas of punishment such as transforming prison into a hell and inflicting punishment with utilitarian precision. Bentham's concept of punishment was one that was impersonal and appropriate to the crime. In the true spirit of Bentham's reforming instinct, he therefore criticised the contemporary method of flogging, since it varied according to the strength of the person wielding the whip. He suggested instead that a rotary flogging machine should be used, so that all offenders could be whipped equally hard.

The example just given illustrates the curious concern for fairness, coupled with the crude psychology that Bentham advocated. However, he also saw an educative role for the legal system, whereby penal laws would be shown to the offender as being rationally right and whereby the subject of laws would be persuaded that any law was actually there to help the citizen towards greater happiness.

5.2   The 'scientific' approach

a) Bentham's belief is that the reasons why we do act, as well as the reasons why we ought to act in a certain way, are the same. These reasons are pleasure which gives us the sense of 'right action' and pain which gives us the sense of 'wrong action'. To ignore this is to 'deal in sounds instead of sense, in caprice instead of reason, in darkness instead of light.'

b) This was to Bentham an empirical truth. However, from this factual position, Bentham jumps to the assumption that people should be governed in order that pleasure be maximised and pain be minimised. This is an assumption of value, since it might equally be asserted on the basis of Bentham's empiricism, that we should be governed in the way that gives most pleasure to the governor(s). He was quite aware of the lack of logical foundation: 'If it be denied me, I must confess I shall be altogether at a loss to prove it ...'

To find a justification for it is difficult, because it assumes the value judgment that government should be for the good of the governed. This may be a useful platform for rational political debate, as suggested by Harrison, but otherwise it is unjustifiable.

c) However, the purity of this utilitarian principle was to be maintained by the strict application of the empirical mathematical counting of the calculus of felicity. The calculus is necessary in order that the very vague proposition of the greatest happiness be converted into a usable measure of human activity. We shall not explore the way in which Bentham sought to calculate these matters.

5.3   Support for Bentham

Bentham did not invent utilitarianism, but was probably the first to adopt it to the exclusion of other moral criteria. The concept of measuring good in terms of happiness had been in existence for a considerable period of time. However, with the empirical revolution, it was adopted by many, including Hume, as being a logically sound framework for measuring human action.

5.4   The problems with Bentham's utilitarianism

The problems faced by utilitarianism are two-fold:

a) *Empirical difficulties*

   i) As we have seen, the relationship between the maxim and government can only be explained in terms of an assumption or value judgment that cannot be rationally sustained.

   ii) The concept of happiness is hopelessly vague and very difficult to measure. Modern utilitarians have largely abandoned happiness as a criterion, for this reason, and concentrate instead on revealed preference, ie what people think will make them happy.

   iii) Finally, there is logical difficulty with employing the same reasoning to explain the different questions of why I do act in a certain way, why I feel I should act in a certain way and why I ought to act in a certain way. These issues of motivation, inclination and obligation are explained by Bentham in the broad terms of pleasure and pain; however, this is to ignore the differences in the way in which people reason about each of these questions. Bentham would regard the differences between these as the result of other people's indoctrination by the opinions of others. However, this is not easily proved in empirical terms since humans characteristically live in social groups and are moulded by others' opinions. As long as man is a social animal, opinions will figure in his up-bringing.

b) *Moral difficulties*

   i) Utilitarianism might conceivably necessitate great misery for the few, which is something that most people find morally unacceptable. Popper suggests that a better approach would have been for Bentham to have aimed at the minimisation of misery. However, this would have been somewhat inconsistent with his preferred economic theory of laisser faire (minimum State interference).

   ii) Utilitarianism bases its tenets on knowledge acquired on past experience yet is wilfully blind to the experience of history. Predicting what will make people happier requires an understanding of what has made people happy in the past. A policy or law might make everybody happy now, such as the abolition of work, but might result in misery in the future.

   iii) Hume was at least appreciative of this. His view of natural rights as the invention of an inventive species and the acquired social knowledge of the past is a sustainable one. Mill ultimately tried to incorporate Natural Rights of a sort into the calculus of felicity on the acceptable basis that: (1) they were shown by history to have a utilitarian value; (2) Mill simply found the idea of untempered utilitarianism too frightening. The problem with trying to incorporate Natural Rights into a utilitarian scheme is that the result is simply the same as arbitrary moral judgment on the basis of received opinion. Hart, who considers this conundrum, observes that although they are fundamentally inconsistent with utilitarianism Natural Rights have a moral appeal.

   iv) One major criticism of utilitarianism is that it does not give us answers to all of the moral issues that face us. Do foetuses count as human beings who are to be weighed in at the felicific calculus? If they are then how do we resolve the question of abortion? Bentham would probably suggest that unwanted children are likely to make society unhappier, but what of the potential millions of unhappy dead babies?

   The Warnock Committee report on *Human Fertilisation and Embryology* (1984) found that: (1) utilitarian calculations on the issue were practically impossible; and (2) even if they were they would not tell the committee whether experimentation on embryos was right. The former is a valid point, but I think the latter is simply saying that, from the utilitarian point of view, it is unlikely that we would like the answer.

   v) The most damning argument against the strict Benthamite approach is that utilitarianism claims to be an empirical explanation based on the way people actually make moral judgments (aside from the influence of others). The fact that utilitarian conclusions seem often to be flatly contradictory of most moral judgments would seem to question, not the soundness of our moral judgments, but of the calculus of felicity.

Furthermore, given the utilitarian choice that seems to emerge in a democratic society, people become more concerned about rights and morality. It seems that 'the pestilential breath of fiction' that Bentham seeks to free us from is what we prefer. This may be because in a doctrine of rights an individual has an inalienable value, whereas in the utilitarian perspective an individual simply has a numerical value. Utilitarianism can thus justify rights (people are happy to have illusions about themselves), to the exclusion of the theory itself, except as a platform for political argument.

5.5 What use is utilitarianism?

The fact that it is logically and morally difficult to accept Bentham's answer to the question 'What ought the law to do?' compels us to judge utilitarianism on its own merits. Hence, of what utility is utilitarianism?

One problem with utilitarianism is that it seeks to answer too many questions with the same evaluative criteria. If we separate the questions we might find what is logically satisfying in utilitarianism and discard it as an answer to questions that it fails to explain.

a) *Why do people obey law?*

i) Bentham, it may be remembered, believes that the reason why people obey law is that it offers a sanction or a reward. The value in this is that it frees us from the naturalistic fallacy that they obey law because they morally ought to. For example, the misconception might be 'People obey laws because laws are the will of God and people by natural inclination obey God'. Utilitarianism acts as an exclusionary reason, preventing us from saying that people predeterminedly obey laws in the way that apples obey the law of gravity. By this we can also say that positive law does not, and should not, describe the way that people behave in a free state of nature.

Laws are thus brought into the arena of human will. Laws are obeyed by choice, and choice is an aspect of human reason. As a logical tool the utilitarian position reminds us that there are reasons for humans obeying laws.

ii) Are the reasons offered by utilitarianism sufficient reason to explain why humans do obey law? Certainly, fear of sanction and the self-interest that is satisfied by reward are strong reasons why people do obey laws. However, it does not explain why all people obey laws. Take Hart's example of the lone smoker, in a non-smoking train compartment. Why in certain circumstances does he not smoke, even though he wants to? The answer is that he thinks he ought not to. Bentham would suggest that this is a misconception on the part of the smoker, he ought to do what gives him the greatest happiness.

This is a strange viewpoint, since it positively encourages a neutral attitude to unenforced rules. Surely legal systems seek to be effective, and in pursuit of this they should encourage people to think that there are other reasons why they should obey the law? Utilitarians correct this position by saying that people do have other reasons for obeying law, in that they think they should obey law.

b) *Why do people think that they should obey law?*

The answer to this may be taken on the empirical level as the reasons people give for obeying law, or the heuristic level, by speculating on the basis of personal experience of deciding whether to obey a law.

We may ignore sanctions, which we have already accepted as strong reasons, and discount habit, which is not a reason why someone does something, but a description of their behaviour. The fact that people habitually obey laws means that they do not think about obeying law and is hardly equivalent to saying that they think they ought to obey it.

If we ask why a person should obey law, the answer normally given is: 'because it is law/right'. The utilitarian takes this to mean that it is productive of the greatest good or happiness. (Happiness, however, is largely abandoned by most modern utilitarians.) This is an altruistic point of view – 'I conform because it is good for other people/makes them happy'. But what is critical is that people actually believe or assume that obeying a rule will produce this effect. On the heuristic level this equates the obligation with its beneficial effect on other people.

What this does not explain is the obedience to law by people who neither fear sanction, expect reward, are unreflective (habit) or are being altruistic in the above respect. Such people think they ought to obey law because there is an obligation to obey law or they think that the law has a moral value which carries with it the moral obligation. This is not necessarily the same as saying that they do obey law (habit) unquestioningly, but that the fact that something is law means that no further reason is required for obeying it. This is to say that people respond to law as duty-imposing in its own right. To say something is law is to say that it carries with it the obligation to obey, irrespective of any further reason. We are conditioned to react to law in this way. This approaches the argument put forward by Raz that we will see in the next chapter.

One point to note is that Hart, Milton observes, is a utilitarian of sorts and advocates some of these utilitarian positions, but also accepts an internal aspect to rules.

Thus, although utilitarianism in its refined form can bring out a plausible explanation of why people rationally obey rules, it does not usually explain non-rational feelings of absolute moral or legal obligation.

c) *What laws should we make?*

The utilitarian answer might be taken to be 'Those that promote the greatest happiness/good.' The defect in the happiness principle has been pointed out. The latter seems to be a very reasonable proposition, but we have seen that the problem with this proposition is the difficulty of finding a viable criterion for determining what 'good' is (see Chapter 2); whether it be harm to society, harm to the actor. Strictly speaking, Bentham, although he advocates the maximisation of happiness, was not in favour of enforcement of arbitrary moral standards that had no harmful effect. Thus, private sexual morality would not have been enforceable on Bentham's criteria. Yet people are eager to normatise certain personal moral standards. Overall happiness might be augmented by the outlawing of various practices that people see as immoral.

It is thus hard to exclude the dimension of morality from even a utilitarian evaluation. However, what is more worrying is that certain legal reforms would be justifiable on the collective good criteria, yet conflict with our moral feelings. Euthanasia, not only for the elderly, but for all of the sick and the disabled, could be justified as taking a burden from society, removing genetic impurities from the gene pool and saving the old and the ill from suffering. Slavery could be justified for the lowliest in society – a slave-owner is likely to feed and house his property if he can get work out of it and if it has economic value. Empirically speaking, historical research has shown that slaves in the part of America researched had a better quality of life than poor white farmers (Popper). Why not then re-introduce slavery, for the common good?

It is these issues of morality that the utilitarian principle cannot comprehend. We will deal further with this issue in Chapter 17.

5.6 Conclusion

Pound comes to certain conclusions on the value of utilitarianism:

a) Utilitarianism emphasises the social purpose of law. The expository theory of the utilitarians strips law of any external moral justifications and redirects our attention to its instrumental nature.

b) The censorial aspect of utilitarianism emphasises that law ought to be in the interests of the governed rather than those who govern. By denying moral ideologies, it deprives a ruling class of the claim that they have moral superiority for non-rational reasons eg the Divine Right of Kings.

c) Utilitarianism emphasises that law should be an agent of societal progress. However, Pound observes that the claims and demands of individuals tends to have a 'warping' effect on law. I take him to mean by this that there is a tendency for legislators to take into account the claims of interest groups. For example, we speak of vested interests having an effect on the law, eg the 'tobacco lobby' seeking to restrain the legal restriction of the encouragement of smoking. The utilitarian view is that we should do things, not on the basis of moral claims, such as the right to free choice, but on the effect of a law on society. This 'filters out' unmeritricious claims, minimising the 'warping' of the legal system's social purpose.

d) The search for an impartial criterion for moral judgments is prompted by the urge to give people's claims an equal chance to be considered. Thus, rational arguments, rather than old prejudices, may be employed when deciding what law should be. They also emphasise that the legislator has to compromise between the individual claims of citizens in the light of general social needs.

e) The fundamental difficulty is assessing the value of the individual, as balanced against the good of society. Are there any areas where the law should not interfere? Are there any circumstances where the law should guard the claims of individuals absolutely? These are primarily issues about the nature of rights (see Chapter 15).

f) Equally, should we treat a law-breaker in accordance with what would be for the societal good or should we treat him according to the most appropriate action for him as an individual? The judge who employs utilitarianism when faced with an inadmissible confession, should for society's good still admit the confession so that the transgressor may be convicted. Why then do judges feel constrained to act according to rules of procedure that favour the individual? Utilitarianism seems inadequate to explain the judicial commitment to rules. The judge feels that he is obliged to obey rules even if he thinks that a rule's application will be prejudicial to societal good in a particular case, or even if he feels it will be bad in all cases.

The nature of some legal obligations, the reactions to rules and the reasons for those reactions are issues that will be addressed in the next chapter. The individual's place in a system of rules and the issues of rights is largely a question of justice (see Chapter 17).

Utilitarianism has a place in the history of legal development and may be employed as a critical test of non-rational claims, but it does not provide all the answers to the questions that we ask. Nor does it fulfil the expectations that humans rightly or wrongly cherish as being 'rights'. Moreover, I think Stone is correct when talking about the 'happiness' based utilitarian ethic, to observe that happiness is not always achieved by pursuing happiness. Happiness is accrued incidentally to other activities as an incentive for doing things of independent value, eg procreation!

6 POSITIVISM 3: RULES

6.1   Introduction

The inclusion of 'rules' in this broad category of positivism is somewhat problematic. Positivism is a term that Summers would gladly see us abandon as being misleading. I am tempted to agree with him on this; however, the term positivist is useful as a word for broad classification purposes. Positivism has a concern with legal statements as they are, as opposed to evaluating them, as Natural Lawyers seek to do, or doubting their absolute truth, as realists tend to do. Jurisprudence based on the analysis of legal concepts and statements is not exclusive to 'positivists' and, as such, there is a separate section on the analytical approach to jurisprudence in which considerable weight will be accorded to some of these 'positivists'.

However, the analysis of legal systems in terms of rules, tends also to be one that represents an advance on the imperative theory, but which still quarantines moral aspects of law, as being distinct.

The student might ask 'What is the difference between a rule and a command?' I would suggest that there need not be any difference, except in the 'focal meaning' of the two terms. To employ the term command or imperative is to render legal systems so-described open to falsification and ambiguity.

a) A command is psychologically and conceptually associated with a will. If I command you to do good, the fact that I command you, requires you to conform with what I conceive of as 'good'. The proper fulfilment of a command is thus relative to the degree that I conform, not to the words of the command, but the meaning that the person commanding has ascribed to it. Thus, if I am commanded to be reasonably careful, the criterion of reasonableness must be the subjective view of reasonableness that the person commanding entertains. Rules are generally acted on as if their meaning is an objective one. Thus, if we play a game of chess, we might look at a rule-book and argue over what the 'correct' interpretation is, as opposed to what the inventor of the game intended.

b) Because of the logical independence of rules, when it comes to interpretation, the identity of the author is unimportant for understanding their validity. The identity of the author may, however, give us an idea of whether a rule has conformed to any procedural requirements that allow us to identify whether it is a relevant rule. Thus it becomes of secondary importance to establish the existence or importance of the author.

For these, if no other, reasons, the concept of a rule provides a better framework for understanding law than that of a command. There still remain, however, the considerations of efficacy, validity and coherence. It is these considerations which are well-served by the rule-based theories that we are about to encounter. Notably, there is a greater deal of sophistication in these theories, although they are not necessarily more complex than the imperative theories.

6.2 Hart

Raz identifies three views of legal statements that are the premises of Hart's analysis of legal statements:

i) The existence of law may be ascertained by reference to social facts. Law itself is a complex social practice and therefore Hart, somewhat misleadingly, describes his *Concept of Law* as an 'essay in descriptive sociology'. Hence statements about law can be either true or false.

ii) Legal statements have a normative dimension that can only be explained in terms of normative propositions. This means that legal statements are statements about how people ought to behave, so that in order to understand law we can only reduce these legal statements to 'oughts' – Hart employs the concept of the rule.

iii) The nature of legal obligation and the force of law does not presuppose the existence of moral values. The effect of this is to establish the mutual independence of moral and legal values, not to preclude moral considerations from the making or the obeying of law.

One might add a fourth observation made by McCormick:

iv) Law in more complex societies is built upon the interplay of different kinds of rules and thus has a 'systemic quality' that further differentiates it from other social rules, such as rules of morality.

a) *A definition of law?*

Hart in *Theory and Meaning in Jurisprudence* claims to apply the Wittgensteinian approach. He does not start with a definition of law, since this would be to presuppose that the word law actually represents constant and verifiable facts. If we look at Austin, for instance, who Hart is very critical of, we can see how basing a concept of law on an exclusionary definition (law is the command of a sovereign) is a diversion from the truth, rather than an explanation. Therefore, although Hart is in favour of theorising, he is not in favour of 'theorising on the backs of definitions'. By avoiding using a definition of law, he seeks to avoid the problem of committing himself to ideas that cannot be universally sustained.

Instead Hart's jurisprudence is built on basic concepts, which are aspects of the way in which a legal system might manifest itself. However, the core concept is that of the rule.

b) *The four different types of rule*

Hart envisages that a legal system has four different types of rule:

i) Primary rules

All legal systems can be assumed to have, to a greater or lesser extent, rules concerned with actually regulating normal societal behaviour. These rules might be 'do not steal' or 'keep goats out of other people's gardens'. It might be noted that in Chapter 3 we considered Hart's minimum content of Natural Law. The rules derived from the facts of human existence that constitute this would normally be present, reflected in primary rules. Thus, since humans are physically vulnerable, there might be primary rules against killing and maiming. Since there are limited resources, there might be rules against theft (or against private property).

Primary rules are at the heart of legal systems and in primitive societies may exist on their own.

Secondary rules

ii) Rules of change

These are rules with two levels:

- Rules of change allow individuals in society to change their legal relationships with each other. Thus, if there is a primary rule that requires people to honour contracts, there might be a rule of change that prescribes how contracts are to be made.

- In a more developed legal system, there might be individuals who have the role of making new laws and repealing old ones. Rules of change could prescribe the procedures for changing law.

Rules of change are secondary in that they presuppose the existence of primary legal rules and are charged with the purpose of making them work more effectively.

iii) **Rules of adjudication**

Equally, for primary rules and rules of change to work well, it might be necessary for there to be procedures for verification of a breach of primary rules etc and rules prescribing how the offender should be judged and punished. This does not necessarily suppose the existence of an institution that corresponds to the judiciary. One might look at some of the early English self-help laws of vendetta for an example of rules of adjudication without the requirement for a judicial institution.

iv) **Rules of recognition**

We will consider these further. However, it suffices to say that a rule of recognition provides the criteria for identifying what is to be regarded as a valid legal rule.

c) *Effectiveness and the separation from moral law*

It is not enough that these rules exist in some form or another. They must themselves be social practices in order to genuinely amount to law. Therefore there are three requirements that need to be observed:

i) Those rules that are valid according to the legal system's ultimate criteria should generally be obeyed.

ii) The rules of adjudication and change should be accepted as common standards by both the general public, and, if they exist, people charged with legal 'jobs'.

iii) At least the rule of recognition should be accepted from what Hart terms the 'internal point of view'. (We shall return to this in a minute).

Obviously, if a legal system is not developed enough to have secondary rules then the second two considerations need not apply. Hart cites an example of a legal order that lacks these complexities – namely international law. International law consists of various primary rules relating to the behaviour of states. However, it has no rules relating to how states are to be judged or how the legal order is to be changed, nor has it a rule of recognition.

While Hart would accept that International law is not a legal system in that it lacks the systemic quality that is brought about by the interaction of primary and secondary rules, it is nonetheless law. We might remember that to Austin, international law was 'positive morality' rather than law.

This leads us on to an interesting question: If rules by themselves can be law, then what is to distinguish legal and moral rules, especially in a primitive society? The first point that I think Hart would make, is that in the absence of a rule of recognition, it is unlikely that the society itself would draw a distinction. Certainly, in primitive society much of positive morality and law is fused and indistinguishable. But to Hart the outsider can see some conceptual differences between laws and moral rules:

i) Moral rules are important, whereas legal rules are of varying importance, depending on their subject matter. Some legal rules are relatively 'trivial'.

ii) Moral rules are not susceptible to change on the basis of expediency, whereas legal rules are.

iii)   Moral offences have a voluntary character. Moral standards are frequently self-imposed and a critical element of moral judgment is based on whether someone was aware that something was wrong.

iv)   The form of moral pressure which gives force or sanction to moral rules is 'different'.

I am bound to observe that these are, in themselves ethical, if not moral justifications, rather than logical ones. The importance of moral rules is: (i) dependent on how high a society or individual values morality; (ii) equally variable. One might pick up a twenty pence piece from the ground and consider oneself fortunate, yet one is aware that it is not, strictly speaking, one's own property. The fact that it is impossible to find the owner of the coin and that it is not significantly valuable tempers our moral judgment. However, if we found a bar of gold we would have greater moral pangs about simply keeping it.

Certainly, moral rules are immune from change through expediency, but only if it is accepted that moral rules derive from a different process than normal practical reasoning. Some empiricists would doubt that morality is anything more than enlightened self-interest, which is tantamount to expediency.

There are other potential criticisms of Hart's separation of law from morals, but Hart does accept that this is primarily a moral argument, for reasons we have discussed earlier (Chapter 1). However, I am inclined to feel that Hart's four 'cardinal' features that separate law from morality are in themselves a rule of recognition that he is superimposing on all law in an illicit fashion. It may be that he has involuntarily hit on the conceptual link between law and morality that he denies. Some legal systems have, as part of their rule of recognition, an incorporation of moral codes. For example, the American constitution, by which all American laws gain their validity, is a moral code. It may be that all legal systems must address the question of whether to bind themselves to a particular morality, such as the Americans, or separate moral systems from their core to allow morally independent judgment.

It may be that the conceptual link between law and morality might be thus illustrated; the rules of cricket, chess or computer programming essentially relate to morally neutral issues, but laws relate to issues whereby a legal system cannot escape moral judgment.

d)   *The internal aspect of law*

Hart's choice of rules as the building blocks of his concept of law is, as we have already noted, not merely accidental. The important aspect of rules is, to Hart, the way in which a person responds. Hart insists that law cannot be understood simply from the external point of view. The fact that law commonly has sanctions does not explain what goes on in the mind of a person who obeys the rule and never gets to the point of having a sanction visited upon him.

The human attitude to social rules is, to Hart, the focal sense of law. If a smoker is alone in an Underground carriage, where smoking is prohibited, why is it very likely he will still not smoke? Thus, rather than relying on habitual obedience, as Austin does, Hart prefers to have a view of law that can explain rule-based behaviour in more psychologically realistic terms. In response to legal rules, therefore, 'there should be a critical reflective attitude to certain patterns of behaviour as a common standard, and that this should display itself in criticism (including self-criticism), demands for conformity, and in acknowledgments that such criticism and demands are justified, all of which find their characteristic expression in the normative terminology of "ought", "must" and "should", "right" and "wrong".'

It is only on the basis of these actual statements of actors in the social world that we can understand how people react to law. Moreover, for a legal system to be genuinely effective, at least the officials in a legal system should have this critical reflexive attitude. It is from this that laws gain their normative effect.

This view seems a realistic sociological observation, which indicates that people are expressing an attitude of willingness to be guided by legal rules. However, these observations beg the question – is Hart saying that people are expressing a moral judgment of law? Raz seeks to address this question:

i) Hart separates legal from moral obligation, so therefore '[o]rdinary legal discourse consists of internal statements and those, though expressing a practical attitude of acceptance of the law as a guide for behaviour, do not necessarily express moral grounds.' However, this is a difficult position to maintain.

ii) When people speak of other people's obligations to obey law Raz believes that often, though not always, people are making moral claims. Sometimes people may require someone to obey the law because it has a direct or indirect effect on the speaker, but the language used is that of the general 'rightness' of obeying law, which sounds like a moral claim.

iii) Raz postulates a dilemma. 'Either all legal statements are statements expressing moral endorsements of the law or not all legal statements are internal statements as understood by Hart ... Hart rejects the first horn of the dilemma and he is surely right to do so. Clearly many legal statements do not express a moral position either way. This fact is not disputed by Natural lawyers and is indeed accepted by Finnis.' McCormick concludes, as does Raz, that Hart does not adequately explain 'what is denoted by rules being generally "accepted", "supported" by criticism, "supported" by pressure for conformity and so on'.

One must conclude that what Hart is striving to do is to give expression to man's instinct for social cohesion and emotional urge for normativity. This is at least the conclusion of McCormick. We seem once again to be returning to the issue of law and morality! However, the fundamental search is for the nature of legal obligation.

Hart thus sets the foundation for the important questions about the nature of rules, by indicating that legal theory must comprehend the way in which people respond to rules, as opposed to the content of rules. We shall return to this question later in this chapter.

e) *The rule of recognition*

Hart has postulated interesting answers to several questions which it might be worthwhile recapping:

i) Hart has accounted fairly acceptable sociological criteria for establishing whether a legal system exists in factual terms, ie his criteria of effectiveness.

ii) By employing the concept of rules, together with the internal reflexive attitude, Hart has posited an answer to the question of what gives law its normative dimension. In addition this provides for the logical independence of law from its author. Thus, in order to understand why we must obey law we are diverted from the answer 'because the sovereign so commands', which begs the question of why we should obey him. It also resolves the distinction between power and authority. To say that law rules through fear is neither rationally nor sociologically acceptable as a truth.

iii) By explaining the interaction of primary rules and rules of adjudication and change, he explains the cohesion and unified purpose of a legal system at any given time.

However, there remain two issues that are desirable to account for in a legal system.

Officials of legal institutions and lawyers are obsessively concerned with the concept of 'valid' law. This is a question of utility rather than logical necessity. How do we know that an Act of Parliament of two hundred years ago should be applied? Should we take cognisance of the Inland Revenue claiming to raise a tax that Parliament has not authorised? Validity as a criterion of legal usefulness allows lawyers to see a continuing cohesion over time as well as providing a criterion for excluding 'irrelevant' rules. This is to be distinguished from the issue of validity based around the question of general legal obligation.

However, it is therefore clear that it is merely useful, rather than necessary for law to:

i) Provide a guide for the lawyer as to what he should 'properly' consider as law (ie as valid).

ii) Provide a guide for the lawyer as to how to relate present laws to those of the past and future. Such a guide seeks to explain the continuing validity of laws as well as legal institutions. It explains why we obey the Parliament of today, even though it is not comprised of the same people or elected on the same basis as two hundred years ago.

A primitive society that has no special legal officials will not be concerned with what is valid law (in the sense of (i) above), since it only concerned with validity in terms of generally creating obligations. Equally, the second requirement assumes an empirical history of law-making, which is not necessarily a feature of all legal systems. Austin sought to explain the continuity of legal phenomena by saying that people were in the habit of obedience. However, this defies logic; how can one be in the habit of obedience to a new king? Hart terms this 'too simple a notion'. Instead he suggests that in some instances we can look to another explanation, which is couched in terms of rules.

The rule of recognition is a rule that is employed to determine what rules should be enforced. What it exactly is, defies even the descriptions of Hart, but the following are the salient features, as far as I can tell:

i) In the English legal system, we might take the rule of recognition as 'what the Queen in Parliament makes is law', but since it is not the only law-maker, the rule should also stipulate the other law-making bodies and their relative importance. Obviously, in view of this, certain rules of change might become mixed up with the rule of recognition. For example, the courts can make new law in the form of precedent and Parliament can change it because it is a superior law maker.

ii) The rule or recognition thus confers the power on legal institutions to exclude that which does not accord with the rule(s) of recognition. However, the situation becomes a little more problematic when we consider whether there is an obligation to obey it. The student will remember that the third criterion of efficaciousness was that the rule of recognition is accepted. Thus, there must be an obligation to obey the rule of recognition.

iii) The rule of recognition is not necessarily expressed or written down, in fact Hart asserts that frequently it is not. Therefore we must rely on observation of the behaviour of people engaged in the legal pursuit to see it manifested. Now the student might find it perplexing that Hart is postulating an unwritten and unexpressed rule, that can only be inferred from the behaviour of those who are bound to obey it. The rule is therefore little more than the coherence of practice of personnel involved in the administration of the legal system.

iv) The rule of recognition carries with it another somewhat difficult aspect. It is neither valid nor invalid, but is simply an ultimate rule from which the importance of every other rule may be deduced.

The burning question (if we can be this enthusiastic) is whether the rule of recognition is a valid jurisprudential concept. There are thus two questions to be addressed:

i) *Does the rule of recognition succeed in answering the questions of validity and continuity?* The rule of recognition certainly explains that jurists do treat certain sources as valid. By expressing this behaviour in terms of an unwritten rule, Hart, suggests Harris, is reducing it to the internal reflexive attitude alone. The effect of this is to say that jurists (a) all adopt the same rules as valid (b) feel they should continue to do so and would criticise a judge who deviated from the norm.

ii) *What is its value?* The rule of recognition does not amount to a posited rule, but is instead descriptive of a social practice or custom. It is merely a logical convenience rather than an explanation and, as such, adds very little to our understanding of legal systems, other than that legal institutions develop customs or conventions of conduct, which they preserve.

We will encounter Kelsen's basic norm in the next chapter which superficially bears a resemblance to Hart's rule of recognition. However, the functions ascribed to Kelsen's norm make it logically indispensable to his theory. Hart's rule of recognition describes the way in which legal systems do behave, but is entirely disposable.

6.3 The contribution of Hart

a) Hart's *Concept of Law* has been described by Finch in a favourable and, I think, an accurate way:

> '... What cannot be denied is that Hart's concept of the union of primary and secondary rules has been thought provoking. No one else has offered a substitute which, with equal brevity, sets out the crucial features of a legal system. It may be that they are too complicated to be capable of a few terms without serious distortion.'

b) A crucial feature of Hart's jurisprudence is the avoidance of 'closure'. Hart does not claim that his 'essay in descriptive sociology' encapsulates all that there is to law. He avoids definition and instead focuses our attention upon the central puzzle of how legal statements act on behaviour but concedes that '... as we move away from that centre we shall have to accommodate elements of a different character'.

c) Hart drags positivism away from its obsession with coercion and the assertion that external pressure is the only force of law. Moreover, his conception of a minimum content of Natural Law bridges the credibility gap between legal naturalism and positivism. The aspect of law as a human activity is very apparent in Hart's separation of the concept of being obliged to obey and having an obligation to obey. The inner response to rules which represents the latter undoubtably is a development on the crude psychology of the imperative theory, which depends on the former.

d) Following Bentham, Hart recognises that power is 'broken into shares' in a legal system. The distinction between laws that regulate human behaviour for the sake of regulating human behaviour (primary rules) and laws that regulate human behaviour for the purpose of making law itself work better is a valuable one.

e) Hart's refusal to undertake the task of definition means that he provides us with the identikit pieces with which to analyse a variety of legal systems. Thus, his theorising may be added to or substracted from, without detracting from its general tenor.

One might eulogise further about Hart's contribution; however, these seem to be the major advantages. The shape of Hart's theory means that criticisms of it seem to add to and refine the concept, rather than break it down.

6.4 The problem with Hart

The criticisms of Hart generally centre around the lack of detail that Hart employs in his exposition of *The Concept of Law*. This, in itself, is not a real criticism, since, as we have noted already, he does not claim to be defining law or to be including all the relevant information. However, there are some significant oversights:

a) *Is law a system of rules?*

Hart's theory is based upon the central tenet that the focal point of law is rules. There are two major critics of this emphasis:

i) Lloyd points out that it is the institutional frameworks of law that root it in a society, hence he would like to see an institutional account of law, explaining courts etc.

ii) Dworkin criticises the sole employment of a concept of rules, in that principles, as well as rules, are used in adjudication. We will consider the Hart-Dworkin debate further in Chapter 19, however it is just fair to point out that Hart's theory is not one of adjudication and therefore principles are not focal to the whole issue of law. What Dworkin means by 'a principle' is something like the legal concept that a man cannot benefit from his wrong-doing.

Thus, in *Riggs* v *Palmer* (1889), a man was, on this principle, prevented from inheriting his grandparent's estate, because he had killed that grandparent.

b) *Does Hart explain rules adequately?*

There are aspects of Hart's explanation of rules that cause some puzzlement:

i) Hart's Rule of Recognition is self-evidently problematic. Its precise role and necessity is unclear, as is where it belongs in the legal system.

ii) McCormick and Raz are not sure that Hart has succeeded in convincing us of the nature of the internal aspect of rules. Hart seems to suggest that there is a non-moral dimension to the critical reflexive attitude, but this is not explained.

iii) Dias, amongst others, is concerned that although the rules theory is anchored in sociological fact, it does not distinguish legal rules from other rules that work in the same systemic way. Fuller offers Hart an answer, suggesting that what Hart has failed to give sufficient account to is the social purpose that law has. A clarified sense of purpose would differentiate law from other rules systems.

iv) Dias is also concerned that Hart gives inadequate attention to the obligatory nature of secondary rules. Hart tends to emphasise that they are power-conferring. However, this is I think to emphasise a conceptual distinction between primary and secondary rules. In practice the distinction is finer.

c) *A concept of law without a definition?*

Although Hart is quite right to suggest that definitions can be misleading, a working definition is desirable. To a certain extent Hart strays away from descriptive sociology to make positive claims about the nature of law. For example, his fervent separation of law from morality amounts more to a definitional claim than a description, since certainly Raz is not convinced that Hart adequately explains how this separation comes about. It is perhaps better to admit to a definition with all its defects and assumptions, than claim to work without one, yet harbour a 'secret agenda'.

6.5   Raz

Raz goes a long way to answering Hart's critics. He identifies three main features of analytical jurisprudence:

'One concerns the special features of the judicial process and of judicial reasoning. The second encompasses the discussion of legal concepts (eg rights, duties, ownership, legal persons) and of types of legal standards (rules and principles, duty imposing standards and power conferring standards). The third range of problems revolves round the idea of a legal system and the features which distinguish such systems from other normative systems ...'

This is an altogether more detailed and rounded conception of law, which seems to encompass some of the issues 'left out' by Hart. We shall endeavour to see how Raz has addressed some of the critical questions that we asked of Hart.

a) *Demarcation of law*

A criticism of Hart was that he failed to distinguish law as a system of rules from other social rules. Raz employs several different approaches to this questions:

i) Rax does not deny that there are moral features of law. However, in *The Problem about the Nature of Law* (1982) Raz proffers a useful distinction between legal rules and moral ones. This centres on what one might call the difference between the legislator's duty and the judge's duty. (These are terms imported from ethics, rather than from Raz.) When we are deciding what rule to adopt, we are concerned to ask what general reasons there are for adopting it. This is a purely deliberative phase, characteristic of the legislators' job, although judges are equally faced with it at times.

However, there is a transition from deliberative to executive behaviour. Once it has been decided to adopt a decision in a legal system, then it becomes regarded as settled or decided. An appeal to law is thus an appeal to something that has been settled or 'laid down' (as is the derivation of the word 'law').

Practical reasoning of the deliberative kind is excluded. We no longer ask what are the reasons for this rule, we simply ask 'what is the meaning of the rule?' The fact that a rule has been decided excludes or overrides any further general consideration of the reasons for the rule, whether they be of a moral or practical nature.

ii) Raz employs the concept of a rule of recognition, but his view is that a rule of recognition is a question of fact. If people actually recognise and apply the rule of recognition, in that they adopt only rules made in a certain way, then it exists.

Moreover, while Hart is unsure whether the rule of recognition is a legal rule or not, Raz affirms that it is, regardless of whether it is merely customary or conventional. Thus, the rule of recognition represents a legal rule by which it can be determined (a) what sources of law are; and (b) what the hierarchy of legal sources is.

b) *Efficacy*

i) Raz quite sensibly asserts that for a legal system to exist, it must be effective. Therefore, we look to social facts to verify whether a legal stem exists. 'Whether a legal system is in force depends on its impact on the behaviour of people in the society ... [N]ormative systems are existing legal systems because of their impact on the behaviour of individuals, because of their role in the organisation of social life. Consequently, when we look at legal systems as systems of laws ... we should look for those features which enable them to fulfil a distinctive role in society. These will be the features which distinguish legal systems from other normative systems.'

ii) Raz concedes that this is an assumption, and not an uncontroversial one at that. However, the 'institutional' approach, coupled with a sense that law has a distinct purpose, is one that avoids requiring that legal systems be identified by their content or by their morality. It is thus a very positivist approach. However, as already noted, 'those features which legal systems must possess to fulfil their unique social function entail that they also have certain moral characteristics'.

iii) As a consequence of this second criterion of function, which is determinable by reference to the institutions required to achieve it, Raz asserts that one of the defining features of law is its institutional system.

- Raz determines that the institution that most readily indicates the existence of a legal system is a *Primary Institution*. A primary institution is recognised by the way that it performs its function, which can be broken into four categories:

  - they are concerned with authoritative determinations or decisions;

  - they make these decisions about normative situations (situations where the question may be 'ought he have done it?' or 'should he do it?')

  - they apply pre-existing rules or norms;

  - their determinations are binding.

  The most obvious example of this is a court, though this is not the only thing that a court does. Yet these features are critical for it to be said that a legal system exists, rather than any particular form of institution, such as a court.

- Simply speaking, law must actually provide a method for settling disputes, but also provide guidance because institutions must decide on the basis of pre-existing rules. This means that their decisions will be regular and therefore predictable. Thus, legal systems are not systems where officials can settle problems in whatever way they think is fit. Law is distinguished from absolute discretion.

iv) It is possible that two sets of rules may contend for the title of legal system in one society. In such a situation, reference must be made to purely societal facts and attitudes, as well as to the effectiveness of constitutional law, ie whether it is obeyed, in order to decide which one is the prevailing system.

In conclusion, efficacy and demarcation are very strongly linked because what demarcates law from other things is that it achieves (ie is efficacious) its unique social role (ie its purpose). In many ways therefore, Raz is approaching the formulation suggested by Fuller that the existence of a legal system is a question of achievement of purpose, although Raz clings on to the issue of societal effect.

c) *The uniqueness of law*

As we have seen, Raz asserts that law has a unique social function to perform. He employs the following criteria that amount to exclusive and necessary characteristics of law:

i) Legal systems are comprehensive

Most normative systems do not claim authority to regulate every aspect of life; however, law does. Morality has nothing to say about what colour to paint my house, yet a legal system could. Cricket rules accept that they apply only to cricket and not to tennis or driving. A legal system, however, claims to have the authority to determine what we say, do in bed and, in terms of mens rea in criminal cases, even judges us by our thoughts and intentions.

Raz points out two critical points, however:

- A legal system need not actually regulate all aspects of social life, but simply claims authority to do so.

- Not all systems that claim authority to be comprehensive are legal systems; it is simply one necessary feature of a legal system.

ii) Legal systems claim to be supreme

As a logical sequitur of the above, a legal system must also claim to be supreme. 'All legal systems ... are potentially incompatible at least to a certain extent.' Legal systems may adopt the norms of other legal systems, may co-exist with other normative systems, but must, if they are to be comprehensive, reserve the right to exclude the binding application of any other rule.

iii) Legal systems are open systems

A feature of legal systems is that they can, to a certain degree, be open. What this entails is the adoption of norms, already present in society, to which the legal system gives binding force. An example might be the societal institution of 'the promise' which is a normative convention that most legal systems adopt and enforce, under given circumstances. The more of such societal and other norms that a legal system adopts, the more open it is.

iv) In conclusion – 'law claims to provide the general framework for the conduct of all aspects of social life and sets itself as the supreme guardian of society.'

6.6 Raz's formulation of validity

As we have observed, there seems to be a concern, particularly among lawyers, to have a vision of what makes law valid. Raz's formulation of validity is a complex one to be found in detail in *The Concept of a Legal System*. I will only seek to represent a simplified model that may help the student read Raz's theory with a greater sense of direction, than going to it 'fresh'.

One might determine that there are three levels at which we can view legal validity.

a) On a sociological and descriptive level, it might be said that a legal system is valid if it is effective. This makes more sense if we remember that, for Raz, effectiveness is the achievement of law's unique social purpose. The achievement of that purpose depends on primary law-applying institutions determining cases on the basis of the rules.

b) This requires that there be an acceptance of these rules as valid rules on the part of the primary institutions. This may be for three reasons:

   i) The members of the institution morally endorse the value of the rule, ie it is valid because it has moral authority. Obviously, it would be factually unrealistic to suggest this applies to all rules.

   ii) There may be a rule of recognition which states that all rules made in a certain way are to be treated as valid. Therefore, although a rule might not have moral authority in itself, it may be valid because it is of a class of norms recognised as being valid. It is therefore because it belongs to a valid legal system that this kind of rule is valid.

   iii) A rule may be alien to the legal system, but in an open legal system, as defined above, this will be a valid rule, even though it does not belong to the system, if it is enforced by the legal system. Therefore, although private international law is not part of the English legal system, its rules are nonetheless treated as valid.

The latter two have *systemic validity* because they either belong to or are enforced by the system. A type (i) rule may also be valid because it belongs to the system, but it has the additional authority of a moral endorsement.

The question therefore becomes, 'What is validity, if it is not a moral endorsement?'

c) Raz therefore asks, 'what does it mean to say that a legal system is valid?' To explain his complex reasoning I might contrast the following reasons why a woman refuses to marry a man:

   i) 'People do not get married these days!' Now, this is not a valid argument. Just because other people do not do something is not, in itself, a reason for not doing something. The statement is not a valid argument because the question is a normative one – 'Why should we not get married?' to which there should be an answer that is a reason rather than a description. One might as well say: 'We can't get married because I am not married.'

   ii) 'I am already married. If I married you as well I would be a bigamist!' This does not mean that the woman does not want to get married, but there is an exclusionary reason, a particular rule, which prevents further action. The argument is a valid argument and gives a reason why she cannot get married. However, it is not necessarily a reason that she morally endorses. She might believe that having more than one husband is perfectly moral, but she accepts that there is a rule that prevents her from having two husbands.

   iii) 'I am a radical feminist and believe that marriage is an instrument of sexual oppression!' This is a valid argument in that it is based on a moral belief. It is also an exclusionary reason.

All of these are answers to a normative question – 'Why should we not get married?' The first statement is only a valid argument if there is a further reason why she should behave like other people. As such it is a statement that is *conditional on the existence on a valid reason*.

The second statement states a valid reason that is based on an exclusionary rule (against bigamy), but does not commit the speaker to a moral acceptance that the rule is a correct one. The rule is valid in the sense that the person feels bound by it, but not necessarily because of moral endorsement. It is therefore *morally detached*.

The third answer is a *committed statement* in that it morally endorses a reason that the speaker not only feels bound by, but also agrees with.

d) *How does this help us understand validity?*

To state that law is valid is tantamount to saying that there is a good reason why it should be obeyed. This is to be differentiated from saying that law is effective, which is tantamount to saying that law is obeyed. The former statement is normative, in that it says that it should be obeyed. The latter is descriptive in that it says that law is obeyed.

Raz concludes that to say law is valid is a normative statement, either of a detached or committed kind. However, as we have already seen, for rules to amount to a legal system, they must be effective. Thus:

i) To say that law is valid is a normative statement, implying that there is a good reason for obeying it.

ii) It is also a statement dependent on the existence of social facts (the adoption of rules by primary institutions).

iii) To say that law is valid does not necessarily mean that the speaker is morally endorsing the law, but simply that there is an exclusionary reason for obeying it.

Raz's systemic approach also explains, in part, the coherence of law. However, it is his theory of normative statements that is most elucidating.

6.7   Is law a system of rules?

In our account so far I have used the word 'rules' to distinguish law from imperatives and to reinforce what Hart termed the internal and the critical reflexive attitude. However, Raz sees problems in Hart's adoption of rules, for reasons already stated. Most significantly, the requirement for criticism and support of rules that is central to Hart's theory, leads to an ambiguity between moral and non-moral reasons for action. Usually, language employed to criticise other people's behaviour is on the basis of moral claims (whether genuinely felt by the speaker or not).

As we have just seen, Raz seeks to distinguish between morally committed normative statements and morally detached statements. To explain people's response to law, we can only really talk in terms of the reasons upon which they act. These reasons are not always spoken, so Raz formulates a theory of reasoning to accommodate this fact. This speculation about what people think, as opposed to what they say or do, is termed an 'heuristic approach'.

a) *Practical reasoning and norms*

'[I]ntuitively, it is always the case that one ought to do whatever one ought to do on the balance of reasons.' This is the core of Raz's theory of practical reasoning. For Raz reasons can be separated into first and second order reasons.

An example of the way in which these things work might be the following:

'I have bought some 1934 champagne. Because I like champagne I have a first order reason for drinking it. However, there is a second order reason why I should not, in that I promised my friend I would buy it for him to drink.'

Raz elucidates further:

'People have an obligation to keep their promises. This entails that they are not at liberty to break their promises whenever they find, all things considered, it will be the best thing to do so. But this does not mean that they ought to keep promises come what may. The presence of reasons of another kind will justify breaking the promise.'

Thus, to continue our example, although a promise might be a second order reason that excludes further deliberation as to whether I want to drink the champagne (I should not, since I promised it to my friend), it may be that there is another obligation involved. For example, the doctor has ordered my friend not to drink, so that keeping my promise would result in harm to him.

For Raz, the existence of a legal rule gives us a second order reason that tips the balance of reasons why I should or should not do something. Second order reasons are weightier than first order reasons and fundamentally affect the way in which we decide what to do. However, laws are not the only second order reasons, moral rules are equally to be regarded as second order rules. Thus, Raz comes to an interesting conclusion for a supposed 'positivist'. Courts, when they adopt valid rules in order to decide a case, apply legal rules because of the rule of recognition, which is a second order reason to exclude other non-legal rules. However, the rule of recognition is not the only second order reason that the court considers. Ultimately, a judge may be faced with a law that he should apply because it is validated by the rule of recognition, yet he feels that it is too immoral to apply. This is tantamount to saying that there is a stronger second order reason of a moral nature.

In consequence, Raz contends that the acceptance of rules of recognition is a moral decision, not just a matter of fact as Hart asserts. It must be made clear that obviously people do not always act in accordance with the rules that they should obey and as such this acceptance need not be morally right, it simply has a moral dimension.

b) *Reasons and rules*

Raz contends that normative statements are statements that imply or express the existence of second order reasons. By reducing statements to this Raz is able to unravel some critical questions.

i) Not all normative statements are expressed as rules: there are also principles, imperatives and permissions.

ii) Not all reasons for action are expressed, yet they are commonly obeyed because the reasons are self-evident eg we need not be told to avoid pain!

iii) The fact that people do behave in a certain way is not in itself a reason why people should behave in a certain way.

iv) A good reason may exist for someone not to do something, notwithstanding that he always does it. A reason is a concept and does not require that it be acted upon for it to exist.

Thus, Raz rejects Hart's narrow concept that law is a system of rules and instead employs the concept of the norm, which is essentially a second order reason for action. Principles, rules, imperatives, permissions and even personal maxims are norms. Second order reasons are reasons in themselves. As such we do not ask, 'Is there a good reason why the law imposes a duty of care?' We simply think, 'I have a legal duty to be careful'. When a rule passes to the executive stage it becomes fixed and there is no point considering the deliberative reasons for which it was made when deciding whether to obey it.

Although norms are the product of practical reasoning, such as the laws of negligence, they are in themselves to be regarded as secondary reasons, because they have been determined or fixed when the norm passes from the deliberative to the executive stage. Raz goes on to elucidate and individuate the various kinds of legal norms.

i) Mandatory norms (including rules)

These are norms that provide exclusionary reasons for behaving or not behaving in a certain way. They often are expressed as conclusive reasons for behaviour as in the example of the girl who will not marry, because she is already married. She might have equally said 'because the law prevents me'.

ii) Permissions:

- Weak permissions – If there is no legal norm that either permits, forbids or empowers a person to act, the person may be said to have a weak permission to do something. There is thus no positive reason for doing something entailed by a weak permission.

- Strong permissions – If there are second order reasons, such as rules that prohibit an action, a strong permissive norm allows one to ignore the rules against doing something. Thus, there is a positive norm that allows one to do something.

iii) Power conferring norms

Raz indicates that there are powers to create and abolish norms and also powers to change the way in which norms apply to individuals. For people to have power, ie to be able to do things that alter the nature or application of norms, there must be a second order reason why they, as opposed to other people, can do this. These second order reasons for the power to change existing norms are therefore termed power conferring norms. These include the power to legislate and the power to make contracts.

6.8   Evaluation of Raz

Even this fairly involved account of Raz does not adequately give a picture of the complexity or sophistication he has brought to Hart's humble conceptual approach. Raz's concept of practical reasoning is not derived from linguistic philosophy, but actually contributes new ideas to it. McCormick views Raz's theory as 'unquestionably the best defence yet' for the positivist thesis. This makes criticism of Raz's theory rather difficult and any critique offered here is bound to seem a little facile. However, some observations might be offered.

a) Raz allows that a legal system can co-exist with another legal system, but at the same time suggests that there is a potential that these may be mutually exclusive. Raz does not provide the jurist with a formula by which he might determine which legal system he must obey. Instead Raz suggests that the choice of which rules to recognise is a question of political morality.

b) Although he goes a long way towards differentiating legal from other normative systems, a certain element of his differentiation is an assumption that legal rules are unique. But none of his criteria of comprehensiveness, supremacy and openness, truly differentiates law from all other normative systems. Even when we apply the matter of 'authoritative determinations' and look for effects on behaviour, one cannot help thinking that the same could have been said of the Catholic church a few centuries ago. It might be that Raz would regard the Catholic church as a legal system, but I do not think this is sustainable. However, to be fair, there are not that many other normative systems with the features that Raz identifies.

c) Raz asserts that lawyers make a moral choice to accept the rule of recognition (this is a simplification of his position). This may be falsified by the existence of coercive forces that are external to the legal system. Take, for example, a country controlled by secret police and clandestine coercion. Superficially, the judiciary may be applying the law through choice, but fear may be their motivation for doing so. Social and political coercion is very real in certain countries. Does this affect the validity of law? Just as moral and legal rules might be second order reasons for acting, might not duress also be so?

d) Following on from the above, I would be interested to know whether legal norms are generally to be regarded as weightier second order reasons that moral norms. This is a critical question. By a legal system's claim to be supreme, it would seem that legal norms should be viewed as superior second order reasons. I am not sure that Raz is clear on the issue, since he suggests that the judiciary is still able to take account of other second order reasons.

e) Though this is extremely unfair, I would suggest that Raz's conception is just a little too ambitious. From the student's point of view it might be that Hart's account is a necessary starting point. Raz, with his complex theory of practical reasoning, is possibly asking the jurist to focus a little too much on the heuristic and sociological aspect. The theory seems to have too many open questions of sociological fact. One yearns for a theory that gives straight yes-or-no answers and is not too conditional on complex sociological questions. This is a simplistic attitude, but it also appeals to the lawyerly instinct in me!

7 POSITIVISM 4: PURE THEORY

7.1   Introduction

The Pure Theory of law is more or less exclusively associated with the Austrian juristic, political and pure philosopher Hans Kelsen. Like a lot of things about the Pure Theory, the student should not take this at face value. Adherents of this theory are numerous, including Ebenstein, Merkl and Radbruch, However, the strength of Kelsen's innovative approach has meant that little has been added by others and consequently most discussion and criticism has been aimed at Kelsen himself.

The second misconception arises from Kelsen's use of Kantian language and methodology. This should not concern the student too much. Kelsen's theory is marked by several propositions, some appropriate to Kant, but all appropriate to Hume:

a) There is a fundamental gap between 'is' (factual statements) and 'ought' (normative statements).

b) In consequence the validity of normative statements can only derive from other normative statements.

c) Normative statements are made by human beings and thus are an aspect of subjective human will.

d) The only law is positive law, ie that made by people. There are no 'natural laws' therefore. (Kant believed that the only truths are moral truths and as such there is an absolute moral law.)

e) Objective facts may have an effect on each other in terms of causality. There is a law of gravity that causes apples to fall. Kelsen asserts there is an equivalent but different relationship between norms. Thus, 'If X circumstance occurs, then you ought to do Y' is a grammatical expression of this *imputation*.

f) The object of legal science is to understand the way in which law works, irrespective of content. The attempt is to explain law in terms of the laws of imputation and, as such, jurisprudence should be a *normative science*, as contrasted to the descriptive sciences that are used to explain facts, eg chemistry, biology etc.

7.2   Normative science

Kelsen points to a fundamental difference between factual reasons for action and normative reasons. It might be illustrated thus:

'The reason I moved was that I was about to be crushed to death by a falling elephant.'

There is a combination of reasons here. There is the fact that an elephant is about to fall, from which we can infer a descriptive 'ought statement'. A falling elephant ought to crush anyone to death. But this is not a reason for action, without the desire to preserve one's own life. As a result of my desire to live, I act by a norm: 'I ought to avoid standing under falling elephants.' The reason for my action is this norm that is attributable to my will. There is no causal relationship between the fact of a falling elephant and my voluntary act of avoiding it. Relationships of causality are factual ones, based on the laws of physics. Kelsen's assertion is that people's reasons for action may be expressable in terms of normative statements. Law can be therefore described in terms of normative reasons rather than of the acts that are the responses to these norms. Thus, if we simply look at posited legal norms, we might find an answer to the question 'How does law work?'

7.3   The purity of the Pure Theory

'The Pure Theory of law is a theory of positive law. As a theory it is exclusively concerned with the accurate definition of its subject matter. It endeavours to answer the question 'what is law?' but not the question 'what ought it to be?' It is a science ...'

The objective of the Pure Theory is not to describe the way in which legal systems work, or what institutions normally are to be associated with law. Kelsen is not even concerned with what considerations a judge takes into account when he decides a case. The Pure Theory is solely concerned with legal reasons for action. Kelsen seeks to rationally reconstruct the way in which legal authority is transmitted in legal systems. In order to achieve an understanding of the way in which law itself works, Kelsen seeks to escape from any fallacies and judgments that might obscure the truth.

7.4   Kelsen's norms

The building block of the pure theory is the norm. Kelsen's concept of a norm is a rather difficult one. It might be explained thus:

a) A norm is 'the meaning of an act of will'. Therefore a norm is the meaning of a real person's wishes. All norms therefore:

   i)   must have an author;

   ii) must have been deliberately made to express what one person wants another to do.

b) However, Kelsen is not interested in the people or methods that are responsible for the creation of the norm itself. He is solely concerned with legal rules, principles and permissions in themselves.

c) Since norms are the meaning of an individual's act of will norms are usually subjective. If I say 'Keep off the grass!' that is the expression of my own wish. But the characteristic of legal norms is that they have an objective quality.

d) Legal norms are objective because they are made by a person who is himself acting in response to another legal norm. The authority for one legal norm is thus another norm that permits a person to make another norm.

If we take an analogy; a judge may order a person to pay a fine. That order is a norm, since it is telling a person what he ought to do. It is objectively valid because there is another norm (for example a statute) that permits or requires the judge to act. Kelsen is only concerned however with the judge's order and its relationship to the statute. Moreover, since Kelsen is not concerned with specific substantive law, he is not interested in the content of the order or statute, but simply the general normative nature of these expressions of will.

It will be clear from the example that norms are arranged in an heirachical structure; one norm is authorised by a higher norm, which is itself authorised by a higher norm and so on. However, it must be remembered that the authority for a norm can only be another norm. One cannot therefore relate the ultimate authority of the law to a fact. Kelsen regards the imperative theory, which relates the validity of law to the factual existence of an ultimate author (such as Austin's sovereign) as fundamentally wrong. The only reason why a sovereign should be obeyed must be another norm.

If I say that I should obey the law because it is made by Parliament, the only objective reason for me to obey Parliament is that there is a rule that exists that says I should. There may be other reasons why I might obey the law of Parliament. I might believe that Parliament represents the electorate and therefore I should obey it. However, this is a norm of political morality, not a legal norm and therefore is not relevant to the study of legal norms. Alternatively, I may look for a legal norm that authorises Parliament to make law such as a constitutional norm.

7.5   The structure of normative systems

Legal systems do not have an infinite number of posited norms. Normally, the constitution is the highest positive norm. However, the reason for obeying the constitution must be another norm – there must be a legal reason in the form of a norm that explains why I should (legally) obey the constitution. This will be the *basic norm* or the *grundnorm*.

It will also be noted that the constitution tends to be very general. For example it may prescribe the way in which laws are made and by whom. However, it will not tell us what a judge should say in a particular case. Therefore, Kelsen observes that higher order legal norms tend to be general, allowing numerous possibilities for the legislator. Parliament can make a law on hanging as easily as it can make a law on gardening, such is its general constitutional power. The choice of what possible norm to create is a matter that is concerned with non-legal considerations, since the only legal considerations are those specified in the superior norm. Kelsen therefore states that the choice of which norm to create or apply is, within the parameters laid down in the authorising legal norm, a political one.

The second facet of the norm-creating process is that as we go down the chain of authorised norms, the content becomes more specific. Parliament can do practically anything, but the courts can only apply precedents or statutes and as such are more limited in the possibilities of creating new norms.

A disciple of Kelsen, Merkyl, describes this process in what he terms the 'Steps and Stairs Theory'. He asserts that each stage of norm creation adds more to the content of norms. As such he disputes the traditional distinction between legislators and norm-appliers. While this might be seen as an interesting view, it is not a 'pure' one. A higher norm may simply specify that it is to be repeated in a lower norm, without any addition to it.

7.6   Law as a social technique

The form of a legal norm is a conditional one. 'If A happens, then B ought to be/may be done.' Kelsen does not take this to be a prediction in the way that Bentham seemed to. A prediction is a descriptive statement of factual probability, not a normative one. Kelsen sees norms as simply authorising reasons, which stand by themselves, irrespective of whether they are acted upon. To understand this distinction, the student should refer to the introductory chapter (1.3(c)).

Kelsen is also aware that law is a means to an end; that of societal regulation. However, as already noted, Kelsen is interested solely in the means. He observes that a feature of law is that it is coercive. At the end of a chain of norms, there is usually a norm that directs a norm-applier when faced with a particular factual circumstance, to issue a norm authorising coercion. An example might be a judge who is authorised by statute to fine someone if he has been speeding. However, the last norm in the chain will be the judicial order (norm) that says the particular offender should pay the fine. This *concretises* the chain of norms.

There is no point in having law as a social technique if it does not address itself ultimately to a specific factual circumstance in society. Law would not be law if it was simply there to authorise lawyers to authorise other lawyers and so on ad infinitum. The norm that addresses the specific social circumstances (eg the act of speeding) roots the legal system in society as a normative social technique. The student must not, however, take Kelsen to mean that the norm need ever be applied, which is a question of factual efficacy. Kelsen is simply pointing out that there should be, in the chain of norms, the authority to apply the law to specific social circumstances. Kelsen is not describing an effective legal system, but simply the conceptual structure of a legal system, which obviously should address itself to social fact.

Another essential feature of law as a social technique is that it seeks to make people do things. Law is not concerned to just inform people of what their legal duties are, but also to ensure that they do behave in certain ways. Therefore norms can be explained as having the following elements:

a) a statement of the circumstances when the norm applies;

b) a statement of what action is prescribed by the norm in those circumstances. A legal norm may (to simplify Kelsen) prescribe the creation of another norm, or, in the case of a concretising norm, prescribe actual coercion.

7.7 Law as a coercive order

There are two aspects to Kelsen's concept of the normative force of law:

a) *Sanctions*

Kelsen's attitude to sanctions is one that attracts considerable criticism. Kelsen asserts that the essence of law is coercion. The fact that people are required to act in a given way is itself coercion, even if they 'voluntarily' act in this way. This is a very Kantian assertion, in that it rests on the supposition that human beings have free will. If a person thinks he ought to do something because another wills him to do it, then he is not acting freely. Kelsen differentiates the normative force of law from the force of other normative systems, such as morality, on the basis of this coercion. Moral law requires people to do what is right, requiring them to be coerced by their own conscience, an aspect of their own will. Law requires people to obey because of the objective validity of law. This is not a description of the way in which these systems actually work; a person may obey a law because it binds his conscience and may abide by a moral code because of social pressure. What Kelsen is saying is that coercion is the normative force that law logically purports to rest upon. Law is coercive because it demands obedience in spite of a person's ability to act on his conscience or according to his own preferences.

Although coercion need not be physical, Kelsen asserts that it normally is of a physical nature in the form of either a reward or a sanction. This is a philosophical rather than descriptive account of the force of law which theoretically, rather than sociologically, explains the normative basis of law.

b) *The delict*

Kelsen observes that it is an ironic use of language when we speak of 'breaking the law'. For him the thing that justifies the existence of a rule is the action that it seeks to prevent. This is a reasonable assertion – why compel breathing by legislation?

A delict is thus the action that satisfies the condition in a norm. The condition, it may be remembered, says that 'If X happens, then ...' Thus, the likely effect of a delict, with relation to a concretising norm, will be the visitation of a sanction. The term delict is, for Kelsen, equally applicable to the breach of a civil legal rule, as to a criminal one. The effect of Kelsen's sanctionalist approach and his concept of delict will be examined later.

7.8 The Basic Norm

It may be remembered that Kelsen asserts that a normative proposition can only be derived from another normative proposition. It also may be remembered that law claims to be objectively valid, ie one should obey it because there is a rule that says you should obey it, which itself rests on a rule. Thus, in theoretical terms an objective norm is one that is based on an infinite regression of norms. However, law does not have this infinite regression, but stops at a constitution. Kelsen tackled the problem of what the reason is that we should regard the constitution as valid. The answer he suggests must be another norm that has the effect of saying that the people who drafted the constitution ought to be obeyed when they make constitutions. It must be noted that a reduction of this to a rule saying 'the constitution should be obeyed' would be senseless duplication and would not be necessary in a state where the constitution is habitually obeyed. But then this is to stray out of Kelsen's theoretical and normative world. The content of this ultimate norm depends on the content of the legal system that it authorises.

The Basic Norm is thus the normative reason why legal norms are legal. By tracing law back to one norm we can decide which norms belong to a legal system, since all the legal norms of one system derive their validity from it. Kelsen asserts that all discrete and objective normative systems have a single Basic Norm.

The problem with the concept of a norm that authorises the highest norm of positive law, is that by definition it cannot be positive. Is there a norm written down somewhere that says we should obey the people who made the constitutions when they make constitutions? Kelsen does regard norms that originate in custom as being positive legal norms. They are norm-creating when a common behaviour pattern becomes adopted as a standard. Thus, it is clear that the Basic Norm is not the same as Hart's rule of recognition that exists as a sociological/behavioural fact.

The Basic Norm is a theoretical necessity, required to explain the objective validity of legal systems. Most jurists do assume that legal systems are valid. This amounts to saying that jurists presuppose the existence of a norm that authorises the highest norm of positive law. As such the Basic Norm is simply a fiction that allows students of law to analyse law as an objectively valid system. Kelsen would urge us not to go in search of a Basic Norm and certainly he would not expect a judge to take into account the existence of it, since it is not positive law. The status of the Basic Norm is similar to a mathematical axiom that although not logical, is necessary to complete the logical theory of mathematics. For example, nought to the power of nought is one. It is essential for mathematics to have this answer yet it is illogical. Nothing, multiplied by nothing, no times is the expression of not doing something – it has no factual value. I would suggest to the student that this is the same nature as the Basic Norm. The only logical explanation for the objective nature of law as a logical normative system is such a hypothesis.

The Basic Norm is a very little understood but much criticised concept, but it is the only logical explanation to the view that law is objectively binding in philosophical terms. To summarise:

a) the Basic Norm is not a positive legal norm;

b) the Basic Norm is the presupposition of jurists who look at law;

c) it is equivalent to saying that for any normative statement to be objectively valid, there must be a normative reason even if we cannot see one;

d) without such an assumption, the jurist merely describes a sociological phenomenon that has no real meaning;

e) as such it is a transcendental legal logical norm ie it explains the logic of legal authority.

If the student is confused, he is in good company since there are many critics of Kelsen who share this confusion. Simply speaking, if one asks a lawyer in his legal capacity what reason he has for doing something he might say it is a statute. If you ask him why he should obey the statute he will say that the reason is the constitution. If you ask him why he obeys the constitution he will not say that there is no reason, but the only legal reason he can give you is that he just should: that is the nature of constitutions. He may give historical or political reasons, but these are not legal reasons. There are non-legal reasons why he obeys statutes, but he gives you the legal reason, because that is the point of acting in a legal capacity. That you 'just should' obey the constitution logically supposes that there is a reason, without knowing what that reason is. The lawyer is not concerned with what it is in terms of legal argument, but the legal theorist who seeks to explain legal norms should at least account for this attitude.

7.9   The relationship of a legal system to other normative systems

a) *Morality*

Hart is much perplexed by Kelsen's assertion that law and morality do not conflict as normative systems. Kelsen returns to the is/ought distinction to explain this. Norms and duties have a dual existence:

I might say 'You must stand up!' That is a norm, whether or not it is heard or acted upon. Conceptually and grammatically, it is not a factual, but a normative statement. Equally, a law that says 'Kill your brother!' is conceptually a norm and if made pursuant to the normative requirements of the legal system it is legally valid. However, most moral codes would say 'Do not kill your brother!' If we ask what the law requires us to do, it is clear; I must kill my brother. In deciding what to do I am aware that the law says I have a duty to kill my brother. I am aware that morality also says I have a duty not to. I can know and accommodate both norms as reasons for acting. All this is on the normative level.

Whether I believe I have a duty to obey them is a question of my state of mind, a factual rather than normative issue. I can believe that I have a duty to the law and an opposite moral duty. A duty exists on two levels: as the meaning of a statement that says you have a duty, or alternatively as a belief in the mind of a person. The former is the content of a norm, the latter is a matter of the sociological/psychological effect of a norm. Kelsen is only concerned with the former kind. The law does not recognise that a moral duty is appropriate to deciding whether someone has a legal duty.

For this reason Kelsen views the conflict between moral and legal duties as the coincidence of normative forces acting on the same person.

b) *Other legal systems*

Just as legal normative reasoning does not presuppose moral obligations, so an individual legal system does not take into account other foreign legal duties as a matter of legal consideration. For example, in the law of evidence, relevant foreign law is a question of fact, rather than law. What one ought to do legally in England is what English law says one should do.

The student will be aware that in England European law is treated as having primacy. This aspect relates to the change in the constitution that regards Europe as an authoritative law-making body and as such it is subsumed under the Basic Norm. It indicates, however, a tendency of jurists to see law as part of a worldwide phenomenon. Kelsen thus moves towards a juristic description of a legal world, where legal reasons are unified under the Basic Norm of international law. We will consider this further a little later.

7.10   Private and public law

Kelsen disputes that there is a natural legal distinction between private and public law obligations. He simply sees this as the law reflecting the political and social ideology of the distinction between law and State.

Public legal relationships tend to impose norms on citizens without the citizens having significant say in the content of those norms, eg a tax demand. On the other hand private law obligations tend to have a mutuality, whereby both parties have a say in what their obligations will be. Kelsen is clearly thinking of contracts here.

Private and public law obligations consist of norm-creating acts. However, public law indicates an inequality in the status of parties, that is a reflection of the political order.

7.11   Efficacy

It was Lauterpact who drew Kelsen's attention to the fact that a distinctive feature of law, as a normative system, is that it is actually adopted as a prescriptive system. One might sit down and write a whole system of 'laws', but it it is never actually practised, it is not dignified with the status of a proper legal system. Thus, an essential feature of legal systems is that legal norms are actually employed as prescriptive norms.

This represents a fundamental difficulty for a theory of law that merely describes legal reasons for behaviour. In order for law to be genuine, then, legal reasons should have an effect on the minds and behaviour of lawyers and citizens. There is thus a parallel existence of law. Law is a system of reasons for action (norms), which has a discrete logic of its own. However, a legal system should also be accepted as having an effect:

> '[T]here must be a certain parallelism ... The tension between the factual and normative must not be too great (if the fundamental rule is to retain its usefulness), just as it ought not to be too small (if law is to remain as distinct from a natural science).'

Lauterpact is here pointing out that while the distinction between law as normative reasons and law as a system of normative effects should remain, there is an unbreakable link between the two. In response to this point Kelsen added that, in order to retain validity, law should be 'by and large' efficacious.

Much criticism has been directed at Kelsen on this point and it clearly disturbed him that his normative theory accommodated a sociological prescription. He did not develop this point, leading to people asking 'How many people need to disobey law before it ceases to become efficacious?' It is submitted that since Kelsen was engaged in describing the normative science of law, he is unlikely to engage in the explanation of the descriptive sociological aspect of law. Kelsen should have simply pointed out that the descriptive sociological aspect of law, ie its effect, was as essential to a concept of law as the normative reasons why people thought they had to so act. However, this would have been to ignore the fact that jurisprudence requires the legal system to be by and large 'effective' if it is to consider a legal system is valid. Thus, Kelsen's theory seeks to accommodate another theoretical presupposition of juristic thinking that law can only really be law if it is used.

I cannot help feeling that it is self-evident in a dynamic normative system such as Kelsen's that this is so. To put it simply, a person does not embark on the study of a complex series of reasons for behaviour, if that behaviour does not in any way correspond to those reasons. We do not study the legal system postulated in Plato's Republic, because it does not exist as an aspect of real human behaviour.

The criterion of efficacy therefore sits very unhappily in the Pure Theory; a problem which Kelsen recognised, but could not resolve. The answer must be that both lawyers and jurists presuppose that when they prescribe a legal reason for action there is at least the potential for someone to obey it.

7.12   A résumé of Kelsen's approach

Kelsen, with the exception of the criterion of 'efficacy', seeks to understand legal normative reasons. If the student wishes to understand this he must think of his study of law to date. A judge will take into account various factual, moral and political reasons for making a decision in a case, but the reason why he is considering the case in the first place and the sole legal reason for him having the authority for him so to do, are the relevant norms (eg statutes) that require and authorise him to act. Thus, Kelsen seeks to explain not the reason why a judge gave a certain verdict in a case, but the reason why, in legal terms, he has the authority to do so. In legal terms, the reason why a judge may decide a murder case is because the law requires him to do so, irrespective of whether he does or does not actually so act.

In view of Kelsen's claim that he is only engaged in the normative science of jurisprudence, it is remarkable that he is criticised by people on descriptive sociological terms. Perhaps the greatest example of this is documented in Hart's essay *Kelsen Visited*. Hart observed that Kelsen agreed with everything that Hart was saying, yet Hart could not understand Kelsen. We only need to look at the aims of their two theories to see how this arises. Hart claims to be engaged in 'descriptive sociology' following an analytical and linguistic train of thought. Hart asserts that one understands the meaning of legal statements only in the context of their use. This binds him to understanding legal theory in terms of the way people do behave and the reasons that they exhibit for their actions. On the other hand Kelsen is committed to understanding the conceptual meaning of legal reasons for action, divorced from the effect of those reasons on human behaviour. It is the difference between the computer programmer and the computer manufacturer. Both are essential to computer science, but are engaged in understanding how to make a computer work from different perspectives. One looks at the internal logic, presupposing that a machine exists that is capable of running the programme, the other looks at the problems of building the machine, supposing that someone has written a programme to run on it. However, that people are aware of the distinction allows them to work more effectively.

In the light of this proposition, it will be clear that those people who do not share Kelsen's philosophical point of view and who view legal norms as effects on behaviour as well as reasons for behaviour, are bound to get muddled over the theory. Hart points out that he fell off his chair when Kelsen vehemently reminded him 'Norm is norm!' However, as the rest of the essay illustrates, Hart still did not appreciate the distinction between a rule of law in the descriptive sense (the expression of a normative reason) and a rule of law in the descriptive sociological sense (the expression of a normative reason that has an effect).

7.13   Criticisms

Wilson described the criticisms of Kelsen as a log-jam. Ebenstein suggests that the Pure Theory has created a 'storm' all over the world. That Kelsen is important is beyond dispute. However, there remains considerable dispute as to what Kelsen is actually saying. I think this stems from the practical attitude of Anglo-Saxon jurisprudence. Kelsen is a positivist in the sense that he believes that the only real law is made by humans. He is, however, concerned to examine positive law as a logic system, rather than a social practice. One of the problems with Kelsen is that he gradually refined and added to his theory so that criticism of Kelsen has been described as 'stamping on quicksilver'. The issue has frequently been not, 'What is Kelsen saying that is wrong?' but 'What is Kelsen saying?' As a result there is a considerable difference between criticising the Pure Theory and criticising what one thinks it is.

a) *Sanctions*

There is much criticism of Kelsen's view of law resting on sanctions. Kelsen assumes that law is not a voluntary order. The purpose of law is to make all people behave in a way that they do not already behave. However, it does not seek to achieve this by convincing people that the content of law is 'right' and binding on the conscience, as moral systems do. Instead law indicates some objective reason why people should act, rather than a subjective reason, such as the dictates of conscience or an independent desire to act in accordance with the law. Kelsen is not saying that people do obey law for this reason, but that it is the reason law gives is the threat of coercion.

Thus, Lloyd is critical of Kelsen on the basis that he says that sanctions of some kind (or rewards) are a necessary feature of law. This seems wrong, since we do not consider that people obey law solely because of fear of sanctions. However, this is an evaluation of the effect of law, not the reasons that the law gives. Take, for example, a statute that says simply 'Thou shalt not kill.' Why should I obey it, unless I agree with it? The logic of the legislator is that a person should obey, even if they do not agree with it, so that some motive for obedience needs to be present. This is the result of the fact that people cannot be assumed to do what they ought to, which is the basic assumption of all law.

b) *Delict*

There is, however, a stronger criticism of Kelsen's concept of a delict as being any act that is the condition of the visitation of coercion. The question of the imposition of duties on legal personnel is problematic. Does a judge have a legal duty to apply a sanction? This thorny question is postulated by Woozley, who suggests that if the answer is 'yes' then there must be a legal norm, accompanied by a sanction, which itself presupposes an official with a legal duty, stemming from a sanction-based norm. This would be a 'vicious regress' back to an ultimate permissive norm with no sanction attached.

The question can only be answered if we address Kelsen's view of legal duty. Kelsen sees duty as having three facets of existence:

i)   the belief in a person's mind that he should do something;

ii) the existence of a norm that says a person ought to do something;

iii) other considerations of fact and belief that represent non-legal norms.

Kelsen is concerned with legal norms (ought statements), not people's beliefs or reasons for people's beliefs. The mistake is to view a sanction as a norm. In the Pure Theory, the imposition of a sanction is a specific category of action that the law requires. Thus, if we examine Kelsen's formulation that a judge should issue a sanction in the event of a delict, there are two normative statements here:

i)   by implication, the delict should be avoided by the citizen;

ii) the sanction should be applied by the judge.

For Kelsen, an obligation cannot stem from a fact, but simply from a norm. The sanction does not create legal obligation, but is the intended effect of a norm. Woozley is surely viewing norms as predictive, ie likely to be acted on. He is talking about the reason why people are psychologically likely to act in a certain way. If we ask 'Does the judge have a legal duty to apply a sanction?', the answer in a normative sense is yes, since there is in existence a legal norm saying that he should. The difference between Kelsen and Woozley is the difference between someone saying that you have a duty, and you believing that you have the duty that a person says you have.

What is unsatisfactory about Kelsen's approach is that it presupposes the sociological jurisprudence exists that explains why a judge believes he ought to comply with the norm. He simply gives the positive legal reason why he should. If this does not seem to be satisfactory, then it is a criticism of the limits of the Pure Theory, rather than its accuracy.

A further criticism of the concept of delict is that it does not differentiate between administrative acts of coercion, such as a compulsory purchase order, and a punishment. Lloyd finds it difficult to understand, however, things such as the compulsory evacuation of a building in the case of fire are not regarded by Kelsen as delicts. I think, again this is more to do with the limits of the normative approach.

If we take Packer's classification of coercion into compensation, regulation, punishment and treatment, we can see the problem. The Pure Theory does not allow a norm to rest on a fact, such as a prediction that people will react to a legal norm on the basis of psychological fact. This is tantamount to asserting that the reason why I ought to obey something is that I am likely to obey if I am approached in a punitive way. This explains a sociological fact, but is not a normative reason why people ought to obey. Kelsen's differentiation of coercive measures resulting from a factual, rather than behavioural contingencies is logical in normative terms. Take these two examples:

> 'If a fire breaks out, bring everyone out of the building.'

or

> 'If a person sets fire to a building, arrest him.'

There is no implied norm in the first instance that fires ought not to start, so that there cannot be a delict if it happens. The normative content is simply that the official ought to empty the building. In the second instance there are two norms; one that people should not set fires, the breach of which is a delict; one that officials should arrest people who set fires.

Again the Pure Theory is logical, but it is not legally descriptive, emphasising just how much of law depends on extraneous sociological and psychological facts. It does not explain why people think they ought to obey the law, but merely the positive legal reasons why they ought to.

Exactly why it is reasonable within the logic of the Pure Theory to base law on the coercive concept of sanctions, which presupposes a psychological fact, is unclear. Kelsen imports this from his philosophical distinction between law and morality, but it is fundamentally a psychological and historical fact that belongs in sociological jurisprudence, rather than normative jurisprudence under Kelsen's own criteria. It is an example of the type of norm that a legal system does have. If it is permissible to say that there are coercive norms, then one may further individuate them into punitive, administrative etc. Kelsen is right to say that these do not belong in normative jurisprudence, but neither on his own terms do sanctions, other than to make an ideological point. That point is that law is not based on moral acceptance.

c) *The Basic Norm*

To summarise the volumes of criticisms directed correctly or incorrectly at the Basic Norm would be impossible. The student should be encouraged to read these. I will simply deal with the two most virulent; one in the context of theory and one in terms of practical application. These are not the only flaws in the Basic Norm, but indisputably they must be seen as denying the whole value of Kelsen's exercise.

i) *Kelsen's imperative fallacy*

Wilson seems to have performed the task of being Kelsen's methodological conscience, seeking to sort out fact from fiction in criticising Kelsen. However, in *The Imperative Fallacy of Kelsen* (1981) he posits the criticism that the whole theory falls apart when we logically pursue the Basic Norm on Kelsen's logic:

- Kelsen is committed to the view that the paradigm of validity and normative logic of law is the norm. Norms are always the meaning of an individual's act of will and therefore are usually subjective. What makes a norm objective is that it is regarded as being binding by the parties to it and third parties. However, the only reason why it can be objective is if there is a norm that gives authority to the maker. In logic, a norm can only derive objective validity from another norm. A judge's authority stems in normative terms from the existence of a norm that empowers him to make norms.

- Kelsen thus locks himself into the potential for an infinite regression. One norm is authorised by another and so on. But this is in stark contradiction to the reality of legal systems. Either law is not objective, which contradicts the whole concept of law as fixed rather than voluntary rules, or it is not logical in the normative sense. Kelsen thus seeks to reconcile the juristic belief that law is objective with his logical premise that a norm can only derive from another norm if it is to be so. The only way to reconcile this is to say that the ultimate norm necessary to validate the constitution exists in juristic consciousness, but is a fiction since it does not exist as a positive norm. Basic Norms are not written down somewhere and they are not posited by jurists. The latter statement is Kelsen's assertion, based on the fact that jurists do not give the law its objective character, because they assume it is objective already!

- Kelsen's Basic Norm thus contradicts reality, because it does not exist, and it also contradicts the logical premise that norms are acts of human will. In a despairing attempt to improve on the theory, Kelsen suggests that the fictional Basic Norm has a fictional author, presupposed in juristic thinking!

This is little different from Austin's concept of a sovereign, except that it is not based in the world of fact. It is almost as if Kelsen has climbed to the top of his ladder of norms and like Jacob has found God! For this reason Kelsen has been termed by Iain Stewart as being exegetical. However, while a fictional rule may logically make a real rule objective, a fictional author makes all the rules simply aspects of a subjective will.

Moreover, I would assert that the Basic Norm itself has no place in Pure normative logic because its existence is itself a matter derived from descriptive sociology. Legal systems do not have infinite norms, arranged in sequence; fact. Therefore, says Kelsen, there ought to be a norm that is non-positive that ends the sequence. Thus, the normative quality of the Basic Norm is itself derived from fact. One ought (normatively) to obey the Basic Norm because it ought (logically) to exist if law is treated as objective.

- The role of the Basic Norm is thus to reconcile fact (there are a finite number of norms in a legal system) with normative logic (objective norms can only derive from other objective norms). Surely this is to derive an ought from an is. Alternatively, one might see the players in a legal system as all telling each other that law is objectively valid, thus simply perpetuating a myth. This would amount equally to deriving an ought from an is: 'You should treat the law as objectively valid because everybody thinks you should.' This is deriving a normative statement from a factual one.

- The relevation of the Basic Norm is thus that law, although being sociologically normative does not comply with the laws of normative logic. In a review of Lloyd's *Introduction to Jurisprudence*, as much was observed by King. Lloyd, like Kelsen, is committed to the fact that normative logic can explain legal logic. King reiterates Wittgenstein's comment that the role of philosophy was to help the fly get out of the bottle, yet the application of normative philosophy still leaves the fly buzzing in the bottle. One might more usefully forget the question of validity, as Hart largely does, and look instead for behaviour that indicates sociologically, that people regard law as objectively valid.

ii) *The rule of recognition vs the Basic Norm*

Many have observed the similarity between the rule of recognition and the Basic Norm. They are indeed complementary, but exist in different spheres. The Basic Norm exists in the logical reconstruction of law in the mind of the jurist, examining law. The rule of recognition exists as a description of normatising behaviour amongst legal practitioners. While the rule of recognition may pose certain problems, it at least has some basis in fact. The Basic Norm is the best illustration of the fact that legal logic is based on a non-logical premise. The answer might better be found where Raz searches, in practical reasoning.

I feel that very soon the is/ought distinction will be largely discarded as a foundation of legal logic. People, for practical purposes, do treat facts as normative reasons, which is tantamount to Raz's notion of secondary reasons. That something is law is a sociological fact, that people think this a reason for acting in a certain way, is a deduction of a norm. As Hume might say, law could be the invention of a naturally inventive species; subjective will that is, for practical purposes, treated as objective, because it achieves the desired result of normativity. Never mind the logic, see the effect!

Kelsen's Basic Norm seems to be an effort to superimpose a system of logic on a subject matter that is treated as having a logical foundation, but instead has a practical one. As such it fails to be describable as a closed logical system, which is surely what Kelsen is attempting. Nonetheless, Kelsen is valuable for showing us why we need to look elsewhere and certain aspects of his theory hold good nonetheless.

ii) *The practical implications of the Basic Norm*

Kelsen insists that lawyers apply positive legal norms and consequently, since the Basic Norm is not positive, it is of no use to the lawyer. However, this has not stopped the Basic Norm actually being used by courts on the basis that Kelsen asserts that the theoretical basis of law is clearer in revolutionary situations. It has been argued that lawyers should turn to legal science for help. However, it is strange that they should seek to employ a concept which on its own premises is self-contradictory, cannot exist and whose meaning can only be inferred from fact situations, and which is merely a jurisprudential aid to reasoning.

Kelsen rejected Stone's assertion that jurisprudence might be a source of legal norms as 'foolish opinion'. Certainly, to employ a legal theory that claims to describe law as it is (positivist) cannot answer a normative question, 'What is the law that I must apply?' However, the appeal of a Pure Theory, which makes no moral or political presuppositions, was too strong in the post-Revolutionary situation following Rhodesia's unilateral declaration of independence from Great Britain. By applying a Pure Theory, how can a court be accused of making a political judgment?

In *Madzimbamuto* v *Lardner Burke* (1968) and other contemporary cases, the question was raised of which legal order should be obeyed, when a revolution claims to have displaced an old order with a new legal order. The judges in these cases embarked on a juristic search for the legal answer, as if hidden in the nature of law was a rule that addresses what to do in the case of successful revolutions. This seems to be characteristic of lawyers, who largely seek to avoid political and moral decisions by seeking a positive legal explanation why they have to suspend their personal judgment. Not surprisingly, this was criticised in juristic terms, the main criticism being neatly summarised and discussed by Harris in '*When and Why Does the Grundnorm Change?*' (CLJ) 29 (1) April 1971. In brief the following observations have been made:

- Eekelaar suggests that Kelsen points out that for obvious reasons, when a legal order is no longer effective it cannot be valid. This does not mean that a new claim of legality, by a new effective order, is a valid claim.

- The decision to treat the new, post-revolutionary law as valid, entails moral and political questions, not just that of effectiveness. Such is the observation of Dias, among others.

- It is only if the law is applied by the court, and then evaluated, can it be said that a legal system is 'by and large effective'.

- The Pure Theory describes the logical assumptions of jurists examining valid legal systems in force and as such it presupposes that the system is efficacious. Harris ascribes this argument to Brookfield.

- Harris makes the following observations: 'If there is a single political maxim underlying legal positivism, it is that: 'propaganda and gestures apart – "legality" without force is nothing worth.' Harris is pointing out that while positivism can tell you that you have a valid legal system when you have it, it is not the purpose of positivism to say whether it is valid if you do not believe it is. The frightening revelation is that the positivist conception of validity is based upon what people assume to be valid. Raz is surely right to say that ultimately a court's acceptance of a legal system as valid is a moral decision.

d) *The unity of the law*

One problem that has perplexed critics of Kelsen is his assertion in later writings that all legal systems could be seen to be subsumed under one Basic Norm. I think that the essence of his argument is somewhat less difficult than that postulated by Hart in his essay on Kelsen's concept of legal unity.

Kelsen suggests that in the modern world jurists must perhaps look at national law being validated by international law. To illustrate what I think he means, take the following example. An English legal theorist may be asked, 'Why is the law in England valid?' His probable answer is that it is made in accordance with the procedural requirements of a valid constitution. He is here presupposing the Basic Norm of national law, that the authors of the constitution were vested with the authority from a fictive norm, to make a valid constitution. Alternatively, it might equally be said that under international law the English system is a valid one, according to the Treaty of Montevideo and the like. If this is so he is presupposing that international law is valid. Why should he take the second course, to the exclusion of the first? Certainly, the modern jurist is aware of the validity of other legal systems. French law is valid in France and is recognised by the English legal system as being valid in France. How then can the English law recognise the validity of French law?

Kelsen offers two approaches. Firstly, we might see French law as being valid in France because the English legal system has recognised it as such. In this case the validity of French law is dependent on the validity of the English legal system as being empowered to recognise the validity of other legal systems. This is itself dependent on the validity of the English legal system generally, which stems from the Basic Norm. Thus, the English jurist would regard French law as being valid under the English Basic Norm. This would be a somewhat nationalistic approach for a jurist! The jurist is willing to accept the validity of English law, and if English law recognises foreign law as valid, then foreign law may also be valid.

In the more realistic alternative, the jurist looks on all legal systems equally. He realises that most are valid and mutually recognised as such. Since they seldom conflict or overlap in their jurisdictions, there is a coherence to them. Why are a multiplicity of legal systems all valid for each different area? The answer may be taken to be that they are internationally linked by international law. This is a simplification of Kelsen's argument, but I find his argument more plausible than some people may. The only criticism I might have is that some legal systems are viewed as nationally valid, but invalid internationally, such as that of Kampuchea. Thus, most legal systems may fit into the unity of international law, but some are potentially independent.

Equally, the subsumption of valid foreign law under the English Basic Norm would not apply to the Rhodesian independence situation. The problem is thus not resolved. The dualistic order, whereby countries are valid under their own Basic Norm, as well as those rules of international law authorised by international law's Basic Norm, is not logically replaced by the Unity of the Law thesis, I feel.

International law is itself problematic, since it may be viewed as being customary and bilateral, thereby subsumed under all the Basic Norms of individual countries. This may be illustrated by the fact that the constitutional power to enter into treaties is exactly that. Our government may enter into a treaty because the constitution has given it the power. The act is therefore only valid under the national Basic Norm. Thus, each party to international law invests its constitutional authority in the creation of international law by treaties and protocols. As such, we might say that international law has no single Basic Norm, but is authorised by the sum of national grundnorms.

Kelsen admits that the development of international law is weak, with the crude sanctions of war and economic isolation that cannot really be effective against some powers.

The unity of law is therefore a problematic postulate, since the identity of one Basic Norm cannot be factually ascribed to either international or domestic law.

7.14 Evaluation of Kelsen

The verdict on Kelsen is very divided, with Raz declaring that he has done nothing new, while Dias views him as offering the 'most refined development to date of analytical positivism'.

a) A strong criticism of Kelsen must centre around his purely logic based theory, as Laski has pointed out. The Basic Norm, for example, is an account of juristic psychology, rather than a conceptual explanation of law as it is. The fact that it exists only in the juristic consciousness does not explain if and why law is valid, but merely that jurists regard it as such.

b) The necessity for sociological jurisprudence is very strongly underlined, particularly since the question of effectiveness can only be accounted for in factual terms, rather than in normative logic.

c) Dworkin's criticism of Kelsen is that the Basic Norm fails to account for the existence of policies and principles as part of the adjudication process. I think that this is not necessarily so. A norm of common law could quite easily be a principle, though I would suspect that Kelsen himself would view policy and principle as being outside pure legal reasoning.

d) We have seen that there is much criticism of the emphasis of Kelsen on coercion. Kelsen certainly does not see general laws as being addressed to the public. The emphasis on coercion is perhaps because Kelsen takes the legal view of law as the correct one, rather than a broader sociological view. I think that the premises of his theory justify this; however, the absence of a sociological aspect of law gives us a very limited picture.

e) The Basic Norm conception is useless as an analytical tool in times of revolution and is unnecessary as an analytical tool in times of stability. Further, it fails to fulfil its function in logic, since it is not logical and cannot genuinely be related to the authority of real legal norms. It simply exists as a fiction in the rational reconstruction of the legal order in the mind of the jurist. It does not explain why judicial logic holds the system to be valid.

f) Kelsen, above all other jurists, seems to have appreciated the subtle core of normative statements, probably because of his philosophical training. Although his theory is a complex one, its analysis is one that illuminates the inner logic of law.

8 EMPIRICAL METHODS IN JURISPRUDENCE 1: SOCIOLOGICAL JURISPRUDENCE

8.1   Introduction

Although this section passes under the heading of sociological jurisprudence, there are several quite different approaches, with differing labels that are subsumed under this heading. To differentiate them is hard, since they encompass various 'schools of thought' themselves. All of them share the attribute of applying methods of social enquiry in order to elucidate the role of law in society. For the student's convenience, I shall seek to divide the ideas conceptually into three strands of approach.

a) *Sociological jurisprudence (Idealist)*

In this area I include those thinkers who either:

   i)   base their analysis of society on Idealist historical information;

   ii) base their analysis of society on an economic or political theory.

b) *Sociological jurisprudence (evaluative)*

In this section I include those thinkers who are primarily concerned with whether law is sufficiently reflective of societal needs.

c) *Sociology of law*

In this section I include those thinkers who are concerned to apply social scientific methods to explain laws and the reasons for laws in their social context.

These groupings, particularly the first two, are necessarily somewhat arbitrary. There are numerous other ways to view the sociological approach, but these groupings are intended to marshal rather diverse subjects into manageable categories.

8.2   Sociological jurisprudence (Idealist)

a) Auguste Comte is credited with inventing the term 'sociology', denoting the scientific analysis of society. The student will already be aware of the belief that scientific method was the one appropriate to the study of all phenomena that flourishes to this day. However, the study of society did not necessarily start with Comte, although he represents a good starting point for our purposes.

Comte's espoused theory was that the appropriate method for study of society was by observation, experimentation, comparison and historical method. This is not dissimilar to the broad principles of modern sociology, although it has been somewhat refined.

A fundamental problem that plagues early sociology was the dire state of historical knowledge, based on 'official versions' of history and broad and somewhat idealised views. This necessarily prejudiced the works of early sociologists.

b) Scientific theories developed in the nineteenth century, alongside crude economic ones, also influenced the views of sociologists, with Herbert Spencer espousing 'social Darwinism' that contrasted with the historical idealism of other thinkers, but was based on little more truth. Equally, based on the idea that self-interest dictates social responsibility, the laisser faire attitude that economic and social forces will necessarily order society for the better, was adopted by Adam Smith, Ricardo and, to a certain extent, Bentham. The followers of such theories were less interested in legal control as in deregulation of trade, which was viewed largely as the answer to most social evils.

c) Bentham, followed by Jhering, adopted a utilitarian approach, based on the satisfaction of human wants. Law, by the coercive methods that we discussed in Chapter 4, would be the instrument of order by which society could balance the needs of the individual with the needs of society.

d) Eugen Ehrlich placed considerable emphasis on the diversity of social institutions with coercive or normative force, directing attention towards institutional rules and practices that are parallel, but not part of the law. These almost constitute private legal systems. This insight is a useful one and its reflection is to be found in the growing interaction between legal institutions and social ones. For example, we might now find that professional rules and standards are widely reflected in judgments in the law of negligence. Equally government has begun to delegate legislative powers to agencies, even of a private nature. The Financial Services Act 1986 delegates the power to legislate and make rules on investment practices. The holders of these powers are private limited companies that are the evolutionary forms of independent professional investment bodies.

However, Ehrlich took his analysis further. Although he conceded that the law had its own professional approaches to social problems, he emphasised that true law was 'living law', ie the interests and practices in society, and as such most legal reform was simply the accommodation of 'living law' into these rules. Ehrlich urged the lawyer to gain his understanding and weight his judgments by the interests in society, thus moulding 'book law' to the living law.

Clearly, Ehrlich overlooked the fact that legislation itself has an effect on practices and seeks itself to balance interests. However, we cannot be excessively critical of him, without taking into account the rapid progress and complexity that was a feature of his times.

e) All the above theorists share a fairly remote and instrumentalist view of law. Law was seen as subservient to greater social forces that would set the legal agenda. The concept of social progress and the 'rightness' of the forces within society seem to reflect the economic and political change in the nineteenth century. However, such approaches contribute little to our understanding of law's place in society. Indeed, one feels that it is possibly dispensable.

f) It may be noted that historical and empirical fallacies are not confined to this section. Durkheim, who will be considered a little later, based much of his argument about the role of law on assumptions and somewhat dubious historical data. His concept of society bears closer resemblance to an organism, with collective thoughts expressed through law. Equally, Weber, whose importance is significant, still, as Lloyd points out, remains bound to the laisser faire ideal. It seems hard for a sociologist to approach the status of law in society without bringing with him unfounded preconceptions or quasi-empirical theory.

8.3 Sociological jurisprudence (evaluative)

The informal group of social scientists considered in this section are primarily, though not exclusively concerned with the 'effectiveness' of law. Principally their aim is to focus on the 'gap' between 'law-in-theory' and 'law-in-action'. The reason for this concern was largely a reforming instinct. A second concern relates to the nature of society – does society have a common interest expressed through law, or does it represent some sort of conflict within society?

There are three thinkers whose importance is predominant in this area: Pound, Weber and Durkheim. Pound is to be regarded as more or less synonymous with the term 'sociological jurisprudence'. Weber's contribution is indisputable, since his methodological improvements and refocussing seem to pave the way for a true sociology of law. However, Weber must be viewed in the context of responding to the legal sociology of Marx. For practical reasons, it is therefore necessary for the student to refer to Chapter 13, since Marx's concept of law and state, although properly a sociological and economic analysis, deserves special attention.

Finally, Durkheim is an appropriate figure of focus. Marx, Weber and Durkheim might be together categorised as legal sociologists, marking the transition to a sociology of law, away from the traditions of sociological jurisprudence.

a) *Introduction to Roscoe Pound's theory*

The extensive writings of Roscoe Pound spread as they are over a long period of time represent the culmination of the legal philosophy of the past. Pound was an academic lawyer and an advocate for socio-legal studies. His concern was to examine 'law in action' as opposed to the dry topic of 'law in books'. Again it should be emphasised that his primary concern was with law reform and his theory ought to be read with this in mind. He was developing a technology to redraft the law to take account of social reality. He saw 'law as a social phenomenon' which translated into policy action, and meant that in the making, interpretation and application of laws due account should be taken of law as a social fact.

The fact that he was by training a botanist may, it has been suggested, explain his tendency to engage in classifications. Having said that, I cannot imagine a situation where a candidate will be examined on his/her ability to recite the various classifications that Pound developed. If you have the pleasure of my lecturing then it is at this point that I invariably refer to my notes. It is not expected that you would learn these by rote. What is required is an overview of his aims and of his general categorisations.

Nonetheless for the sake of a complete record the following represent the task of the purposes of the legal order:

i) Factual study of the social effects of legal administration.

ii) Social investigations as preliminary to legislation.

iii) Constant study of making laws more effective.

iv) Study, both psychological and philosophical, of judicial method.

v) Sociological study of legal history.

vi) Allowance for the possibility of a just and reasonable solution of individual cases.

vii) A Ministry of Justice to undertake law reform.

viii) The achievement of the purposes of the various laws.

In order to achieve these purposes of the legal order it would first be necessary to achieve the recognition of certain interests which operate on different levels. These levels are the:

- Individual
- Public
- Social

Secondly, it would be necessary to arrive at a definition of the limits within which such interests will be legally recognised and given effect to. And thirdly, the securing of those interests within the limits as defined.

Again we stay with these lists in order to identify what would according to Pound be required in order to achieve this. He listed the following as necessary:

i)   Preparation of an inventory of classified interests.

ii)   Selection of interests which should be legally recognised.

iii)   Demarcation of limits of securing the interests so selected.

iv)   Consideration of the means whereby laws might secure the interests when these have been acknowledged and delimited.

v)   Evolution of the principles of valuation of the interests.

As stated above, in doing this rather protracted task Pound sought to harmonise 'law in books' with 'law in action'. It is not at all clear that he has succeeded in this aim or indeed that anyone could have succeeded. However, in order to give due regard to his attempt we shall examine his efforts in this further. In particular we shall examine his concept of social engineering and the balancing of conflicting interests and the use of his jural postulates in the achievement of the balancing act.

b) *Conflict or consensus model*

In order to understand the working of Pound's theory it would be necessary to discuss the rather broad distinction that runs through sociology of law and sociological jurisprudence – namely whether society is essentially a reflection of the consensus or of the conflict model. Although this may appear rather a general discussion in the middle of Pound's theory, it is the first point in the text where we come across this matter and it is one to which we will regularly return.

i)   A consensus model is one which sees society as having shared values and traditions, and law serves the interests which are to the ultimate benefit thereof. Law, therefore, may be seen as a value consensus, representing the shared values of the society, and adjusting conflicts and reconciling interests to match with the consensus. Such a model may be seen, explicitly or implicitly, in the works of Pound and Durkheim.

It is also the basis of the framework provided by Parsons and developed by Bredemeier. Parsons views the legal system as having a function of integration, of preventing via the set of rules the disintegration of social interaction into conflict. He splits the legal from the political system: in the former, the courts hold centre stage with their work of interpretation; in the latter, the legislature formulates policy.

Pound put it thus, 'The success of any particular society will depend on the degree to which it is socially integrated and so accepts as common ground its basic postulates'. Such a view postulates that law adjusts and reconciles conflicting interests according to the requirements of social order.

The problem with this view of society is that in effect it is a representation of a static and homogeneous society where such a society does not exist.

ii)   A conflict model, on the other hand, suggests that society involves not a value consensus but a value conflict; that law, rather than reconciling conflict interests in a compromise, instead imposes one interest at the expense of the other. Such a model is expounded by Quinney, and of course, the Marxists.

Which is a correct reading of the English legal system? Both views can claim support from particular pieces of evidence; either showing a social consensus (major crimes, civil liberties protection?) or rules that are the product of conflict (rules of property and contract). Lloyd and Freeman suggest that research rather supports the conflict model (see their *Introduction to Jurisprudence*, p572).

Is the conflict a simple one, with one ruling class (of which judges are a part: see JAG Griffith's *The Politics of the Judiciary*), or competing interest groups with varying amounts of power? Theorists differ; it might be pointed out that if the latter position is accepted, the question arises as to how far different is that from a compromise/ consensus position?

c) *Social engineering*

Following very much on the consensus model of society and in explaining the process of the balancing of conflicting interests, Pound has used an analogy with engineering. He sees the task as one to build as efficient a structure of society as possible, which requires the satisfaction of the maximum of wants with the minimum of friction and waste. Thus by identifying and protecting certain interests the law ensures social cohesion.

The idea of the balancing of conflicting interests was derived from Ihering and can be stated as the giving effect to as much as possible of conflicting claims 'which men assert de facto about which the law must do something if organised societies are to endure.' Harris has observed that it is not a full blown theory of justice. Harris has stated that Pound's theory 'equates justice with quietening those who are banging on the gates' in that achievement of one's interests depends on articulation of those interests. Those interests are subject to manipulation through advertising campaigns for example. The role that advertising plays in shaping desires is discussed by Stone in chapter 9 of *Human Law and Human Justice*.

i) Balancing of conflicting interests

It would be appropriate to examine further the notion of the balancing of conflicting interests. In doing so Pound looks at actual assertion of claims in a particular society as manifested in legal proceedings and this of course includes rejected as well as accepted claims.

Again there is more classification involved. However with this matter it is worth learning the three different levels on which Pound identified interests operating. These are:

- Individual interests – these are claims as seen from the standpoint of individual life. The following are examples:

    - Personality, eg interest in person, honour, privacy;

    - Domestic relations, as distinct from social interest in institutions such as family, eg parent;

    - Interest of substance, eg property, freedom of association.

- Public interests – these are claims asserted by individuals but viewed from the standpoint of political life. These are less important but would include:

    - Interests of the State as a juristic person; looking at the personality of the State (note: this is not relevant in Britain); and

    - Interests of the State as guardian of social interests. According to Dias there is here an overlap with social interests.

- Social interests – these are the most general and according to Pound the preferred level on which to balance conflicting interests. They are claims as viewed of in terms of social life or generalised as claims of the social group. This includes the social interest in:

    - General security, ie to be secure against threats to existence from disorder and matters such as health;

    - Security of social institutions, which acknowledges the existence of tension and the need to protect religious institutions;

    - General morals, ie such matters as prostitution and gambling which are said to be offensive to moral sentiments;

- Conservation of social resources, this is comparable to Rawls' 'just savings principle' and is in conflict with the individual interest in one's own property;

- General progress, which would cover free speech and free trade (but nonetheless ignores the tendency for resale price fixing); and

- Individual life, according to which one should be able to live life according to standards of society.

These are just examples. The important point according to Pound is that these must be balanced on the same level otherwise the decision is already made in that if this were not done the preference for type of interests would dictate the outcome of the supposedly scientific exercise in balancing out these interests. It is noteworthy that Ihering did not insist on this when he spoke of balancing conflicting interests. Are you convinced by Pound's insistence on balancing conflicting interests on the same level? Pound has not paid much attention to ways in which one conflicting interest is to be compared with another. Lloyd summed it up thus, '...Unlike Ihering, who assumed that social and individual interests should always be directly compared, Pound insisted that a fair balancing of interests could only be achieved by examining a conflict on the same plane or level.'

ii)   Jural postulates

In circumstances where an accommodation of interests is not possible there would according to Pound be no objective way of resolving disputes. To meet this defect Pound developed the notion of jural postulates as the means of testing new interests. These jural postulates are the presuppositions of legal reasoning which embody the fundamental purposes of the legal system. They are in effect the basic assumptions upon which society is based. One cannot help but conclude that Pound was using a new term to describe something that was already well recognised. He has not discovered the wheel; he has merely called it something else.

Pound's methodology was that of incremental legal reasoning (the whole topic of legal reasoning is discussed in detail in a later chapter). This method of legal reasoning which is well known to common law lawyers would allow new claims only if claims of that sort are already recognised. The speech of Lord Buckmaster in *Donoghue* v *Stevenson* [1932] would represent one of the most famous to adopt incremental legal reasoning. In essence Lord Buckmaster was saying that unless Mrs Donoghue could show that in a previous case a claim such as that she was bringing to the court was admitted then whatever the particular merits of her case her claim would have to be rejected.

According to Pound these jural postulates may conflict although he insists that his do not. Furthermore they may change and would do so relative to the stages in social evolution. I state this here in order to deal with a criticism that was made by the Scandinavian realist Lundstedt to the effect that Pound's jural postulates were nothing more than natural law allowed in through the back door. Lundstedt is wrong in that these jural postulates do not possess the characteristics of natural law. They are not absolute, nor are they universal and indeed, as has been stated, nor are they unchanging.

d)   *Critical evaluation of Pound*

There is much written by Pound and more written about him. It really is not possible to raise all the critical evaluations that have been made. I will here attempt to list some. This list is offered with the usual caveat to the effect that the student should reflect on these before formulating his/her own views.

i)   Patterson, in *Jurisprudence: Men and Ideas of the Law* (1953) describes Pound's catalogue of interests as a rationalisation of the actual.

ii)   Lloyd and Freeman state that Pound's classification of interests 'reads rather like a political manifesto in favour of a liberal and capitalist society' even though for Pound they were seen as objective. A socialist would insert other interests. They add that the classification of interests suffers from excessive vagueness.

iii) With regard to the recognition of interests Dias has argued that there are graduated levels of recognition and cites the case of *Van Duyn* v *Home Office* (1975) which involved the denial of access to this country of a citizen of the EEC who was a member of the so-called Church of Scientology. This would normally be a breach of the rules on freedom of movement within the EEC but Dias points out that while the Scientology 'church' was not outlawed it was however officially condemned.

iv) Dias raises further criticisms when he states that the 'whole idea of balancing is subordinate to the ideal that is in view. The march of society is gauged by changes in its ideals and standards for measuring interests.' Dias is of the opinion that the listing of interests is less important than judicial attitudes towards particular activities. According to him weight will depend on ideal.

v) It could be stated that the recognition of a new interest is a matter of policy as opposed to jural postulate based.

vi) Dias has criticised the engineering analogy as being false in that engineering projects are based on a plan yet the reality is that society changes and that if one is building one builds on shifting ground. Perhaps there are limits to which analogies can be taken. Dias does however argue with some force that law is not a planned enterprise, but rather *ad hoc* attempting to cope with situations as and when they arise.

vii) Pound asserts that claims pre-exist law but often claims are based on law. An example would be with regard to welfare benefits where claimants base their claim on existing rules and regulations.

viii) It is clear that Pound asserted that the nature of a society is one of consensus yet it is less than clear whether or indeed how balancing of interests will produce cohesive society. It could further be remarked that the very process of using law as a tool of social engineering would depend on the credibility accorded to the law. This can be seen in the examples of political trials such as the trial of the Chicago Eight or the Oz obscenity trial where the aim of the defendants was to totally discredit the court. The trials of IRA suspects in Northern Ireland also make the same point. There the defendants seek to deny all legitimacy to the proceedings. In such circumstances social engineering could hardly work.

ix) The law involves considerations of people's needs as well as their interests. This is especially the case with regard to paternalistic laws such as the law on the compulsory wearing of seat belts in cars. The very idea of satisfying people's interests conflicts with a paternalist view of society. The laws forbidding the display of pornography run counter to the satisfying of people's interests if interests are defined as desires, yet there exists powerful argument from a paternalistic point of view to the effect that such laws are necessary.

x) It has been shown, and this point is discussed above, that post Pound socio-legal research doubts whether law is the result of value consensus. The findings of Quinney show that society is better described as founded on a conflict model rather than any consensus as such.

xi) Overall it can be stated that Pound exerted a considerable influence on jurisprudence in that he laid the foundation for post traditionalism. However, according to Alan Hunt in *The Sociological Movement in Law* 'Pound used sociology when he saw fit; he cannot be regarded as having developed a sociological theory of law.'

e) *Weber's response to Marx*

The writings of Marx proposed a revolutionary theory that sent capitalism scurrying for cover. As with any revolutionary theory those at the focus of the revolutionary attack will seek to provide a response. This can clearly be seen with regard to Von Savigny's response to the adoption of the French Code Napoleon in parts of Germany (see chapter 11). In the more modern frame this is also exemplified by the response of the Gulf States to the revolution in Iran. Weber offered a response to the Marxist challenge to capitalism. In assessing the response of Weber it would be appropriate to discuss the nature of that challenge.

Marx thought that capitalism was in crisis. He saw the brutal exploitation of labour in the Lancashire cotton mills and drew a conclusion from this that capitalism was in its last stages on its deathbed. He developed his Marxist theory on the premise that capitalism would not for long survive and that it would inevitably be replaced eventually with a classless society. As part of that attack on capitalism Marx noticed that the greatest revolutionary potential was the working class and that in order to bring about that revolution and the arrival of the stage of socialism, what was needed was to raise the revolutionary consciousness of the working class. This would be done in Marxist terms by dispelling capitalist ideology which he saw as a false consciousness that mystified the working class and legitimated the capitalists' control of the means of production. Marx therefore saw everything in terms of economic determinism whereby the state and the law served the interests of the class that controlled the all important means of production. This crude class instrumentalism was the focus of Weber's remark that 'authority strives for acceptance, not submission.'

Marx thought that the state and the law which represents 'authority' was a tool of oppression in the hands of the ruling class in seeking to dominate the working class. Whilst this view has been recanted upon by more modern Marxists seeking to enter the political agenda of today, at the time Weber was writing he was dealing only with the original works of Marx and Engels. It would not therefore be a legitimate criticism to say that Weber did not take account of something that did not exist at his time. In response to that class instrumentalism Weber observed that 'the search for a single primal cause was futile.' He was thus criticising Marx for the view that economic factors were the sole determining cause of the nature of the society. Whilst saying this Weber recognised that economic factors are important. Nonetheless, it is submitted that the criticism was ill founded. Marx merely said that 'in the final analysis economic factors determine the nature of society'. Thus Marx recognised that other factors were important also.

According to Marx's dialectical materialism (which viewed the history of all hitherto existing society as the history of class conflict) authority through the state and the law was the instrument of those controlling the means of production in the maintenance of their domination over the relations of production, in that it both legitimated and mystified the oppressed class. The mystification operated through the exploitation of the surplus value of labour, and the legitimation was through authority using simple power disguised through use of state ideological and repressive apparatus, such as the 'legitimate' state use of force and the false consciousness that sought to preserve the status quo, such as religion which Marx saw as the opiate of the masses in the sense that it dulled their senses about the reality of their exploitation.

There exists a single thread that runs through Weber's work, namely a response to Marx which he regarded as crude, oversimplified and fundamentally wrong! Weber's response was quite sophisticated. He thought Marx was either dogmatic or vague and totally rejected Marx's unilinear theory. In response to the idea that the state was the tool of the dominant class, Weber sought to speak of legitimate authority. The legitimate authority would strive for acceptance. This Weber proved by examining the question as to why people feel obliged to obey law. I suppose that had Weber the advantage of Hart's work he would have asked why people feel under an obligation to obey. The difference is merely terminological in this context as it is clear that Weber was addressing himself to obligation in substance.

f) *Legitimacy and authority*

Weber addressed himself to the problem of the nature of order. He saw society as a system of ordered action wherein almost invariably the particular order is claimed to be right – that is to say that it is 'legitimised'. Weber recognised that no society could exist for long on a set of static or unenforced norms and it would therefore be necessary to have power or command to change and enforce these norms. For Weber power meant the 'possibility of imposing one's will on the behaviour of another person'. What in essence is new in Weber is that he identified power as a reciprocal relationship, and this is the crux of his debate with Marxism. The Marxist views power as the consequence of control of the means of production and the means of preserving that control. Certainly power is needed to change rules as society develops, as no society can exist on a set of static or unenforced norms. Weber identified two types of power relation both of which were reciprocal. These are monopoly power and power by authority. In monopoly power the seller fixes the price but the buyer wants to pay it. There is thus mutual self interest, where power is based on a constellation of interests. In power by authority the parties – the ruled and the rulers – accept the relationship as legitimate. Focus is directed at the meaning that the ruler and the ruled place on the relationship between them, that is a relationship of legitimate authority. It would then be appropriate to examine the three types of legitimate authority identified by Weber. These are:

i)   Traditional

ii) Charismatic

iii) Legal rational

i)   By traditional authority Weber spoke of the according of legitimacy to that which has always been. This is characterised by a belief in the sanctity of age-old rules. Examples of this would be the aristocracy.

ii) By charismatic authority Weber meant a revolutionary situation where the followers attribute special powers to the leader. It involves an automatic break with the past. Legitimacy is founded in the belief in the authenticity of the leader's mission. An example of this would be Mahatma Ghandi in India. He held no formal office and was certainly not a manifestation of traditional authority yet he was widely obeyed. In that example the obedience was certainly not through any domination through naked power. There is a problem with the question of succession to authority in such a situation although it could be observed that religious leaders have been more successful than their political counterparts in ensuring the succession, a problem faced by, among others, Napoleon Bonaparte. Having said that, it is recognised that there are some notable exceptions.

iii) The third type of authority was the most important for capitalism according to Weber. It is legal rational authority. It was important for the development of capitalism because it provided certainty in law of contract. By this type of authority, the authority vests not in the person but in the office held. It corresponds to our conception of the Rule of Law in which all people are subject to a uniformly administered system of rules and in which all people are subject to the law. The quotation by Lord Denning MR, directed at the Attorney General, of Thomas Fuller 'be you ever so high the law is above you' in *Gouriet* v *UPW* (1977) amply illustrates the sentiment of this type of legitimate authority. It is the office which holds the authority, not the person, and obedience is given to norms not to the person. When Mrs Thatcher ceased being prime minister she lost her authority not because she was no longer Mrs Thatcher but because she was no longer prime minister – she no longer held the office to which authority attaches. In such a system the law serves to repress a conflict of egoistic wills by coercion and rational calculability.

Thus Weber thought that on occasion the ruling class could act in the national interest. That is certainly the language that the government uses. They would never state that the measure is designed to serve the interests of the ruling class at the expense in terms of labour of the working class. Yet what of measures such as the Welfare State, which so clearly are at the expense of those who control the means of production? Marxists today would explain this in terms of the 'relative autonomy of the state' and would view many laws that serve the interests of the working class as actually also serving the interests of the ruling class in having a satisfied and healthy work force which will produce better products.

According to Weber, in order for capitalism to thrive law has to be systemised so as to ensure the predictability of economic relations. In essence this is the point made by the new Marxists who stress the relative autonomy of the state. So long as the state protects economic relations it need not do anything else as far as the ruling class in Marxist terms are concerned. The problem with this idea is that it does not accord with the sequence of events in England where capitalism first took root. Weber acknowledged this and referred to this as an exception to his rule. There was no complete legal codified system in England then (or now). It is actually more than an exception and is probably a gaping hole!

g) *Weber's typology of law*

Weber was a trained lawyer who, as stated, was interested in explaining the development of capitalism in western society in terms of the development of a rational legal order being required to facilitate such a development. He also thought that capitalism developed as a consequence of the practice of what he called the protestant work ethic to the effect that people would work hard and save some of the proceeds of their labour. These proceeds would then be invested to build up capital and hence the rise of capitalism. I would take issue with that hypothesis. In my view the source of the capital required came less from such savings and more from the profits of global trade. The point, though, is not central to the law aspect of Weber's work.

The premise that underlies Weber's theory is what he called *verstehen* by which he meant that a social action could only best be understood by reference to its meaning, purpose and intention for the individual. Hence the remark that in Weberian terms a wink is different from a blink because it is social. A blink is not interpreted to have any meaning – a wink is so interpreted.

Weber offered a definition of his typology of law to the effect that ...'an order will be called law if it is externally guaranteed by the probability that coercion, whether physical or psychological, to bring about conformity or avenge violation, will be applied by a staff of people holding themselves specially ready for that purpose.' In pursuing this he developed a scheme of lawmaking and adjudication that can be represented in the diagram overleaf.

Note: The substantive/formal aspect relates to the extent to which the system possesses the rules and procedures required for decision making within the system. The rational/irrational aspect relates to the manner in which the rules/procedures are applied in the system.

The legal rational form of legitimate domination is impersonal. Obedience in such a system is not owed to the person but is rather owed to the legal order. The legitimacy of the type of political domination is drawn from the existence of a system of rationally made laws which stipulate the circumstances under which power may be exercised. Because the system is rational it is supported. This is, according to Weber, the source of all state authority in modern societies where legal domination is not dependent on the extent to which the law reflects the values of the people who accept the legitimacy of the system. Obedience does not depend on agreement with the content of the law but with the rationality that lies behind its creation and enforcement. This is an important point of much relevance to our study. Do you agree that it is an accurate reflection of the nature of the relationship between the subject and the government in Britain today?

	Rational	Irrational
Substantive	**Substantively rational** There is no separation between law and morals	**Substantively irrational** Cases are decided on their own merits without reference to general principles
Formal	**Formally rational** The legal system contains answers to all legal problems	**Formally irrational** Decisions are made on the basis of tests beyond the control of human intellect eg trial by ordeal.

h) *Evaluation of Weber*

Although Weber's writings are almost a hundred years old there is much that is still very informative as regards modern capitalist society. Weber's distinction between power and authority and his emphasis on the reciprocal relationship acting as a constraint is most illuminating. Further he can be seen as an early advocate of the value free social sciences, a tradition that is now well established in this country. The Marxist would however dispute that such is a possibility. What Weber was saying was that it is possible for the sociologist to carry out value free sociology whilst at the same time realising that the sociologist has his own value judgments. The sociologist is entitled to exercise his own value judgments in selecting the area of research but having done so the research must be carried out in a neutral way. This is a further manifestation of the separation of the 'is' from the 'ought".

Nonetheless there are some aspects that are difficult with Weber's theory. Perhaps Weber took too restricted a view of the relationship between law and domination. He appears to have reduced the relationship to one of a personal nature as between the ruler and the ruled. It is suggested that the process of domination is much more complex than is clear from its formal legal manifestation.

Weber's thesis is based on a laissez faire system existing yet it is wondered whether it could take account of a welfare state system. Perhaps this point has already been dealt with above.

It is submitted that Weber has a good answer to Marx's point on naked domination but more recent responses have shown Marx to be irrelevant in modern Britain. Whilst Weber's views on authority as legitimate, not seeking to oppress but ruling by agreement, are applicable it is suggested that in modern Britain with a share owning population owning their own homes etc the Marxist analysis is no longer relevant. Weber should therefore be seen in his historical perspective as an early but effective response to the challenge of Marxism.

When Weber stated that 'the search for a single primal cause was futile' he was of course criticising the Marxist reliance on the relations of production, yet the criticism is somewhat misapplied. As we shall see in chapter 13 Marx did not actually say that the relations of production were the only causal factor; what he did say was that economic determinism operates 'in the last instance' and as such Marx clearly recognised that other factors are of some importance.

Weber's attack on the Marxist use of models also provides a valuable insight. Weber believed that models are heuristic devices with which to test reality. To the extent that reality does not accord with the model the task of the social scientist is to change the model. Marx took the opposite view. According to Marx if reality did not correspond with the model then the task was to change reality – hence the revolutionary nature of Marxism. This point is developed in more detail in chapter 13.

In his concept of *verstehen* Weber may have placed too much emphasis on the individual mind in an attempt to understand social action.

In his legal rational domination he speaks of the norms being impersonal. It might be argued that they are perceived as impersonal because of socialisation and education. If this is so could it not be argued that obedience is given not to the law but to the media?

His view of the rationality of the bureaucracy perhaps ignores the role of senior civil servants. They have considerable influence even to the extent of persuading government ministers on the content and timing of legislation. If this is so because these discussions are not open the aspect of rationality is lost. If one is to give credence to the television series 'Yes, Prime Minister', wherein in a humorous manner the civil service are seen as manipulating their ministers to pursue civil service policy rather than the policy on which the government may have been elected, the argument gains even more force. Bureaucracy also has a tendency to create self inertia and as such cannot be regarded as totally efficient.

i) *Emile Durkheim's social solidarity*

Emile Durkheim drew much inspiration from the work of Charles Darwin. He was one of the first to insist on studying law in both its social and historical context. He subscribed to a consensus model of society and developed his theory that there exists a connection between law and the forms of social relations. Durkheim was not primarily concerned with law *per se* but was more interested in the study of society. His relevance to our course is that he attributed a central importance to law in the developing of an understanding of social life in general. Durkheim has been labelled an anti individualist. He spoke of the 'primacy of the social' and of the 'collective conscience'. By this I take him to mean that thoughts have an existence separate to the person thinking them. His concept of the collective conscience is important to an understanding of his theory and to what he said about law.

Durkheim engaged in primitivist reductionism using anthropology to assist understanding. He attempted to reduce matters to their most primitive and in his important study entitled *The Division of Labour in Society* (1893) he again joined issue with the Marxist contention on the conflict society stipulating that the social bond is not one of domination but of cohesion. Throughout his writings it is clear, as stated, that he adopts the consensus model which presumes value consensus in the society.

In his study on the division of labour he identified the extent of the division of labour as the way to classify society and in so doing stated that the type of law prevalent can be used as an indicator of the type of social organisation. Hence, law is seen as the external index which symbolises the type of social solidarity. To study society's solidarity we study its law. Perhaps a word ought be said about his use of the term social solidarity. According to Durkheim, social solidarity is a completely moral phenomenon and law plays a central role in the transition from mechanical to organic solidarity. These are the two polar forms of social solidarity and are identified by the degree of the division of labour. In the archaic also known as a mechanical solidarity society there is no division of labour. In these circumstances the people have shared life experiences. Everyone lives a life almost the same as everyone else. In these circumstances Durkheim thought that as people would be self reliant they would not depend on each other to a great extent and that therefore there would be no problem in carrying out severe punishments on those that violated the code of conduct. Law would be repressive and because everyone shared the same life experiences their reaction to deviation from the accepted code would be passionate and knee jerk. In a mechanical solidarity society Durkheim maintained that the collective conscience would be both strong and uniform. On the other hand, in a more advanced society which Durkheim labelled one of organic solidarity there would be a clear division of labour with a high degree of job specialisation. In such a society the people would have different life experiences. There would be considerable social interdependence as the plumber would need the electrician etc. In order to preserve cohesion the law would need to maintain an equilibrium. The collective conscience would be noticeably narrower and possibly considerably weakened when compared with a mechanical type solidarity. The type of law would be predominantly restitutive. That is not to say that there would not still be repressive laws. These would however be purely functional, designed not as a passionate reaction because that would be meaningless where beliefs were not commonly shared, but rather simply and functionally to preserve social cohesion.

In his study Durkheim stated that 'Every precept of law can be defined as a rule of sanctioned conduct'. Within that he identified sanctions as being of two kinds. These are:-

i) Repressive sanctions – whereby there is suffering or loss inflicted.

ii) Restitutive sanctions – whereby there would be a reestablishment of troubled relations to their normal state.

This process with regard to law is an indicator of the change and development of society. As stated, reference is made to the division of labour and in particular to the degree of specialisation in the economy. This is not however the only shift in which Durkheim was interested. He also showed that there would be a corresponding shift from religion to secularism; from collectivism to individualism and from penal sanctions to restitutive sanctions. It is this last shift that is of primary interest to our study.

With regard to the connection between law and morality Durkheim concluded that these were virtually synonymous. He maintained that law is derived from and is an expression of society's morality and that this explains how punishment can be seen as the expression of collective sentiments by which social cohesion is maintained. Again this reflects his consensus model of society. In an interesting passage Durkheim declared that ...'An action does not shock the common conscience because it is criminal: rather it is criminal because it shocks the common conscience'. On the applied level this leads to interesting conclusions. As society progresses the form of punishment becomes less violent because the basic function of the state is to legalise norms. The state is the central focus of attention and is therefore influenced both by public opinion and by occupational groups. The method of enforced compliance engaged in by occupational groups is a further interesting area of Durkheim's study and one that has inspired more recent research into the role of the occupational group as a substitute for the socialising function of the family.

A question arises as to why there is still a predominance of repressive law in an organic society such as modern Britain. By a predominance it is meant that there is more than is necessary to preserve social cohesion. The answer which Durkheim would provide would be that the division of labour has deviated from its original course. There has been a breakdown of socialisation – the occupational groups are not performing their socialising tasks effectively enough. This is explained by Durkheim in a study on suicide as being made up of a series of different factors. These factors are:-

i) Egoism – whereby the individual is isolated and the bonds which hold the group together are loosened.

ii) Altruism – whereby the individual relates to goals above those of the society and therefore becomes too heavily institutionalised.

iii) Anomie – which is a state whereby the individual feels his life lacks meaning and guidance. In his explanation of this Durkheim focuses on man's activity as governed by norms. These norms ought to be integrated and non-conflicting in order that the individual can be properly adjusted to his society. Where these norms are not integrated or where they conflict with one another then the individual will lose his moral guidance because there would be no norms against 'wrongdoing' which would make sense to the individual. In this state the individual is said to be in a state of anomie; he has no identity.

iv) Alienation – the individual who feels that the society is not there for him and indeed is there to exploit him will not identify with the aims of that society. Experience recently in inner city areas in England may be a case in this point, although it may be doubted whether this is not too simplistic an explanation of those riots.

v) Inequality – this is somewhat obvious and reinforces the above. Again on the applied level the implication of all this with regard to crime and the criminal is a view that was fashionable for a while whereby it is not the individual but rather the society which is at fault for crime. It should not be the individual who is 'in the dock' but the society as a whole. It is a failing of us all that that individual was not sufficiently socialised and he had to resort to crime. Not surprisingly this point leads to some substantial critical evaluation being levelled against Durkheim's thesis. What of individual opportunity and propensity? Are all people in a state of anomie potential or actual 'criminals'? How does this explain crime on the part of those who are most certainly fully integrated, such as City crime (insider dealing)? These people would never consider burglary of a bank yet there remains no clear loser when a bank vault is so emptied. Perhaps this may explain why we still do not regard insider dealing with the same opprobrium as burglary?

With regard to the point about punishment Durkheim appears to have a strong point that has perhaps been taken too far. He observed that punishment performs a useful integrating function in society by providing a scapegoat through which the rest can identify with the norms. The criminal broke the norms and therefore ought to be punished because that will act as a cohesive factor with regard to the others. Hence Durkheim was able to argue that ... 'If we didn't have crime we would have to invent it to keep society together.'

j) *Evaluation of Durkheim*

Durkheim's work is important in many respects in spite of what will be suggested are some rather fundamental flaws. He has identified the importance of punishment as a socialising force. He has emphasised the importance of viewing law in a sociological perspective rather than a pure analytical enquiry. However his treatment of law as a completely moral phenomenon does, it is submitted, neglect the extent to which law and morality often conflict. There are other points which can be made about his thesis. I would argue that empirical evidence tends to refute the assumption that in a primitive society there is no division of labour. Even as between the sexes there was a division of labour whereby women tended the home and men hunted. Their life experiences were therefore quite different. It is therefore disputed as to whether there ever was a truly mechanical solidarity society as Durkheim meant the phrase.

Even without this point it would appear that Durkheim has provided no adequate account of how law becomes increasingly restitutive. He has given no description of the intermediate stages between primitive and industrialised societies and has assumed that the change is swift. This is misleading. As we shall see, anthropological studies show that repressive law is less important in primitive society – see for example Gulliver's study of the Ndendeuli (in Tanzania) where it was demonstrated that a group that relied on each other extensively and had a wide shared life experience developed a sort of bargain model as their dispute resolution mechanism. Leon Sheleff has demonstrated in *'From Restitutive Law to Repressive Law – Durkheim's The Division of Labour in Society Revisited'* (1973) that while Durkheim relied on Maine to say that primitive law is repressive, actually Maine said the reverse. Hence a basic premise of Durkheim's work is shattered.

This view of punishment and the role of the law appears to regard the state as the expression of the collectivity, that is to say an instrumental organ being the means by which offenders are punished. This is not the only view of the role of the state in these matters. The difficulty with such a consensus model is the contention discussed in the previous chapter that the state may not be neutral. If one were to accept the conflict model, then a different view of the role of the state would emerge. Durkheim assumes that everyone will identify with occupational professional values but this is not the case. He takes no real account of power, conflict and change, preferring to presume a value consensus without proving the existence of the same.

On a narrower point it could be stated that a view of punishment as being retributive ignores the deterrent, rehabilitative and reformist aspects of sentencing and also ignores the punitive aspect of the civil law (exemplary damages). As has been stated above, Durkheim's view of crime negates the element of individual choice in crime.

From a Marxist perspective Karl Renner has demonstrated the need to distinguish between the form and function of law, a distinction which Durkheim blurred.

8.4   Socio-legal studies

It may be seen that the approaches of Pound, Weber and Durkheim differ radically. Sociological jurisprudence in the manner of Pound has had certain adherents who are worthy of mention. Pound's jurisprudence finds certain resonance in the writings of the early American Realists. But his reformist approach was to be taken up in the writings of Lasswell and McDougal, who espoused the virtues of social progress and enunciated aims and social expectations that should be adopted by lawyers. Once again their thoughts are more reminiscent of a manifesto of social policy than a concrete and applicable formula.

However, the empirical approach that emphasises questions of effectiveness and the 'law-in-action' thesis, has been subsumed into the broader category of 'socio-legal studies'. These empiricist studies, largely centred around the idea of achieving 'social justice', are often based upon positivist sociology, which largely denies any intrinsic normative consistency to law. Law is thus defined as a procedure whose content and effectiveness may be critically evaluated. There is little in the way of a theory of law, but rather it is concerned with need and effect.

Lloyd is particularly critical of experiments such as the Chicago jury project that contrasted lawyers' predictions with jury acquittals. Particularly, the project is criticised as giving insufficient appreciation to the complex role of juries. Ultimately, the approach is the legacy of sociological jurisprudence that is concerned with law as a tool that may be employed for harm or good.

The fruits of the socio-legal pursuit have been noticeable, though, including the Bail Act 1976 and considerable concentration on the provision of legal advice. However, the jurisprudential theory that underpins it is largely an assertion that all that legislators need to know is what the subjects of the law respond to. Law is thus seen as a catalyst for change, but not an independent phenomenon with a distinct place in society.

8.5   Sociology of law

Selzinck demarcates three stages in the application of social sciences to law:

a) 'The primitive, or missionary, stage is that of communicating a perspective, bringing to a hitherto isolated area an appreciation of basic and quite general sociological truths ...' He quickly points out that lawyers have been quite capable of doing this without the help of sociologists.

b) 'The second stage belongs to the sociological craftsman ... He wants to explore the area in depth, to help to solve its problems ...' This probably amounts to the socio-legal studies movement.

c) The third stage might be categorised as the stage of the sociologist of law when he 'addresses himself to the larger objectives and guiding principles of the particular human enterprise he has elected to study.'

He concludes by saying that the sociologist can not only dictate to the lawyer (as the socio-legal studies movement has sought to do) but can learn from law and legal systems in a search for an understanding of the broader context of society. Stone observes that the early reformist drive of sociological jurisprudence was a phenomenon of it its time, when legal reform was most needed. The new approach might be more reflective of law as an institutional part of society rather than a panacea for societal ills. He points out that a more coherent, less ad hoc, approach may improve the methods of societal control through law.

Thinkers such as Black, who advocates a sociological positivism that is not interested in lawyers' reasons, but is more interested in lawyers' behaviour, may be seen as complementary to the pure positivism that, for example, Kelsen might advocate. However, there is a dichotomy of views on whether there can be a sociology of law that can accommodate such notions. Nonet insists that sociology must be informed by jurisprudence, observing further that jurisprudence itself is informed by policy. Disputing the mutual ignorance of the two disciplines, Nonet exhorts:

'We need a jurisprudential sociology, a social science of law that speaks to the problems, and is informed by the ideas of jurisprudence. Such a sociology recognises the continuities of analytical descriptive and evaluative theory ...'

This seems to be the tenor of a new approach to legal theory through sociology. However, its fruits are, as yet, not as substantial as its rhetoric and methodological argument. The approach is however, a welcome one.

9 EMPIRICAL METHODS IN JURISPRUDENCE 2: AMERICAN REALISM

9.1   Introduction

As with many new attitudes and schools of thought, the American brand of realism was a reaction to an earlier school; in this case that earlier school was formalism, which concentrated on logic and a priori reasoning, and was therefore theoretical and not practical or pragmatic. Formalism had no regard to the facts of life experience. Realism, on the other hand, attempts to be both practical and pragmatic, rejecting theoretical and analytical approaches to jurisprudential questions, and attempting to look at the reality: How does law work in practice? One of the factors that may have contributed to this approach in the United States is the rather different traditions of their judiciary. Indeed one of the pioneering realists in jurisprudence was Mr Justice Holmes, a Justice of the US Supreme Court (who was not approved of by the President (Theodore Roosevelt) who appointed him: 'I could carve out of a banana a judge with more backbone'). 'The life of the law is experience', and that experience will show that law is a court-centred activity: 'The prophecies of what the courts will do ... are what I mean by law'.

This concentration on the courts is, of course, partly a reflection on their more important role in the USA, where they have the power to declare legislation 'unconstitutional' and therefore invalid, and are not as strictly bound by rules of precedent as in the UK. Much more of the law is open to judicial alteration: and even momentous issues of great political significance can be decided on by the court (for example, the case of *Brown* v *Board of Education* in 1954, declaring that the provision of 'separate but equal' educational facilities for negroes violated the 'Equal Protection of the Laws' amendment to the Constitution, and thus outlawing segregation).

It is proposed to discuss the two main approaches of the American realists – the rule sceptics and the experimentalists or fact sceptics. This chapter will also touch upon the schools that have emerged from American realism (jurimetrics and judicial behaviouralism) and the final section 9.6 notes the many criticisms of the realists' work and tries to disentangle the extent of the contribution (if any) that they make to modern legal theory. A comparative evaluation with the Scandanavian realists is made in the following chapter.

9.2   The realist approach

In a sentence, the realist approach was to attempt to look at the facts of the legal experience, and not at those things (eg rules) which theory held to be important; the two most important facets of their writing seem to be their rule scepticism and their concentration on the courts' role in settling disputes. The essence of their approach was that there is more to law than the mere logical application of rules. They are not saying that there is no value in the logical application of legal rules to fact situations, merely that if a more accurate prediction of the likely outcome of the case is desired as the practitioner ought so to aspire to provide, then the mere logical application of rules will not provide a sufficiently accurate prediction. The technique in which most students are trained in law schools in this country is logical application of legal rules to fact situations. The student learns the legal rules during the year and in the examination is given the hypothetical fact situation (problem). The student is then required to apply the rules to the fact situation. What the American realists are saying is that that process is not enough. It is clear then that such an approach combines analytical positivism with sociological approaches. It takes the law as it is posited and addresses the question of the factors that will influence those engaged in the application of the law. This is a feature of their approach, namely that they place lawyers centre stage in that they are primarily concerned with the role and behaviour of officials. It is proposed to examine the two approaches of rule scepticism and fact scepticism.

a) *Introduction to rule scepticism*

By way of a brief introduction it can be stated that the rule sceptics acknowledged that it was not possible to deny that lawyers, judges and onlookers described the legal system and the substantive 'laws' in terms of rules: about one minute spent looking at a legal textbook or a judgment would show this to be the case. What the rule sceptics denied was that rules were, in fact, the main operative factor in legal decisions. Other factors, for example, the background and prejudices of the judge, were important. Hence, because most judges are conservative, judgments in the political field will follow the conservative viewpoint; and so on for decisions on trade unions, students, etc. And, of course, each judge will have his own individual beliefs which will, consciously or not, influence his decisions.

Accordingly, as a consequence, rules could not be viewed in the normal way (as reasons for decision, authoritatively laid down; or as binding commands of a sovereign, for example). Instead, they should be seen merely as predictions of what the courts will do. The 'rule' that theft is dishonest appropriation of another's property (etc) is a prediction that in the given circumstances the court will punish an 'offender' for theft.

b) *Gray*

Perhaps the rule sceptics went overboard in their concentration on the courts, and what they will do. If a descriptive formulation of a rule in a textbook does not accord with court practice, it is not a 'rule' at all. In fact, Gray in *The Nature and Sources of the Law* went as far as to suggest that until a statute had been enforced by a court, it was not law at all, but only a source of law. This approach denies the facilitative function of certain statutes eg the Companies Act 1985 – one does not go to a court in order to incorporate a company yet the procedure and requirements for doing that are prescribed in statute. Cardozo J, a critic of realism, has observed that if Gray's thesis is carried to its logical conclusion then 'law never is, but is always about to be.'

c) *Oliver Wendell Holmes J*

Holmes in *The Path of the Law* took the view of 'our friend the bad man', who 'does not care two straws for the axioms and deductions', but 'does want to know what the Massachusetts or English courts are likely to do in fact' – what he feels will happen if he does certain things. Interestingly, this approach would take into account moral factors eg adultery. However it is wondered why Holmes takes no account of 'our other friend, the good man'. According to Holmes then the law is the rules which the courts lay down for the determination of legal rights and duties.

d) *Fact sceptics*

Jerome Frank went further than other realists, in suggesting that it was not in fact possible to predict what courts would do; in each case, everything depended on how the court decided the facts. A short piece (section 9.4) on Frank, discusses this in more detail.

It is not only the actual writings of the realists that are important. The encouragement of systematic and detailed study of the areas they concentrate on has produced much research, and many results. The realists themselves did not, on the whole, engage in such research (Llewellyn's main research, for example, was anthropological), but two new directions, judicial behaviouralism and jurimetrics, can be seen as the outcome of stressing empirical research and predictions of what the court will do. These new directions are the topic of section 9.5.

9.3 Karl Llewellyn's rule scepticism

Llewellyn was a 'mainstream' realist, a rule sceptic; it was he who suggested that, apart from being predictions of what the courts will do, rules are merely 'pretty playthings'.

Alongside this general approach, we can place his more detailed analysis of the functions and techniques of law. Many of his ideas seem rather more theoretical than scientifically or empirically researched, and the conclusion that he reaches (that appellate decisions can be predicted accurately in 80 per cent of cases) seems a little surprising, but much of what he says is interesting. (You might ask yourself to what extent it is novel, and to what extent simply common-sense.)

According to Llewellyn the basic functions of law are two-fold:

1 Aiding the survival of the group

2 Engaging in the quest for justice, efficacy and a richer life

To fulfil these two functions, there are a number of 'law-jobs' which the institution of law has. Llewellyn saw an institution in terms of an organised activity which is built around doing a job. The important aim is to ensure that these jobs are well performed. These law jobs are then the basic functions which the law has to perform. He lists these law jobs in *My Philosophy of Law* as:

1 The disposition of trouble cases which he likened to garage repair work with the continuous effect of the remaking of the order of that society;

2 The preventative channelling of conduct and expectations so as to avoid trouble and looks not only at new legislation but at its purpose.

3 The allocation of authority and the arrangement of procedures which mark action as being authoritative.

4 The net organisation of society as a whole so as to provide integration, direction and incentive.

5 Juristic method as used in law and the settlement of disputes.

His analysis of these is found in his book *The Normative, The Legal and The Law Jobs: The Problem of Juristic Method* (1940) in which he identifies the bare bones aspect of law jobs and that these law jobs are implicit in the concept of a group. The first of these he sees as the most important yet he does not tell us about their interrelationship. He suggests that these law jobs are universal yet this quest for universality has, as Lloyd and Freeman observe, led Llewellyn to concepts of a high level of abstraction.

Llewellyn was concerned to find the best way to handle 'legal tools to law job ends'. Although he suggests that his framework provides a general framework for the functional analysis of law, he suffers from a defect common to other functionalists in that he overlooks the dimensions and structure of power.

The institution of law consists of rules, principles, concepts and an overall ideology; and of various techniques (such as precedent) and practices. Within the set-up of the institution is the body of specialists who carry on the law-jobs, who pass down the skills or 'crafts' necessary to the working of the institutions.

In his concept of juristic method developed in his *Common Law Tradition* he outlines his theory of craft. Here he identifies his period style of judicial reasoning. He identifies two polar positions within this period style and says that judges will fall within that spectrum. This was based on empirical research that he and his students engaged in by looking at the performance of the courts at different times, hence 'period' style. He noticed that from the manipulation of precedent the courts could be classified. At the one pole is his grand style in which judges are less strictly self constrained by the rules of precedent and in his formal style the judge considers himself bound by the rules of precedent entirely. In the grand style the judge will follow what Llewellyn calls a 'situation sense' in order to ensure that a reasonable result is achieved. By identifying a judge's propensity then it may be possible to achieve the aim of the American realists namely the prediction of the outcome of the case. If we know what approach a judge takes we may be able to predict how he will approach a particular dispute.

The most relevant of these 'crafts' in view of the realist concentration on the courts, is the juristic method of decision-making. As has been pointed out, 'reckonability' in case law is high. This, according to Llewellyn, is the consequence of various attributes of the system which tend to stability. (Incidentally, the list of these factors seems to be a good example of a theoretical, rather than empirical, statement.)

Llewellyn has made an important point namely that law is not just about rules and that the prediction of the outline of cases is an important and useful function. However, law is not solely concerned with the prediction of what the court will do about a particular dispute. It is also about behavioural guidance to individuals. On a more specific point Lloyd and Freeman observe that Llewellyn's law jobs overlook the dimensions of structure and power in society. Further Twining, generally favourable, observes that Llewellyn's period style is 'a relatively simple theoretical model'.

As is clear from brief summary, Llewellyn realises that judges do use rules, and also realises that dispute settlement is not the sole function of laws. In adjusting to meet possible criticisms in these areas (the general realist approach ignores any function but dispute settlement in the courts, and derides the use of rules; both of these points can be effectively criticised) the impact of the realist attack is weakened. Law is only partly about predictions of what the court will do (dispute-settlement), it is also about behavioural guidance to individuals; and rules may be predictions – but they are also used by judges. Is this more than just a change of emphasis from traditional thought?

A fellow American realist, although from the fact sceptic aspect, Judge Frank took the view that Llewellyn's work was focused on the appeal courts and took no real account of the work of the trial courts where it was not the application of the rule that was important in predicting the outcome, but the uncertainty about the fact finding process that was the key.

A strong criticism levelled at both the rule sceptics and the fact sceptics is that they engage in over-generalisations in order to make a valid point. Furthermore the judges do use rules to explain their decisions and the judge is judge by virtue of a rule that says he will decide disputes. These are relegated to virtual unimportance in Llewellyn's law jobs theory. To this extent that analysis is defective. Critical evaluations are discussed in more detail below.

9.4 Frank and the experimentalist approach

Jerome Frank expounded a theory more extreme than the general approach we saw in section 9.2. He termed the views of Llewellyn et al 'rule-scepticism': they were concerned to show that the enunciated formal or 'paper' rules did not prove reliable as guides to judicial behaviour, so that uniformities of such behaviour should be studied to achieve certainty of prediction.

Frank considered that such certainty was impossible in relation to trial courts: the writings of the rule sceptics concentrated on the upper courts, not the 'sharp end'. In the lower courts, prediction of the outcome of litigation was not possible. The major cause of uncertainty is not the legal rule (either the 'proper' or the 'real' version), but the uncertainty of the fact-finding process. Much depends on witnesses, who can be mistaken as to their recollections; and on judges and juries, who bring their own beliefs, prejudices and so on, into their decisions about witnesses, parties, etc. These prejudices are idiosyncratic to the particular judge and jury, and cannot be standardised or predicted. Take for example the trial of Clive Ponting, the senior civil servant charged with an offence under the Official Secrets Act 1911 for disclosing to an unauthorised person (an MP) official secrets connected with the sinking of an Argentinian ship by British forces during a conflict in the South Atlantic. It was not in dispute that he had so 'leaked' the information. His own defence counsel (according to a book the defendant himself wrote afterwards) advised him on the day the jury were due to return their verdict that he should bring a new toothbrush as he would need one in prison. As we know the jury returned a verdict of not guilty. We do not know the reasons for this (it would be an offence to attempt to elicit from the jury their reasoning or their deliberations) but it may be speculated that the jury did not wish the matter of sentence to be left to the judge and so removed that from the bench by returning a verdict which on the face of the evidence and interpretations of the law to that trial was quite unexpected.

I think that this analogy can be elevated to a more theoretical plane by asserting that the uncertainty can also be found in the process by which a judge determines a particular fact to be a material fact. On the basis of the determination of material facts the legal rule will self apply.

This extreme version of realism does have a point to make: the decision in any specific case does depend on findings of fact which can be affected by jury and judge preconceptions and prejudices. Recent controversies over 'jury vetting' (checking by the security services of the prospective members of a jury, to see if a challenge should be made against individual members), the common opinion that a jury is better than a judge for motoring offences, and challenges on appearance of jurors in trials (for example challenging women jurors in rape cases) are all evidence that practitioners are aware of influences on decisions.

Frank does, however, seem to go too far. Many of the objections to realism set out in section 9.6 below apply with added force to the Frank version: particularly the concentration on the courts, and the denial of any place to formal rules are unacceptable. Moreover, it is surely not the case that all questions of fact are unpredictable as Frank describes. Within the bounds (known bounds, incidentally) of the rules of evidence, a professional adviser can make a very firm prediction in most cases of what facts the court will accept as proved, and what rules of law are to be applied to them. Could a thief caught red-handed by two independent witnesses really be told that all depended on what facts a judge or jury found?

Further, many cases never really get to the stage of disputed facts. How is fact-scepticism relevant to a defendant pleading guilty (in a criminal case) or only contesting quantum not liability (in a civil case)? And what of the many cases which go to judges on a basis of agreed fact, to see what the legal rule is? A famous example would be *Donoghue* v *Stevenson* [1932] AC 562.

As perhaps with mainstream rule-sceptical realism, an interesting and important point about the legal process is spoiled by over-generalisation.

9.5 Jurimetrics and judicial behaviouralism

a) *Jurimetrics*

The term 'jurimetrics' was coined by Loevinger in an article in 1949 to mean the scientific investigation of legal problems through the use of symbolic logic and computers. The latter play an interesting part in the legal world.

i) Many law firms and chambers now rely on computer retrieval systems to discover relevant precedents (several systems, including 'Lexis', are available). Key words are typed in ('company' – 'director' – 'fiduciary duty') and the computer finds the cases where these words occur within a set number of words of each other.

ii) Computers can aid some complicated legal processes, such as tax planning, where the relevant information is fed into a programme designed to ascertain the most efficient tax plan. This could save many man hours of calculations.

iii) Computers can take part in investigations – the proper field of 'jurimetrics' – where the data can be quantatively analysed. For example, research on the true realist concern, whether there are regularities of judicial behaviour which could give us patterns to predict.

iv) Computers can deal very quickly and effectively with logical patterns. However, when used as an aid to prediction of the likely outcome of a case, the computer is fed with a plethora of information about the court and behavioural models on which to base its prediction. The behavioural models will look at the group approach of a multi judge court and identify the task leader, whose self perception is as the efficient solver of a given problem, and the social leader, who provides the friendly atmosphere conducive to solving the problem. This group approach however, looking as it does on the inner workings of the group, requires a consistency in the membership of the tribunal. That is not provided by the court. Further, in order for the computer to detect a logical pattern, a precondition would be the existence of consistency in decision and attitude of the court. Here lies the central flaw. Judges are not logical machines – indeed that is the essence of what the realists are saying. Judges have moods, they change their mind and are subject to all the other weaknesses of the human condition.

What realism has done is lead to a systematic gathering and processing of data about the court which in Britain remains only at the level of gossip and rumour. Who is a good judge for this matter? What type of a mood is the judge in today etc?

The purpose behind this approach is clear. It was to aid the advocate. He would ascertain the preferences of the judge and tailor his argument to meet those preferences – this is done of course by better advocates on an ad hoc basis. What the jurimetrics application sought to do was to make this approach more organised.

These developments have led to criticism, and fear of machine justice. Such fears are exaggerated. Computers are useful tools of memory and research, and cannot at present be conceived of as replacing human roles in the judicial process. The real danger from computers now is that to privacy posed by computer data-banks: lawyers have a part to play in controlling this development, but should not be hindered from using computers in (i) - (iv) above by this (different) issue.

b) *Judicial behaviouralism*

This can be seen as the logical follow-up to realist theory: it involves actually carrying out research into how judges behave. A mixture of realist encouragement for such studies and social research techniques for carrying them out can be seen as responsible. The research as yet is patchy, and on appellate court decisions alone, some obvious results (especially those predicting decisions after the cases themselves!) and more surprising ones (Schundhauser found that judges who had sat on lower courts before getting to US Supreme Court level were more likely to overrule than those who had not, and that dissenting judges were less likely to overrule than majority decisions).

An interesting – if one-sided? – English writer's work on judicial decisions adopting a judicial behaviouralist approach is JAG Griffith's *The Politics of the Judiciary*.

Lon Fuller has observed that a defect in this approach is that the behaviouralists put consistency at a premium and that leads to the judicial process being seen as a formalised game of 'snap'.

9.6   Contributions and evaluations

Returning to the general approach (in section 9.2), we must evaluate it, and determine what, if any, contributions this brand of realism has made to legal theory.

Briefly, to recap, the approach we are examining is as follows: legal rules are not the mainly operative factor in legal decisions; because of other factors playing a part it is important to look behind these 'paper' rules for the 'real' rules: uniformities and regularities of judicial behaviour. The 'paper' formal rules are now only useful insofar as they are predictions of what the court will do.

Is this picture of rules, predictions, judicial process acceptable? The most obvious general point is that it involves a total change in the way we all talk and think about law. Textbook writers, judges, practising lawyers and students all view law in terms of rules and exceptions applicable to fact situations. While this is not in itself a damning criticism of the realists, it is clearly a strong indication that there are faults in the realist theory: is everyone engaged in the law perpetrating, or the subject of, a mass delusion?

Imagine first, that you are an individual approaching a solicitor on a non-contentious matter. You want to form a company, perhaps, or carry out properly your duties as executor of a will. If, when you ask what law is relevant to your case, the solicitor talks in terms of predictions of court behaviour, you will be very surprised: after all, you intend to fulfil your legal obligations and not end up in court at all (failing to form the company properly will result in, in any case, invalidity, not illegality or an offence). Surely the law and its rules are as much about these non-contentious matters as about cases that go to court? Non-contentious questions of obligations (as with the trusteeship) and the facilitative 'power-conferring rules' both public and private seem to be obscured by the realist dismissal of rules: this is our first specific criticism.

Much of the law, and much of the importance of legal rules, relates to guiding people's behaviour – allowing them to avoid a failure, to live up to their obligations and duties, and to take advantage of the various facilitative devices, such as wills, contracts and company formation, that the law provides.

Next, place yourself as a litigant in a contentious matter: let us say a plaintiff in a road accident case. Again, if advice was given as prediction of judicial behaviour, something would seem to be missing. Of course, especially in a case involving disputed facts, an element of prediction is involved in any complete advice: considering the evidence that the court is likely to hear, is it likely to find the defendant liable? What level of danger can be expected? But this is not the complete picture. We assume that, given that certain facts can be proved to the court's satisfaction, the defendant is liable (and not just that the court will probably find him to have been so): in fact the reason why the court is likely to find him liable is because he is liable, because he was under an obligation to drive non-negligently which he has breached.

To take another example, we think it perfectly correct to say (in an appropriate case) 'I'm sure X is guilty of theft, but the police cannot prove it and so he will be found not guilty', 'he was negligent, but there were no witnesses', etc.

Rules impose obligations and duties upon people. They have a normative aspect in that they guide behaviour. When they are breached, the question of whether or not a court will enforce the rule is a separate question from whether or not it has, in fact, been breached. Law is then not only about dispute settlement but about behavioural guidance as well.

A further minor point could also be made here. If our contentious litigant was told that there was no 'rule' imposing liability on the defendant, because rules were only predictions, and in his case the defendant would probably not be liable, he might turn his mind to other questions. All is said to depend on the courts/judges: but who are they? Surely they are only judges/courts because rules give them their authority?

Since the emphasis is on the courts, we should next try to look at things from the viewpoint of a judge. The cases, etc cited to him in argument do not bind him, they are merely predictions of what he will do. This ascribes too restrictive a view to the nature of legal rules. Rules bestow authority on judges. They are a judge by virtue of a rule that says they are. They are to decide cases by virtue of a rule that says they are to do so. Their decisions are to be carried out by virtue of a rule that says so.

Frank, who was a judge himself, suggests that a judge must be 'conscientious', but this is hardly coherent: how is he to decide in which way his duty lies? With regard to fact scepticism in general it can be stated that their approach is of no application when there is no dispute as to facts. Take for example the interlocutory proceedings in *Donoghue* v *Stevenson* [1932] where the court assumed the facts as alleged by the plaintiff and addressed the legal question as to whether those 'facts' disclosed a cause of action.

Again we must move back to our criticism that the predictive explanation has missed out the normative aspect of rules, the obligation imposed by them. Furthermore, judges are not only bound by the rules, they have the Hartian 'internal aspect': they accept the rules as a standard and a guide to their decisions. They will decide in a way following the rules, because they accept those rules as a standard to be followed. As Hood Phillips has stated, habits enable external prediction whereas rules provide a justification for acting in conformity and grounds for criticising those who deviate.

Hart has said that the fact that the judge has the last word does not imply that there is no rule. He uses an analogy with a soccer game and states that where a player who gets the ball into the net is offside a referee may still award a goal. This does not negate the offside rule but merely means that it was not applied in that case.

There are cases that do not have a settled rule covering them, and in those cases the judges must make new decisions: almost inevitably, personal viewpoint as well as institutional material will enter their new decision. These are the exceptions; in general, a judge will apply a settled rule, and this brings us to a linked point.

Although there is a degree of uncertainty about the law, there is also a large area which is certain, in which rules are the heavily operative factor in a judge's decision. Indeed as Dias has pointed out, if a judge circumvents a rule (on the rare occasions that he is able to do so) he will do so in a manner that conceals the fact of his doing so, and furthermore legal rules act as a brake on caprice.

Next it has been said with much justification that realism is less a philosophy than a technology. The realists sought to approximate the methodology of the natural sciences to an examination of the workings of the law. However as Glendon Schubert, a judicial behaviouralist, has argued, the realists failed to achieve their objective in that they lacked both theory and method. Of course, as a behaviouralist Schubert was concerned with motivations and attitudes behind judicial decisions.

There are some more minor points that can be mentioned here drawing on the critical literature. Stone, who is quite critical of the American realists, says that they offered nothing more than 'a mere gloss on the sociological approach'. From a Marxist perspective, Ackerman in *Reconstructing American Law* (1984) writes that realism was a culturally conservative theory designed to insulate the common law discourse from the new deal, thus viewing the theory as a response to the economic crisis of the time.

So what of the contribution of the realists? The points made above seem to destroy the realist approach: is this so? In view of some of the points and criticisms made, the realists towards the end of the movement were not as extreme as some of the earlier views. Llewellyn talks about the behaviour-guidance function, and discusses the normative aspect of rules: while 'situation sense' is one operative factor in judicial decisions, the legal rules are another.

Without getting bogged down in too much detail, it is probable that the intention was never to get rid of rules totally, but only to show that there was more to the use of the law than the mere application in logical fashion of legal rules. They have not rejected technical legal analysis but have merely emphasised that it is not enough if we wish to understand how the law works or how to improve the law. From that point of view, many of the realists' ideas are now commonplace – empirical and scientific studies of law in action and particularly judges in action, scepticism about fact-finding processes by judge and jury, realisation that the prejudices, etc of judges do play a part in litigation and decisions, and that judges do have a degree of discretion in some cases. Further, behaviouralism and jurimetrics are two positive off-shoots.

The idea of rules as predictions, the concentration on dispute settlement and the neglect of normative aspects of legal rules, may have been rejected: in lots of other ways, however, the American realists have influenced and made contributions to our grasp of legal theory. Perhaps to such an extent that Alan Hunt in *The Sociological Movement in Law* (p59) wrote that '... In a very real sense we *are* all Realists now if only in the most general context of recognising the need to view law in its social context ...'

10 EMPIRICAL METHODS IN JURISPRUDENCE 3: SCANDINAVIAN REALISM

10.1   Introduction

The other movement of realists consisted of a group of Scandinavian philosophers and jurists. As with the Americans, an overall similarity of approach conceals a difference in detail and emphasis in the writings of the various theorists.

We shall look at the 'identifying characteristics' of the movement's approach, and then concentrate on the three major figures: Hagerstrom (1868-1939), and more recently Olivecrona and Ross. A consideration of the contribution made by the Scandinavians will be followed by a section comparing them to the Americans: do the realists form one movement, or two?

10.2   General approach

It would not be true to say that all the Scandinavians talked about – or even agreed with! – the following points: but they are the characteristic ideas we can associate with the movement as a whole.

a) *Realist*

In a more philosophical way than the Americans, the Scandinavians considered themselves to be realist. They were interested in the legal system as a whole rather than the narrow area of interest adopted by the Americans. In essence, they were talking about law as observable fact (which, of course, makes them similar to the positivists), as part of the world of cause and effect, and therefore legal science as a science of 'causality'. They rejected formalism as in their view it had no regard to the facts of life experiences. In their rejection of a priori reasoning they declared that the method for the enlargement of knowledge was through empirical observation. This is what they meant by viewing law as an observable 'fact'. As we shall see discussed in more detail below, the proof of the existence of law was ascertained through the psychological effect.

b) *Against metaphysics: verifiability principle*

This realism led them to reject as 'metaphysical' anything which did not exist on the level of cause and effect, of empirical reality. They subscribed to the 'verifiability principle' of the logical positivists whereby if a statement cannot be proved by empirical evidence, it is meaningless.

The importance of this principle to an understanding of law is obvious and fundamental. In talking about law, we continually use statements and concepts which do not seem to be 'verifiable' in this way. Many legal rules are based on views of what is 'good', 'bad', 'just', 'right', etc; the rules themselves are phrased normatively, in terms of 'ought', and not 'is'; and we think of legal concepts such as 'right', 'duty', 'ownership', arising from these rules. All of these ideas are non-verifiable, it seems, referring to a different realm of thought from empirical reality, a realm or science of 'ought', not 'is'. Simply they are not rooted in the actual sense experiences.

Such a realm of thought is rejected as being metaphysical. (One can at this point effectively contrast natural lawyers, for whom such a realm of thought does exist and in fact controls our moral and legal rules, etc.) Unless all legal thought and experience is to be rejected as metaphysical, some other explanation of the concepts and rules which constitute it must be given. This is the task that the Scandinavians have set for themselves.

The proof is that it is to be found in the mind of the individual, in psychology. There is no objective criterion of 'good' or 'bad' or 'just', only subjective views; the normative effect of rules of law comes from their effect in psychological terms; and notions such as 'right' and 'duty' can be explained as psychological feelings: a right as a sensation of power, and a duty as a sense of constraint or compulsion. The exact explanations differed from theorist to theorist; Lundstedt in particular was extreme in condemning as metaphysical even the idea of 'normativity'. Ross and Olivecrona were more acceptable in this respect; normative statements are clearly a form of language with an important function, which need to be re-evaluated in the light of verifiability.

c) *Normativity: psychological occurrences*

The meaning of a normative statement according to the Scandinavian view, then, is psychological: X 'ought' to do something because he feels bound to, he has a right because he has a feeling of power, and so on.

The concepts of normativity, of binding quality of law, of the validity of law, are all explained with reference to psychological occurrences. Law takes place through the psychology of individuals. People who have rights feel they have power and people who are under an obligation feel they have to act in a certain way. These concepts are considered in detail by both Olivecrona and Ross, below.

d) *Other points*

The points (a) – (c) above are the main tenets characterising this 'school'. There are other points made in the theories, not perhaps as important, which we should mention before considering the individual writers:

i) *Law as rules about force*

A recurrent theme is that the legal system has a monopoly of force, and that all laws are ultimately backed by the threat of force. We must not confuse this with the view that a sanction is a necessary condition for a valid law: Ross for example, expressly rejects that. Nevertheless, sanctions and force are central to an understanding of how law works. Without the monopolisation of the use of legitimate force psychology would not be effective.

ii) Legal rules as predictions of officials' behaviour

This, of course, is a strong element of American realism 'rule-scepticism'. In the present context, the point is subtly different: while it seems that rules will not be valid unless they are effective predictions of how officials will behave (ie unless they are followed in practice), another aspect must not be forgotten: to be valid, a rule must also be felt to be binding, and therefore be the motivation for obedience. This latter point is not to be found in the American theory.

iii)   *'magic words', legal ritual*

Both Hagerstrom and Olivecrona are concerned with the effect of legal formulae in changing the legal position.

10.3   Hagerstrom

Hagerstrom has been referred to as the 'spiritual father' of the Scandinavian realist movement. The others in the movement took up his ideas and built upon them. It is therefore by way of background information that a brief outline of his views is here discussed.

Hagerstrom rejected the idea of a non-natural sense in which things could exist. So 'goodness' and 'badness' are subjective notions, and similarly there is no reality to the concepts of 'rights' and 'duties', beyond their actual effect in the real world.

An insight into his thought can be gained by looking at his explanation of the 'rights' created by imperative laws. When a legislator, for example, declares that a person has a right (expressed in an imperative form) he has in mind the likely consequences of that declaration, based on his knowledge of the effectiveness of the legal system. Those consequences are two-fold; first, that when certain facts exist, the person with the right will generally enjoy certain advantages against another/others; and second that legal proof of relevant facts in court will enable the person with the right to get at least an equivalent of those advantages.

A legislator will generally also consider that his declaration has the effect of producing a right in a 'supernatural' sense, providing an obligation which exists in some way even if neither of the two consequences above occur: for example, if the person with a contractual 'right' gets neither the advantages (the other side does not perform) nor the equivalent in court (since he cannot prove the relevant facts, eg the formation of an oral contract). We think it perfectly coherent to say that 'there is a contract (and therefore contractual rights), but I am unable to prove it'. Hagerstrom rejects this, because it does not reflect reality, but is elevated above the physical world.

Another interesting aspect of Hagerstrom's work emerged from his study of Greek and Roman law, and concerns the legal use of 'magic words'. He suggests that formal words (for example, in the mancipatio ceremony in Roman law for the acquisition of property and livery of seisin in a medieval feoffment) were taken to have a magical effect in the real world. I think there is something to this view in modern law. Provided the appropriate formula of words is uttered in the appropriate ritual a 'magical' or legal consequence flows. The marriage ceremony is one such example. Uttering the words 'I do' in a marriage ceremony has the effect in the real world of changing your legal status. No actual change takes place – the change is not real but is a change in attitudes. The parties (bride and groom) will treat each other differently and more importantly from this point of view other people will treat them differently and all because they uttered these magic words in a ritual. The law too will treat them differently, for example the husband will be responsible for paying his wife's poll tax, so there can occur the rather ridiculous situation at the moment that where a married woman writes to her local authority the reply is addressed to her husband. That this law dates back to a previous era (1806) when the status of a woman was quite different must be obvious. Another example might be in the incorporation of a company – where the appropriate procedure is correctly adhered to (the ritual) the Registrar will incorporate the company (the magic words) – the legal effect of this is to create a new legal person. Furthermore, I have made reference elsewhere to the word 'law' having a special effect. Perhaps, Hagerstrom has something to tell us about the importance of psychology in this regard.

This view has been questioned in relation to the ancient laws, and is clearly not the case today. One cannot deny the importance of form and language in law (for example, using a seal instead of consideration for a contract, the words of the marriage ceremony), but we no longer believe in any 'magical effect'. The forms of language fulfil an important function, which is discussed by Olivecrona (on 'performatives', below). There is a suggestion that there is a middle ground in the use of language where the language of rights and duties are a separate and legitimate use of language. The argument goes as follows: there is a body of rules which establishes standards. Statements made with reference to these standards are an explanation of rights and duties. These statements take their validity from the sense that they are part of an acceptable body of standards. This is not metaphysics because it is not being said that the body of standards exists. This has been described as a (possible) middle ground. The extremes are firstly where rights exist in an objective fashion – a view that there are objective human rights for example and at the other extreme where a right is a feeling of power. The popular view today is that rights exist irrespective of whether they are accepted. It can thus be said that perhaps the Scandinavians 'threw out the baby with the bathwater'.

10.4 Olivecrona

Olivecrona was concerned with how laws played a part in the world of cause and effect. He also, as with Hagerstrom, rejected metaphysical ideas surrounding the laws; instead he considered the 'factual circumstances' of the law. These circumstances were that a state (not a metaphysical entity in any way; just a group of persons) which has a monopoly of force passes legislation which results in psychological pressure being felt by individuals, who because of that pressure obey the law. The reality is how legal concepts work in relation to constellations of facts, so that a right would have no objective existence but would merely describe the relationship between a set of facts.

According to Olivecrona, a legal rule has two elements, the 'ideatum' and the 'imperatum'. The 'ideatum' is the imagined pattern of conduct, which the rule is meant to bring about. Traffic regulations, for instance, are intended to produce a smooth and safe flow of traffic. To supply a motive, sanctions are directed for non-compliance; the rules relating to these sanctions contain a pattern of conduct for others (ie the police, judges, etc who will enforce the original rule).

The 'imperatum' is the form of expression of the ideatum, ie the imperative. The addressee is told to follow the particular pattern required. These imperatives are 'independent imperatives': they appear to be commands, but no-one actually commands them (the 'will of the state' is rejected as a metaphysical concept); they merely issue forth from the accepted procedures for law-making.

Even power-conferring rules on the Hartian model are imperative, according to Olivecrona; 'performatory imperatives' or ('performatives'), in that something should happen. The imperative form is used: 'if so and so happens, a contract shall be formed...property shall pass...the parties shall be married'.

The above exposition of a legal rule's content comes from the 1971 edition of Olivecrona's *Law as Fact* and is particularly interesting because Olivecrona clearly identifies the individual citizen as the addressee of the independent imperatives. This is in contrast, somewhat, to his own earlier view that in facts laws were addressed to officials, and were chiefly about the exercise of force (which it may be concluded drew heavily for its inspiration on the writings of Hans Kelsen (see chapter 7). Although force is often kept in the background, all laws are ultimately enforced by force: criminal laws by imprisonment, civil laws by execution of judgments (by seizure of goods, and imprisonment etc). The relationship of force and law is that the law 'consists chiefly of rules about force, rules which contain patterns of conduct for the exercise of force'. As Hagerstrom demonstrated a duty arises out of an individual's psychological response to coercion. By this is meant, clearly, those laws addressed to officials, to ensure that they enforce the patterns of conduct expected of individuals. In this version, these latter patterns of conduct are only 'aspects' of the rules about force, which are for Olivecrona 'primary'. In this way

Olivecrona sought to explain the attitudes and responses of those to whom the law is directed.

The later shift in addressees (from officials to individuals) should not obscure the importance of force to law. A necessary condition of effective legislation is an organisation to enforce them by force if necessary; and laws are 'about the exercise' of that force.

As we have seen already, the Scandinavian view of normativity is a psychological one: a 'valid rule' is one that is binding; and a rule is 'binding' in terms of the compulsion felt by individuals. Olivecrona considered the psychological processes involved in the legal experience; three aspects are worth noticing:

a) *Legislation and judge-made rules*

Both legislation and judge-made rules are effective because officials and individuals feel bound by them (although the effect of judge-made rules, because of the uncertainty inherent in them, is less formalised and certain). For statutes, 'the fulcrum is the act of promulgation'. Since officials accept the constitution, rules which are passed in the proper procedure automatically are accepted as binding. In fact officials will generally rely on the conscientious collection of official copies of statutes and so will not in fact check to see if they have been properly passed. In English law, judges must rely on the correctness and validity of an Act of Parliament which expresses the correct passage and is kept in the correct places, *BRB* v *Pickin* [1974] AC 765, and individuals will simply accept the appellation 'law'.

Judge-made rules (which must be seen as legislation and not as inferences of 'what law is') depend for their effectiveness on whether (because of the judge's renown and reasoning) courts and writers are prepared to accept them as 'law'.

b) *The law and fear of sovereigns*

The law and the fear of sovereigns (that force which ultimately enforces the law) are the main cause of our moral standards. Rather than in each instance making a calculation about whether or not obedience to the law is worthwhile, the independent imperative form of law is absorbed into our minds (as we grow up). The situations then enter our minds with an imperative symbol stamped on them: you shall not steal! This is wrong! This process is 'internalisation'.

c) *Performatives*

Performatives (power conferring rules) seem to work in the same way as legislation: the expression of the words of marriage in the proper procedure and place change the status of the couple by producing psychological effects in them and other people. In short, people treat them and think of them as married, and that is the reality of the married state.

10.5 Evaluation of Olivecrona

It is not possible fully to evaluate Olivecrona without critically considering the overall Scandinavian position, and that consideration is left to section 10.8. However, some specific criticisms must be made. Most importantly, Olivecrona's generalisations were the result not of research but of guesswork. Do we really have our moral standards formed in that way, as a result of legal rules? Most of us would think of the process in reverse: it is because murder is thought immoral that it is a crime, and *not* because it is a crime that it is thought immoral, surely? Also, if we all live in the same legal system with the same laws, how do people's views come to differ? Pornography is banned in this country, yet some people consider it to be morally acceptable.

Another criticism relates to the importance of force in the theory. Surely saying that all views are 'about force' is not only an exaggeration but misleading. Laws are about providing a standard of conduct for the people in society, and the rules of enforcement are to uphold that standard. Perhaps this explains Olivecrona's later shift to considering individuals as the addressees of law: rules to individuals are not secondary, but primary. (We have made similar criticisms of Bentham and Kelsen; and see Ross below.)

Finally, is it correct to treat 'performatives' as just another form of imperative? Isn't this similar to one of the flaws in Austin's theory (treating all laws as commands), again missing the different function of such laws (as giving people a particular facility, rather than imposing a duty on them)?

Olivecrona spoke of the internalisation of norms which leads to the development of moral standards. According to him law is valid because it is felt to be and the binding force of law is a reality only in the minds of the subjects. It is thought that this places too great an emphasis on psychology without actually understanding psychology. Is it not the case that in psychology an understanding requires there to be a norm (in the sense of a normal) whereas in reality can it be wondered whether there exists such a 'normal person'? Doesn't psychology need a point of reference that is not determined in the Scandinavian theory?

10.6 Ross

Ross has provided what is generally regarded as a better developed explanation of law than that of his colleagues in the Scandinavian school, and one that is strikingly similar to that of Hart. Much influenced by logical positivism and therefore rejecting metaphysics and attempting to explain law as a social fact in a positivist way, Ross again attempts to explain the normative quality of law in psychological terms. Ross' work can be read in *Towards a Realistic Jurisprudence* (1946).

a) *Scheme of interpretation*

Drawing on an analogy of a chess game, Ross sees the rules of both chess and law as explaining behaviour which is otherwise inexplicable. Ross takes this from the viewpoint of a third person – a spectator. There is no reality apart from the experiences of the two players. The moves themselves mean nothing. Ross sees the primary rules as directives which are accepted by both players as socially binding. It is important to distinguish between the rules of the game and the rules of skill. A bad move may still be a permitted move within the rules. The effectiveness of these rules of the game are established by observation. However, like Hart, Ross is also interested in the extent to which the rules are regarded as binding. Here Ross would adopt the introspective method – this is concerned with the psychological state of mind of feeling bound. In Hart's *Concept* the internal aspect may coincidentally involve feeling bound or compelled but it is coincidental and not necessary. The internal aspect performs an altogether different function that is providing both a reason for following the rule and for criticising those who deviate from the rule. Why should a particular move in chess remove a piece from the board, and (applying the analogy) why should a particular document, plus certain factual circumstances, cause a judge to order compensation, one might ask? The explanation is in terms of law as a 'scheme of interpretation'; valid law is that set of normative ideas which can be used to interpret law in practice. So, the judge orders compensation (law in practice) because of a particular normative idea (eg breach of contract followed by damages, an 'ought'): all such normative ideas together constitute valid law. This interpretative scheme enables us to explain the behaviour of judges, and to predict it. Thus like the game of chess where one knows the rules one can comprehend the actions – what had previous to comprehension appeared to the external observer to be mere regularities of conduct.

b) *Valid norm*

A specific norm exists if it is both followed and felt to be binding, and followed because it is felt to be binding. Logically, this obedience is obedience by judges: as with Olivecrona, Ross sees laws as about the exercise of force, and therefore as primarily addressed to officials to order the application of that force. In his later work (*Directives and Norms*) he does accept that psychologically – as against logically – there are norms addressed to individuals, which are grounds for the reactions of the authorities; but the 'secondary norms' addressed to officials to give legal effect to the primary norms addressed to individuals, contain all that is contained in those primary norms, and as such are the ones strictly necessary.

c) *Not behaviouralist*

The notion of 'predicting' in terms of the system, and 'exercise of force' in terms of an individual law could lead to a misunderstanding, viz that Ross holds the American realist line that rules (if anything) are predictions of what a judge will do in the particular case. Such a 'behaviouralist' approach is rejected by Ross; he gives the (fairly traditional but strong) argument that it cannot cope with the difference between a punishment and a tax demand. The important point to emphasise is that valid law enables predictions of the judge's behaviour to be made because the judge feels the rule to be binding: this element is lacking from American realist explanations.

d) *Why are rules felt to be binding?*

The reason that judges feel the rules to be binding is their allegiance to the constitution and the accepted sources of law. Individual citizens obey the primary norms addressed to them from a mixture of motives, fear of the sanctions to be imposed and belief that they should obey the law.

e) *Norms of competence*

Ross does distinguish some norms (those of competence, divided into private and social, or public) which do not purport to obligate the subject, and instead give him the competence to do something (these are what we have identified as 'power-conferring' laws). However, these norms as well are seen as directives to the courts, and therefore as fragments of laws imposing duties (cf Kelsen, Bentham).

10.7 Evaluation of Ross

There is much more in Ross that could be explained, but we have concentrated on the main lines of argument. We can note how strongly in some respects his theory resembles Hart's. Hart has identified as the necessary characteristics of a legal system, the general obedience to the rules by individuals, and the internal acceptance of the secondary rules by officials: Ross also sees a distinction between individuals, who will obey for mixed reasons, and officials, particularly judges, who obey out of allegiance to the constitution and the accepted sources of law. Hart identifies laws which do not impose obligations, as does Ross (a notable advance on Olivecrona, who refers to even 'performatives' as imperatives); and Hart identifies and emphasises the internal aspect of rules, echoes of which can be seen in Ross. The rule for Ross is 'felt to be binding'; for Hart, the internal aspect of a rule involves it being taken as a standard for conduct, an internal statement being one from that point of view. Although Hart sees a distinction (*Scandinavian Realism*, CLJ (1959)), he also sees the similarity (*The Concept of Law,* p243, note to p85).

Several criticisms can be made: Ross takes no account of law that has never been applied by the courts because it is universally obeyed. A major flaw in Ross as well as the other Scandinavian theorists is that they seem to dogmatically follow the tenets of early logical positivism which has been demonstrated to be defective. The idea that there are only two forms of meaningful statement, namely the logical (analytical) and the empirical, must be too restrictive. The heavy reliance on the verifiability principle which has been stated by Schlick as '... (the) meaning of a proposition is the method of its verification...' failed to produce a logical criteria for verifiability. The verification principle is neither analytical nor empirical and therefore, as it exists in the realm of metaphysics, by their own standard the Scandinavian realists must reject it!

Ross's theory can further be criticised. As with Olivecrona, law is seen as rules about force – which can be seen as missing its main function of setting standards of behaviour. The misrepresentation inherent in the 'rules about force' view is reinforced by seeing laws as norms addressed to officials; and a similar misrepresentation of power-conferring laws as part of the same pattern ignores their different function.

A further aspect of his theory and approach can be seen when he noted that jurisprudence should be rooted in empirical study of official behaviour, not norms that ought to be obeyed but those norms likely to be applied by the court. In this way he was similar to the American realists although this aspect is discussed in more depth below.

A further criticism that can be levelled against Ross is that his theory and approach does not take account of how courts justify their decisions, which according to Hart is explicable in terms of the rule. Ross merely states that an understanding of the rule is necessary in order to comprehend the judicial process and to predict the likely outcome of the case. If we know the rules we know what the judge will apply. As Hart has amply pointed out, the concept of a rule involves it being taken as a standard of conduct and not just that it is felt to be binding. Lloyd and Freeman point out a further difficulty with regard to the place of the judge in Ross' theory. The observer will not know if the judge is applying the rule because of 'the experience of validity' or simply through fear or indifference. The theory itself is of no assistance to the judge. When judges read their own decisions they are not predicting their own behaviour. Ross attempts to answer this by drawing a distinction between statements about the law and statements of law. His discussion about validity relates to the former, ie statements about the law. In response to criticism which he felt to be misdirected Ross asserted that the use of the term 'valid' in his account was really a mistranslation of 'in force' or 'existing' law. If this is so then, in this writer's view, Ross has weakened rather than strengthened his argument as he is now in danger of using a tautological definition which goes something like ...'a rule of law is in force if it is applied by the courts...'

Ross went in search of the impossible. He sought a norm that was not normative. He sought to derive validity from application. This was doomed from the start. I think that generally the problem with the Scandinavian realists as a whole is that their theory has not been treated seriously. I think the reason for this is that their theory (if theory it is) is either a statement of the obvious or the ridiculous.

10.8 Contribution to legal theory

It is impossible fully to assess the Scandinavians' contribution, as their works are referred to relatively infrequently in the rest of Europe, and then they are often dismissed briefly. Their main point, that law produces psychological feelings and compulsion and that this is its place in the world of cause and effect, seemed at first to be new and extreme, denying, as Lundstedt did, even the possibility of normativity. Despite their detailed faults, Olivecrona and Ross are to our eyes more acceptable; their interpretation is still a psychological one, but an explanation of normativity within the system is provided, with results that, in Ross, mirror closely the most mature results of Anglo-American positivist analysis. The psychological point is made, watered down, and becomes a useful and acceptable insight.

In other specific ways, there are contributions and speculations that give support to other positivists, by saying the same thing. The parallels between Olivecrona and Kelsen, for example, are as worth noticing (both see law as 'imperatives' issuing from the system rather than an individual; both see law as rules about force, with laws addressed to officials; both see the acceptance/validity of laws within the system as resulting from acceptance of a constitution) as those between Ross and Hart. The emphasis on reality as against 'metaphysics' finds echoes throughout positivism, and the support for empirical study obviously echoes American realism and other sociologists.

The Scandinavians may now be silent and not generally accepted; in various ways their ideas and contributions remain in our legal theory. In an illuminating chapter on their theory Finch has appreciated that they engaged in a 'radical and iconoclastic approach to the traditional problems of legal theory' This description would also apply to the American realists and therefore a brief comparison is discussed in the next section.

10.9 Comparison with American realism

The student can be expected to make detailed comparisons of his own after reading the last two chapters, to answer the question – is there one school of 'realism', or two schools (just joined by a common name)? Two main strands can be identified as an opening to this comparison. First, in their different ways the American and Scandinavians were realists; they were rejecting metaphysical explanations of law like natural law, and trying to explain the law in terms of observable behaviour, in terms of 'cause and effect'. For this reason, research is important and encouraged, although the Americans must be regarded as having the stronger 'hand' on that.

Second, to different extents, there is a concentration on judges. Both Llewellyn's 'rule scepticism' and Frank's 'fact scepticism' result in a closer look at what the courts do, Llewellyn even viewing legal rules as predictions thereof. On the Scandinavian side, Olivecrona and Ross both suggest that rules are addressed to officials. This similarity must not be allowed to mask the fundamental difference; for Ross, judges follow rules because they are binding and cover the case in question determining its results; for the Americans, seeing rules as determining cases in this way is incorrect.

Finch has stated that '... Both the American and the Scandanavian Realist movements are radical and iconoclastic in their purpose, and this attitude is reflected primarily in their respective attitudes to legal rules ...' This is an interesting statement an examination of which would enable a comparison between the two to be made. By way of a summary this comparison could be made as follows.

Both the American and the Scandinavian realists can be seen as a reaction to the rule formalism that preceded and to a certain extent has succeeded them. Their point was that too much emphasis was placed on the rules and not enough on the reality of the legal experience.

Thus the Americans thought that there was more to the legal exerience than the mere logical application of legal rules. Placing the lawyer at centre stage the Americans indeed did smash idols and dispelled the a priori reasoning of the formalists. The rule sceptics denied that rules were the main operative factor in legal decisions; indeed one of their number, Gray, went so far in his *The Nature and Sources of the Law* to argue that a statute is not law but is merely a source of law. When it is applied by a court it is law but then thereafter it reverts to being a source of law for another court. This lead Benjamin Cardozo to observe that for Gray 'law never is but is always about to be'. What cannot be denied is that the approach of Gray is certainly radical and iconoclastic. His fellow travellers in the rule sceptics did not go quite as far along that road as he did. Gray ignored the facilitative function of law yet Oliver Wendell Holmes, considered by most to be the grand old man of the American realists, thought that the law is what the bad man thinks will happen if he does certain things. The law for Holmes was the rules which the courts lay down in the determination of legal rights and duties. Similarly Karl Llewellyn thought that rules are mere pretty playthings in the hands of the lawyers, although in his later work he moderated this stance. He thought that the law is what officials do about disputes.

From an entirely different perspective but no less radical and iconoclastic was the experimentalist approach of the major fact sceptic, Jerome Frank. In his volume *The Courts on Trial* he argued that the rule sceptics suffered from a craving for certainty. He emphasised the need to look at the work of the trial courts as opposed to the appellate courts on which Llewellyn concentrated so much of his attention. Whereas the rule sceptics saw the rule as of assistance in the prediction of the outcome of the case, Frank thought that the rule was of no use in the predictive process. The rules according to Frank are fixed. What leads to uncertainty are the difficulties in the fact finding process both with regard to witnesses and the juries and also with regard to the process by which the judge determines particular facts to be material. Thus there would be no point in examining the rules as this would not give any indication as to how the matter would be decided if it came before a court. Our own law schools have failed to take this into account. In substantive law topics the examination calls for the logical application of legal rules to a factual (hypothetical) situation in order to advise the parties to the dispute. The American realist in answering that type of question would want to introduce matters such as the background of the judge and other personal factors which he would say would also contribute to a decision.

The American realist's approach to rules whilst not universal is certainly very radical and iconoclastic. It is a major departure from anything that went before. It has also given rise to jurimetrics and to studies involving judicial behaviouralism. It has emphasised an important matter, namely the emphasis that a potential litigant will place on the prediction of the likely outcome of the case. Unlike the rule formalist the American realist will not arrive at that prediction solely through the mere logical application of legal rules.

Such an approach is not without its critics. It could be observed that a prediction of the court's behaviour would not be appropriate in non contentious matters. Furthermore, rules have a normative aspect in that they guide conduct; thus law is not only about dispute settlement but is also about behavioural guidance. This side of the law's function is ignored by the American realists. Hart has observed that the fact that a judge has the last word does not imply that there is no rule. He draws an analogy with a soccer match in which in spite of the fact that a player is offside the referee may not see it and still award a goal. The award of the goal does not negate the offside rule. The point was made by Hood Philips that habits enable external prediction yet rules provide a justification for acting in conformity and grounds for criticising those that deviate. This is similar to Hart's observation of the presence in a rule of a critical reflexive attitude. Within the limits of the courtroom I would concur with Hunt who observed that 'we are all realists now'.

The approach of the Scandinavian realists whilst quite different from their American namesakes is nonetheless radical and iconoclastic. The Scandinavians had a deep mistrust of the metaphysical and insisted on verification of any metaphysical notion in the real world of cause and effect. Lundstedt in his *Legal Thinking Revised* argued that legal rules are mere labels and become meaningless if taken out of context. He argued that it was not possible to stipulate that because of a rule a duty arises, because this would be to support a metaphysical relationship that cannot be proved in the world of cause and effect.

Olivecrona saw two parts of the rule, namely the ideatum and the imperatum. By the ideatum he identified the imagined pattern of behaviour that the legislature wants to bring about and by the imperatum he identified the expression of the ideatum. His was essentially an imperative approach although he did not see imperatives in terms of the wish of any person, as Austin so required. For Olivecrona the imperative was independent of the wish of anyone. He viewed his performatory imperatives as a type of power conferring rule yet it is submitted that this is wrong. Power conferring rules are not just another form of imperative. In essence what Olivecrona was writing about was that law is valid because it is felt to be. The binding force of law is a reality only in the minds of the subjects and this is its manifestation in the real world, through psychology. For this reason, Olivecrona had to change his idea of who were the addressees of law. In his volume *Law As Fact* whereas he had previously been similar to Kelsen in that laws were addressed to officials this did not enable him to explain how individuals had feelings of power and of obligation as a consequence of a rule. This would mean that the rule was meaningless. Therefore Olivecrona altered his position and spoke of laws being addressed to officials in the primary sense and to the public in the secondary sense. I cannot escape from the conclusion that his work is largely guesswork and I therefore have little respect for it.

By use of an analogy with a game of chess Alf Ross shows in his work *On Law and Justice* that there is no reality apart from the experience of the players. He approaches the question of verification in a sophisticated psychological way. He distinguishes legal rules from rules of skill and maintains that the effectiveness of a rule can be established by observation. He then addresses the question of why rules are felt to be binding and concludes that the normative quality of law can be understood in psychological terms. Thus for Ross, rules act as schemes of interpretation for particular actions and it is this that enables the explanation and prediction of judicial behaviour. On the basis of the paper rules it is possible to predict what the judge will do. This is because the judge feels the rules to be binding upon him as he has accepted the sources of law and has allegiance to the constitution. The general public feel bound by a variety of reasons.

Law for Ross produces psychological feelings of compulsion and this is its place in the world of cause and effect. Thus a valid law for Ross would be that 'set of normative ideas that enable us to interpret the actions of officials in applying sanctions'. Hence a realistic jurisprudence ought to be rooted in the empirical study of official behaviour and not in norms that ought to be obeyed but rather in those norms that are likely to be applied in a court. In one important respect Ross is similar to Hart and that is that he regards law as a social fact. For him a norm is a directive that stands in a relation of correspondence to social facts. We need to know the rules before we can understand what is happening.

The problem with this radical and iconoclastic approach is firstly, that while some radicals and idol destroyers are widely followed the Scandinavian realists are entirely out on a limb. It would not be discourteous to say that they are not even treated seriously in their own universities. Perhaps this is because they are either engaged in a statement of the obvious or of the ridiculous. Secondly, Hart has pointed out that the importance of a rule is not just that it is felt to be binding but that it is taken as a standard of conduct. The Scandinavians have not dealt adequately with this point.

The point made by Dias that a rule is more abstract than a judicial decision, yet lawyers ought to be concerned with both, is probably a useful synthesis of the contribution such as it is of the realists.

11 EMPIRICAL METHODS IN JURISPRUDENCE 4: HISTORICAL JURISPRUDENCE

11.1   Introduction

The so-called historical school of the nineteenth century, led by the very different theories of Savigny and Maine, shows us that law cannot be fully understood until its historical and social context is studied and appreciated. The natural law emphasis on universality and reason, and the positivist emphasis on law as it is, might blind us to this fact.

In its historical perspective there were two main reactions against natural rights doctrine (the age of enlightenment). We have already examined in detail the reaction that was positivism and the reasons for that reaction. In this chapter we shall examine the other main reaction which may be called romanticism.

I think it is possible to identify several pressing reasons that lay behind the romanticist reaction against the natural rights doctrine, as follows:

a) a reaction against the unhistorical assumptions of natural law which it will be recalled asserted the supremacy of unchanging principles;

b) a reaction against nationalism which promoted the excesses of the French Revolution and the wars that followed that event;

c) a rejection of the idea that the legal system is founded on the basis of reason;

d) a xenophobic reaction against anything French – this is particularly appropriate for von Savigny;

e) a desire to re-emphasise tradition as emerged from a leading anti-French revolutionary work by Edmund Burke entitled *Reflections on the Revolution in France* (1790).

For the purposes of this chapter I have put the theories of von Savigny and of Maine together. In reality I think that they represent two very different approaches to an understanding of law and the legal process. They have in common this reaction against the natural rights doctrine and a desire to emphasise the historical perspective, but I think that that is as far as their similarity goes. I would agree with those who have identified these theories as organic for Maine and mystical for von Savigny, and I will use those terms accordingly.

11.2   Maine

a) *Background*

In the second half of the nineteenth century, Henry Maine's writings concentrated on law in an historical context, stripped of the mysticism of Savigny's 'volksgeist'. The early positivists, while rejecting natural law, still sought a universal analytic definition: political philosophers considered present-day political obligation, and any references to history to bolster their arguments tended to be history 'read backwards' (for example, reading the later developed idea of a contract into the state of nature; and suggesting laws as the commands of a supreme law giver, ignoring the historical priority of custom over legislation).

Maine pioneered a new approach, studying the history of different legal systems and the 'legal' set-up of primitive societies, to enable a full understanding of law.

A great influence on his work was Darwin's *Origin of Species* – the theory of evolution, which dominated thought in every field in the late nineteenth century. In the words of Professor J H Morgan: 'he demonstrated that our legal organisms are as much the product of historical development as biological organisms are the outcome of evolution'. This connection with Darwin is most clearly seen in the evolutionary stage model of development.

b) *Theory*

Studying the early law of Greece, Rome, and the Old Testament, and Indian law (and using as well his knowledge of English law), Maine said that the development of legal systems followed a pattern of six stages. Static societies passed through the first three stages; progressive societies then moved through (at least some of) the latter three. Maine stated that the origins of legal development can be traced to religion and ritual. This can be seen in societies that never developed literacy, at least so far as the majority of their population are concerned. There ritual is used as a means of education in circumstances where it would be futile to reduce instructions to writing. Examples of ritual washing may demonstrate this point. From this initial pool of ritual and religion flowed the stream of the development of the law. The pattern of development that Maine was so concerned to identify, along the same lines as Darwin identified for the development of species, was as follows:

i) *Royal judgments*

Royal judgments, divinely inspired, were the first stage. This has also been described as the stage of Themistes (after the Greek goddess). This should not be confused with the 'command of a sovereign' idea as it was not deliberate law-making, merely dispute settlement. In fact, Maine suggests that Bentham and Austin's description tallies exactly with the facts of mature jurisprudence, but more primitive law is more difficult to fit into the Bentham 'picture'. An example of this would be the story of King Solomon and the two mothers, proposing to divide the live baby in two as the mothers could not agree on who was the real mother. There was no principle or rule that King Solomon was applying. Within the context of Maine's theory it can be observed firstly that it was to King Solomon that the parties turned for a resolution of the dispute and secondly that the decision was divinely inspired in order to draw out the real mother who would rather have her child live but away from her than dead. Whilst this is a good example to illustrate the concept of divinely inspired judgments, it can also be used to defeat the historical/chronological aspect of Maine's thesis. The point is that King Solomon existed after the law had been codified (ie after the ten commandments etc) and not before, as Maine's developmental process would have maintained.

ii) *Custom*

Custom and the dominion of aristocracies follow royal judgments; the prerogative of the kings passes to different types of aristocracies (in the East, religious; in the West, civil or political), which were universally the depositaries and administrators of law. 'What the juristical oligarchy now claims is to monopolise the knowledge of the laws, to have exclusive possession of the principles by which quarrels are decided ... Customs or observances now exist as a substantive aggregate, and are assumed to be precisely known to an aristocratic order or caste.' This is the stage of unwritten law; knowledge of the principles is retained by being kept by a limited number.

Interestingly, it appears that the aristocratic order or caste in England was the judges: 'It is quite true that there was once a period at which the English common law might reasonably have been termed unwritten. The elder English judges did really pretend to knowledge of rules, principles, and distinctions which were not entirely revealed to the bar and to the lay public.'

iii) *Codes*

Next we arrive at the period of the codes - this is when written and published laws replace usages deposited with the recollection of a privileged oligarchy. This is not an era of change, but rather a period at which (because of the invention of writing) the usages are written down as a better method of storage. In Roman law, the Twelve Tables, and in England the gradual move to written law reports, represent the 'codes' stage.

Static societies stop there, and only progressive societies move on. The major difference of the next three stages from the first three is that they are stages of deliberate change. Most of the changes in the content of law in those first stages were the result of spontaneous development – in the (to that time, and to Maine's possibly paternal eye?) very few progressive societies, deliberate attempts are made to alter the law. Social necessities and social opinion are always in advance of the law; to attempt to close the gap, there are three instrumentalities. While one or other may be omitted, their historical order (per Maine) is always as follows.

As stated, it is at this stage that static societies cease their legal development. Further, according to Maine, the progression through the foregoing three stages will be spontaneous. Any further development will require definite acts. Maine identified three further stages, taking account of the development of law to the stage at which he was writing. These are:

iv) *Legal fictions*

That is 'any assumption which conceals, or affects to conceal, the fact that a rule of law has undergone alteration, its letter remaining unchanged, its operation being modified'. Examples would be false allegations in writs to give a court jurisdiction (eg the growth of contract actions from assumpsit pleas) and the Roman 'fiction' (a false averment by the plaintiff which the defendant may not traverse).

This device is now not needed: its day is 'long since gone by'.

v) *Equity*

The development of a separate body of rules, existing alongside the original law and claiming superiority over it by virtue of an inherent sanctity, is a second mode of progress and change. Such a body grew up under the Roman praetors, and the English chancellors.

vi) *Legislation*

The final stage of the development sequence. It is the enactments of a legislature (either an autocratic prince, or a sovereign assembly); these enactments are authoritative because of the authority of the body, and not (as with equity) because of something inherent in the content of the principles. In modern terminology, the authority of the enactments is 'content independent'.

This six-stage development is of the form of law: Maine saw a parallel movement in the context of law in progressive societies from status to contract: 'The movement of the progressive societies has been uniform in one respect. Through all the course, it has been distinguished by the gradual dissolution of family dependency, and the growth of individual obligation in its place. The individual is steadily substituted for the family.' Slavery has been replaced by the contractual servant-master relationship: and women and sons are no longer subject to the authority of their husbands or parents, but can enter contracts themselves. Of course, minors and lunatics cannot: they are still subject to their status, but only because they lack the judgment to make contracts.

In a famous passage, Maine says 'we may say that the movement of the progressive societies has hitherto been a movement from status to contract'.

11.3   Evaluation of Maine

In a single sentence, we may evaluate Maine's contribution to jurisprudence by saying that while his conclusions have not proved (on further examination and evidence) to be correct or to have stood the test of time, his scientific and empirical method was the forerunner of much modern jurisprudence and sociology.

The sequential development of a legal system has been greatly doubted. Malinowski in *Crime and Custom in Savage Society* reveals that considerable latitude is inherent in the content of primitive peoples' customary practices. It is not clear that primitive societies move through the first three stages, nor that they are static (studies of some primitive tribes show use of legislation, for example); nor is it clear that the Anglo-Roman experience of fictions and equity as the first two progressive stages is universally experienced. An evolution along the six-stage pattern should not be expected for every legal system. Anthropological studies have now somewhat discredited Maine's conclusions or at the least led to a thorough reappraisal of the findings.

Perhaps the problem was that Maine sought to identify a pattern – a law of the historical development of law – and that he sought such a pattern of legal development through a comparative examination of a few different systems. Of necessity some of this research was second hand, eg his study of the Old Testament (he could not have engaged in a field study!). However, while it has been said that many of his conclusions are now doubted, his method provided the framework for the early anthropological studies, many of which set out to prove or disprove his findings. He can be seen then as an inspiration for anthropology which only really developed into a separate branch of learning after his work pointed the way.

On the 'status to contract' movement, criticism has centred on later developments taken to disprove the movement. The Welfare State, employment protection, statutory implied terms in contracts etc – all relatively recent developments – are evidence, it is said, that we have moved back to status. This is not an argument which strictly hits Maine, who was talking of developments up to that date: in any case surely these pieces of legislation are making the individuals' freedom to contract more real? If I am contracting with a monopoly and must use their written terms, am I really 'contracting' at all? Was a nineteenth century factory hand really 'free' to bargain with the factory owner?

Clearly there has been a change since the 'laissez-faire' of the nineteenth century; it does not seem to be too difficult to argue that it furthers the movement Maine saw, rather than reverses it.

Finally, we must emphasise that Maine was the start of anthropological and sociological studies of law. His particular conclusions have been discredited; his influence was immense. His view of history was, according to Dias, more balanced than that of others of his time. This is particularly so with von Savigny whose mystical theory we shall now consider.

11.4   Von Savigny

Savigny was a Prussian aristocrat, writing in the first half of the nineteenth century in reaction to what any aristocrat in Europe would have regarded as the excesses of the French revolution, in particular their method of dealing with the French aristocracy. Not peculiar to von Savigny, he was hence very much a man of his time, influenced by, and absorbing, many current ideas and feelings. This perspective ought not to be lost on those reading his work.

a) Intellectually, the eighteenth century had been dominated by the Age of Reason, and the 'natural rights' doctrine. The reaction against reason took two forms. One, positivism, we have already considered; the other was the romantic movement, based on feeling and imagination in the arts, literature and learning.

b) One particular writer who foreshadowed Savigny's thought was Herder, who stressed that each nation and era had its own unique character. This character and the national spirit ('volksgeist') should not have a universal natural law imposed on it, since this would affect its free development. The idea of a unique national spirit which must be respected is the basis of much of what Savigny says.

c) One reason for the reaction against the Age of Reason, etc, was its part as an origin of the French Revolution. Antipathy to all things French was also important in Savigny's rejection of the idea of imposing the French 'Code Napoleon' on German law: it was to stop this development that Savigny wrote.

d) Finally, the long drawn-out Napoleonic Wars had increased nationalism throughout Europe, and particularly in Germany where anti-French feeling was strong. His *On the Vocation of Our Age for Legislation and Jurisprudence* contains a powerful argument against codification and in particular the proposal by Thibaut to adopt the Code Napoleon in Prussia. Briefly, his argument was that the character and national spirit (*volksgeist*) should not have a universal natural law imposed upon it. Savigny's central idea was that law is an expression of the will of the people; it does not come from deliberate legislation but as a gradual development of the common consciousness of the nation. He expressed it thus, 'The spirit of the people gives birth to positive law' and in another passage, 'The nature of any particular system of law was a reflection of the spirit of the people who evolved it.'

e) Savigny saw the historical development of law as follows:

    i) Law originates in custom which expresses national uniqueness. The principles of law come from beliefs of people.

    ii) At the pinnacle stage juristic skills are added – codification, articulating the volksgeist, merely giving technical and detailed expression to the volksgeist.

    iii) Decay.

f) More important than his historical development notion are the underlying implications of his theory. These are:

    i) Law is a matter of the subconscious.

    ii) Law making should follow the course of historical development.

    ii) Custom is superior to law which must conform to the common consciousness.

    iii) Volksgeist cannot be criticised for what it is, namely the standard by which laws are to be judged.

    iv) If law is a reflection of the volksgeist law could only be understood by tracing its history.

It would be appropriate to examine his theory in more depth. Since Savigny was opposing codification, a good starting point is his attitude to reform and codification. He was not opposed to either reform or codification, but for them to be successful the strands of development and continuity in the country's laws had to be understood.

A major feature of his theory was that the law was the expression of the spirit of the people, the 'volksgeist'. Law did not come from deliberate acts of legislation, but from a gradual development of the 'common consciousness' of the nation, which is reflected in judicial decisions, and should be reflected in legislation. The time for codification is when the legal system has added the technical skill of specialist lawyers to the nation's convictions.

Such views are strange to the English reader and it may therefore be appropriate to include here a few extracts from von Savigny in order that, as it were, he may speak for himself. Thus he wrote:

    'In the general consciousness of a people lives positive law and hence we have to call it people's law. It was by no means to be thought that it was the particular members of the people by whose arbitrary will, law was brought forth ... Rather it is the spirit of a people living and working in common in all the individuals, which gives birth to positive law, which is therefore to the consciousness of each individual not accidentally but necessarily one and the same ...'

'When we regard the people as a natural unity and not merely as the subject of positive law, we ought not to think only of individuals comprised in that people at any particular time; that unity rather runs through generations constantly replacing one another, and thus it unites the present with the past and the future. This constant preservation of law is conditioned by, and based upon, the not sudden but ever gradual change of generations ... '

From his study of Roman law and its history, Savigny concluded that law originates in custom, with the work of lawyers a later step. In fact, for both law and nations he saw a three-stage developmental process. First, principles of law from the convictions of the people, second, law reaches its pinnacle, with juristic skills added to these convictions. It is at this stage that codification is desirable, to retain the perfection of the system. The third stage is one of decay.

The juristic skills in the second stage, do not, according to Savigny, pull law away from its customary roots. The jurists are an actual part of the people, and represent the whole: 'The law is in the particular consciousness of this order, merely a continuation and special unfolding of the people's law – in outline it continues to live in the common consciousness of the people, the more minute cultivation and handling of it, is the special calling of the order of jurists.'

As has been noted, legislation does not play an important role. It is in fact inferior to custom, and often is just a speeding up of the gradual process of assimilation of real norms and institutions into the legal framework.

11.5 Evaluation of von Savigny

We should not doubt the important point inherent in Savigny's version of historicism. The particular history, situation and values of a country do manifest themselves in that country's laws in many ways. In the UK, for example, one thinks of rules about the Monarchy, the House of Lords, the Privy Council: in fact for many countries their constitutional laws and conventions will have been shaped by history and political values. Many other examples could be found.

However, it is clear that this truth is obscured by the obvious flaws in Savigny's discussion of the 'volksgeist'. The whole concept of the 'volksgeist', the spirit of the people, is difficult to accept for most societies. Nineteenth century Germany may have fitted the concept, but it is hard to think of a modern country of which the same can be said. Many countries have groups of different races and different cultures, different religions or totally different political persuasions: differing 'spirits' exist even in countries with strongly totalitarian governments (eg Poland). While Savigny allowed for 'inner circles' of groups and localities within a country, his theory cannot accommodate these many countries where a 'choice' of 'spirits' exists.

To be more specific with examples: when 'Jim Crow' legislation discriminating against negroes in the USA flourished, was that part of the 'Volksgeist'? Is the apartheid legislation in South Africa part of the 'volksgeist' too? The strongest churches in Europe seem to exist in Eastern Europe: is the legally-imposed Communism (atheistic, of course) part of 'the spirit of the people'? What would Savigny have made of the laws of Nazi Germany?

Further points of criticism should be mentioned. According to Savigny, the technical law which is the result of the juristic skills is as much part of the 'volksgeist' as the 'common convictions' of the first stage of development. It might be easy to fit laws against murder into the mould of common consciousness, and other types of laws – family laws, for example, allowing divorce but not abortion. Note, however, that some of these laws appear to be universal (and so not unique to one 'volksgeist'): only the details differ from society to society. Can the same really be said for technical institutions, such as the fee simple, the secret trust, promissory estoppel, bills of lading? And tax legislation? Also, what about those laws which seem to be contrary to the common consciousness – the abolition of capital punishment, allowing homosexual acts, entering the EEC, are all English examples which spring readily to mind.

The reply that Savigny might give to those examples could be that they corrupt the proper historical process, as deliberate law-making out of tune with the common spirit is a mistake. Surely though, deliberate law-making (by both legislature and courts) to lead public opinion in new directions (and to introduce technical laws which the 'common consciousness' has not concerned itself with) is an aspect of the legal experience – particularly of modern systems – which the Savigny theory underplays. The abolition of capital punishment, perhaps, can be seen as an attempt to educate people, and change the customary way of thought; similarly to an extent the introduction by legislation of the Welfare State.

It could be argued that in certain circumstances there are laws which do indeed reflect the constitution which is a political development. Take the example of the personal status laws in the Republic of Ireland. There that country has a strong Catholic tradition and the vast majority of its citizens are observant Catholics. Its laws forbid divorce, abortion and contraception. Is this a particular manifestation of that country's volksgeist? Perhaps the concept of the volksgeist identifies a continuity in tradition in any society but it suffers from very serious consequences. It assumes that every people is an identifiable entity possessing a separate metaphysical personality. On the applied level this has disastrous consequences for humanity. It allows for those who would argue that the involvement of those outside the volk leads to a corruption of the sacred volksgeist and enables those people so arguing to call for the exclusion or worse of those perceived of as corrupters. The examples of Nazi Germany's treatment of the Jews and of South Africa's treatment of non whites demonstrates this point. It is not here argued that von Savigny was a racist in the modern sense of the word but it can be attributed to his writings that they laid the intellectual groundwork for racial purity theorists that were to follow him.

It is also possible to raise several more specific points in critical evaluation of von Savigny's mystical theory. One could identify many universal laws, eg against murder are not unique to a given volksgeist. It could be stated that to explain technical laws as being developed by juristic skills from a revelation of the volksgeist is fanciful – it rather reduces the draftsmen into nothing more than mediums at some circus.

Savigny extrapolated his volksgeist notion into a sweeping universal and treated it as discoverable – thus adopting an a priori preconception.

There exists some evidence which shows that codes have been transposed without difficulty, eg Egypt's adoption of French codes which seem to work well there, yet the two 'people' cannot be more different in background, culture etc. See also Lipstein's study of the reception into Turkey of Western laws under Kemal Ataturk. This however does not entirely defeat the argument that Savigny was making. Perhaps his theory could be likened to a medical analogy. He stated that reforms that went against the stream of the volksgeist would be bound to fail. In the same way it might be argued to follow the analogy that a body will reject an organ that is transplanted but which is incompatible with the body system. He was not engaged in a rejection of all reform. Indeed he would admit reform if it was based on historical research that showed that it would be compatible with the volksgeist.

It is not clear who the 'volk' are whose 'geist' determines the law nor is it clear whether the volksgeist may have been shaped by the law rather than vice versa. This theory ignores the point that law has an educative function such as the Sexual Offences Act 1967 among other measures of the first two Wilson governments that were designed to change perceptions and attitudes – in the example cited towards homosexuality. In pluralistic societies such as exist in most parts of the world today it really seems somewhat irrelevant to use the concept of the volksgeist as the test of validity.

Savigny venerated the past without regard to its suitability to the present, eg in Roman law the notion of privity of contract would not admit 'negotiable instruments'. Generally although Romanticists look to history their concern is with the present. Perhaps the essence of their point is that the national character influences some types of laws more than others and in particular those concerned with personal status.

One might conclude this evaluation with the words of Dias who put it thus, 'Savigny's work, on the whole, was a salutory corrective to the methods of the natural lawyers. He did grasp a valuable truth about the nature of law, but ruined it by overemphasis.'

12 EMPIRICAL METHODS IN JURISPRUDENCE 5: ANTHROPOLOGICAL JURISPRUDENCE

12.1   Introduction

In the last chapter we looked at the historical school and the works of Sir Henry Maine. One of Maine's great contributions was to prompt others to study the 'law' of primitive societies, to see if they reflected his, or another, pattern of evolutionary development. Maine was only correct if study could show that primitive, static societies did in fact go through his first three stages of development, and then progressed no further. As we shall see, many of the studies that have followed, have invalidated Maine's sequence, but that does not deprive him of the achievement of being the first in a new and important field.

Anthropology has obvious links with sociology. Maine was also a forerunner of that field, the whole historical/anthropological approach emphasising that law differs with different societies, and at different times gave an impetus to consideration of how society affects law, and what part law plays in society. Further, the pattern of development in the two fields bears an overall similarity: early pioneers in the field, leading to studies often very much from a legal point of view (cf sociological jurisprudence), overtaken by studies from a wider viewpoint (cf sociology of law) and attempts to answer the general questions which caused the interest in the first place.

There are two points to bear in mind as we look briefly through the history and development of the anthropological 'school'. Does looking at 'law' in primitive societies help us to understand them? Perhaps, more important, does it help us to understand our own societies and to be better able to analyse properly our own concept of law?

Harris in *Legal Philosophies* identified two approaches to the study of primitive law. Firstly, the study of primitive society using conceptions of law derived from our own society. Secondly, to mould a conception of law broad enough to encompass the ways in which primitive peoples themselves see their own arrangements.

12.2   The anthropological 'school'

No attempt will be made to cover all the writers, viewpoints and contributions of the 'school' (this writer had the 'honour' of studying this topic for an entire term during his undergraduate degree course); rather, an overview of major figures and the sequence of development will be tried.

a) *Maine et al*

Maine and other early anthropologists in Germany and the USA were much influenced by the evolutionary fervour produced by Darwin's *Origin of Species*, and produced grand schemes of development of law, with different systems for different types of development (cf Durkheim, chapter 10).

While most 'researchers' in the period immediately following Maine depended mainly on secondhand knowledge, not actually observing in situ themselves, two things were discovered of great importance. In even the simplest societies, regularities of behaviour could be observed, and yet often these societies had no visible means of enforcement. These discoveries open up the questions still central to legal anthropology; how does social control work in such societies? Do different forms of organisation and control go with certain stages of development in, or types of, societies?

The basic answer of early researchers such as Rivers was that 'obedience' to the regulations or customs was automatic and unthinking: later anthropologists have criticised this conclusion. It seems at least strongly affected by 'ethnocentrism', ie a bias towards the forms and culture of one's own culture – in this case, our own English-type forms of law, with courts, Parliament, statutes, etc. 'Ethnocentrism' involves looking at the situation in the primitive societies through the eyes of an Englishman, and attempting to recognise courts, rules, prisons, or their equivalents. Often, in these early and later times, a definition of 'law' was chosen, in an attempt to categorise and arrange the material provided by the primitive societies.

Anthropology is not just about law, indeed law represents a very small part of anthropology. It should therefore be borne in mind that we are examining a relatively minor part of a very wide discipline.

b) *The two approaches*

Ethnocentrism was a great problem with early theories, and has remained one since. It has two distorting effects. First, if we define 'law' in order to decide which material in a society to study and write about, we will tend to distort that material by taking it out of its context, ignoring its relationship to other normative material in that society; and second, when we try to fit the material into categories to explain it, we will again distort it, by arranging it in ways that suit us rather than the material and the way it is used by and appears to the society itself.

An early example of this was Evans-Pritchard's study of the Nuer people; he said that they had no 'law' because there was nothing to fit the definition of law as social control through systematic application of force by society: no one had the authority to adjudicate. By looking for western institutions and concepts via that definition of law, Evans-Pritchard's view of the material was distorted.

Malinowski's study of Trobriand Islanders, *Crime and Custom in Savage Society*, was a major step forward. He actually studied the islanders by personal observation, so that his material was authentic; and he strongly criticised ethnocentric factors in earlier works. His own conclusions have themselves been criticised; from his studies, he concluded that the observable behaviour came about not automatically, but via continuous control mechanisms, especially the ever-present possibility of the withdrawal from reciprocal economic arrangements which were central to the islanders' livelihood. Such reciprocity he identified as the identifying characteristic of law.

Simon Roberts, in his introduction to legal anthropology *Order and Dispute,* has identified two main approaches following Malinowski: 'law-centred' studies inspired by western jurisprudence is one approach, and wider studies of order and dispute is the other.

c) *The first approach*

The law-centred studies are those which attempt to define law, and how the simpler societies fit into that picture. Obviously the criticisms of ethnocentrism mentioned above could well apply. Apart from Malinowski's definition mentioned above, Bohannan sees laws as institutionalised customary norms (custom redefined in legal institutions, and turned upon social conflicts custom can't resolve 'double institutionalisation'), Gluckmann as being defined by reference to recognition by judges, Hoebel by coercive enforcement, and so on. It is proposed to examine these in more detail and then to draw a general conclusion.

i) *Malinowski*

In addition to the foregoing about Malinowski, it can here be added that while primitive communities generally do not have any specialist vocabulary in order to distinguish legal from non-legal rules in the manner available in the language of an advanced society, Malinowski in *Crime and Custom in Savage Society* sought to identify some crucial feature of primitive life by applying some distinguishing characteristic of 'law' which for him was reciprocity. He identified the following characteristics:

1) Rules are felt and regarded as obligations and rightful claims.

2) Rules are sanctioned not by mere psychological motive but by a definite social machinery of binding force.

3) Social machinery is based upon mutual dependence and realised in the equivalent arrangement of reciprocal services.

ii) *Bohannon*

Bohannon in *The Differing Realms of Law* (1965) has criticised Malinowski's approach as being too undiscriminating between customary norms as a whole and law in particular. He preferred to define law in terms of institutionalised customary norms. According to him 'Law comes into being when customary, reciprocal obligations become further institutionalised in a way that society continues to function on the basis of rules.'

Thus according to Bohannon, for law to work there must be:

1) a way of disengaging disputes in a particular institution and engaging them in a legal institution;

2) a framework for handling the dispute and coming to a decision;

3) a way of re-engaging it into a previous non-legal institution.

Bohannon maintains that this process of double institutionalisation explains why law is behind contemporary thought in society. The problem with this explanation is that there is no central focus in primitive society to facilitate this re-institutionalisation.

iii) *Gluckman*

Gluckman in *The Judicial Process Among the Barotse of Northern Rhodesia* (1967) shows that it is obedience which is contemplated, not disobedience, in a society that rests on reciprocity but also possesses a mechanism to deal with disputes, which he observed had developed 'the reasonable man test' quite independently of the English judiciary. This assertion has given rise to much dispute and is discussed below. Gluckman's study identified the task of dispute resolution for the Barotse as involving:

1) reconciliation rather than ordering of sanctions;

2) sanctions will be applied only where reconciliation has failed or is not possible.

The obedience to the custom rested on the reciprocity of services.

iv) *Pospisil*

Pospisil in *Anthropology of Law* suggests that primitive law is essentially a matter of degree which can be isolated by reference to a cluster of differentiating criteria among which he listed:

1) authority

2) universality

3) the sense of obligation

4) sanctions.

He did however focus on the disposal of disputes rather than behavioural guidance.

v) *Hoebel*

Hoebel in *The Law of Primitive Man* saw coercive enforcement as the sole badge of law. He observed that 'The more civilised man becomes, the greater men's need for law – law is but a response to social needs.'

In another illuminating passage he stated that 'Without a sense of community there is no law – without law there cannot for long be a community.'

Hoebel listed the four functions of law for primitive man as:

1) defining relationships amongst the members of society;

2) taming naked force and directing it to the maintenance of order;

3) the disposition of trouble cases;

4) the redefinition of relationships as the conditions of life change.

Harris finds this list more illuminating than those concentrating on the content or the institutions of primitive 'law'. Hoebel criticises both Maine and Hart's view of the static nature of primary rules (due to the absence of a secondary rule of change). In a customary society of the ideal type there would be no perceived tension between what is practised and what is thought to be right. Harris further observes that there would be no self conscious creation of rules. This is however an ideal type from which the real world differs.

It has been pointed out that if the community being studied does not distinguish law from other customary norms, then why should the observer? Barkun in *Law Without Sanctions* argues that our notion of law is too professionally orientated. In a manner similar to Ehrlich's 'living law' approach, he sees law as a product of the society and does not confine it to the courtrooms.

The extent to which these studies are ethnocentric and flawed by that, varies. On the one hand can be put studies prepared for the practical purposes of informing western officials, with the job of enforcing local customs and laws, what those laws were: these studies tended to be lists of laws in English type categories, and therefore very much subject to the second pitfall of ethnocentrism (distorting information by putting it in inappropriate western categories). On the other hand, even some studies which confined themselves to 'law' and what were seen as legal institutions were of value and interest.

Malinowski studied why people followed the patterns of behaviour in the society studied: Gluckmann and the Llewellyn-Hoebel study *The Cheyenne Way* looked at what happened to disputes and conflicts. From the latter, we can see that even primitive societies do alter the law (there, as a result of disputes); Gluckmann's study of the Barotse in Northern Rhodesia explored how rules actually affected decision making.

In considering language Bohannon maintains that one cannot juxtapose one language to another, since there is no possibility of true translation this would have the effect of negating the use of language. Bohannon denies the possibility of cross-cultural knowledge and in order to reinforce this descends into the pessimism of infinite relativism. Bohannon then speaks of the use of a folk system relying heavily on the use of folk terminology. Gluckman developed an analytical model in an attempt to avoid stagnation, engage in comparative studies and educate against ethnocentrism. In doing so Gluckman may have been presumptive in that his descriptions are not total (is it possible to have total descriptions?) and that therefore his analysis is engaged too early. Further, his description stage suffers from the problem of ethnocentrism as in the eyes of the describer rests the description. This can be represented on the following diagramatic representation of Gluckman's analytical model.

Gluckman's analytical model

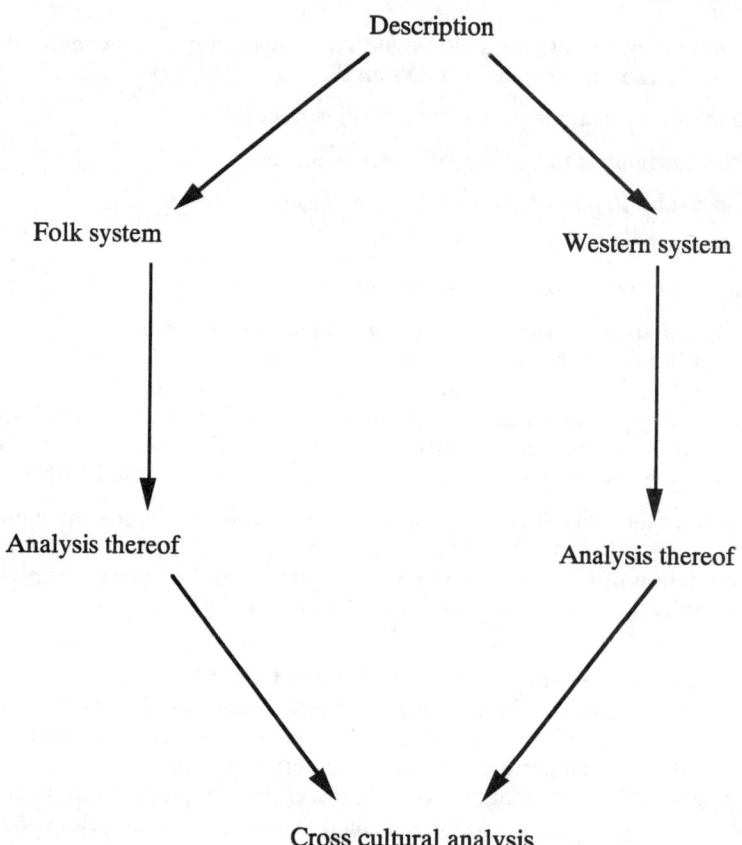

Description

Folk system   Western system

Analysis thereof   Analysis thereof

Cross cultural analysis

d) *The second approach*

If a wider approach is taken to avoid the danger of ethnocentrism created by using a definition of law (which danger does not always, as we have seen, actually occur), a similar problem is reached. Some boundary to our study must be set: if we are not imposing our own limited view of law, we must still decide which features of the simple societies we want to study. Roberts suggests that the best framework is to look at order – the way order is preserved in society; and dispute – how disputes are considered and solved. Freed from the corrupting influence of our ideas and rules, courts and coercion, a more complete and correct picture of primitive societies can be acquired, without distortion.

Studies following this wider approach have found wide variety between societies. Various factors push them into considering the processes of the society and how they affect the individual and how he views them; particularly, disputes are seen as a necessary part of society, and are considered from a longer-term perspective: attempts to compromise, various forms of outside intevention, and how the society returns to normal. In some societies, discussion is not used to settle disputes – force is!

These wider studies enable better perspectives to be gained, and ultimately answers the questions of how societies are controlled, and whether different legal mechanisms and organisations are present in different societies.

12.3 Evaluation

The outline of anthropological thought related to law given above is sketchy and brief, but raises interesting topics. The two approaches are complementary, I think; the wider based studies of dispute processes (particularly in societies without institutions and formal rules) introducing an element missed by narrower attempts to study the law and legal system – even those that manage to avoid the dangers of parochialism. It is interesting to ask whether more is learnt about primitive societies or our own by the various writings. While much can be learned about the societies themselves, a lot can also be learned about ourselves. The wider perspective enables us to see that law is not unique, and that our type of legal system is far from being so. Primitive societies with their wide variety of methods show us that courts and strict laws are not the only, or even the best, way to control society and deal with disputes. Above all, perhaps the importance of negotiation and conciliation found in many studies contains a lesson we could certainly benefit from.

Although there is also a wide variety of content of 'laws' in primitive societies, it does seem clear that something like Hart's 'minimum content of natural law' is a universal feature.

Findings such as Llewellyn's and Hoebel's (that the Cheyenne did create new rules) and the decreasing attention paid to evolution, have led to Maine's actual conclusions not now being accepted. The continuing vitality of the anthropological approach remains as a monument to his innovative work.

I am of the opinion that it would be more useful to address an evaluation of anthropology of law in the form of an analysis of its usefulness to the student of law in an advanced post industrialised society. This is really the only possible question that can be asked on this topic, however the question is actually worded.

12.4 Anthropology of law – a waste of time?

Whilst studying anthropology of law the relevance of the topic is often called into question by students. An examination of both the potential contribution of anthropology on the macro and micro levels would be particularly imformative. There are many sceptics yet it is acknowledged that there are some lessons that can be drawn from the study of the law and legal systems of more primitive peoples and that there have been instances when these lessons could have been well learned in our own society.

A large number of students of jurisprudence, who while they may have their doubts about the whole topic of jurisprudence as a compulsory paper on an LLB degree would most certainly be sceptical of the inclusion within the syllabus of the study of anthropology of law. The basis of that scepticism lies in their view that anthropology has nothing to add to an understanding of our own law and legal system other than to provide a light diversion into the world of *National Geographic* magazine. I would dissent from that view but would nonetheless admit that there are important limitations to the study of anthropology of law. These limitations would not in my view be so strong as to negate the usefulness of the study of anthropology. In holding such a view I would not restrict the usefulness of anthropology to merely providing an understanding of how other people organise their legal systems, interesting though that itself may be. Even those who regard anthropology as a waste of time would concede this point. Having said that it is admitted that there may well be better ways to spend one's time when engaged in the study of law in society. That is not the same as saying that anthropology is a waste of time because anthropology, it is submitted, can add a dimension to the study of law in our own society that cannot be found in any other discipline.

It is at once clear that the central issue involved is the legitimacy of cross-cultural comparisons and the adequacy of drawing conclusions for our own society from anthropological studies. It is on this premise that I will assess whether anthropological studies do have much to offer the student of jurisprudence.

At a funeral oration for the Athenians who died fighting for Athens, Pericles said, 'Our institutions are not borrowed from those around us; they are our own, the creation of Athenian statesmen; an example and not a copy.' I would take the view that that quotation has a lot to offer on the legitimacy of the application of 'lessons' from anthropological studies to our own society. I take Pericles to say that a conclusion about cheese will not assist in an understanding of wine. I will however indicate those areas where it is my view that anthropological studies may contribute to a greater understanding of our own society, including the legal system.

One of the main difficulties with anthropological studies is the tendency that they have towards ethnocentricity. This involves the study of others through concepts developed by ourselves. On the other hand it could be said that on the micro level at least, phenomena in our society also occur in primitive societies. In primitive society the study of these common phenomena may be more simple since they are less likely to be complicated and obscured by the complexities of an advanced industrial society. This view looks to the study of primitive society as if it were a laboratory for the understanding of our own society. The validity of this approach in itself is highly suspect.

Even if this 'laboratory thesis' is accepted, then the scientist/anthropologist will still have to develop a mechanism for the avoidance of the tendency towards ethnocentrism by which the scientist will largely invalidate his study as he takes law out of its context and arranges his observations according to preconceived yet inapplicable notions. Malinowski attempted to get around this defect in his study *Crime and Custom in Savage Society*. Perhaps the only effective way is through the avoidance of translation! In his study of the Barotse of Northern Rhodesia (now Zambia), Max Gluckman came across the notion of 'the reasonable man' which he observed was employed in the same way as in our courts to arrive at an objective test by which to assess the conduct of the defendant. Bohannon isolated the problem as being one of language, hence the point above about translations. He claimed that Gluckman analysed the Barotse according to the doctrines of the common law which is clearly not applicable to them. Bohannon insists that if there is to be any potential for anthropology to truly understand any tribe then it must use tribal terms and not western concepts. The solution proposed of developing a computer language is unsatisfactory as it would have to be programmed by someone who has his own notions and certainly more importantly, it would be read and understood by comparison with already existing notions in the original language of the reader.

I do not think that our advanced post industrial society developed tribunals because Laura Nader found that the Zapatec Indians had developed something performing a similar task to what she identified as a tribunal, any more than I would think that because the Eskimos resolve disputes through 'song contests' by which the person who uses the best insults wins, that would be an appropriate method of dispute resolution in our society. Yet it clearly is adequate for their society.

Some of the approaches adopted in the anthropological studies may be of use in an understanding of our own society but these could well have developed without engaging in anthropological studies.

Although Durkheim tried to make a distinction between mechanical solidarity and organic solidarity type societies, it has to be observed that western industrial society has both restitutive and repressive laws and that both of these are expanding. That fact does not necessarily defeat the usefulness of Durkheim's model in helping us to understand the difference between the two types of laws, but the conclusion drawn by Durkheim has been proved wrong.

If the models used in the anthropological method from primitive societies are applied to advanced post industrial society then that exercise may well enhance our understanding of our own society through sociological inquiry. It is my view though, that the conclusions reached in the anthropological studies are inapplicable to our own society so far as the institution of law is concerned and I take it that that must be the prime area of interest of the jurisprudence student. In *The Law of Primitive Man* Hoerbel has said that 'the more civilised man becomes, the greater men's need for law – law is but a response to social needs.' He thought that the institution of law was a necessity. He observed that without a sense of community there is no law and that without law there cannot for long be a community. The Andaman Islanders (in the Indian Ocean) have no suprafamilial authority. There social control is exercised by and within the family. However, in our society the individual is independent of both the family and the clan. Such a mechanism as is applied in the Andaman Islands would be wholly inadequate here.

It ought to be said that anthropological studies can show us that conclusions that are relevant to primitive societies are not relevant in our advanced society. Felsteiner's study, *Influences of Social Organisation and Dispute Processing* shows that the form of dispute settlement flows from the social organisation. He distinguished between TCRS ('technologically complex, rich society') and TSPS ('technologically simple, poor society') and observes that cross comparisons between these are of very limited value. Perhaps von Savigny had a point in this regard when he noted that each society develops the law it needs and that indeed law is a reflection of the particularities of each society (the volksgeist).

Anthropological studies do have certain advantages not least of which is that it provides us with an understanding of law in societies other than our own. Certain heuristic devices have also been developed through anthropological studies and these may well be useful models for a study of law in our own society. At the micro level anthropological studies have pointed to the working of some aspects of our own society. Gluckman's model of testing not only cases, which undergo a transformation when taken to court, but also looking at rules and praxis (the way people act under the law) does not however explain the purpose of law but is useful as far as it goes.

Take for example Gulliver's negotiation and adjudication models where he observed that in adjudication the dispute is settled on a 'zero/sum' basis where one party wins and the other loses whereas in negotiation the dispute is settled on a 'mini/max' principle where both parties minimise their loss and maximise their gain. Perhaps in industrial relations (and in particular the fiasco surrounding the Industrial Relations Act 1971) where the relationship is one of reciprocity a lesson might have been learnt from anthropological studies that in such circumstances adjudication is not an appropriate mechanism for dispute resolution and preference given to negotiation. The industrial relations court had an impossible task, not because of the law, but because of the nature of the reciprocal relationship that the law was attempting to regulate in a compulsory adjudicatory method.

Rather than focus considerable attention and resources on anthropological studies it would be preferable to pay greater attention to sociological inquiry into our own society from the point of view of the needs of the jurisprudence student. In particular one would look for an inquiry into the nature of our state; the form and function of law; the source, distribution and location of power in our society and the study of conflict in our society. Admittedly, these are rather parochial issues; however they represent a view that although lessons can be drawn from primitive societies such as that coercive law is not always the best dispute resolution technique, these lessons are already drawn and these anthropological studies merely cloak a conclusion in a robe of authority. Our society had already 'invented' tribunals long before Nader told us that they were a good way of resolving certain disputes.

I would conclude that the only really interesting anthropological study would be one carried out by a person from another type of society. His findings would tell us more about our own society than any anthropological study we would carry out on his society. I am therefore drawn to a conclusion that the insights to be gained from anthropological studies are of little advantage to the student of jurisprudence who is interested in studying the law in his own society.

13 MARXISM 1: NINETEENTH CENTURY AND APPLIED MARXISM

13.1   Introduction

To identify the 'genuine' Marxist attitude towards law is a difficult task. The writings of Marx (and Engels) have spawned as much diversity and factionalism as the Bible. The Marxist approach might, however, be summed up as being centred on a particular notion that society and history are governed largely by economic and material factors.

In common with other nineteenth century theories based upon social analysis, Marx's own views on law denied that it was autonomous or objectively separated from society. Law follows and reflects the material forces of society to an extent that he views ideas of legal objectivity as simply 'legal fetishism'. For this reason, a brief account of the Marxist theory is needed as a background to understanding Marxist jurisprudence.

13.2   The Hegelian dialectic

Marx and Engels' philosophy was based on the insights of Hegel who viewed all aspects of civilisation, including law, as having a defined place in the progress of the human mind towards freedom. He used as his model of historical progress the concept of the dialectic. The dialectic theorises that progress is a result of conflicting forces, in Hegel's theory, ideas. The clash of contradictory thesis and antithesis results in a sort of compromise called the synthesis. The synthesis is reacted to by another antithetical idea resulting in another synthesis. Thus, through the process of conflict society progresses towards the truth.

Marx was a law student and initially influenced by the German Historical School, although he moved towards the Hegelian left. The influence of Hess is apparent, who viewed law and morality as disposable when people are freed from their lack or self-awareness. Under the influence of Fuerbach, Marx adopted the view that Hegel had made a mistake in viewing the dialectic as one of ideas; instead ideas were the product of social life and as such the dialectic of history was one of social conflict.

Thus, Marx's dialectic materialism sees history as conflict resulting in a synthesis. Ideas are the awareness of the social situation and as such are a result of social conflict. Social conflict arises from economic differences; thus ideas, including law, are predominantly expressions of the economic conflict in society.

The processes of history see the development of feudalism, which historically resolves itself by dialectic means into capitalism. In feudal times the feudal lords dominated the means of production, land, and were therefore in conflict with serfdom. The development of better means of production results in a shift towards capitalism, where the bourgeoisie, owning the means of production, dominate the working class, the proletariat. Ultimately, this conflict will result in revolution of a violent or non-violent kind that will cause the overthrow of the bourgeoisie and bring about the dictatorship of the proletariat. thus, the means of production will be returned to the people who produce, resulting in the eradication of repression and a communist state, where neither state nor law will be necessary.

Since ideas are reflections of social conflict, they are incomplete and partisan. Law is simply an aspect of these false ideas or 'ideology'. The makers of law, as with other ideas, are subliminally influenced by social conflict. As a result law rides on the processes of historical materialism.

13.3   Law as superstructure

Marxism sees society divided into base and superstructure. The base is the actual relations between people involved in production, the economic structure of society. The dominant class in a society is the class that is the exploiter in these economic relationships. Superstructure represents:

a) A reflection of these relationships in legal and political forms.

b) The dominant class's view of the world.

c) The development of awareness of social conflict, resulting in a critique of the above.

Law represents a mirror of inequalities in society, often obscured by the ruling classes' presentation of it as impartial and detached. Thus, Marx speaks of the laws of contract. They seem as if there is an equality of bargaining power. However, the reality of relations of production is that the employer is more equal than the employee. The judge may believe that he is working with objective categories, but they are simply the product of the economic forces. Thus, law is 'false consciousness'.

Consequently, we can expect that in feudal society, where the emphasis is on the retention of land, that this will be the role of law. Equally, in capitalist society, commercial relationships will be much of the concern of law. This view is the 'crude materialist' approach. However, Marx and, to a greater extent, Engels, concede that other factors influence the base, such as tradition, which will be reflected in superstructural institutions such as law. Thus, the material and economic forces are the ultimate, rather than the only, determining factors in the progress of laws.

13.4   Law as ideology

Marx and Engels view opinions and beliefs about law as ideology. By this they mean, as Kolakowski puts it, 'false consciousness or an obfuscated mental process in which men do not understand the forces that actually guide their thinking, but imagine it to be governed by logic and intellectual influences.' Ideology might be the product of the dominant class, who are normally, by virtue of their opportunities, the dominant intellectual class. Thus, Victorian 'morality' might be one classic example of ideology. Equally, the commonly held views about the nature of the world are likely to be ideology, since these will normally be warped by a lack of awareness of social conflict. The broader contributions of the arts and sciences would to a certain extent fall into this category.

13.5   The tension between material forces and ideology

There is, to a certain extent, a contradiction between the influence of economic forces and the 'false' nature of legal ideology. Engels brought this contradiction out in his letter to Conrad Schmidt:

'The determining element in history is, in the last resort, the production and reproduction of real life. More than this neither Marx nor I have ever asserted. If therefore someone twists this into the statement that the economic element is the only determining one, he transforms it into a[n] absurd phrase. The economic situation is the basis but the various elements of the superstructure ... constitutions ... forms of law, and even the reflexes of all these actual struggles in the brains of the combatants: political, legal, philosophical theories ... and their further development into systems of dogma – all these exercise their influence on the course of historical struggles ...'

Thus, law can itself exert influence on the base in three ways:

a) Law has a crystallising effect that maintains traditions, customs and religious conceptions. These are restrictive on the achievement of awareness of class struggles and as such hold up the inevitable processes of history.

b) The more antagonistic the forces in society, the more law seeks to achieve a compromise of conflicting interests.

c) The demystification of law has a critical effect on raising class consciousness necessary for revolution.

Marx was not unaware that he himself was contributing to ideology and that his terms were quite frequently like those used by a 'feudal jurist'.

Thus, by the end of Marx's life, Engels commented, 'We the "revolutionaries", the "rebels", are thriving far better on legal methods than on illegal methods and revolt.'

However, although Marx and Engels see law as having a relative degree of autonomy, they scarcely give a definition of law, rather seeing it as:

a) An ideological cloak that hides the 'truth' about social conflict either by compromise or conservatism.

b) As an aspect of state control. The Marxist perspective of law is dependent on the Marxist conception of the state.

13.6   The state

Marx writes that 'The state acts as an intermediary in the foundation of all communal institutions and gives them political form. Hence there is an illusion that law is based on will, that is on will divorced from its real basis, free will.' The state is thus an 'illusionary community serving as a screen for the real struggles waged by classes against each other'. It is political in character and an instrument by which the real relationships in society can be controlled, either by the ruling class or on their behalf. 'Because the state arose from the need to hold class antagonisms in check, but because it arose, at the same time, amid the conflict of these classes, it is as a rule, the state of the most powerful, economically dominant class, which through the medium of the state, becomes also politically dominant, and thus acquires new means of holding down and exploiting the oppressed class.' So says Engels in the *Origin of the Family*, prompting the notion that the state, and its means, including law, is an instrument of class oppression.

However, where the struggle within society is strong, there may be a need to allow the state autonomy. Thus, the ruling class may, as was the case after the coup d'etat of Louis Napoleon, place the apparatus of state in the hands of an autonomous bureaucracy. The state is nonetheless a means of coercion and therefore alienates people and is alienated from people.

In summary therefore:

a) The state is a means for furthering economic domination.

b) The state acts to mediate in class tensions, maintaining the inequalities in society.

c) The state takes on a more or less autonomous role, depending on the relative strengths of classes in conflict in society.

d) The state is thus a means by which people are prevented from achieving genuine freedom.

In his earlier writings Marx expresses his views on bureaucracy: 'wherever the bureaucracy is a principle of its own, where the general interest of the state becomes a separate, independent and actual interest, there the bureaucracy will be opposed [to the cause of the citizen]'.

13.7 The withering away of the state

The state and its instruments, such as the judiciary, is in Marxist theory, was doomed by the dialectics of history. The state is a particular manifestation of the oppression of the ruling class. The ultimate overthrow of the ruling classes by the proletariat might employ the state as an instrument for bringing about total awareness, under the dictatorship of the proletariat. Lenin was to transform this idea when his time approached to apply Marxism. Ironically, Marx claimed not to be a Marxist since Marxism was to be applied revolutionary theory. He was perhaps wise to so distance himself.

13.8 The emergence of dichotomy

Marx's and Engels' philosophical theory was one open to multiple interpretations. Before we turn our attention to the main current of Russian Marxism, it is interesting to see how Marx's ideas had affected both believers and non-believers.

Kelsen, in *Socialism and the State,* criticises Marxism on the basis of its Utopian view that the state could be abolished, since law will be necessary until such time as humans are transformed into angels. In response, Adler, an Austro-Marxist, simply asserts that this is exactly what Marxism entails. It is this aspect of the Romantic ideal in Marxism that is perhaps abandoned in Leninism.

Lenin was faced with the practical problem of applying Marxism. For a while he had been in sympathy with the social democracy characteristic of people such as Kautsky, which advocated universal suffrage. However, certain conclusions became apparent to him, as Kolakowski points out:

'If law, for instance is "nothing but" a weapon in the class struggle, it naturally follows that there is no essential difference between the rule of law and an arbitrary dictatorship ... When his adversaries were able to point out that he was in conflict with something Marx had actually said – for example, that "dictatorship" did not mean arbitrary despotism – they were proving Marx's own inconsistency rather than Lenin's unorthodoxy.'

Lenin thus began to see the state and laws as means to ends, as instruments of the struggle for freedom. This contrasts with Marx, who saw the ends as predetermined by economics.

The dichotomy mentioned in the heading was thus between those who advocated the gradual reform of capitalism and the utilisation of the legacy of the bourgeois state, and the pragmatists, exemplified by Lenin.

13.9 Lenin's theoretical contribution

a) Lenin's ideal was a pure democracy, at first conditioned by coercion, but ultimately achieved without restraint. Equal pay and elected officials feature in his Utopian view in *Materials Relating to the Revision of the Party Programme*. The party would be the educating force, bringing the oppressed the self-awareness that would prompt the arrival of the socialist state. This would necessitate a 'transitional proletarian state'. However, it is his approach to law that concerns us. In the proletarian state the judiciary would be elected by the workers. However, Lenin's theoretical attitude to law was already less than Utopian from my bourgeois point of view.

b) Lenin had the following attitudes to law, that were built upon after the Russian revolution:

   i) Categories such as freedom and human value were to be qualified by the question of what class they serve. Thus, bourgeois freedom is a tool of the bourgeois class struggle.

ii) International law is not a matter of concern. Lenin would cite Clausewitz that 'War is simply the continuation of policy in another form.'

iii) Democracy and its institutions are simply the legal expression of class conflict. In the light of this, the bourgeois state should be smashed immediately to be replaced by the proletarian state that would wither away.

iv) The proletarian state is necessary to remove the traces of bourgeois values and as such democracy can only come about when capitalism has been eradicated by the dictatorship of the proletariat.

In *The Victory of the Cadets and the Tasks of the Workers' Party* he states 'Dictatorship means unlimited power, based on force, not on law.' He frequently reiterated this view.

v) The blueprint of this was found in his 1918 party programme:

'Abolition of parliamentarianism (as the separation of legislative from executive activity); union of legislative and executive state activity. Fusion of administration with legislation.'

vi) In a letter to Kursky after the revolution, Lenin wrote 'the courts must not ban terror ... but must formulate the motives underlying it, legalise it as a principle, plainly ...'

These principles were carried into action in the Russian revolution. This reformulation of Marxism might best be termed Marxist-Leninism. This doctrine of law was transmitted to Stalin, when Lenin died. It is interesting to note that the official support for Marxist-Leninism was only withdrawn in 1991.

13.10 Pashukanis

Pashukanis was the head of the department of legal studies in the Soviet Communist Academy. His *General Theory of Law and Marxism* is thought to be representative of the legal theory of the 'Thirties. He argues that, not only the content of legal norms, but the form of them, are intrinsically linked to 'fetishist commodity relations'. Law was created, therefore, as an instrument of trade that was extended to personal and other relationships. Legal relationships reduce humans to abstract juridical categories, according to Pashukanis. The continued existence of law in the USSR was, thus, a sign that the society was still in a transitory stage.

A similar approach is taken by Stuchka, who suggests that law is the weapon of class struggle and as such is necessary to fight hostile forces and saboteurs. Stuchka was a member of the Cheka, the Soviet secret police. The task of the Cheka was to fight against the forces that sought to overthrow the proletarian state. To further this end, Lenin had proposed an amendment to the criminal code which permitted draconian punishment for anyone whose statements might objectively serve anti-revolutionary forces. Ultimately, such a law is a strict liability catch-all! Such approaches became the norm under Stalin whose contribution to Marxism was the adding of numbers to a manual on the Marxist ideology and reducing the numbers of Soviet citizens by millions, which was termed 'socialist legality'.

13.11 Post-Stalin

Up until the 1990s, the Soviet government had not lost sight of the revolution and future communist state. They saw the Soviet Union as an 'all-people's state', and no longer a workers' state: the internal enemies of the workers are sufficiently under control for the state to be considered classless. The concept of a classless state, even an all-people's classless state, does however, run counter to the strict reading of Marx (the state comes from class division and inequality). Similarly, there is no justification in Marx for the 'developed socialist society' once claimed in the USSR as a necessary step on the road to communism.

Clearly, a communist state has not arrived in the USSR, and law has not 'withered away' even to the extent foretold by Lenin and Engels. The state remains important; so does law. The Soviets have given many reasons for the continued existence of the state and law. These may be summarised as follows:

a) Capitalist encirclement where there is an external physical threat. This was relied on by Lenin and Vyshinsky. The immediate post revolution experience of the USSR and the Nazi invasion lend force to this.

b) Law is an important lever in establishing the foundations upon which communism will be built. This is a notion developed by rather more sophisticated theorists Ioffe and Shargorodskii than existed at the time of Stalin.

c) Ideological tool enabling re-education of the masses who have been exposed to ideology

d) Parental law – inculcation of communist morality. There is lots of propaganda ensuring citizens are aware of the law, the aim being an internalisation process (cf Olivecrona), the law inculcating the dictates of communist morality. As Lloyd and Freeman point out in their *Introduction to Jurisprudence,* p 997, the legal process itself has an educational role. Courts go out to the provinces, and there is considerable lay participation. A question which arises here is why is there still a need for this seventy years after the revolution?

e) A more sophisticated and longer lasting explanation can be that law is necessary for the administration of a complex society and the central planning of the economy. These are reasons to which the question in (iv) above could not apply.

f) Because the process spoken of by Marx of the spread of the revolution has not taken place the USSR maintain that they require the state and law to act as a defence against any reassertion of bourgeois materialism.

13.12 Alternative 'schools' of Marxism

Whether the Soviet experience was applied Marxism or simply a totalitarian empire that adopted an ideology that suited it, is a matter of hot debate. The virtual collapse of the Soviet empire has witnessed that as with the failure of revolution to materialise in the West, the predictions of the Soviet ideologues was to be unfounded. We shall discuss the effects of these changes in the next chapter.

However, independently of the Soviet development, Marxism was and still continues to be an important analytical framework. It is worthwhile addressing some of the alternative conceptions of Marxism. This we shall do in the next chapter, since the Marxist trends that have developed in capitalist societies have been of use as critical, rather than political tools. It has been suggested by Lloyd and Freeman that it is possible to use the Marxist attitude towards law as a jurisprudential guide, without necessarily accepting the predictive aspects of the theory. It is submitted that in the light of recent developments, this is possibly the most useful way in which we can employ the Marxist perspective of law and state.

14 MARXISM 2: CONTEMPORARY TRENDS IN MARXISM

14.1   The failure of applied Marxism

It may well be argued that Marxism, like God, is dead. However, like religion Marxism claims considerable intellectual support. The experience of Marxism would seem to refute the intellectual adherence to the idea. In Eastern Europe the communist state has withered away in a manner not anticipated by Marx. In China, the crude Maoist Marxist theory is becoming diluted by capitalist reforms, while the recent experience of Ethiopia suggests that the Marxist state is not the reforming success anticipated even in the third world. However, it is easy for Marxists to argue that this is not 'real' Marxism, but the adoption of a label in order to sanction a different political regime. There are certainly contradictions, as witnessed by the Soviet experience. Whether these are the failings of the theory or corruptions of it, I will leave the student to judge.

a) *Ideology and economy*

Lenin differed from Marx in his belief that political power, rather than economic forces, could influence the coming of a socialist society. As a result, it might be suggested, the Russian revolution may not have been the outcome of the inevitable forces of materialist history, but an ideological coup. This argument would be suggesting that Russia was seeking to run before it could walk. Certainly, most Marxist states have developed in societies throwing off feudal or colonial power, rather than capitalist orders. However, Marx was aware in later life that Russia was a likely place for a communist revolution. Ideology, rather than historical materialism, was the dominant force behind most of these revolutions.

The Leninist-Marxism of the Soviet Union further 'subverted' the laws of history by restraining the development of production by centralised planning and under-investment. Much of the means of production in Soviet society has remained the same as it was in the distant past. Such restraint on technology is, to a certain extent, to restrain one of the essential elements in the evolutionary process of history according to Marx. However, it might also be said that the progress of society towards socialism will never happen because the constant advance of means of production through technology means that surplus capital will always be accrued. Thus, if a person in an unregulated socialist society invented a new way of manufacturing food more cheaply, that used less labour, he would exploit this and recreate capitalism. The only reason why Marx does not envisage this happening is because he believes that in a post-capitalist state everyone would act in harmony according to the maxim 'from each according to his means; to each according to his needs'. It must be submitted that this Romanticism is not an accurate reflection of human nature as it is now.

b) *The proletarian revolution*

Marx believed that it was only when the proletariat became 'aware' that the revolution would take place. However, the Soviet revolution happened before such awareness came about. It may even be suggested that such an awareness is not necessarily a feature of historical development into communism. The anti-communist revolution, although spearheaded by intellectuals, such as Havel in Czechoslovakia, is largely a proletarian one.

The development of a bureaucratic caste in Russia was a predictable part of the retention of the state structure. Lenin was aware of this himself, as was Stalin. However, their solution was the imposition of more bureaucracy. It may be submitted that, on the death of Stalin, there was a complete bureaucratic takeover and the subsequent legal reforms and limited 'rule of law' were merely to protect their interests. As we saw in the last chapter, Marx was well aware that the bureaucratisation of a state adds to, rather than detracts from, conflict in the state.

c) *The Soviet state*

Lenin's concept of the proletarian state which protects its own interests is in Marxist thinking inevitably self-perpetuating particularly when bureaucratised. The identification of the 'real' proletariat with the state is a feature reminiscent of the adoption of Natural Law theories such as divine right, to sanction older totalitarian regimes. Stalin stated that he was, himself, the proletariat. Furthermore, he believed that the proletariat in Russia were too uneducated to produce their own ideas, but would simply emulate capitalist ideology. Consequently, the state justified its existence as being the conscience of the proletariat, until such time as they became 'aware', yet intellectual autonomy was prevented, thus stopping the proletariat from developing this awareness. This inevitably became the justification for the continuation of the state.

It is interesting to note that Marx, in his early critique of the German press laws, asserted that censorship can never be in the interest of the state, since it is thereby blinded to the conflicts that threaten it. It may be contended that this prediction was accurate with regard to the Soviet empire.

A further observation is that the state in Hegelian views tends to get stronger with the forces of history. Hegelianism was the foundation of fascist theories of law and state. It may be that the Hegelian notion of the laws of history is a more accurate prediction than the Marxist one. However, the Marxist experience seems to confirm that the state is an alienating feature that falsifies production relations and increases conflict.

The Italian Marxist Gramsci directed this criticism equally at Marxist and fascist states:

> 'It is regressive when it aims at restraining the living forces of history and maintaining outdated anti-historical legality that has become a mere empty shell ... when the party is progressive it functions "democratically" ... when it is regressive it functions "bureaucratically" (in the sense of bureaucratic centralism). In the latter case the party is merely an executive, not a deliberating body ...'

Gramsci rejected the 'scientific socialism' of Lenin, which advocates the indoctrination of the proletariat with the 'correct' doctrine. He saw this as anti-historical and anti-democratic.

d) *International order*

It is submitted by many Marxists such as Renner that the worldwide, or even national, revolutions expected by Marx were averted by the effect of colonialism. The modern world is viewed in terms of global, rather than national, economic forces. Even in the post-colonialist world, we still benefit from the effects of economic colonialism, which increases surplus in capitalist societies, thus funding the reform of capitalism.

The Soviet Union as an element in the economic world was, in economic terms, doomed since it continued to have to compete in global economic markets for commodities that were 'necessary'.

e) *The change in 'necessary' commodities*

In Marx's time technology promised to be able to deliver the answer to people's basic needs: that of health, housing, food etc. However, technology has the remarkable side-effect of creating new needs. The utilisation of technology for 'need' functions such as communications, transport, domestic efficiency, creates demand for televisions, cars, washing machines etc, which in the modern world are viewed as necessities. Needs can therefore be seen, in the technological age, to increase at an ever greater rate than means. Thus, the producers' wares are always insufficient to satisfy demand. I feel it is the development of technology that inevitably falsifies the means-needs beliefs of Marxism. If technology can supply a commodity, then it is no good saying that 'you do not need this', since this is viewed as economic oppression. The consumerist aspirations of those in communist society, as much as the urge for free thought and democracy, must be seen as an important factor in the decline of communism in the Eastern bloc.

14.2 The implications for law of Marxist-Leninist 'contradictions'

a) In the absence of human perfection, law is necessary for the purposes of ensuring that distribution of commodities according to needs.

b) It seems fairly obvious, even from the British point of view, that administrative and executive action requires internal objective regulation and has a tendency towards bureaucracy. Rules are necessary if any kind of normatisation is required, including 'scientific socialism'.

c) Stalin and Lenin thought that social coherence will progress largely from political domination through 'scientific socialism'. The 'socialist legality' of 'scientific socialism' inevitably assumes the continued existence of social diversity and may be said to perpetuate social conflict. Part of the inevitable definition of law is that, as Kelsen pointed out, people do not always obey it. Therefore the claim to have achieved an 'all-people's state' accepts the necessity of continued legal control to achieve socialism.

d) According to Marx the state does not wither away because of ideologies, but as a result of economic forces and the real relations in the base. Thus, the idea that law may be used to stimulate the withering away of law, which is at the heart of scientific socialism, is an obvious self-contradiction.

e) It is clear from the Soviet experience that social deviance is not necessarily a feature of class conflict, but may be related to other social phenomena.

14.3 The failure of the revolution to materialise in capitalist countries

What is particularly damning about Marx's predictions is the failure of revolution to take place in developed capitalist countries. As a result, it is asserted by some Marxists that the 'reform of capitalism' is to be blamed. However, the reform of capitalism may be seen as stemming from a duality of forces. On the one hand, capitalist forces are viewed as bribing the proletariat with reform in order to retain their economic dominance. On the other, some Marxists and socialists have seen the reform of capitalism as the way in which socialism may be brought about. As such, Marxist conceptions have crept into the everyday language of capitalism. We need only to hear the language of current English conservatism to realise that the 'classless society' on the basis of minimising state intervention in economic affairs appeals equally to Marxist ideology and to capitalist laissez-faire philosophy. I am not suggesting that the Conservative Party are Marxists, but that 'class conflict' and economic oppression are still considered to be real issues. Ironically, socialism seems to advocate the increased use of legal intervention in modern 'democratic' society. It may be suggested that the democratic reforms which enfranchised the working class have instigated a 'weak instrumentalism' in the proletarian use of law.

As a result, there seems to be some point in a continued evaluation of law in the light of Marxist jurisprudence.

14.4 'Modernised' Marxist conceptions of law

a) *Historical influences on modern Marxist criminology*

While Engels saw crime as a result of the 'demoralising' effect of the condition of the poor, Marx was also aware of the parasitic 'lumpen proletariat' that are the criminalised class. A consistent criminology was not, however, a feature of early Marxist thought. Nonetheless, the sociological evaluation of law tended towards an analysis of the correlation between crime and social conditions. Additionally, the feature of 'social alienation' due to economic disparities is to be found stressed in some sociological studies. Consequently, in the last twenty years there has been more interest in Marxist thinking and its application to crime. As a result there has been a 'rediscovery' of 'non-orthodox' Marxist jurisprudence of which the following are influential examples:

i) Karl Renner, a Marxist, yet also a noted Austrian statesman, began to emphasise the way in which law could be useful in the manipulation of material conditions. His *Institutions of Private Law and their Social Functions* affirmed that law could mould the social conditions of a society. Renner emphasises that the relationships between law and economy are subtle ones. He views the base-structure distinction as a metaphorical one that illustrates the division in society.

ii) The 'Frankfurt School' of critical theory used Marxism as an analytical tool, but incorporated philosophical and psychological learning in their search for understanding.

- Horkenheimer, in *Study on Authority and the Family* introduced the conception that law and other political institutions increased in importance as 'socialising' or normatising as parental authority is transferred or declines. All the contributors to this study saw social relationships as being bureaucratised, while individuals were increasingly controlled by law. This was the result of the effect of mass media and other technocratic controls, which sought to create a false culture amongst the mass of society, using utilitarianism and pragmatism. People were being turned into consumer robots.

- Of particular interest to criminologists are the methods of Adorno, who used empirical methods to understand what factors contribute to the obedience of some individuals to authority and what creates deviance.

- Similarly, Fromm's post-Freudian analysis of society and the urge for social order is an interesting one. Capitalism liberates creative forces and gives men the awareness of their individual dignity and responsibility. However, they also become aware of the competing and conflicting human interests. As Kolakowski describes his theory:

    'Personal initiative has become the decisive factor in life, but increased importance also becomes attached to aggression and exploitation. The sum total of loneliness and isolation has grown beyond measure, while social conditions cause people to treat one another as things and not persons.'

Fromm's conclusion is that, to coin a phrase 'All you need is love'. It might be argued that Fromm over-emphasises the humanist tendencies in Marx's writings; however his views are nonetheless influential in understanding social deviance.

The Frankfurt School consisted of other, very interesting thinkers such as Marcuse. However, the relevance of these is limited for our present purposes. The publication of their journal had a considerable effect in 1960. Its criticisms of institutional values and its emphasis on a revolution of 'minorities', together with cultural reform and mental reflection were imported into America as a result of the war and have had a considerable effect on both society and the interpretation of society.

b) *Modern Marxist theory of law and state*

i) 'The new criminology'

The approaches of social scientists investigating the nature of crime was beginning to be questioned in the 1960s. The Marxism of the above thinkers led Marxists such as Quinney to view some elements of crime as being 'proto-rebellion' against falsified values. The radical movement that asserted the 'rights' of gypsies, homosexuals, drug-users and so forth required an understanding of the relationship between criminality and the state value system. Thus, Taylor, Walton and Young, in *The New Criminology* called for a fully social theory of deviance that would demonstrate that criminality was 'politically, economically and socially induced' by material forces. They identified the relationships between law and the means of production as follows:

- English civil law is largely centred around the three concepts of:

  1) Property;

  2) Rights of possession;

  3) Contractual obligation.

  All these things favour the accumulation and retention of capital.

- The criminal law has a preoccupation with property crimes, such as theft, criminal damage etc. The concept of equal treatment before the law means that the existing economic distribution is maintained. This is precisely the Marxist thesis.

However, it has been pointed out by some that the law also protects, to a greater or lesser extent, the working class from having their meagre resources taken by the rich. However, the economic relationship with law is thus tenuously established. The view that the law is somehow impartial and separated from economic forces becomes less tenable. However, this does not exclude the moral element involved in the making of criminal law. This view is rather too simple.

One application of Marxist theory is the suggestion that crime is largely the domain of surplus populations that have no real role in the means and relations of production – the unemployed and unemployable. This lumpen proletariat certainly exists in modern society and is the source of much crime. However, it does not account for the violence of the so-called 'lager-lout' of the mid 1980s, who, rather than being poor and unemployed, tended to be well-paid working class, falsifying the 'demoralisation' as well as the lumpen proletariat thesis.

ii) The function of a capitalist state

Hall and Scraton argue that in modern democracies, the state is viewed as being bound by the will of the people, but urge us to look at what the state does. Their argument is more complex:

- The principal purposes of the state are economic ones.

- The capitalist state is as its label implies 'capitalist' ie committed to individuals being able to make profits if they have the means to. It lives on the extracted surplus of these profits and its health and importance is measured by the production of the country.

- Therefore it employs law to do that which will help in the maintenance of this system.

- Consequently, employee share participation on the small scale that we see in current English society represents an incentive towards better productivity. Education models the new minds necessary for modern production techniques. Even unionisation allows for easy collective bargaining and normatised protest.

This view I think is sustainable without any implication of 'conspiracy'. It differs from the Marxist conception of law as purely an economic reflection of the present, but is compatible with the view that law, state and economic activity act in a certain amount of concert. This view is somewhat at odds to the crude class instrumentalism of Quinney who views law as simply the weapon of the ruling class.

With more subtlety, Miliband argues that the predominance of those in judicial positions are of a particular class and inclined towards their cultural views. This is true, as the profession itself accepts, although the judiciary do have remarkably broad minds considering their backgrounds! However, there is an institutionalised distinction to be found in a system that sends a lawyer who has embezzled client funds to an open prison and a person who steals a car to a more secure one. Presumably the latter is more likely to escape!

iii) The structuralist approach

For Poulantzas, the law and state are the mediators that legitimise existing relationships within society, although not all of them. Thus, dominant economic classes can claim that the law is concerned with the 'general interest'. Contrary to being synonymous with classes, the law treats, according to Poulantzas, everyone as an individual of equal status, thereby blinding us to the economic domination of a class of people. Thus, legal concepts such as citizenship, equality before the law and rights amount to an 'isolation effect' by which people lose sight of a minority that own the majority. However, it might be pointed out that this does not account for the welfare rights that exist to protect the less fortunate parts of the population. Poulantzas' 'structuralist' approach is therefore limited.

14.5   A critical evaluation of main Marxist conceptions

Marx himself argued that every movement is a product of its own time. Questions have been raised as to whether the same can legitimately be said of Marxism. Was the theory a product of its time?

In his analysis of capitalism in crisis Marx identified certain important issues and offered an explanation of them in terms of a conflict theory ('the history of all hitherto society has been the history of class struggle'). He developed a science of historical materialism that offered an explanation for everything in economic terms. This was and to some remains attractive. The question is to what extent is it still valid. The response could be addressed in Marxist terms by looking at changes in society in economic terms and observing that as our society has changed from the rather naked exploitative capitalism of the mid nineteenth century through the Welfare State, working class participation and more recently the advent of the Thatcherist enterprise culture, the distinction between working class and capitalist class has become blurred. Workers now own shares, if not in the recently privatised concerns then in their own workplace. The real distinction in Britain today seems to be between those who have a job and those who do not – between the working class and the non working class.

The explanation offered in original Marxism that the state and law are but parts of a superstructure that is reflective of the economic base – the relations of production – concerned itself to show that the superstructure served those that controlled the means of production. This class instrumentalism is rather crude and more recent studies such as those of Ralph Miliband have sought to 'update' Marxism by showing that the relationship is more symbiotic, resembling more of a partnership rather than a position where one determines the other. In essence what Miliband is trying to do is to show that Marxism can explain modern phenomena and is not restricted in time to the last century.

Another modern Marxist, Alan Hunt, has sought to explain modern events in the post industrial society in terms of economic factors and of the conflict theory. This is a clear attempt to show that Marxism is relevant and can enter the current debate rather than address itself only to rather obscure and historical points. The argument used by modern Marxists is that unless they can offer such an explanation then their theory will lapse into obscurity and they will be excluded from the current political debate. With regard to criminology, Taylor, Walton and Young as Marxists have sought to participate in current debates the agenda for which is not set by Marxists, and have developed an approach to criminology that does not just call on the rather simplistic Marxist explanation of crime but seeks to explain crime in more complex terms whilst remaining faithful to the essence of Marxism as they see it – namely the importance of economic factors and the conflict model of society.

Lloyd and Freeman, who are not Marxists, argue that it is legitimate to accept Marxist analysis without Marxist conclusions. That is to say that Marx identified important factors at work in society and that his explanation of naked capitalism in the mid nineteenth century is essentially accurate. If that is the case then Marxism has only a value in terms of the historical development of ideas whose time has since passed, rather like the explanation of the flat earth society. The student of jurisprudence need not then be concerned with Marxism. Marx would reject such an approach. As has been stated, Marx attempted to provide an explanation for everything. Marx would see ideology as a product of economic factors. He argued that those who control the means of production also control mental production and that truth would not be truth until applied. Such would then see the discrediting of Marxism in economic terms as an ideology or false consciousness designed to mystify the exploited class and to legitimate the position of the dominant class as those who control the means of production.

Hence whilst it is probably accurate to argue that original Marxism as an analysis of naked capitalism is dated and not therefore of much relevance to the modern student, it is rather the analysis of the modern post industrial capitalist state that remains of considerable importance. Here Marxists, rather than Marx, speak of the relative autonomy of the state, the explanation of which can be found in Poulantzas' *Political Power and Social Classes* wherein it is pointed out that the state that is also the Welfare State and the state that provides for laws on consumer protection that appear to be in the interests of the working class, remains the state of the ruling class. The Marxist explanation of the separation of state from civil society, which observes that those who govern are not those who control the means of production, points out that in the capitalist mode of production there is no need for those who own the means of production to rule just so long as their rights in capital are protected; the state can otherwise be relatively autonomous. This can be summed up in the phrase of Sigman that the capitalist class 'rules but does not govern'.

Whether these approaches are correct is a matter for considerable argument. The student of jurisprudence must recognise the importance of that argument and therefore there is much in Marxism that is still relevant to the student of jurisprudence. The fact that half the world subscribes to what it terms Marxism even though Marx might have difficulty in so recognising it further reinforces the argument as to its relevance.

The theme which therefore runs through this discussion is that whilst original Marxism may have little to offer by way of explanation of those matters that properly concern the student of jurisprudence today there has developed from that Marxism a new Marxism that does attempt to offer explanations in Marxist terms of developments in modern British society. If for only this reason Marxism is still relevant.

14.6   Evaluation

We have outlined Marxist views on law in a capitalist society. Briefly, law is one of the institutions of the superstructure of a society; the superstructure reflects the base, the relations of production; this is because the dominant class control law and state and uses them to oppress the workers. Is this view satisfactory?

a) *Is there a clear base-superstructure division? Is law just part of the superstructure?*

In the theory, the *base* of the society consists of the relationships of production, ie the relations between the owners of the means of production and the workers; this economic base is reflected in the superstructure of the society, of which law is a part. In fact, the real situation is more complex than this simple model suggests. Law plays an important role, not only in the superstructure, but also in the base. It defines the relations of production and upholds them. In capitalism, one side of the relationship is the owners' side: ownership is a legal concept, with large bodies of law defining it (law of real property, of personal property, of conveyancing) and enforcing it (law of theft, to prevent appropriation; trespass, to prevent improper invasion: conversion, etc). Further, owners frequently rely on forms of combination which are defined and controlled – and to an extent aided, in tax terms – by law (partnerships, companies). Money is raised through institutions controlled (to an extent) by law (the Stock Exchange, banks), ownership is subject to removal by law (compulsory purchase, bankruptcy, insolvency).

On the other side, the workers – what counts as an employee, rather than a contractor, is defined by law; combinations of workers are controlled by law (trade union legislation).

The relationship between the two sides is defined by law (contract of employment), and is subject to legal control (employment protection legislation giving protection from redundancy and unfair dismissal; fair wages control; Factories Acts and Health and Safety at Work Acts controlling conditions of work; a complex network of torts and immunities relating to strikes, picketing and other industrial action).

Law, then, is an integral part of the base. Collins suggests that this criticism is not a fatal one: law can be understood as superstructural in that it reflects the dominant ideology; but it closely governs the relations of production (presumably thereby reflecting the relations of production) and so acts in the base.

b) *Law reflects the economic base: class instrumentalism*

Law is held to reflect the economic base, and the dominant ideology: this works through a process of class instrumentalism, ie the law is used by the owners to oppress the working classes. Does this analysis fit the facts?

In some areas of law, it clearly does. Recent Employment Acts removing immunities from strikers fit the model. So does the lack of a required minimum wage, complex company legislation (which allows for flexibility in setting up companies, and by limited liability allows owners to attempt to make profit without risk, allows for access to money via the Stock Exchange, without losing control of the company, and allows, if carefully planned, for lower taxation levels), insurance laws (to allow risks to be minimised), banking laws (to give further access to required capital), commercial laws, and so on. A whole battery of laws exist to allow owners of the means of production to combine and make agreements between themselves and with workers, allowing for the maximum possibility of profit-making with the minimum risk. One could clearly analyse all this as the dominant bourgeoisie ideology at work.

Other laws, however, are not as easy to fit into the picture. Some laws appear to contradict it even in the economic base. Employment protection legislation which gives workers the right to have details of their contracts, and to payments for unfair dismissal and redundancy; the Health and Safety at Work Act, protecting workers at their place of work; and immunities for workers involved in trade disputes from actions for various economic torts, thus in effect giving a right to strike. Other laws, acting clearly in the superstructure, contradict the general picture of a dominant class oppressing the working class: consumer protection legislation including the Sale of Goods Act and similar statutes, and the various provisions of a Welfare State (National Health Service, National Insurance, Social Security). There are also laws in other areas which seem remote from the class oppression picture altogether – family laws, crimes of violence, wills, charities, and so on. Another view would be that these laws protect monopoly since they make it more expensive for new enterprise to 'get started' by raising the capital cost of establishment in compliance with safety and consumer legislation.

Can a Marxist properly explain all these laws? Taking the third category first, those laws appearing remote from class conflict, there is a ready answer for many of them. We have seen that the dominant class ideology will support the retention of the status quo. For this reason, laws against violence and against sexual crimes, and laws relating to family, etc, can be seen as part of the social fabric, preserving the present stable social order and an acceptable level of community morality. They prevent social unrest and disquiet from rising to too great an extent. It is rather more difficult to justify charities, or even freer moral laws re homosexuality/abortion, on this rationale: perhaps these can be seen as sops to the conscience of various groups in society. The institution of probate and intestacy allows the means of production to be preserved in the families of the dominant class.

The contradictory laws in the superstructure can be explained, by a Marxist, in different ways. They can be seen as proving that the dominant class does not control each and every law passed by the legal system, but allows it relative autonomy, ie only preventing the passage of laws which would be harmful and ensuring the passage of vital laws, allowing any other laws to be passed. This can be accepted, just about, as an explanation of the Welfare State. Although the owners will have to pay a large part of the cost out of profits, they do benefit, because they and their workers are kept healthy and alive between jobs, and they can manipulate the tax system so that the working classes bear a large proportion of the cost themselves. Whether relative autonomy could be used to explain consumer protection legislation must be regarded as more open to doubt, since it is clearly harmful to the owners of productive means not to be able to sell their products as they wish. A further possible explanation is that these superstructural laws are sops to the working classes, given to keep them happy and to prevent them forming a coherent class consciousness (a necessary prelude to revolution). This of course, can be used to explain away any contradictory laws, even those of the first type (ie those forming part of the base). A third possible explanation is that these laws are concessions wrung out of the dominant class by the developing consciousness of the working class. The dominant class, however, retains overall control of the system. Presumably the recent anti-union legislation can be seen as the dominant class reasserting its position, when the present economic climate makes the concessions unnecessary (a recession obviously works against working class solidarity, since personal concerns such as getting and keeping jobs become more important). The contradictory laws in the base could also be explained thus, as concessions wrung out of the ruling class.

Are these various explanations satisfactory? Can all laws be justified as being oppression – directly or indirectly by preserving the status quo – of the working classes, or instances of relative autonomy, or sops to the working classes, or concessions wrung out of the dominant class?

Obviously these questions are empirical ones. There is at least one counter-interpretation. This view would say that the various types of contradictory law merely show the theory to be incorrect. Whatever the earlier capitalist situation, in a developed capitalist society – by electoral reform and other means – the working classes now play a full role in the law-making process, and the distribution of benefits and burdens in society take their interests into account as well as the interests of the owners. The Welfare State, consumer and employee protection are simply manifestations of the concern of the law-making process with the interests of the working class and the poor. Further, it is a mistake to see law simply in terms of the power balance between the classes. Doesn't law have other functions, like simply regulation of law and order and upholding commonly upheld standards of decency and family life?

Do you find this – or another – counter-interpretation more convincing than the Marxist theory?

c) *Class reductionism*

One final point of evaluation, and then we can move from the capitalist state, which has taken up the majority of our time on Marxism, to the revolution, when law and state will wither away.

This point concerns the Marxist division into just two classes, the bourgeoisie and the workers. In present-day Great Britain, for example, many pressure groups and interest factions play a part in the political and legislative process, lobbying MPs and party leaders. What is more, sometimes those from the same Marxist class will take differing sides. For example, agricultural owners and fishing boat owners will often clash with developers of land and/or seaports; a good case in point is the damage done to some fishing ports and livelihoods by entry into the EEC (which has imposed quotas), which entry was, of course, supported by most industrialists. Further examples of conflict within the Marxist classes could be given. To avoid the charge of 'class reductionism' (ie over-simplifying the class position by seeing only two classes), a Marxist would have to argue that pressure and interest groups are just short term, and are not as fundamental as the real classes. Class conflict, in the sense of conflict within the classes, arises because of a lack of class consciousness, not sufficiently developed in the working class and not required at present in the bourgeoisie, who can afford to wrangle and still dominate. Is this answer convincing? Could a Marxist give any other answer?

Charges of class reductionism have another aspect too. The two class divisions can now be seen to be a simplification because many members of the working class now form part of the ruling class. Pension funds and trade union funds, building societies and banks all invest in, own shares in and therefore partly own, companies, etc. The money of these various funds comes from the man in the street, who also sometimes saves more directly by buying shares himself. Most working people own at least a stake in the means of production. In fact, the people at the top of the big companies often own little or no stake therein. The controllers of the means of production no longer necessarily own it. Further, the institutions which might be included in a wider version of the ruling class (see, for example, Griffith's *The Politics of the Judiciary*, especially the last chapter) courts, civil service, police, armed forces, etc, cannot really be seen as having a different ideology from the ordinary person: and remember that the ordinary person controls, ultimately, by the power of the ballot box.

Isn't seeing capitalist society as divided into two classes, the owners of the means of production and the workers, thus a gross misinterpretation?

15 ANALYTICAL JURISPRUDENCE 1: LEGAL CONCEPTS

(A)   RIGHTS

15.1   The philosophical premises of rights

a) When philosophers have problems they often retire to a hypothetical 'desert island'. If the student wishes to understand the philosophical premises of the concept of 'rights' I would advise him to do the same. If a man is alone on a desert island is he likely to use the concept of 'rights'? From a purely practical stand-point there is no reason why he should; due to his isolation he may do whatever he pleases. From a moral perspective he should do what he thinks is right. Now here begins the problem. The Natural Lawyer would argue that there are laws that transcend laws posited by will. Let us suppose that Natural Law requires that a man should take from his environment only that which he needs for a comfortable life – that he should not 'rape' his environment. As well as for reasons of enlightened self-interest in areas of finite resources, this proposition has a certain 'natural' force to it. In the moral codes of many societies, it is improper to 'rape' the environment. Indeed, modern law is becoming more 'environmentally friendly' due to the warnings of science. If such a rule may be taken to be a tenet of Natural Law, then our 'Robinson Crusoe' becomes involved in the philosophical premises of rights. It may therefore be stated that:

   i)   He is allowed to take what he needs for a comfortable life.

   ii)   He is not allowed to take more than this.

Could we therefore say that he has a 'right' to (i) and 'no right' to (ii). Certainly, in common parlance, we could say this, but does a permission carry the full force of a 'right'? Do we invoke the concept of 'right' simply to denote that we are permitted to do something? I think not. Normally, we will employ the concept of 'having a right' when there is something that might prevent us from doing something that we feel we are allowed to do.

b) Imagine our Robinson Crusoe is a vegetarian on the grounds that he feels that eating meat is immoral. However, there is no vegetation on the island, only chickens. He might employ the concept of 'having a right' in solving this dilemma:

   i)   'My conscience tells me that it is wrong to eat chickens.'

   ii)   'Natural Law says that I may use what is necessary for a comfortable life.'

   iii)   'Natural Law gives me the right to eat these chickens.'

Now a sceptic might say that he is not deciding this on moral grounds, but because he is hungry and is therefore putting aside his scruples. This might be true, but it illustrates that rights are more than permissions in that they have a normative force that may exclude restraining factors. In Dworkin's terms, they are like 'trumps' that have a special feature of over-ruling some other considerations.

c) The student might think that this is rather a weak example. Our Crusoe is not really invoking a right, because it is his own conscience that he is 'trumping'. He is simply using the concept of a right as a justification for something that he thinks would normally be immoral. Normally rights are associated with social situations. However, Natural Law theories carry with them the characteristic claim that they are 'superior' either morally or logically, to normal legal orders, and as such an appeal to Natural Law is an appeal to something that ought to 'trump' normal legal obligations. As such, it is frequently asserted that there are 'natural rights' that are more morally or rationally compelling that positive legal norms.

However, as we have seen, proving the existence or content of Natural Law is a little difficult. Therefore, we might seek to show a humanistic concept of rights.

d) Gerwith, in *An Epistemology of Human Rights*, adopts what might be termed as a 'heuristic' argument, that does not presuppose the existence of a natural law, but rather stems from logical propositions about people's normative reasoning. For our purposes, I will simply borrow a few of the concepts that he employs.

Imagine our Robinson Crusoe is eventually picked up by a ship. He has lost all of his scruples and no longer even subscribes to Natural Law. He simply does what he wants, and since all he could do on the desert island was eat, drink and sleep this did not provide any great problems. He therefore subscribes to the maxim:

     'I should do what I want to do.'

The captain of the ship that picks him up asks him where he wants to go. This proves a problem since he wants to go both to London and to Paris. He has conflicting desires and, as such, must make a decision about where he desires most to go. Thus, his maxim changes to:

     'I should do what I choose to do.'

This means that he must have reasons and preferences of some kind that allow him to make the choice, even if it is being bound by the toss of a coin. He is thus responsible in a weak sense that he can give a reason (whether or not it is a good one) for why he has decided between two conflicting desires. However, what one man chooses to do might prevent another man's choice from being fulfilled. Crusoe may wish to go to London, but the captain might be intent on going to the Maldives. As a rational human being he may decide where he wants to go, in the same way as Crusoe may decide what he wants. However, as a captain he has the ultimate decision of where to take the ship because he has a right under maritime law. Obviously, without making a choice, he cannot exercise that right. It is the presupposition of a right to act, that a person is free to choose how to exercise that right. As we have already pointed out, there is also a presupposition that there is a conflicting reason for why a person should not act in a certain way that a right allows him to act. We can therefore say the following:

i) The concept of a right presupposes that the 'right-holder' has the ability to choose how and whether to act in a certain way.

ii) A right also presupposes something that might prevent a right-holder from acting in the way that he chooses to act.

iii) It is the right that determines that the free choice to act in a certain way is a stronger reason for acting (i), that the reason for not acting (ii).

iv) A right does not presuppose that reasons for not acting (ii) will not actually prevent a person's choices from being fulfilled; it merely determines that a person should be free to choose to act in a certain way and ought to be allowed to act according to his choice.

v) Thus, rights are normative, rather than factual.

However, it is obvious that this analysis does not explain everything:

i) Where do rights come from?

ii) Why should we be bound by rights?

iii) Why are there conflicting reasons for action?

iv) Do animals etc have rights?

15.2 The contradictory nature of rights

It may also be observed that in my loose interpretation of the background to rights there is the strong possibility of contradictory outcomes. Rights claimed in modern society have a contradictory quality about them. We can easily place strongly affirmed rights in direct conflict:

a) People claim the right to life yet there is also a claim of a right to abortion.

b) People claim the right not to be killed by another, yet there are also claims to a right to die.

c) People claim the right to free information, yet there is also a claim to privacy.

These are but a few examples. The claim to right is thus ultimately a claim to self-determination, which can produce logical contradictions and is itself in contradiction to the aspect of social control by law. However, the contradiction is one of degree. Thus, the issue of rights in the social context is one of balancing conflicting claims and determining which claims have priority.

15.3 The place of law

It is submitted that law has a special function within this framework. Law presupposes free choice at least to the extent that by implying that you ought to obey, you might otherwise choose to do something else.

However, law restricts the way in which you may act in certain circumstances, even to the extent of physically restraining you. Thus, the law itself claims that 'the citizen ought to do as the law chooses, regardless of whether there are other non-legal reasons for doing otherwise'. The origin of the right or authority to make law has been intermittently discussed, since this is the question of the authority to make law and of the obligation to obey it. However, it begs the question, 'Does law extinguish individuals' claims to rights?' The question may be broken down further:

a) Are there strong normative reasons for law to prefer an individual's choice to the prescriptions of legal norms? This must be considered the normative jurisprudential question of rights.

b) When a legal system concedes the existence of rights, what does this mean and what does a legal right do? This is a question of analytical jurisprudence.

15.4   Some contrasting views on rights

The legislator's duty, in ethical terms, is to society as a whole. Yet society is made up of interest groups and individuals. The immediate need of society may be seen as being in irreconcilable conflict with that of the individual. When should an individual or class claim of right be upheld in spite of the interests of the 'whole' of society?

a) *The Marxist perspective*

The orthodox Marxist perspective on morality and rights stems from two premises:

i) Morality is an ideology that derives from the particular stage of development of productive forces of a society. Thus, Marxism cannot criticise the infringement of 'rights' of works in capitalist societies in moral terms. The critique of capitalism is a scientific one.

ii) Man in socialist society requires no such ideology because he will naturally orient himself to social usefulness.

As a result, Marx views morality as relative to the particular stage of societal development and human rights as an ideology that alienates one man from another. As we have observed, rights presuppose restraint and conflict, mediating between them. Such alienation and mediation are seen by Marx and Engels as delaying revolutionary change to a society where conflict no longer exists. To adhere to a concept of 'right', is to adhere to a maintenance of the status quo and unequal distribution. Marx denies therefore that there are strong normative reasons for rights that can be accepted by law, since law merely shields the interests of the dominant class.

b) *Bentham*

Bentham, as has been observed in the chapters on imperative theory and utilitarianism, completely rejects the concept of rights as anything other than fantasies of the mind. To Bentham rights derive entirely from the law and are legal constructs. However, it must be remembered that Bentham is sceptical about the concept of morality as a whole. Human beings act on the principles of pleasure and pain. It would seem to be vastly illogical that the interests of the rest of society should be subverted for the pleasure of an individual or class of individuals. The crude utilitarian perspective sees the legislator's duty as being solely the maximisation of pleasure in society, potentially at the expense of the rights of the minority.

However, this does not mean that all utilitarians follow this rather simplistic view. It is possible to demonstrate that a presupposition of 'weak' rights is compatible with the utilitarian perspective. We shall investigate the rights vs utility debate a little later on.

Bentham himself subscribes to the view that an individual should be granted the maximum independence that is conducive with his fellows in society, but he still reserves the right of the state to intervene on behalf of the collective good.

c) *Natural Law*

In Chapter 3 we discussed the views of Natural Lawyers, who tend to view Natural Law duties as ones that transcend legal duties. By appeal to Natural Law, we might have rights that exist independently of law that we would expect law to fulfil. However, it has been observed that Natural Law proofs tend to be open to empirical attack. In order to assert the existence of natural rights one needs to believe in Natural Law. Faith, either secular or religious, is a strong normative reason for an individual to expect rights, but not for an agnostic society to accept those rights. A further problem with Natural Law is that historically, the distribution of rights has been uneven and thus a recipe for the denial of rights to some in favour of the privilege of others.

d) *The common sense approach*

Both Hume and Hart suggest that there are certain empirical facts about the nature of the human condition that one would normally expect to see responded to in legal or moral systems. These amount to their respective theories of Natural Law. Inevitably, if we look at history, we can see that certain legalised actions have been ultimately detrimental to societal interests. Thus, genocide, torture and certain other extremes of state action in the name of society have served no particular benefit to society. In these terms, it is common sense for a historically informed legislator to avoid such excesses. Moreover, this is linked to a weak moral argument that law, while necessary to mediate between conflicting wills, should leave a certain amount of moral autonomy to the subject.

The common sense approach does, however, rely on practical reasoning and experience. This means that pragmatism can 'trump' this conception of rights. The torture of a terrorist may save the lives of hundreds of potential victims of a bomb that he has planted. The argument against doing so is largely a moral one.

We shall explore interest theories and Hart's will theory in greater depth later on, since they are concerned chiefly with the nature of rights actually found in law, rather than the reason why law should have a concept of rights.

15.5 Liberalism, libertarianism and utilitarianism

In all of the above theories the main contentions are egalitarian ones, although of subtly different perspectives. The arguments that we shall analyse are those of the three jurists most strongly engaged in the rights debates. It must be remembered, however, that these are equally theories of justice, so that if the student seeks the background to the argument he should refer to Chapters 17 and 18.

a) *The three 'egalitarian' starting points*

In order to clarify the positions of these three political philosophies we might simplify the egalitarian approaches adopted by each:

   i)   Liberalism

   Dworkin suggests that people should be treated by law with equal concern and respect.

   ii) Libertarianism

   Nozick sees each individual as ultimately free, with certain inalienable rights that are to be protected by the law.

   iii) Utilitarianism

   Hart suggests that a modern form of utilitarianism gives equal weight to the equal interests of everyone.

Although I have termed these as egalitarian, the theories simply imply that in some particular aspects, people are to be treated as equal in the eyes of the law. The irreconcilable conflicts between these views will become apparent soon enough. However, this does lead us to the question of whether we can envisage rights as being held equally by all persons, that is, the question of 'generic' or 'human rights'.

b) *When may a right be claimed to be objective?*

To assert that there are rights that are equally held by all is more than a subjective claim to have a right. I can claim that I have a right to wantonly kill all my neighbours with a chain-saw, but do I have such a right? This is a return to the question of the objectivity of normative assertions. There are two ways in which we might claim that we have an objective right:

i) If others recognise that I have such a right. This is what might be termed a conventional
    right. However, the fact that something is conventional is not a reason, in itself, why a right
    should be observed.

ii) Because there is a good reason, independent of whether it is observed, for people to respect a
    right.

In terms of our categories of liberalism, libertarianism and utilitarianism, we can see that these
reasons are of variable relevance.

The utilitarian, working on the expressed preference of individuals, will find reflected in his
considerations principle (1), if the majority feel that a person has this right. Thus, when asking
everybody in society, 'Should we ban homosexuality?, if the majority who express a preference say,
'No, homosexuals have the right to sexual freedom', then the law will respect that right.

The libertarian would answer the question by saying that the law may only intercede to protect the
rights of other individuals. If homosexuals do not infringe the freedom of others, then they should
not be banned. This completely ignores the first principle, but adopts the second principle in a
specific way: 'People have the right to do anything that does not interfere with the freedom and rights
of others.' We shall examine a libertarian view of what people's rights are in a moment.

The liberal would seem to adopt a combined approach. Most liberals tend to advocate the
majoritarian considerations that utilitarianism supports against a claim that people have a residual
right to liberty in the libertarian sense. However, if the majority were to say that we should ban
homosexuals, yet there is, in Dworkin's words, a 'good reason' that suggests the law would be
'wrong' to do so, then it is asserted that homosexuals have a right to their sexual freedom. That
good reason would seem to be that the majority decision would not result in homosexuals being
treated with equal concern and respect if they were to ban homosexuality.

Thus, depending on one's political philosophy, a right may be objectively based on one or both of
these principles. The common denominator between these theories is, however, that all three are
based on the equal value that is placed on the individual, albeit that the values attributed to
individuals are different – equal say in decisions, equal right to act freely, equal respect and concern,
respectively.

Thus, the theories have in common that members of society ought to be regarded as equal in one
respect or another. However, this is where the similarities end.

15.6 The critique of utilitarianism

Both Nozick (libertarian) and Dworkin (liberal) are not fully satisfied that the principle of utility, ie that
of maximising the common good, provides the answer to rights problems. Indeed, principles of utility
find it very difficult to accommodate the concept of rights, although Hare suggests that they possibly
can by proceeding from the presumption that people are of equal value.

However, as Hart has recognised, the modern critique of utility, on the basis that it 'fails to take rights
seriously' has not been exceptionally successful in proving its point. Utilitarianism claims to be a
politically neutral theory of justice, yet it is claimed that it can become corrupt if it does not
accommodate rights.

The criticisms that we will consider are specifically those advanced by Nozick and Dworkin. They stem
from radically different perspectives. On the one hand Nozick rejects utility to an extreme degree, while
on the other Dworkin accepts utility as a 'background for decision-making' that may be 'trumped' by the
holder of a right. We shall therefore consider the criticisms separately.

15.7 Libertarianism: Nozick's theory of rights and the minimal state

The opening argument of Nozick's *Anarchy, State and Utopia* is the following assertion:

  'Individuals have rights, and there are things no person or group may do to them [without violating these rights] ... Our main conclusions about the state are that a minimal state limited only to the narrow functions of protection against force, theft, fraud, enforcement of contracts, and so on, is justified; that any more extensive state will violate persons' rights ... and is unjustified.'

Consequently, the state may not coerce individuals to help others and may not 'protect' an individual from himself. Such a view would seem to be diametrically opposed to that of the utilitarian. Rawls, who criticises utilitarianism because it does not give sufficient priority to rights, is criticised by Nozick for advocating that a priority in state considerations should be the minimisation of violations of rights. This is because, on the basis of Rawls's argument, an innocent man might still be punished in order that a rampage of vengeful citizens might be prevented from violating the rights of still more people. Nozick views the trading off of the rights of the individual in the interests of the rights of the many as 'a utilitarianism of rights'.

Nozick's position is immovable; people cannot be treated as anything other than ends in themselves. The state and law must not violate the individual's rights, even if it is to avert the violation of the rights of others. The side-constraint of all state action is that the state's duty is primarily not to violate an individual's rights. Nozick's argument is that the individual cannot be forced into sacrificing his rights for the community, even if as a free agent he might sacrifice himself for another.

However, Nozick's consideration of utilitarianism is on the basis of the automatic assumption that it is not worth considering. Thus, his critique occasionally becomes absurd in the extreme:

'Maximising the average utility allows a person to kill everyone else if that would make him ecstatic, and so happier than average.'

While his attention to social, rather than individual concerns, is evasive:

'The question of whether [never violating the individual's rights is an] ... absolute, or whether [this principle] ... may be violated in order to avoid catastrophic moral horror, and if the latter, what the resulting structure might look like, is one I hope largely to avoid.'

Nozick's rejection of utilitarianism is thus on the basis that 'individuals have rights'. What are these rights and how do they come about? The answer is that people (i) have a right to liberty (ii) have a right to the fruits of their labour. One person cannot have rights in another person. The function of the state is to protect the legitimate distribution of assets.

We will look at Nozick's principle of distributive justice in Chapter 18; however, some consideration of his theory of rights is pertinent here.

a) *Liberty*

Nozick cites Locke's idealist 'State of Nature', where every individual acts as he sees fit, 'without leave or dependency upon the will of another man'. Such individuals subscribe to the law of nature that 'no one ought to harm another in his life, health, liberty, or possessions.' The function of the minimal state is thus to guarantee the laws of nature with minimal interference with individual liberty.

Nozick does not explain why people have the right to liberty. In the philosophical premises discussed in the first part of the chapter (accepted in Nozick's discussion of Hart's fairness principle), I asserted that the language of rights is not meaningful in a Robinson Crusoe situation. If a person is free to do as he chooses, then the question of 'rights' has no real meaning. In a social situation, a claim of right is to assert that:

i) What the 'right-holder' claims is his right;

ii) Is to be preferred against the counterclaim of another.

Nozick is therefore asserting that the right of freedom is a right that prefers the individual's claim of freedom of action, against another's claim that he might restrict that freedom. Yet is this not to contradict the freedom of another to act? If my freedom to act in the way I choose is to be preferred to your freedom to choose to restrict my action, do I not therefore assert that there are limitations on your freedom of action? This would contradict the assertion that all people have the right to act freely. This, Nozick explicitly accepts by postulating that Natural Law states that we cannot use our freedom of action to endanger the life, health or possessions of another. The law is justified to compel obedience to these conditions.

This would seem to solve the problem. However, if I have access to food and you do not, yet I refuse it to you, do I not do as much harm as I would have done, had I stolen your food from you? Freedom in a social context depends on the absence of monopoly. We have seen that Nozick criticises the utilitarian on the grounds that he would allow one man to kill everyone for the maximisation of his pleasure. Yet Nozick would allow by default one man, in the name of his individual liberty, to allow all others to starve!

The individual in society, or even in competition, is dependent on either the compromise or weakness of his fellows for his own survival. Since Nozick rules out physical violence as in violation of the rights of others, man is thrown back on the distributive justice of his fellow men.

A further point to note is that a man may become comparatively freer in his opportunities, if he sacrifices his complete autonomy and co-operates with another. In modern society, the benefit of communal action is manifest. One man cannot in his lifetime build all the things that he consumes or uses in his everyday life. However, neither can I enter into a voluntary transaction with all those from whom I might benefit. Nozick seems to deny non-consensual co-operative action. If the value of a man's contribution to a particular goal is greater than the benefit that he, as an individual, gets from the common pursuit of that goal, it would be wrong to force him to engage in it. Yet people are unable to guage the benefits that they get from society in any direct way, and are not always the judge of their own best interests. Nozick simply views people's interests at their own concern. However, in a society people's interests are interdependent. My well-being is not only my own concern, but my family's, my employer's, and those people I am philanthropic towards. I am an individual only because I have a discrete and valuable place in society.

b) *Property*

We shall investigate Nozick's concept of property in Chapter 18, so my observations here must be brief. The cry of Anarchists such as Proudhon and Kropotkin is that 'Property is theft!' The basis of this is that, by asserting that I may have a sole right to an object or commodity, I may be denying another what he needs. The true libertarian must presuppose that no man has the right to deny another his liberty. A fundamental precondition to liberty is that a person must be alive. Thus, a precondition of liberty is the satisfaction of the basic needs of life. Basic commodities and means of survival must be distributed not according to the means of acquisition, as Nozick suggest, but on the basis of the needs. Most libertarians therefore assert that the right to liberty determines that the individual has the right to the necessities of life, by which he may obtain liberty. Nozick believes that the free market naturally will tend to the satisfaction of needs. He presupposes that minimum needs are satisfied, so that law should not interfere to ensure it.

c) *Conclusion*

Although we shall revisit Nozick's theory I cannot but endorse the view of Lukes that he does not appreciate the nature of the individual as a social being. In terms of supplying us an answer to the problem of the nature of the legislator's duty, his theory simply endorses the rights of those who have already got rights. He endorses the inequalities in society on the weak assertion that to interfere would be to damage the rights of some in order to benefit those that have no rights.

15.8 Liberalism: Dworkin's theory of rights and justice

Dworkin's ambit as a writer stretches beyond legal theory and the judicial role, and into the realms of political philosophy. As in those other areas, his work is novel and challenging. His work is considered at various points throughout the course and just because there is not a specific chapter devoted to his work the student should not underestimate the importance of his views to this course as a whole.

So far as his views on justice are concerned he argues that the state should be politically neutral; it should not choose between conceptions of the good. This is liberalism, a view shared by Rawls. According to Dworkin, it rests on a principle that the state should treat everyone with equal concern and respect. This principle he illustrates in his discussion of auction equality on a desert island. This discussion justifies redistribution, and points to a majoritarian democratic process.

In that process, decisions should generally be decided upon the basis of utility. However, the state must not infringe on rights. There is no right to liberty generally, nor to specific liberties; rather, rights relate to those decisions likely to be made on the basis of 'external' rather than internal preference.

We now look at these things in more detail.

a) *Political neutrality*

Why should the state be politically neutral?

i) There may be pragmatic grounds, ie to foster social co-operation, but if this is so, it would not require the prohibition of state use of particular conceptions of the good life, only some forms of restraint. And, of course, it by no means follows that a person, in the absence of state-employed conception of the good, would be free from other external influences, eg that of social environment, family, culture, etc.

ii) An argument for political neutrality might be made from the Kantian principle of autonomy, that they should be treated as 'ends in themselves'.

Of course, there are the practical difficulties. Not only must people be allowed to choose freely, they should be given as large a range of choices as possible (what Raz has called a 'grant equality of opportunity'). But to provide choices for some individuals may close-off or limit the options available to others (eg Arts Council grants to provide 'culture for the people' as opposed to other forms of recreational activities). And is not the valuing of an autonomous life a conception of the good itself? Perhaps it ignores, or fails sufficiently to emphasise, the more social aspects of human nature.

b) *Auction equality*

Dworkin attempts to design a system which will give effect to the basic principle of a right of everyone to equal concern and respect.

If we imagine a group of people on a desert island which has a limited amount of resources, an initially plausible method of distribution would be by auction. At this stage we assume that all the arrivals on this (previously uninhabited) island have an equal number of bargaining 'counters', all have the same talents and abilities though all have different tastes and ambitions. Clearly, if they value a particular good enough (or more than anyone else) they will pay the most for it and so obtain it. Suppose, therefore, we can reach a situation where, after this exhaustive auction, no one envies the bundle of goods that someone else possesses.

Now, states Dworkin, if we imagine a more realistic situation where people differ not only as to their tastes but also as to their talents, some re-adjustment will be required. For Dworkin, the problem of any system of distribution is how to be sensitive to tastes. He adopts the familiar position that unequal resources are justified if they result from differences in taste (or ambition) but not if they are derived from the fact that some people are more able, clever, strong, etc, than others. There is little argument for this premise but it may be supported to rely on a claim, like that of Rawls, that differences in ability are simply 'arbitrary from a moral point of view'.

For Dworkin, therefore, a powerful conception of equality of opportunity is required, one that allows for a constant readjustment of wealth patterns diachronically (over time) to ensure that at no stage do inequalities of resources arise merely as a response to people's differential talents. So some comprehensive system of income tax is clearly envisaged and considered to be legitimate.

The point is simply this. If A and B are equally talented but A is lazy and fritters away his abilities and resources while B works hard to invest his goods and to use his talents to the full, it is quite justifiable that B is better-off financially. Not so, according to liberal theory, if the reason for the disparity is that B is actually more talented than A. In this way, Dworkin's liberalism attempts to steer a course between allowing individuals a measure of free choice (to follow their aspirations) and compensating them for their 'natural handicaps'. Of course, all this is not simply the logical follow-up to a theory of equality as the mainstay of the theory, as Dworkin claims – it rests upon a particular idea of liberty (as taste-sensitive) which needs to be argued for, independently. That is, precisely what do we mean by a right to (equal) concern and respect?

c) *The political process – the derivation of rights*

Dworkin sought to modify the initially plausible idea of a majoritarian political system as the most satisfactory arrangement for the liberally-minded island-dwellers. He wished to avoid any major concessions to a utilitarian theory that might follow from the use of such an arrangement.

According to Dworkin, 'personal preferences' are those of an individual relating to his own enjoyment of goods and opportunities. External preferences are those of an individual that relate to how others should run their lives. Clearly the principle of political neutrality forbids the use by the state of such external preferences.

But in any decision-making process, how are such considerations to be filtered out?

The sort of problem that worried Dworkin was described by him as follows: Suppose the state can purchase a theatre or swimming pool but not both. Against the vote of those who wished to build a theatre would be the votes of those who had a personal preference to swim, and also of those who, while not wishing to swim, simply thought that swimming was a more desirable activity. Dworkin said that such an inclusion of external preferences led to 'double-counting'.

It is difficult to see why, though. Each person has one vote – surely he is not limited to voting only on those matters in which he has a direct interest? Why can he not use either an external or personal preference, or both? After all, it is the votes and not the preferences which count. As Hart points out, when an activity is impeded by state action, it is not necessarily because the majority saw it as inferior, but simply that the minority failed to secure enough votes.

At any rate, Dworkin wanted to use a mechanism which would prevent decisions being made with respect to certain kinds of activities, likely to be restricted by a conglomeration of external preferences. That is to say, some interests and actions would no longer be a subject for legislation – they would be removed from the ambit of the majoritarian process altogether. Such protected interests are, of course, Dworkin's rights. They are necessary to give full effect to the fundamental rights to equal concern and respect. In a sense, then, Dworkin would see such rights as unfortunately necessary – because of the vagaries and possible utilitarian implications of a majoritarian system – rather than a natural feature of human existence (see for the latter view, Nozick, *Anarchy, State and Utopia*). Dworkin gives us no exhaustive list of such rights but refers us favourably to that contained in the US Bill of Rights. Analytically speaking, Dworkin defines a right in this way:

> 'If someone has a right to something then it is wrong for the government to deny it him even though it would be in the general interest to do so.'

While Dworkin maintains that some activities are protected by the idea of rights as trumps not because they are more valuable than, for example, increases in the general welfare, but just because they preserve the basic right to equal concern and respect, surely some value comparison is necessary. How can a deep equality compel us to accept a certain list of rights without more?

At times it is difficult to resist the temptation to see the basis for such rights not in Dworkin's objection to preferences of an external nature but rather his hostility towards preferences with a particular content (ie anti-liberal preferences). If this is so, then there is an implicit value-judgment at work.

d) *The nature of Dworkin's rights*

Notice that Dworkin allows rights to be restricted in two cases:

   i)   On grounds of principle, to protect another right;

   ii) On grounds of policy, to prevent an emergency of some kind.

Of course, under escape-clause (i), much depends on the list of rights chosen and how we assess the conflict between rights. If the latter is assessed by reference to the relative utility of each right, then clearly some utilitarian argument is allowed to enter the picture. Clearly utilitarian arguments present themselves in the case of escape-clause (ii), where the exercise of the right would have disastrous consequences for the general welfare.

In addition, of course, under (i), any right may presumably be restricted if its restriction furthers the basic right of all to equal concern and respect. This is really Dworkin's justification for a policy of reverse discrimination which, while trampling on the individual's right to be considered on his merits (the existence of which right Dworkin conveniently doubts) furthers the overall goal of a basic equality for the whole community. Such reasoning is highly uncertain, however. At the very least the utilitarian or goal-theorist will find ample room to manoeuvre within Dworkin's theory.

e) *A right to property?*

As a liberal-egalitarian Dworkin is distinctly uneasy about the existence of such a right (contra the libertarian Nozick). He rejects it by claiming that he cannot think of any argument to show that a political decision, limiting such a right-protected activity as the accumulation of property, is likely to be giving effect to external preferences, hence no need for special protection. But why not?

Consider minimum wages legislation. May many such measures not be passed on the basis of the external preferences of those who, while not directly affected by such legislation, approve of a better standard of living for the workers who are directly affected?

Dworkin might reply that such legislation is required to further the basic good of overall equality, but that assumes that there is a prima facie right to property in the first place, which he seeks to deny. One has some sympathy with Hart's view, that we cannot escape, as Dworkin's purported derivation of rights from equality attempts to do, the assertion of the value of such liberties as compared with advancement in the general welfare however fairly assessed. In other words, in placing emphasis on right-protected activities, Dworkin is simply valuing them as worthy, as conceptions of the good that ought to be fostered.

f) *The Dworkinian proviso*

There is another dramatic weakness in Dworkin's idea of political neutrality. He tells us that liberals can legitimately support (and enforce or provide for) a particular cause, like conservation of the environment, not because it is regarded as a superior form of life, but because the situation is such that a form of life, desired and found to be satisfying in the past, may no longer be available for future generations. If such a life-form or life-style (eg enjoyment of the countryside) does disappear then liberalism should attempt to maintain its existence.

Thus, we should keep open as many options as possible. However, this raises a number of problems.

   i)   Can we distinguish between providing that a life-plan is not excluded from the choice of future generations, and affirmatively fostering life-plans already excluded by society (ie reviving 'old options')? If we cannot, is political neutrality really being preserved?

   ii) How do we assess when, and to what degree, a life-plan is about to be closed-off?

There is a dilemma for Dworkin here. If he wishes to take account of the possible interests and choices of future generations, then conceptions of the good must not only be preserved for them – others may need to be fostered to ensure that they have as wide a choice as possible. But if so, then surely the principle of political neutrality has been violated? The alternative is simply to ignore the future, but is that what Dworkin wishes us to do?

This is rather similar to the difficulty encountered by Haksar who says that the state may legitimately give inferior status to a particular form of life (eg bestiality), not because we wish to force people to be better or more worthy individuals (an idea which Haksar rejects) but to 'provide a decent and morally healthy environment for the coming generation'. Of course this amounts to an espousal of paternalism, if not now, then for the future.

g) *Liberalism defined*

Can we therefore accept such a strong and optimistic form of liberal theory? Apart from its internal inconsistencies, Dworkin's analysis of liberalism does differ importantly from those of other like-minded theorists. Some see not equality but liberty as the basic principle and then, as Gutterman points out, call equality into aid as an instrument by which such liberty can meaningfully be exercised. Dworkin has given us an interesting theory as to what is constitutive of liberalism, and what it means to 'take rights seriously', but he has not avoided the pitfalls of value-judgment. That is because an appeal to value, indeed perfectionist, considerations cannot be avoided. In the end, as always, it is up to us to judge its intuitive appeal.

15.9 Evaluation of Dworkin's theory

In a welter of detail, it is easy to lose sight of basics. Dworkin's basic argument is that society should be governed on the basis of equal concern and respect; that this requires a tolerant liberal society in which everyone's conception of life is given equal weight; that this can best be achieved by a majoritarian political process, within the qualification that decisions antecedently likely to be made by external preferences are forbidden as interferences with rights.

At first sight, Dworkin's viewpoint is an attractive one, promising to justify our present political process but to support an acceptable list of human rights. However, Professor Hart, in 'Between Utility and Rights', *Columbia Law Review* (1974), has subjected it to devastating criticism. Some of the points he makes are:

a) Dworkin's 'rights' are limited to those decisions likely to be taken by external preferences in a majoritarian society. It does not cover situations of tyranny and authoritarianism; it also means that where people are more tolerant, there will be fewer, not more, rights (as less external preferences decisions are likely).

b) Allowing external preferences to be taken into account is not 'double counting' at all, as Dworkin suggests. It is merely counting the interested person's internal preferences, and the disinterested person's external preferences, once each.

c) Isn't the vice of some decisions reached by external preferences the decisions themselves, and their non-tolerance, and not the process by which the decisions were taken?

d) Similarly, isn't the denial of freedom in, say, laws against homosexuality best seen as a denial of freedom and fairness, rather than a failure of equal concern and respect on the basis of double-counting?

The argument, then, would seem to be at least seriously flawed. That might be a pity, since Dworkin's theory would produce results that would be for a democratic liberal acceptable.

One major point that emerges from all these discussions on justice throughout the last three chapters might be this: that, at the end of the day, isn't it true that (for all their arguments and justificatory reasoning) each theorist derives those principles of justice which satisfy his own value judgments?

15.10 Limitations on rights

Given that, like motherhood, one is generally in support of the existence of people's rights, the question arises as to whether there exist any circumstances where it would be desirable to limit those rights on the protection of which importance is placed. Having addressed the main views on the normative question of what rights ought to be, I would now like to approach the question of the limitations on rights from a substantive law angle.

However this cannot be divorced from the theoretical background which is discussed above. I have elaborated on this question primarily from the liberal perspective because it is from that perspective that this question is problematical.

In order then to answer the question a distinction would have to be made on the type of rights that one is prepared to override. Not all rights are overridable with legitimate justification. I have in mind the ones mentioned above as non-derogable. However the European Convention provides that in certain circumstances other rights and freedoms may be justifiably overridden. It lists two other categories of rights. Firstly, those that are subject to limitation or restriction and secondly, those that are derogable in times of war or other public emergency threatening the life of the nation. However such derogation is legitimate to the extent strictly required by the exigencies of the situation. The jurisprudence of the Council of Europe allows a certain margin of appreciation to the state concerned in the determination of how far this goes: see the *Greek Junta Cases* and *Ireland* v *The United Kingdom*, concerning conditions at prison camps in Northern Ireland. Dworkin would view the restrictions on rights in line with the derogation clause of Article 15 of the European Convention as a restriction on policy grounds whereas with regard to other restrictions such as that contained in Article 17 as one on grounds of principle.

Article 17 provides that the rights contained in the Convention cannot be pleaded in order to defeat the exercise or enjoyment of rights by others. There are ample case authorities illustrating the legitimacy of the denial of rights to those who seek to deny the rights of others. The *Federal German Communist Party Case* (1957) illustrated the denial of the freedom of association to an organisation which it was thought sought to deny the right of others. More recently the case of *Glimmerveen & Hagenbeck* v *The Netherlands* shows that the right to free speech does not extend to racists calling for the expulsion from the Netherlands of a racial group. In those circumstances one would support the jurisprudence of the organs of the Council of Europe in their justifiable overriding of the rights of some.

Thus Dworkin's rights thesis sees rights as trumps placing individual rights over considerations of general welfare and that these rights ought not be interfered with unless one is faced with the type of situation covered by either Article 15 or 17 of the European Convention. The problem is that such a view is not devoid of political considerations, whatever Dworkin may say about the political neutrality of the state in this matter.

Conclusion

Any discussion on rights is inevitably going to make political assumptions. It is on these political assumptions that most criticism is made. What is clear from Dworkin and to a certain extent a view now hijacked by the new left is that rights are anterior to law. When rights can justifiably be overridden depends then firstly, on political assumptions about the nature of rights, secondly, on the type of rights whether substantive or procedural and thirdly, on the circumstances one is minded to allow for such restriction.

15.11 Analytical and normative jurisprudence

So far we have examined the normative jurisprudence of rights which is essentially an action based exercise looking at the rights that people have or ought to have. It was said that normative jurisprudence was about the moral foundation of rights. Now we shall turn to the analytical jurisprudence of rights. Analytical jurisprudence concerns itself with analysis of concepts. It is essentially a 'dry' matter addressing itself to the problem of definition. Although we did not address the subject at the time as such the imperative theorists can be regarded as engaging in analytical jurisprudence in their search for a definition of 'law'. Later, we shall look at another concept, namely legal personality, from the point of view of analytical jurisprudence. At the outset I would state that in my view it is neither entirely possible, nor it is submitted would it be desirable, to separate analytical and normative jurisprudence, the reason being that in my view normative jurisprudence gives meaning to the exercise of analytical jurisprudence. Before examining what a right is it is desirable to ascertain what rights ought to be and who ought to have them and when, that is to say under what circumstances it would be 'legitimate' to restrict or otherwise limit the enjoyment of those 'rights'.

15.12 Hohfeld's scheme of jural relations

Within the area of the analytical jurisprudence of rights the starting point for any study must be, according to Lloyd and Freeman, the work of Wesley N Hohfeld. Hohfeld's writing on the subject of rights was undertaken at the early years of the twentieth century and it could indeed be said with some justification that he has made a considerable though hardly acknowledged contribution to our understanding of law. In his work, *Fundamental Legal Conceptions As Applied in Judicial Reasoning*, Hohfeld stated that the aim of his theory was to clarify different kinds of legal relations and the different uses to which certain words that are employed in legal reasoning are made. He sought to expose the ambiguities and to eliminate the confusion that surrounds these words. He was concerned to give meaning to the phrase 'X has a right to R' and to explain the set of jural relations that such a statement gives rise to. That objective can be achieved by the concept of right (which he also referred to as a claim; of privilege (liberty); of power and of immunity. These he saw as the lowest common denominators in which legal problems about rights could be stated. That proposition is one that is not without criticism. Indeed the contention of his critics is that whilst his scheme works for some propositions in which the phrase 'X has a right to R' could be fitted; it does not always work because his scheme could not take account of paternalistic criminal law. It is proposed to deal with this criticism in more depth below.

For Hohfeld these words (claim; privilege; power and immunity) are to be explained in terms of correlatives and opposites, as each of these concepts has both a jural opposite and a jural correlative. These contain eight fundamental conceptions and all legal problems could be stated in their terms. They thus represented a sort of lowest common denominator in terms of which legal problems could be stated. This he did by method of the following:

Jural opposites – right/no right; privilege/duty; power/disability; immunity/liability

Jural correlatives – right/duty; privilege/no right; power/liability; immunity/disability.

These terms can be defined as follows:

i)   By a right (claim) he meant that everyone is under a duty to allow X to do R and that X would have a claim against anyone from everyone to enforce that right.

ii)   By a privilege/liberty he meant that X is free to do or refrain from doing that which is the subject of R. Y has no claim against X if X either exercises or refrains from exercising that liberty.

iii)   By a power he meant that X is free to do an act whether or not he has a claim or a privilege and that this act would have the effect of altering the legal rights and duties of others.

iv)   By an immunity he meant that X is not subject to anyone's power to change his legal position.

v)   By a duty he meant that Y must respect X's right.

vi)   By no claim he meant that where X has a liberty Y has no claim that X should not exercise that liberty.

vii)   By disability he meant that the party has an inability to change another person's legal position.

It is important to emphasise that Hohfeld was examining legal rights and that the meanings attributed to his terms are technical and do not necessarily accord with their common usage.

Dias utilises a model developed by Glanville Williams which can be set out as follows:

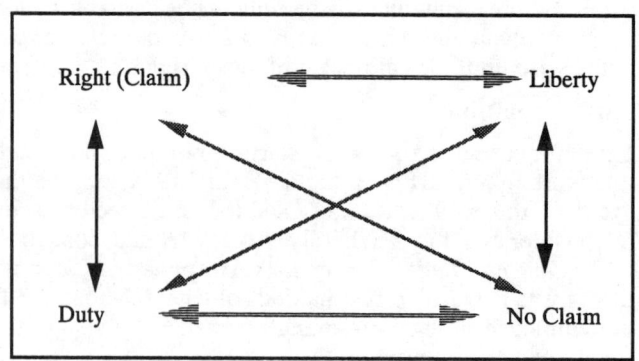

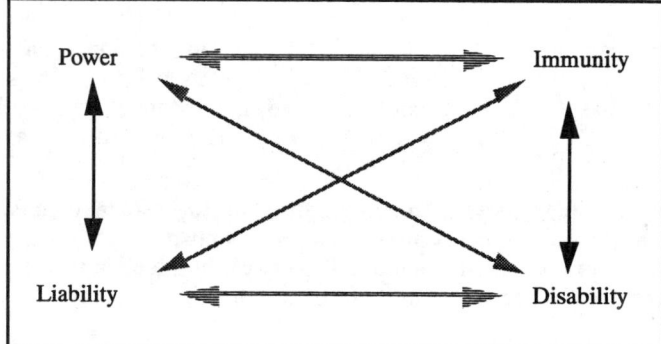

Changing jural relations

Key:

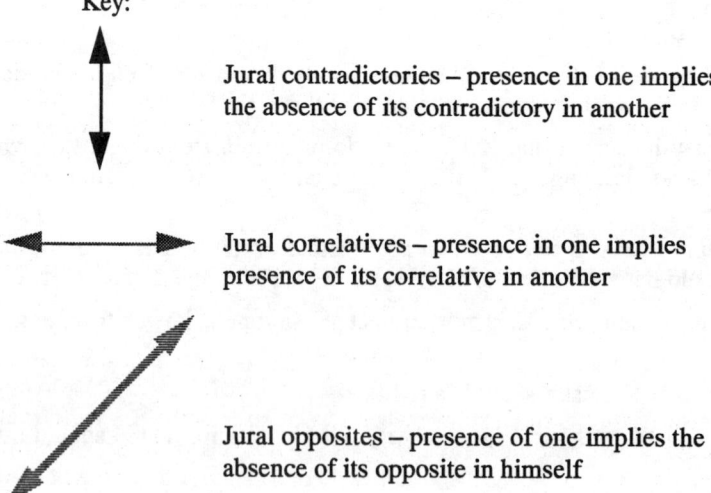

Jural contradictories – presence in one implies the absence of its contradictory in another

Jural correlatives – presence in one implies presence of its correlative in another

Jural opposites – presence of one implies the absence of its opposite in himself

The problem with this diagram is that while it appears to work on its face it does not use the same terminology as Hohfeld himself used and has therefore perhaps added to the confusion. On examination of the Glanville Williams diagram the arrows for jural correlatives are inverted with the arrows for jural contradictories. On the definitions offered by Hohfeld for his own terminology (see page 175) it would appear that a claim could not be regarded as the correlative of a liberty in the sense that the presence of a claim in one implies the presence of a liberty in another. It is submitted that the relation between a claim and a liberty is better described in Hohfeldian terms as a jural contradictory in that the presence of a claim in one implies the absence of its contradictory (a liberty) in another. This point is not however settled.

The aim of Hohfeld was to provide a model for the correct solution of legal problems and to make that solution easier and more certain. He would advocate that the judge and the legal theorist employ the above scheme in order to ensure greater understanding of these legal concepts. He wrote of the need to use the term 'right' in a very strict sense and not indiscriminately to cover a privilege, power and immunity. Nonetheless, it would not be necessary to Hohfeld that the legal practitioner actually employ the terms claim, power, etc so long as he thinks in terms of Hohfeld's scheme. It is thus possible to think Hohfeld without talking Hohfeld. This in my view adequately deals with the criticism of Hohfeld that he has adopted an unusual terminology which it would be naive to expect the legal profession to adopt overnight. Indeed Hohfeld's scheme was developed seventy years ago and still nothing much has happened by way of the legal profession adopting his terminology in the effort to clarify legal problems. Nonetheless, his contribution has been quite substantial although underrated to date. His scheme provides an excellent starting point for any theoretical discussion of rights. The major problem from this point of view is that of accepting the utility of a pure analytical approach to the question of a concept such as rights. As stated above it would be my view that an analysis of rights in the analytical sense would be determined by a prior position adopted by reference to the realm of normative jurisprudence. By normative jurisprudence in this context I understand the premise to be the moral foundation of rights – an examination of what rights people have and what rights they ought to have. Without this premise what 'right' would the analytical jurist examine?

As Dias observes, it would be necessary to view the relationship between the jural relations at rest and the changing jural relations in a temporal perspective in which he noted that a change in the power/liability relation will have a 'knock on' effect on the claim/duty relation. The power/liability relationship would be anterior to the claim/duty relationship since the claim/duty relationship would be created or amended by the power/liability relationship and would reflect any change therein. An example would be in the adverse possession of land. Here a change in power/liability where formerly the tenant could exclude the squatter has now changed and the squatter gains title to the exclusion of the tenant. Thus T previously had power ie the facility to alter another's (S) legal status. On the running of time S now acquires power and T is under a liability. This would then lead to a change in the claim and duty relation. From the sociological point of view it is relatively easy to accept that there will be changes in power relations. If not the society would be entirely static. Dias observes that changes in power are anterior to changes in claims. This seems to me to be quite acceptable.

15.13 Evaluation of Hohfeld's scheme

Whilst Hohfeld's scheme of jural relations is useful not only for illustrating the different forms which the word 'right' can take it also illustrates the interrelationships between these words. It is thus useful for distinguishing between claims, liberties, powers and immunities but it is argued that it would also be both necessary and desirable to retain a general concept of 'right' to denote institutions such as ownership or possession. As Cook, who was the editor of Hohfeld's work and generally sympathetic to his task, observes, Hohfeld mistakenly considers all rights as sets of any number of his four elementary rights, namely: claim, privilege, power and immunity. Rights are not sets of these. Their possession entails the possession of other rights or of powers and duties. For example, the concept of ownership includes rights of possession, transfer, sale, hire, use and enjoyment. Thus ownership creates a set of claims and powers. The concept of ownership can be seen as a set of rights. It does not denote the relationship between the owner and the tangible object.

His contribution has been useful although the difficulty is that it is not as widely used as he would have advocated. Nonetheless, as Lloyd and Freeman observe, it is the point to which all lawyers return. They perceive the value of his analysis in enabling the reduction of any legal transaction to relative simplicity and precision and in the enabling of the recognition of its universality.

Harris identifies three important advantages to his approach. Firstly, that it enables real normative choices to be disentangled from verbal confusions. Secondly, that if lawyers and judges were to employ his terminology that was not too far removed from that already employed then clarity would reign. The third advantage lies in their use. Hohfeld believed that juristic problems concerning the nature of compound concepts could be dissolved.

Although he has been criticised for insisting on correlativity in situations where correlativity is hardly present, eg the criminal law, the implicit answer that Harris finds in his defence of Hohfeld is that all litigation cases involve two opposing parties and as such viewing these concepts as correlatives is in that frame quite meaningful. It does however make an explanation of rights in rem impossible. Nonetheless, there are important criticisms of Hohfeld's scheme. In that he purports to analyse fundamental legal concepts he does so without taking account of any concept of law. He fails to provide an explanation of the process by which those conceptions are given their legal character. He further assumes that there is only one concept of duty. It is said that this is because his examples are drawn from civil and private law.

In criminal law his scheme hardly works. This it is submitted is because of the nature of the duty under criminal law. Whilst, as Harris observes in defence of Hohfeld, Hohfeld was concerned with the lowest common denominator in litigation, this would not in my view be applicable in a prosecution. The duty is not owed to the prosecution but to the society as a whole. That duty does not give rise to a right in anyone. Hohfeld's scheme is designed to cover one to one relations and not the relations between an individual and the society. Furthermore, it is suggested that with respect to paternalistic criminal law such as the laws that govern the wearing of seat belts in cars and the law of murder which forbids the defence of consent of the victim, the nature of the duty is one that the individual owes both to the society and to himself. As such when an individual has both a claim and a duty with regard to the same thing the scheme would be without application.

Roscoe Pound in *Legal Rights* noted that some of Hohfeld's conceptions are without what he called 'juridical significance' yet in a generally appreciative work Pound suggested that had Hohfeld lived he would have dealt with this point.

It could be argued that Hohfeld's scheme lacks any utility in that where a case is decided without the use of the scheme of jural relations then that scheme is superfluous, yet in those circumstances where the case is not in accord with the scheme then it is said that the scheme is wrong. Any theory should be subjected to the test of utility particularly a scheme that purports to offer a practical solution to a real problem. It is submitted that if the foregoing is correct then that would represent a major defect in the application of the scheme of jural relations in practice.

In spite of these criticisms, viewed in a chronological frame his contribution has been substantial. There have however since his work been further developments and elucidations such as the works of Hart and MacCormick on rights. They benefited from having available to them Hohfeld's analysis.

15.14 What rights do – choice protection or interest protection

In this context the debate between Hart and MacCormick over the role and nature of legal rights is particularly informative. The essence of the debate should be viewed within its political perspective.

a) *Hart's will theory*

Hart views rights as legally protected choices. He emphasises the power or option of one person to waive someone else's duty. Thus having a right is to do with the legal or moral recognition of some individual's choice as being pre-eminent over the will of others as to a given subject matter in a given relationship. This is applicable in the civil law area in matters such as contract. The essence of the holding of a right is that the holder has the choice whether to waive the duty owed to him. The connection with Hohfeld's scheme of jural relations is apparent in that such a view assumes a correlativity of rights and duties. In this theory the choice could be expressed in Hohfeldian terms as the choice of whether or not to exercise that right or power or privilege or immunity. A problem with this approach is that it makes the enforcement of a duty conditional on the exercise of a choice or will of a person other than the person who is under the duty. Y will only be under a duty if X who has a right in respect of that duty decides to exercise that right. A difficulty that Hart readily admits with this approach is that it fails to take account of the fundamental rights of the individual as against the legislature. For this right Hart invokes the 'immunity' as defined by Hohfeld.

b) *MacCormick's interest theory*

MacCormick criticises Hart's theory on the grounds that there are some rights which do not seem to involve the exercise of a choice at all. He argues that, particularly in the area of paternalistic criminal law, the law limits the power of waiver without destroying a substantive right. An example would be in respect of assault or of murder. The law will not admit the consent of the victim in defence to a prosecution. MacCormick argues that if one cannot consent to assault it follows that one is not exercising a choice on the right to freedom of the person. MacCormick maintains that the nature of rights can be viewed as protecting the interests of the right holder.

Looking at the difficult example of the 'rights' of a child MacCormick draws a distinction between the substantive right and the right to enforce the substantive right. He shows that the child possesses the substantive right to have its interest protected but lacks the right to enforce that right – the right to enforce is exercisable by the child's guardian on behalf of the child. Further the child cannot in fact nor in morals nor in law relieve his or her parents of their duty towards it. MacCormick then prefers the view of rights as protecting certain interests in the sense that either moral or legal normative constraints are imposed on the acts and activities of other people with respect to the objects of one's interest. Hart admits that if rights are all about choice then a young child would not possess any rights in that sense. As to the question of the protection of the child, Hart maintains that rights are not the only moral basis for protection and that other factors such as humanity, love and compassion also provide the basis for protection. If that is so then there would be no need for a formal assignment of rights to the child on its attaining the age of choice – perhaps the traditional 'key of the door' or other ceremonies of attaining adulthood also imply an assignment of rights from the parent to the child. Until that assignment of rights the parent would act as the child could have acted had it possessed the power to choose. A problem with the idea that rights are founded on love, etc is that it is impossible – I think! – to enforce love. Where there is no love, compassion, etc then there would be no protection of the child. Perhaps in reality that is what happens but it is not reflective of the legal position as the recent events in the Cleveland 'child abuse' inquiry demonstrated.

Hart rejects the view that rights are legally protected interests because he maintains that the interest analysis does not explain rights independently of duties – if a right is merely a protected interest then rights can always be expressed as a reflex of duties. MacCormick gives an example of the right of succession in intestacy. He shows that such a right cannot be rephrased in terms of the rights of the personal representatives because the right vests at death – prior to these duties. MacCormick maintains that the idea of correlativity obscures the fact that duties are imposed in order to protect rights. There may however be a problem with identifying the beneficiaries of a duty. In his book *Central Issues in Jurisprudence* Simmonds uses the example of the crash helmet law whereby all people riding on a motor bike are under a legal duty to wear a crash helmet. Who is the beneficiary? Surely not the manufacturers of crash helmets? MacCormick may not be entirely correct in his contention that the power to waive a right is not a necessary part of a right but is just something that a right often includes. In support of that contention he demonstrates that in certain circumstances it is necessary to override freedoms – for example, in contract the freedom to contract the terms is overriden by the recent consumer protection legislation. Simmonds sums it up thus, 'Even if

MacCormick has provided a convincing case against the correlativity of rights and duties it is by no means clear that he has provided a convincing alternative'.

MacCormick does admit the importance of the will theory in the explanation of rights. He put it thus, '...it cannot be denied that the central point of the theory is that apart from children and incapacitated persons the holder of a legal right is empowered in law to choose whether he should avail himself of his right on a specific occasion by insisting on performance of the correlative duty'. If that is so it might be assumed (albeit wrongly, it is submitted) that Hart and MacCormick's theories are compatible, but that would be to fall into the linguistic trap which was so much the concern of Hohfeld. For MacCormick the difficulty is in the absence of choice with regard to children's rights, the argument going that those rights are among those referred to by Hart in a footnote in his notion of immunity rights dependent upon individual benefit. In the Hohfeldian sense the rights of children as envisaged by MacCormick are claim rights whereas Hart's are immunity rights. Hence while both rights are fundamental and important they have different lowest common denominators.

By way of cross reference, attention should also be paid to the question of judicial discretion, as the issue there raised is whether there is always a legal right to cover every legal question to be adjudicated. Traditionally the answer has been that there is not always a right answer and that the judge is left with an area of discretion within which to decide the case before him. As is examined later, this question has been reassessed recently by Dworkin. Dworkin has suggested that the institutional materials always yield principles which give one party a right to the decision in their favour. It is not proposed to enter into a discussion on this issue here but to defer until the later study unit.

(B)   LEGAL PERSONALITY

15.15 Introduction

A right is not the only legal concept to have attracted much jurisprudential discussion. Another such concept is that of legal and especially corporate personality. Why are certain bodies treated in law as 'persons' and some bodies (trade unions, partnerships, unincorporated associations generally not? What (if anything) does it mean to say that a company is a 'person'?

I will look at the issues in four sections. First, I will look at the different types of legal person known to English law; second, I will evaluate the usefulness of the concept of personality with particular reference to corporations aggregate; third, I will outline various theories which purport to explain the concept, and finally I will join Professor Hart in suggesting that perhaps the theories obscure more than they illuminate.

15.16 Different types of legal personality

There are three types of personality recognised in English law; in relation to any question, you should ask yourself if it is about one or all three.

a) *Human beings*

No distinction is drawn in law between legal and natural persons. Hohfeld sees human beings as merely a multitude of claims, liberties, powers etc. But it should be noted that the notion of a human being is more flexible than might be thought. We shall examine some of these:

  i) *A foetus* – what is the legal status of an unborn child (pre-natal deformity? child destruction?) The example of the legal personality of a foetus has raised interesting and emotive questions recently. In the case of *C v S* (1987) the question arose for consideration. Briefly, in that case a man who claimed to be the father of a foetus attempted to prevent the mother of the foetus from proceeding with an abortion after their relationship broke down. His grounds were to invoke the criminal law against the destruction of a child 'capable of being born alive' (s1 Infant Life Preservation Act 1929). The rather controversial interpretation given to that phrase by the House of Lords need not detain this text. What is of importance is the observation that it took the father (or any other interested person) to bring the action and not the foetus, yet if the foetus had been a legal person it could have brought the action itself. Practical problems of instructing solicitors, etc from the womb can in this legal system be overcome – there are procedures to enable the incompetent to be party to actions. The implication though is wide. The foetus would have a separate legal personality to the mother carrying it. The mother would merely be a walking incubator for another legal person. The mother would owe that person a duty of care that would give rise to that 'person' having a cause of action where, for example through smoking cigarettes, the mother caused the foetus damage. If the foetus is a legal person then it would be party to an action to prevent an abortion, etc. I would imagine that other factors will be considered in seminars – enough for present purposes to raise the questions. By way of anecdote for those interested I understand that although the House of Lords held that the foetus could be aborted as at the stage of gestation that it had reached, it was not capable of 'sustaining' life if born. The mother continued with the pregnancy and the child is being brought up by the father – (a happy ending?).

ii) *A dead person* – legal personality extends to those humans who are alive and of an existence independent of their mother. What is the position with regard to the dead? They have legal interests, such as that their wishes as expressed in their will are carried out, for example. The law has studiously avoided any definition of death – see *R* v *Malcherek & Steel* – probably for the very sound reason that advances in medical science and technology would outstrip the capacity of the law to keep pace and we would arrive at a situation, as we have for example in criminal law, where the definition of insanity has become fossilised in 1843 (*McNaghten's case*) in spite of very considerable advances since then. So what quite constitutes legal death is not that clear. I think that the proposition stated at the start of this sub-section to the effect that so far as natural persons are concerned a prerequisite of legal personality is independent live existence is true. The dead may have certain rights, to have their property disposed of according to their legal wishes, but that is as far as it goes.

iii) *A married couple* – the former example that used to be used was that a husband and wife were treated as one person for certain tax matters, eg mortgage interest relief and the filling of tax return forms that required a wife to disclose to her husband all the sources of her taxable income because the husband was under the legal duty to declare that income of his wife to the Inland Revenue. That position has been changed in the Finance Act 1988 although aspects of it have not at the date of writing entered into force. I do not envisage this rather antiquated rule that regarded a wife as an appendage of her husband being revived.

iv) *Status* – another flexible aspect is that there are different relationships to think about - status (parent, slave, consumer) and capacity (the same person can have two or more in some factual situation; trustee and beneficiary, shareholder and employee and company director, for instance).

b) *Corporations sole*

A corporation sole is a person with a perpetual existence, ie an office, the personification of an official capacity. Examples are parsons, bishops, the Crown (the Queen has a different personality for each country where she is the monarch). The main rationale behind the corporation sole is that the continuity of jural relations, such as the holding of property, is made possible. This need hardly detain us further.

c) *Corporations aggregate*

These are companies or other corporations created by charter, statute or under the Companies Acts. They are treated as persons in law unless the contrary is stated (statutes use 'individuals' if they mean humans and unincorporated associations but not corporations). Some unincorporated associations are given some of the incidental benefits of corporations but they are still not 'persons'. Partnerships, for example, can issue writs in their own name and can make contracts, but the individual partners remain fully liable as individuals.

15.17 Is legal personality a useful concept?

The flexibility of treatment given to the notion of a human being is useful and corporations sole have their limited effectiveness allowing in the continuation of property ownership and contractual relations. This question as to the usefulness of the concept of legal personality is, though, most relevantly considered with regard to the corporations aggregate.

a) *The uses of corporations aggregate*

These have been stated as:

i) *Convenience*

The convenience offered by conferring powers and liabilities on a unit rather than on each individual shareholder involved (imagine suing British Telecom if it were otherwise!).

ii) *Limited liability*

Shareholders do not attract liability except to the extent of their respective shareholdings, and directors and employees are only liable for their personal negligence; this is subject to the frequent requirement of personal guarantees, from participants in small companies.

iii) *Perpetuity of succession*

This applies on death, retirement, sale of shares.

iv) *Ability to sue*

Can sue or be sued, can own property (this is really an aspect of (a)).

v) *Separate ownership*

Ownership and control can be separated, allowing investors to risk their money but under the control of expert management. In many public quoted companies, ownership and control is totally divorced in this way.

vi) *Other advantages*

Generally, an individual trader can escape personal liability (subject to personal guarantees) and it is easier for a company to raise capital than for a sole trader. Note though that the courts do sometimes lift the corporate veil (there is a list of instances of this in Dias). Note also that some of the advantages can be achieved without a separate personality being used. For example, writs can be served on partnerships, and property is often held by some only of the partners. This allows ownership to be passed more easily. Also, a big partnership will often split its management from the bulk of the owning partners. Think also of the special treatment of trades unions and employers' associations in English law.

b) *Problems with corporations aggregate*

Corporations aggregate also raise the following problems:

i) *Groups*

English law has difficulties in dealing with the idea of a group of companies: for most purposes they are treated as separate units rather than as a collective entity, which is most unrealistic. Some inroads have however been made into this problem; group companies now submit consolidated accounts and are taxed as a unit, for example.

ii) *Inflexibility*

Even small companies have to fulfil statutory requirements suitable for much larger outfits. The present government is committed to relaxing some of these requirements and it is already the case that small companies have to submit less complete accounts, for instance.

iii) *Unfairness*

Small creditors never have security and so can lose heavily in an insolvency. There are some restrictions in the Insolvency Act 1986 on directors involved in just setting up a similarly named company in such cases (only time will tell on their effectiveness) and there are various possibilities of penalties or civil remedies (including disqualification) against directors involved in an insolvency see the Companies Directors Disqualification Act 1986. But these generally will not benefit small unsecured creditors, who can't afford to rely on them. It is a myth that a customer or supplier is safer dealing with a limited company than an individual trader or partnership – often the reverse is the case.

iv) *Inconsistency*

It is not at all clear why some legal rules and regulations apply to all companies but not to other (often larger) organisations which organise themselves as partnerships. Often the choice of business medium is based on taxation considerations rather than on which medium is more suitable in terms of its inherent characterstics.

15.18 The theories – what theories are used to explain legal personality?

There are four main theories for us to consider, albeit in each case rather briefly. We will try to analyse for each theory which elements of the law it can, and cannot, account for. None of the theories performs spectacularly well!

a) *Fiction theory*

First, we will look at the 'fiction theory', supported by Savigny and in England by Coke, Blackstone and especially Salmond. Juristic or artificial persons are only treated as if they are persons, under this view. They are fictitious, not known as persons apart from the law. The law gives them proprietary rights, grants them legal powers and so on, but they have no personality and no will (except to the extent a will is implied by the law). This is an obviously flexible viewpoint, since it can account for any apparent inconsistency in legal treatment by simply saying that they are only treated as persons 'to that extent'. The doctrine of ultra vires, under which a company cannot do anything not authorised by its memorandum of association might be thought to support the fiction theory, on the basis that the law only gives personality to the limit of the memorandum, and so might the doctrine that a company is separate from its members, epitomised in the leading case of *Salomon*. This case shows the law treats the company as a separate unit, even though in fact it is not, especially in the one-man company cases like *Salomon*.

Further support for this theory could be claimed from the criminal law, which originally accepted that a company could not commit a criminal offence which depends on mental intention. The fiction view explains this on the basis of the 'will' of the 'person' only being that given by law, and therefore presumably being limited to lawful intention. Recent developments show a more pragmatic and sensible approach to the question of corporate liability, with companies being subject to more criminal liability (and also subject to liability for the torts of their servants). Also, the cases where the law allows the corporate veil to be turned aside can be explained as limitations on the grant of the fictitious personality.

Acceptable explanations, then, are provided by the fiction theory for many aspects of company law (although many of them can be explained acceptably by other theories, see below).

However, no explanation is given of why the law uses the idea of 'personality'; is there an essential similarity to real persons or not? Hart has emphasised some of the faults raised in relation to this theory, particularly the illogicality involved in denying that a company can commit certain crimes because it has no 'mind'.

Some other theories are similar to and bound up with the fiction theory, notably the concession theory (that legal personality flows from the state) and the symbolist theory of Ihering.

b) *Hohfeld's theory*

This theory is not mirrored in English writing on the subject. Since only human beings have juristic relations, one must, according to Hohfeld, explain companies in a complex way by looking at the capacities, rights, powers and liabilities of the individuals involved. This view is clearly related to Hohfeld's analysis of rights; however, it again fails to give us an explanation of why the notion of a company is used, the notion of a separate personality.

c) *Realist*

This view sees an 'artificial person' as a real personality, having a real mind, will and power of action. It is associated with Gierke, Dicey, Pollock and (though Hart doubts it) Maitland.

If independent power of action was the only requirement of our definition of a 'person' and 'personality', perhaps an artificial person would qualify (but has a company really got a power of action independent of its members and officials?); surely though there is something more. To say a corporation is a real person implies an individuality, and that implies some consciousness, experience, inner unity. Some groups may seem to have such a unity and consciousness – one could talk of such a feeling over the reaction to the Ethiopian famine crisis, for instance – but do all legal personalities fit? Surely a corporation sole (consisting of successive holders of one office) hasn't a 'consciousness', nor has a multi-national company, nor even a small company? Perhaps a university might be thought to fit?

In any case, even if the legal personalities could be counted as real persons, a further problem arises. If a two-man company is a person in reality, why not a two-man partnership? If a one-man company, why not a one-man business? If a university, why not a private law college, one that is unincorporated? The 'realist theory' fails to explain why the legal definition of personality does not match the extended realist definition.

Returning to some of the aspects of English law already considered, realist theory can account for the ultra vires doctrine (the real personality constituted by the company as set up by its documents), albeit rather weakly (isn't it a weakness to have to refer to legal documents to establish the limits of reality?); but it can't successfully accommodate the tearing aside of the corporate veil. If the company is a real entity distinct from its members, surely it should always be viewed as such and not sometimes viewed as a collection of its members?

Finally, realism can account for those instances where criminal law applies to a company: can it account for those when it doesn't (if a board meeting orders an execution, the company isn't guilty of murder: why not)? The reason why it would not in the likelihood of a board resolution so ordering be guilty of murder is that it is incapable of forming the necessary mens rea for murder. Obviously, considerations as to suitable penalty will also be relevant (it is impractical to imprison a company!) The recent suggestions of possible prosecution whether public or private against a ferry operating company for corporate manslaughter as a result of suggestions in the inquiry into the events at Zeebrugge demonstrate an actual example of the criminal law responsibility of a corporation.

Hart has raised some additional points. The theory (as with the fiction theory) has illogical barriers; for example, it has been suggested that a company cannot be bound by an agreement with another company because that would be degrading, and the realist view has difficulties with a one-man 'technical' company – isn't such a company not a real entity but just a convenient device for the individual proprietor?

Linked to this theory is the 'organic' theory, the name of which is quite accurate and suggests that a company acts through the various organs that constitute it. In this theory the board of directors will take decisions concerning the day to day running of the company whereas the general meeting will take decisions concerning the constitution of the company. So long as the proper decision is taken in the proper way by the proper body it will be considered at law as the act/decision of the company.

d) *Purpose*

The final view is the purpose theory developed by Brinz and in England by Barker. On this view, only human beings are persons, but the law protects certain purposes other than human beings. The creation of artificial persons just gives effect to a purpose (for example, a charitable corporation is created to give effect to various devices by which the law aids the charitable cause). So company property is held not by a person, but for a purpose.

This view has a fundamental flaw. It does not answer the question. It is obviously true that companies and other artificial legal persons are given their status for a purpose (or various purposes). The question remains, why call them 'persons'? What aspect of these entities makes them so akin to real people that the law uses the same name and to a great extent applies the same rules?

A purpose view can explain the ultra vires doctrine (a company is limited to its express purposes, as mentioned in the memorandum), and even the tearing aside of the veil (the countering weight of other legal purposes), cannot explain the concept of an artificial person.

Our conclusion at this point is that none of the various explanations given of the nature of corporate personality is satisfactory.

15.19 Do the theories obscure?

Both Paton on *Jurisprudence* and Hart in his inaugural lecture at Oxford, *Definition and Theory in Jurisprudence,* think that the answer to the question is yes, because the theorists, in trying to ascertain what is the nature of corporate personality, are asking the wrong question. Paton writes that seeking the essence of, the connecting factor between, the various different types of legal persons, natural and artificial, is the wrong approach because there is no connecting factor except the similarity and treatment meted out by the law to the different persons.

Hart's views are somewhat different. The slim booklet setting out his inaugural lecture (which is also set out in his *Essays on Jurisprudence and Philosophy*) is well worth reading. Briefly he considers that the question 'what is corporate personality?' is seeking the wrong type of definition.

Just as with other concepts found in law, such as a right or a duty, corporate personality has no straightforward connection in the world of fact, nothing to which it corresponds. It should not, therefore, be defined in the same way as the table or chair you are sitting at or on, since these things do have an item to which they correspond in nature – they exist and can be touched in the real world of scientific cause and effect. Hart goes on to say that the theories which we have looked at above are often in the clouds and do not deal with practical realities.

What then is Hart's alternative? Well, he says, picking up an idea that he attributes to, among others, Bentham, corporate personality and the other legal concepts should be defined not by looking just at the words themselves but rather by considering a characteristic sentence in which they appear and then explaining the conditions under which the words are used – under what conditions does the law ascribe liabilities to corporations? By this method we can avoid questions such as those relating to a corporation's supposed will.

Hart in *Definition and Theory*, pp 17-18 imagines an innocent lawyer from Arcadia to whom the notion of a legal or corporate personality is introduced for the first time. He would learn what types of legal personality there were and the forms of statement in general use by which rights were ascribed to Smith & Co Limited in circumstances in some ways similar to and in some ways different from those in which they were ascribed to Smith as an individual. He would see that the analogy was sometimes thin but that given the circumstances set out in the Companies Acts and in the general law the statement 'Smith & Co Ltd owes White £10' applied as directly to the facts after its own fashion as 'Smith owes White £10'.

On his return to Arcadia he would tell of the extension to corporate bodies of rules worked out for individuals and of the analogies followed and the adjustments of ordinary words involved. He would, in short, have explained corporate personality without any need to get into the confusing and obscure theories which I have set out above. In Hart's words 'we could make the simple Arcadian feel the theorist's agonies only by inducing him to ask "what is Smith & Co Ltd?" and not to admit in answer a description of how, and under what, conditions the names of corporate bodies are used in practice, but instead to start the search for what it is that the name taken alone describes, for what it stands, for what it means'.

In conclusion, if one accepts Hart's position then the question of the nature of legal personality will be seen as a red herring.

16 ANALYTICAL JURISPRUDENCE 2: LANGUAGE AND LAW

16.1   Introduction

It is plain to any student of law (or indeed of jurisprudence) that there is something 'puzzling' about legal language. As Glanville Williams points out in *Language and the Law*, many of the problems that lawyers and jurists face are problems of understanding language. He therefore suggests that an understanding of semantic philosophy would be of help to elucidate the language 'puzzles' of law and jurisprudence. In this chapter we will consider two approaches that have taken up the challenge of semantics in the search for the truth about law.

16.2   Hart's use of linguistic philosophy in legal analysis

Hart reminds us in *Definition and Theory in Jurisprudence*, that jurists such as Bentham have long been aware of the dangers of words. Hart, however, addresses this problem with considerable veuve. So successful has Hart been, that semantic analysis has become a feature of modern positivism. MacCormick suggests that it is necessary for positivists to have some outlook with regard to the philosophy of language. Why then is language so important to Hart and positivism?

16.3   Refuting essentialism

a) Essentialism is a term employed to denote two ideas that are related, but distinct. On the one hand there is the view that behind every noun there is an actual reality that it denotes on a physical or metaphysical level. Thus, in the same way that when we say 'box' we can find a reality that is some sort of receptacle, behind the word 'right' there is a real metaphysical entity, floating around on a metaphysical level. Obviously, if this is so, then it might be possible, by reason and philosophy, to gain an understanding of what this 'reality' is. There is a strong relationship between this notion and some early Natural Law theories which saw an ideal legal system residing in some metaphysical supermarket.

b) The second strand of essentialism is somewhat less troublesome, and may be found reflected in some 'positivist' thinkers. This sees a word as denoting a common factor or essence intrinsic to a class of objects, things or practices. By a process of logic, this essence might be distilled out from other factors in order to express the real nature of the word. Thus, some Natural Law theorists as well as Austin and even Kelsen seek to give the concept of law an essential unity. A commitment to the search for such logical unity need not entail a belief that concepts have a reality lurking in obscurity, but does commit one to the view that there is one 'right answer' to the question, 'What is law?' or 'What is a legal system?' This is a commitment to the view that one central idea can be and is shared by all people who use the word 'law'. This idea might be expressed in the form of a definition.

c) There is an essential (forgive the pun) problem with this. One might easily describe a material object, such as 'my dog Fido', but when does a description become a prescription? For example, if I seek to define what weeds are, at what point do I stop merely describing the features of what are commonly regarded as characterising weeds, such as a tendency to stifle other plants and infest lawns? Surely the definition of a 'weed' is a plant that I do not wish to cultivate, ie a weed is a plant I should not grow. Similarly, by defining what law is, can I not tend to slip into saying what ought to be regarded as law? This is, for the legal 'scientist', an unpardonable sin. The legal scientist seeks to describe what law is, not what we ought to regard it as. Thus Hart, following linguistic philosophy, particularly that of Wittgenstein, seeks to escape from this by asking, 'What is the word "law" used (in legal discourse) to denote?' Furthermore he eschews definitions, instead concentrating on the 'focal' usages. He does not posit a definition of what law is, which requires a 'linguistic recommendation', ie suggesting what it is appropriate to call law. Rather he engages in a description of legal discourse seeking to ask what certain key concepts are being used for. Hart describes his concept of law as an 'essay in descriptive sociology' since he is attempting to view law as a form of linguistic behaviour from which we can infer certain attitudes (see Chapter 6 for an account of the critical reflexive attitude, which Hart regards as the focal area of law). Thus, for Hart, the nature of the jurisprudential enquiry is a search for the revelations of language use.

d) It may be noted that one would expect this to limit Hart's conclusions to the English-speaking legal system. The specific nature of language means that concepts, especially legal ones, do not translate easily. Hart is a scholar of considerable ability, but the linguistic variations of countries would suggest that his task is quite a considerable one if he wishes to arrive at a general theory of law. In order to overcome this, Hart commits himself to the concept of rules, which, it might be suggested, is a partial lapse into essentialism. Dworkin criticises positivists for their search for an illusionary unity in law, which seems exactly what the positivists were trying to avoid. Dworkin, in *Law's Empire*, addresses the difficulty of definitions in an interesting way. He posits an 'abstract definition' which he suggests is fairly uncontroversial, and upon which he does *not* built his theory. Instead it is employed as a 'plateau for argumentation', that is a starting point for discussion of legal theories, rather than as a limitation of such a discussion. Whether he is successful or not, (and some, like N E Simmonds, suggest he is not), this is a different approach to overcoming the problem of essentialism.

16.4 Hart's approach

a) *A summary of why definitions 'don't work'*

'Descriptions of methods [of deciding cases] actually used by courts must be distinguished from prescriptions of alternative methods and must be separately assessed.' Hart's statement in *Problems of the Philosophy of Law* epitomises the positivist conception that law must be studied scientifically. The linguistic philosophy of Wittgenstein and of J L Austin seems to offer a method of determining objective meanings of concepts and words, rather than prescriptions of what that word should mean. For example, if one looks the word 'law' up in a dictionary, why is that not a sufficient definition to work from? The answer is that the dictionary provides us with a view of what is regarded as the 'proper' use of the word, rather than what the actual use is. For this reason, definitions in the dictionary are changed when they cease to be descriptively accurate statements of how people do use the word.

b) *The meaning of legal concepts*

Hart sees actual legal 'speech acts' as being properly 'legal' in the context of their use. When one says, 'I have a right to silence' it presupposes rules, currently regarded as expressing a reason for action. Thus, isolated concepts are not 'essentially' legal, but legal because they refer to other things that are legal. The distinctive feature of legal discourse is that it employs concepts that are not properly explicable in terms of everyday definitions. Therefore one should not seek to understand the word 'contract' when used in legal discourse, in any other way than by reference to the rules that require performance of obligations embodied in the totality of legal discourse. Thus, for Hart, law is self-defining and legal concepts are legal because they 'belong' to legal discourse. Law concepts belong to a 'language game' called 'Law', rather in the same way as the meaning of 'Park Lane' on a Monopoly board is only explicable by reference to the rules of that game. While both 'contract' and 'Park Lane' have counterparts in ordinary discourse, they are separated by their usage in a different 'form of life'. The relationship between a legal word and its ordinary counterpart might thus be merely that of analogy. If we look at the concept of 'reasonableness' under the Wednesbury rules, we find that the analogy with the everyday usage of 'reasonableness' is very slim. Similarly, if I have a piece of paper that I think is a contract, that says 'contract' on it and looks like other contracts I have seen, it may still not be a contract, legally speaking. Ordinary reality is thus only the same as legal reality, when ordinary reality accords with the rules of the game of 'Law'. This analysis would accord, I am sure, with what the student has been told about law.

c) *Rules*

Hart talks of rules, but what are these except being mere words? To this the answer is that 'speech acts' are part of a larger pattern of behaviour. Thus, there is the requirement that there is an understanding of what a rule means, how it will be/has been applied, and what 'breaking' or 'conforming' to the rule means. Hart gives a clue to his view of this process in *Signs and Words* where he indicates that there should not only be a speech act or sign (the actus reus), but the speaker should have had the intention that those words be understood and responded to in a certain way (like a denial of consent in a rape case). Furthermore, the respondent should be aware (mens rea) that the speaker intends that he (the respondent) ought to act in accordance with the rule, without necessarily acting in that way. I have put these legal terms in parenthesis in order to help the student understand the relative mental positions, but also to illustrate how Hart's conception of human communication seems to be informed by legal convention, rather than human convention. The problem is that, like 'yes means no' rape cases, different words mean different things to different people in different situations. Hart's language game has thus postponed the problem of definition, rather than avoided it entirely. Different fact situations in law may seem to fit rules differently; sometimes clearly within a rule, sometimes not so clearly. This is a lot to do with the complexity of the subject matter that law seeks to regulate. In Monopoly, being entitled to a salary is as simple as 'passing Go', there are not very many other variables in the actions that the rules of Monopoly govern. However, a claim for payment under a contract of employment requires rules in the legal game that cover the infinite variables of employer-employee relationships. A verbal formulation of legal rule must seek to anticipate this, yet must be finite enough to be comprehended. Thus, things might seem to fall clearly into the rule because they are directly anticipated, while other circumstances need to be related to the rule by wider reasoning. This facet of rules is what Hart terms their 'open texture', which embodies clear or focal cases, that are directly equivalent to the formulation of the rule and penumbral areas that are related to the circumstances envisaged by the rule, but are not clearly anticipated by it. Hart's assertion that the judge uses his discretion in the latter instances is critically discussed in Chapter 19.

Simply stopping at this generalisation is, some would say, to postpone and then ignore the question. Hart is merely saying that some usages of a word are obvious, while others are less obvious. The meaning of a legal concept is thus understood in factual terms as where reality obviously corresponds with the legal rules that define that concept. The meaning of the word 'contract' becomes, in this analysis, what is obviously a contract to a contract lawyer. However, it is also what a judge, in his discretion, when considering a document that falls less obviously within the rules, thinks a contract ought to be. Thus, the meaning of a legal term is the legally obvious meaning it has, together with the meaning that a judge might give to it. This is a simplification, but it illustrates a problem with the approach. Certainly lawyers deal with definitions that have a possibility of multiple meanings, some more obvious than others, and seek more concrete judgments from other rules, but surely the meaning is better expressed by the motivation and ideology behind the rules of contract, eg 'A contract is a means by which mutual undertakings that accord with legal institutional requirements may be institutionally guaranteed.'

An alternative criticism is put forward in a fascinating, though technical, article by Goodrich, *The Role of Linguistic Legal Analysis*. The argument of this critic is based upon developments in linguistics which would seem to emphasise that a 'speech act' cannot be isolated from its social, ideological and material context, since these have a bearing on the interpretation of words. Some legal-linguistic thinkers, such as Lenoble and Ost, deny that any word can ever have a consistent meaning since contexts are always variable. This radical relativism defies practical use; however, it serves to indicate that the meaning of law as opposed to its expression in words or on paper is the interpretation given to it by an individual. When the positivist says law is what positive law is, then he can do nothing but show us what the expressions of law are, or he may seek to do what Hart pursues with 'sociology', which is to say this is what I think other people think, because this is generally what they do/say.'

16.5 Evaluation

Hart's linguistic analysis does not seem to explain the meaning of the legal game and its constituent concepts, but merely explains how to find out how the game is played. Hart is fond, as was Wittgenstein, of the games motif, yet games are often described in terms of their particular purpose. Even esoteric games such as cricket can be described in terms other than their rules either by their purpose (a combination of athletic skill, tactical ability and chance pursued by competing groups of individuals for pleasure and/or profit) or analogy (the Englishman's version of baseball). Surely these are more elucidating than what Hart would postulate: 'primary rules interacting with secondary power conferring rules (if there is an umpire) in more developed contests, where there may be consideration of human vulnerability (such as is found in the "bad light" rule and others in cricket).'

Hart's linguistic approach might be seen as having lost something of the 'spirit' of the legal enterprise. Much criticism of Hart's linguistic approach comes from those with an orientation towards 'Critical Legal Studies' such as Goodrich (cited above). However, others, such as MacCormick and Dworkin, who are not averse to a linguistic analysis of some kind, view Hart's views as descriptively inaccurate, rather than methodologically flawed in its linguistic premises. Each critic of Hart has, however, his own agenda. The Critical Legal Studies Movement seeks to develop new ways of reading law so as to evaluate it in the light of reforming goals. Dworkin emphasises that judges search for political morality and principles in their decisions to the aim that judges continue law in a democratic and rights orientated genre, likening the process to literary analysis of a 'chain novel'. MacCormick searches for narrative coherence to explain how laws interact, in search of the key to legal reasoning.

16.6 Jackson's 'Law, fact and narrative coherence'

While Wittgenstein concluded that philosophical discourse should best take place in poetry (leading to suggestions that he was 'mad') and Iain Stewart and Peter Rush see Kafka's novel *The Trial* as a significant contribution to jurisprudence, Jackson sees a humble, but significant role for analysis of legal discourse. He sees social sciences and social psychology as a means of describing the way in which lawyers seem to reason, but he does not see it as providing the answer to how lawyers actually make decisions. This combination of linguistic and other enquiries into signs and narrative meanings of behaviour is termed 'semiotics'.

Jackson sees legal discourse as a form of 'story telling'. Law students, when they learn to 'think like lawyers', are actually being encouraged to 'internalise a set of frameworks of understanding which represent the conventions of that particular profession or "semiotic group" … a set of narrative frameworks regarding the legal recognition of typical behaviour patterns.' He adds that these 'stories' are related with accompanying judgments of institutional approval or disapproval. Thus, the student who has a vast resource of legal stories with 'happy endings' in terms of a judgment in favour, or 'horror stories', may learn to expect in analogous stories, analogous endings. The following are interesting among his conclusions:

a) Legal statements seem to be encoded messages that call upon the listener to bring into play his prior knowledge of legal 'stories' that he remembers. Furthermore they have a purpose relating to practical action.

b) Jackson sees legal adjudication as a series of interlocking narratives. The book is primarily an attempt to reconstruct the common law trial process, although it concentrates on the adjudication process, which is the point at which a judge seeks to logically justify his position.

Semiotics claims to be a multi-disciplinary approach to legal analysis, but one which concentrates on the language element of law, simply because language is so much of the law. The advantage of the approach is that it does not exclude other disciplines such as history and social psychology, factors ignored by Hart which caused much criticism of his approach. However, it does not sacrifice 'reasons' given in legal statements for valuations from those disciplines. This is probably why the critical legal theorists are critical of Jackson, even though there is a shared resource of information for both lines of enquiry. For all the limitations of the semiotic approach that Jackson represents, there seems to be common sense in an approach that combines linguistic analysis with other disciplines. Moreover, I think the analogy with 'stories' is a strong one, especially considering the common law orientation towards case law. Stories are constructed on the basis of credible (or incredible) events that seem coherent if they conform to the genre. Furthermore, this approach advances our understanding of the quality of law that refers to previous cases (stories) and statutes (new story lines) in a way that is natural and elucidating. The semiotic approach, or more broadly, the literary approach (as exemplified by Dworkin in Chapter 19), seems to be an interesting direction for jurisprudence to take, since law is the result of human creativity, a fact that may account for the difficulty that has being experienced by those who seek to treat legal material in a 'scientific' manner (eg Kelsen).

16.7 Is legal reasoning logical?

The question of the logic of legal reasoning is perhaps more properly a question of the adjudication process. However, express legal reasoning claims to be logical. If adjudication is something more than the telling of 'tall tales', we would expect that legal reasoning has a foundation in deductive logic. Thus, we might ask the question, 'Is legal reasoning logical?'

In Professor Griffith's view, as expressed in *The Politics of the Judiciary*, legal reasoning is nothing more than a smokescreen for a political decision. However most writers concentrate on examining the form rather than the content of the reasoning and it is here that consideration can be given to the question as to whether legal reasoning is logical. As to form then, legal reasoning can take either a deductive or an inductive form. By deductive is meant that a logical necessary conclusion is drawn from major and minor premises; by inductive is meant that propositions are arrived at after collection and sorting of data. The former, deductive reasoning, may well be true of factual propositions but is not available in normative terms. This was demonstrated by David Hume in his *Treatise on Human Nature* in which he denied to the natural lawyer the use of the deductive syllogism. As for the inductive form, this would closely resemble the type of reasoning used in the common law with reference to the reliance and emphasis placed on precedent as authority.

The observation that legal reasoning is not logical stems from the premise that as the tools of the law are words and that as these words are not instruments of mathematical precision, then it would not be useful to apply logical reasoning to the resolution of legal problems. Words possess an 'open texture'. There is in the words of Hart a penumbral area of doubt as to their meaning. It is in these penumbral areas that legal problems arise for if the matter fell within the core of meaning of the word(s) then there would hardly be more than a trivial dispute involved. Where the matter falls within the penumbral meaning then it is said that logical reasoning is less useful than the employment of legal rules which act as a means for deciding disputes. This is not to say that the method of resolving disputes on the basis of legal rules is arbitrary. Lloyd and Freeman see legal reasoning as essentially a justification for a value judgment. Rules of law are not linguistic or logical rules. They continue that the choice of which rule to apply '... is not logical in the sense of being deductively inferred from given premises, but it has a kind of logic of its own, being based on rational considerations which differentiate it sharply from mere arbitrary assertion.' Hence the logic is that they are not arbitrary but rather that in law reasoning is done by analogy and that there is a certain 'logic' to that process.

MacCormick in *Legal Reasoning and Legal Theory* takes the view that in the litigation of a question of law deductive reasoning is not possible. An example would be the case of *Donoghue* v *Stevenson* (1932). Here no amount of logical reasoning would have produced Lord Atkin's formulation of the neighbour principle. Lord Atkin almost gave the game away when he said '... I do not think so ill of our jurisprudence as to suppose that its principles are so remote from the ordinary needs of civilised society and the ordinary claims it makes upon its members as to deny a legal remedy where there is so obviously a social wrong ...' The essence of his technique, now widely used in duty of care cases, is to use previous cases as examples rather than as authorities. This allows the court to find new duty of care situations in circumstances where these are not contradicted by previous authority. The speech of Lord Buckmaster, dissenting, adopts an alternative view, being one of incremental legal reasoning by which any new proposition must find support in an already existing authority. This can be illustrated in the passage where he said, '... The law applicable is the common law, and though its principles are capable of application to meet new conditions not contemplated when the law was laid down, these principles cannot be changed nor can additions be made to them because any particular meritorious case seems outside their ambit.'

The attack on the proposition that legal reasoning can be logical in any but trivial cases finds further support in the area of statutory interpretation. The golden rule of statutory interpretation (see eg *R* v *Allen* (1872)) illustrates the way the application of a literal meaning of a word can lead to absurdity. The circumstances under which the court would consider the consequence to be absurd are not found in any logic. A comparison of the case of *R* v *Allen* and *Fisher* v *Bell* (1961) illustrate this point. In the former case the court was concerned that the legislature may have enacted an absurdity in that according to the literal meaning of the words the offence of bigamy could not have been committed and so they applied a varied meaning to give effect to the intention of Parliament as they perceived it. Yet in *Fisher* v *Bell* the court did not concern itself that the offence of offering for sale of a certain type of knife could not be committed as the statute was worded. That merely led to the amendment of the law by a further Act of Parliament. The point being made here is that the circumstances where the courts will follow one meaning in preference to another cannot be logically determined.

MacCormick sees legal reasoning not as logical but as 'consequentialist'. In this way he seeks to explain the difficulty identified above. Nonetheless, even within the consequentialist school no matter how desirable the consequences may be, no reasoning is legally permissible unless it is either authorised by a legal principle or is analogous to an existing legal rule.

Harris in *Law and Legal Science* suggested that legal science 'constructs' the law according to four logical principles. These he identifies as (a) exclusion – by which he means that the law is identified by a finite set of sources; (b) subsumption – that rules originating in an inferior source must be subsumed under rules originating in a superior source; (c) derogation – which stipulates a priority amongst rules depending on a ranking of sources; and (d) non-contradiction – which insists that any other contradiction must be eliminated.

We can therefore see that both Harris and MacCormick argue that it is part of legal reasoning to eliminate logical conflicts between legal rules.

Nonetheless it has been argued that logical reasoning need not be coherent. Even so the system of precedent is intended to be coherent in that it attributes a rational purpose to the law. What is clear is that these coherence and consequentialist arguments are not dictated by logic. Because as Holmes J said 'the life of the law has been not logic but experience' we can conclude that if a matter has come to litigation, it would tend to indicate that it could not be resolved by logical reasoning.

Whilst our conclusion would depend on the premise as to how we defined logical reasoning if we adopt the definition that it is deductive reasoning, then we would conclude that legal reasoning is not logical reasoning.

17 JUSTICE 1: THE PROBLEM WITH JUSTICE

17.1   Conventional theories of justice

17.2   Definitional delimitations

17.3   Utility as the sole valid evaluative criterion?

17.4   Criticisms of utilitarianism

17.5   An outline of some different types of theories

17.1   Conventional theories of justice

There is a universal appeal to justice. All persons are aware of the need for justice, yet there is no agreement on the nature of justice or what arrangements constitute a just ordering of society. Hence justice, Hart suggests, is shared as a concept; however, there are many conceptions of justice. Justice, on this analysis, would defy definition. The purpose of this chapter is to illustrate some of the conventional theoretical approaches to the question of the nature of justice.

17.2   Definitional delimitations

David Hume wrote that justice can only be meaningful in conditions of moderate scarcity. In his view, a conception of justice is inapplicable where there would be no resources because the population would be starving and shelterless. The issue would be one of survival, rather than justice. On the other hand, where everyone has everything they want, then distributive justice (as opposed to procedural justice) would be unnecessary. Justice in this sense can be seen as the justification for the distribution of resources in society. Distributive justice is concerned with the distribution of both material resources and legal rights to material resources.

Aristotle sought to draw a distinction between distributive and corrective justice. The former idea is concerned with the fair division of benefits and burdens – giving to each according to his just deserts. Corrective justice seeks to ensure a fair equilibrium by redressing any unfair distribution. The latter might be seen to be more properly the occupation of the courts, while the former is more properly an issue of political or social justice.

A further distinction may be made between procedural and substantive justice. Procedural justice might be viewed as expressing the tension between what Herbert Packer terms 'due process' and 'rule of law'. 'Due process' is concerned that people, when faced with the courts, should be treated in accordance with the procedural requirements laid down by a particular legal system. This ensures that the rules are not 'bent'; however, it may allow a mass killer to be set free on a technicality. 'Rule of law' conceptions of procedural justice entail the primary motivation of the courts being the punishment of the wrongdoer if it is clear that he has broken the law, irrespective of procedural technicalities. However, although this might correspond more strongly with the popular idea of justice, it does present a 'watering down' of the checks that are designed to prevent the innocent being wrongly punished. One might also refer to Fuller's 'inner morality of the law' as providing a theoretical framework for procedural justice. In essence procedural justice is therefore a concern with how legal rules are applied.

Substantive justice, on the other hand, is concerned with the content of a law itself. It is a question of juxtaposing the existing legal system with ideals or standards of political morality. The difference between issues of procedural justice and issues of substantive justice can be illustrated by the contrast between a just decision in a court and the justness of the law that the court has upheld.

We shall briefly consider conventional attempts to construct theories of social justice in this section. Issues, particularly of procedural justice, are discussed in the chapters on adjudication (Chapters 19 and 20). In the next chapter, more innovative approaches are considered.

17.3 Utility as the sole valid evaluative criterion?

Bentham insisted that the principle of utility be the sole valid criterion for the evaluation of a just measure. He also stated that to prove the rightness of the principle of utility is both unnecessary and impossible. It is wondered whether it is unnecessary because it is impossible. This is a matter that is crucial to an appreciation of utilitarianism. The arguments can be summarised as follows.

There is much appeal to the idea that the sole valid criterion for the ascertainment of what is just is the application of the principle of utility. This principle that sees a measure as just if it has a tendency to increase happiness or to reduce pain is one that we apply in our daily lives. We undergo dental treatment in which pain is inflicted in order to alleviate a long term toothache. That we therefore apply a utility calculus to the decision whether to undergo that dental treatment explains why the idea is attractive on the social level. A further advantage to utility is that it is secular and does not require any understanding of abstract principles. It is a simple way of telling the difference between what is right and what is wrong.

The concept of the principle of utility was developed out of a distaste for the use to which natural rights were put as the criterion for the evaluation of justice. In spite of certain clear appealing aspects whenever the principle of utility is put into practice, I find it to be defective. I would not therefore be happy to accept the principle of utility as the sole criterion for the evaluation of what is just. My objections are manifold.

One difficulty is that there are two types of utility. The total utility looks at the total level of happiness and says nothing about the distribution of happiness among the population. As such it could allow for slavery in that it has the potential of increasing the total of happiness in the world. On the other hand average utility fares little better. With the same example of slavery, average utility would hold that slavery is just so long as on average happiness is increased. This could be achieved if the slave owners had greater happiness than the slaves had misery.

Mill made it clear that regardless of the various pleasures and pains that would enter the equation, the only thing that the utilitarian would be interested in calculating would be the consequences. Thus the means always justifies the end so long as the end has the tendency to increase total or average happiness. From a deontological point of view this is entirely unacceptable; as Lumb has observed it can be used to justify the arbitrary deprivation of human rights. Indeed it will be recalled that Bentham regarded natural rights as 'nonsense on stilts'. The criticism against the application of the utility principle is that it can lead to the most horrendous outcomes. Torture would be regarded as just so long as the victim divulged information that lead to a greater happiness. With regard to terrorism, a suspected terrorist could justly be tortured if that torture actually led to him disclosing the location of a bomb providing he disclosed its location in time for the premises to be evacuated with no loss of life. It is the actual consequence that matters and not the intention behind it. Thus it would not avail a utilitarian to plead that the terrorist died during interrogation but that the torturer had intended to get the relevant information from him. Good intentions do not count. I have a major problem with this suggestion. I have been asked what I would do if I were in a position of being able through torture to attempt to extract information from a terrorist that related to say, for example, the fate of someone close to me. I probably would torture in order to obtain the information, but I would differ from the utilitarian in that I would not regard what I was doing as just or right but as an unjust necessity.

The problem is with regard to consequences. These consequences can only be ascertained as they happen. They will only happen if we do the act. If the consequences turn out to have a negative effect on the felicific calculus then what we have already done is unjust. The utility principle thus provides no guide to action but a mere *ex post facto* criterion for the evaluation of past events. This is a severe limitation on its applicability and cannot be satisfactory. If we are to seek to do justice we must have a means of finding out what would be just before we do the act and not only afterwards.

A deontological approach would hold that there are criteria for the evaluation of what is just that have no connection to the consequences. An appeal to absolute values would be one such approach that would from the point of view of the sanctity of the human being probably hold that torture is unjust no matter what the circumstances. It would degrade not only the victim but the torturer and the entire society through guilt by omission to prevent. However this is exactly the very notion that the utilitarians rejected. Bentham thought that the two sovereign masters of man were pain and pleasure and therefore designed his felicific calculus around his fourteen pleasures and twelve pains. Why should we be limited to these? Dworkin has argued for the use of preferences instead in an attempt to salvage something from the criticisms of utilitarianism. As will be seen, Dworkin's own proviso changes much of utilitarianism.

Other criticisms of the use of the felicific calculus in this way would address the issue of the impracticability of its application. In order to assess whether a measure is just or not, a mammoth task of calculation would be involved, taking into account everyone affected and the impact on their pain and pleasure. If this were actually adopted then there would be little to do other than to continuously ask everyone what are the effects etc. It would rather be like the painting of the Forth River Bridge – once completed it is time to start all over again. This of course rests on an assumption that I would not even be prepared to go along with. The assumption is that pains and pleasures are measurable. I simply do not accept that they are scientifically measurable and even though Mill developed certain rules of thumb to guide the calculation, these are not real substitutes for the actual ascertainment of the result.

If these were the only criticisms of the applicability of the utility calculation I would take the view that they would be enough to destroy the utility of the calculation for the ascertainment of what is just. They are not the only negative aspects of the felicific calculus in practice. As Rawls has observed, utilitarianism fails to account for the separateness of persons. It regards persons as mere receptacles for the pain-pleasure calculation. Thus Rawls writes in *A Theory of Justice* that the utilitarians assume just that as rationality requires the making of small sacrifices for longer term gains so it also requires a trade-off of the welfare of some against the welfare of others. This idea of trading off the welfare of some against the welfare of others conflicts with our moral intuition.

Rawls' second objection to utilitarianism is that it seeks to define the right in terms of the good. Utilitarianism begins with an account of good and defines as right that which brings about the good. Herein is the anomaly because utilitarianism takes account of unjustly obtained happiness. According to Rawls, '... Justice is the first virtue of a social institution in the same way as truth is the first virtue of thought. And like truth, justice is uncompromising.' What is good must therefore be defined in terms of what is right hence utilitarianism is unable to satisfy this requirement of justice. I would therefore reject the application of the principle of utility as the sole valid criterion for the evaluation of justice.

17.4 Criticisms of utilitarianism

In the preceding section I have considered many of the criticisms that have been made of utilitarianism within the context of its use as the sole evaluative method for assessing justice. These are not the only criticisms that have been made of this very influential theory and it is proposed to discuss a few of the other criticisms in this section.

a) As has been demonstrated, the modern theories, particularly Rawls' can be seen as attacks on utilitarianism and attempts to remove it from its pre-eminent position.

b) The criticism mostly made of total utility is that it ignores the lot of the average person: if by increasing the total population by a large number the total utility can be slightly increased, society should follow a programme of encouraging production of children, even though on average everyone's lot will be less happy. For this reason average utility is preferable, but this too is unacceptable. For a start, how does one measure utility or happiness or welfare: is it psychological, is it based on want, satisfaction or what? How does an unemotional man's quiet happiness measure against the super-sensitive person's ecstasy? How does my enjoyment of a plate of fish and chips relate to the satisfaction of a country walk, or a symphony, or solving a chess puzzle? (A distinction is made between act-utility and rule-utility, the latter asking not if a particular sentence of capital punishment is utility-maximising, for example, but whether the effects of the rule leading to capital punishment as a whole are. Does this make measurement any easier?)

c) Assuming a measure can be found, we still must face the fact that utility is not a theory which should be acceptable. Three points can be made:

   i) Some preferences or wants must be disregarded for reasons of consistency: for example, preferences for anti-utilitarian arrangements (for example a ban on alcohol for religious reasons); or more fundamentally, desires for a state run according to the rules of a religion, even if that did not match happiness or want maximisation.

   ii) Utility would offend our intuitions of justice, because it would countenance unacceptable inequality. We should test all possible conceptions of justice against our own convictions of what is right in particular situations; when we apply utility to one or two factual situations, we can see that it goes counter to these convictions. To take a simple case, of a slave-owning society: should we keep slavery? Assume that we are measuring utility in terms of satisfaction of wants or preferences. If 20 per cent of the population are slaves, they would have to feel four times as strongly about becoming free as the 80 per cent slave owners feel about life without slaves. It is not implausible to assume that slavery will be kept. Thus, utility will frequently accept situations where the majority benefit from the poverty or oppression of a minority.

   iii) A more complex example can lead us to a further point. Should discrimination against blacks be illegal? A decision on this question, on any utility scale, will take into account the views (wants, happiness, preferences) of those who see blacks as unequal, and therefore less deserving of respect: the very decision will therefore be based on an unequal view of blacks. And yet, utilitarians would claim to be egalitarian in that each person is counted as the same weight. The discrimination decision clearly does not give them that weight.

   Dworkin argues that this latter point extends to all 'external preferences' for his attempted rescue of the utilitarian position. Other types of rescue attempt can be made: one perhaps stronger than the others. This is to mix utility with another factor, a minimum standard: once the minimum standard is reached for all, decisions are taken on the basis of utility. This attempt fails: it answers the major thrust of the second criticism (against allowing poverty), but does not meet the third criticism (against external preferences).

d) Hart's criticisms to the extent that they are not already mentioned can be stated briefly as follows:

   i) Hart believes that while justice is an aspect of morality it is yet different from other aspects of morality such as right and wrong, good and bad. He gives the example of a father who maltreats his child and states that it would not be correct to describe this as unjust – it is bad or wrong but not unjust. Hart therefore observes a distinction between a bad law and an unjust law. This is a distinction which utilitarianism does not recognise.

   ii) Hart further observes that there can often be a conflict between justice and other values such as freedom. The unfettered freedom to compete if not regulated by law is bound to lead to injustice because all persons are not competing on equal terms. Hart observes that law resolves this conflict by means of anti-monopoly laws so restoring some semblance of justice at the expense of freedom.

   iii) There is also a conflict between justice and the common good. Most of the social services are financed out of the income of the rich and the wages of the working population. Justice is not done to these people but the common good requires the provision of facilities to the poorer members of the society.

iv)   There can also be no criteria for administering justice when the goods are indivisible. The example of scarcity of kidney machines is an example – by what criteria are those who can use these machines chosen?

v)   Utilitarianism in its calculations treats people equally but equal to nothing. Individuals are not separate persons, just a means to an end. Their value is not as persons but as experiencers of pain and pleasure.

e)   Stone argues that even if it is accepted that each person deserves their happiness so that their happiness is a good to them, how does it follow that the general happiness is a good to the aggregate of all? Further, Stone observes that hedonism assumes that pleasure is found by being sought, but pleasure comes as an incidental to the seeking of other things rather than as the intended result of the search. His critique of hedonism continues that pain and pleasure are nothing but the names for an infinitely perishing series of feelings, hence hedonistic morality seeks to realise an idea which can in itself never be realised. It is striving towards an impossible future.

f)   Utilitarianism views the community as a mere aggregate of the individual members. This is seen in the discussions on the separateness of persons. This is mistaken. It takes no account of the logical priority of the community over the individual, as was seen in the discussion on torture. Bentham's extreme individualism is open to objection. It is submitted that it is only in the context of his community that an individual is recognisable as such. It is only in this context that he can be spoken of as a moral being. Further, a person's identity is inseparably connected with their status as a member of the community so that their nationality, family background, education, career et al describe him or her as a person and must involve a reference to the context of the community in which he/she lives. This is especially so because the idea of a community implies a high degree of cooperation and mutual trust among its members who share certain common standards. This means that justice is based not on an individual utilitarianism but on the existence of a community where the machinery of distributive justice is dependent upon the degree of mutual cooperation among its members.

g)   Utilitarianism has been severely criticised by many because it looks at wants, desires and preferences (however these are formed and determined) but takes no account of necessities.

h)   Fuller has argued that utilitarianism says nothing about the distribution of goods in the society.

i)   Hume's rationality argument shows that reason cannot tell us what we ought to pursue but only how to attain ends we have already chosen.

Moral beliefs are based on preferences which are neither reasonable nor unreasonable – they are facts of human nature. Utilitarians argue that human action is rational in that it is geared to the pursuit of happiness/welfare.

j)   John Finnis argues that reason indicates certain goals that ought to be pursued and that happiness/welfare is but one of these. Finnis' goals are incommensurable ie they cannot be measured one against the other. Accordingly, an attempt to maximise would not make sense. He sees these goals as having a more complex bearing on the individual than a simple felicific calculation leading to 'maximisation'.

k)   By way of an evaluation I think we can say that utilitarianism was attractive as a secular philosophy in that it was not tied to any religion and that in interpreting a pluralistic society it demonstrated the possibility of taking account of different views. It represents a common currency we can all agree on, that is, that we use it with reference to our own decision-making process with regard to our own lives. The theory looks attractive but on analysis proves defective. There are too few ideas in utility to meet the demands of a modern society. It must therefore be rejected. In the following chapters we shall consider some more modern theories and assess their usefulness.

17.5 An outline of some different types of theories

I have already considered utilitarianism as a theory of justice. In this section, I will briefly sketch the outlines of some alternative conceptions of justice, and try to discover their bases and starting points. Many writers have put forward ideas of justice in social arrangements, and it will not be possible to consider them all; it is worth at the outset sowing a seed of scepticism and doubt. Can any of the theories discussed below in reality be termed anything other than subjective? Aren't all the arguments aimed at showing 'what justice is', really only showing good arguments for a particular arrangement, and not conclusive arguments that that argument is the uniquely correct 'just' one?

In this section I shall briefly consider social contract theories, natural rights theories and Marxist theories. In fact the first two go together very often, as we shall see; we differentiate them now because the modern theorists Rawls and Nozick (Chapter 18) do not combine them, but use a social contract and natural rights model respectively.

a) *Social contract theories*

These base the justice of society's organisation on the fact that the individuals in the society have – or would have, or may be presumed to have – entered into a contract agreeing that society should be so patterned. It is often unclear whether the contract or covenant is thought actually to have existed: in its modern exponent, Rawls, it is clear that it is a hypothetical justificatory construct.

b) *Natural rights theories*

These emphasise the importance of society being formed in such a way as to protect and not enfringe upon 'natural rights', rights which people have either from God or from their nature. These theories are one type of natural law theory (in itself, I suppose, one could view natural law as a theory of justice, judging human laws against the divine or reason-based standard).

The major exponents of social contract theory in its first heyday in the seventeenth century also placed great emphasis on natural rights: because of their different stresses it seems right to consider Hobbes' as a social contract view, and Locke's a natural rights one, but both included the idea of a state of nature including natural rights, and a contract leading to civil society.

    i) Hobbes: Hobbes argued that men had their natural rights in a state of nature. Since men had a tendency to compete and infringe on the rights of others (and, in the famous words, the state of nature would therefore be 'nasty, brutish and short') they would find this state of nature unsatisfactory, and would therefore wish to join a society where the urge to competition was controlled and restrained by a political sovereign. This sovereign could become so by force or by contract, it didn't matter: people in the state of nature would be prepared to covenant or contract to transfer their natural right to protect themselves, and all their powers to a sovereign. They are then subject to an all powerful unlimited sovereign (cf Austin), subject to political obligation because of a contract they had made or would be prepared to make. On the applied level I think it is clear that Hobbesian philosophy has been and is used by military dictators following a coup d'état in order to justify their actions. So long as the absolute ruler (Leviathan) maintains order then his rules shall be obeyed as being just, for he has improved the lot of men by removing them from anarchy. The justification for despotism is obvious. Military leaders do indeed argue that the reason for their takeover is to preserve order or to prevent the country from 'slipping into anarchy'.

    ii) Locke: In the state of nature, man had rights including that of appropriation of land. The two limits to this (to prevent waste, and to leave enough and as good for others) can be shown to be removed by the advent of money, leaving an unconditional right of appropriation, along with a right to protection of life, liberty and estate. Man could live in the state of nature, but some will try to gain property by trespass rather than just acquisition. Locke has a more optimistic view of man in the state of nature. There is a need simply to channel men's natural goodness. To protect their property, men will enter into a covenant agreeing to a civil society. This society is there to ensure natural rights, and the state is still subject to them; if the state passed laws infringing these rights, rebellion would be justified. All law then must conform to the standard of natural rights. The application of this theory justifies revolution in the face of tyranny. Locke's discussion of certain rights which cannot be assigned to the state has laid the foundation for the recent re-emergence of the concept of inalienable rights in human rights treaties, such as the right to national self-determination.

iii) Rousseau: A third theorist tying social contract and natural rights was Rousseau, whose work was seized on as a philosophical justification for the French Revolution. By the 'social contract', a man transferred his rights not to an actual sovereign but to society which was the 'general will': to obey this was to obey oneself. The state should grant the citizen his freedom and, if it did not, it could be overthrown or revoked by the 'general will'. The state held these rights on trust. The society is just to the extent that it follows the conditions which the contracting members would impose and accept. If it does not do so, like Locke, Rousseau would justify rebellion.

c) *Marxism*

I have already considered Marxist theories of law and the state (Chapters 13 & 14 infra). It is not proposed to repeat that discussion here. What will emerge from a discussion of a Marxist conception of justice is that it is a collectivist theory and that it maintains that a just ordering of society occurs when each contributes according to his ability and receives according to his needs. An example of an attempt to organise on such a principle would be the National Health Service in Britain (at least still at the time of writing!) Those who are earning contribute whether or not they are ill. Those who are ill receive (eventually?) treatment as often as necessary regardless of their contributions, if any.

Since these theories are included for background information it is not proposed to examine them in depth; however, some critical evaluation will point to the content and structure of the more modern theories that do represent a part of the course. At first, difficulty might be seen in relating these theories to our theme of justice, since Hobbes for example concentrates on political obligations to the state, not the obligations of the State to conform to standards of justice. Clearly the 'natural rights' stress of Locke does suggest a standard of justice, viz a society will be just if it respects the natural rights of its citizens (similarly Rousseau); this is the view of Nozick (chapter 18). However, although Hobbes does not allow the social contract to be used in the direction of obligations of the state, it seems that individuals who were contracting in such a way would lay down conditions to control the state, and determine how it would operate. So the social contract model suggests a standard of justice as well, viz a society will be just if it follows the conditions which contracting members of society would impose and accept. This sort of approach can be seen in the work of Rawls.

Those are only a few of the types of individualistic theories of justice. Others include *perfectionism*, which organises things to promote a particular good or value, and *intuitionism*, which denies that any acceptable complete criteria of justice can be worked out, and therefore results in each decision being made by the intuition of the decision taker. The former is only acceptable if we accept the idea in question; the second only if no complete criterion proves satisfactory.

18 JUSTICE 2: MODERN TRENDS

18.1   Modern theories of justice

18.2   Rawls' theory

18.3   Evaluation of Rawls

18.4   Nozick's theory

18.5   Evaluation of Nozick's theory

18.1   Modern theories of justice

This chapter gives an outline of two modern theories of justice, developed partly as a reaction to, although to a certain extent developing out of, the conventional conceptions presented in the previous chapter. However, they represent very different accounts of how justice should deal with the problem of the individual. While Rawls seeks to provide for a social, or distributive justice, Nozick stresses that the individual's rights are of paramount importance, even to the extent that it may cause the suffering of others.

However, the theories are to a great extent inspired by political standpoints. Therefore, I suggest that the student should be left as the arbiter of the question, 'Is this justice?' The contrast is quite a stark one, so that the differences between the two positions should be fairly clear.

18.2   Rawls' theory

The most complete argument for a theory of justice is possibly that provided by Rawls, who argues for his two principles of justice in *A Theory of Justice* (1972). His theory is of justice as fairness, accepting those principles that would result from an 'original position'. In this 'original position', the parties set out, subject to conditions considered reasonable and fair, to agree the principles by which their society should be organised. It is thus a social contract position, although the contract is a hypothetical one.

a) *Method*

Rawls accepts Hart's distinction between concepts of justice and conceptions of justice. He agrees that any theory of justice must deal with both of these. By a concept of justice Rawls means the role of its principles in assigning rights and duties and in defining the appropriate division of social advantages. This is essentially an objective phenomenon. By a conception of justice he means the interpretation of the role of these principles in particular situations. He acknowledges that this is much more subjective.

Rawls' theory in its own terms is designed to cope with situations where mutually disinterested persons put forward conflicting claims to a division of goods and services under conditions of moderate scarcity. His theory is of no application in conditions of total scarcity eg Mozambique.

His method is to test all the previous theories and from their defects to extrapolate a superior theory. Whilst he states that his is the best (not surprisingly) he acknowledges the existence of other theories. His starting point is a rejection of utilitarianism.

i) *Rejection of utilitarianism*

The first half of the book is directed at a rejection of the earlier theories. We shall concentrate on his comments with regard to utilitarianism. Classical (total) utility is easily dismissed, since it supports an increase in population even if average utility would be thereby decreased. Average utility is more of a problem; Rawls has criticisms of it. Some of these are general, in terms of allowing sacrifice of persons for others: we have already discussed utility in this light. Some are specific to the OP, and why the POP would not choose it. The veil of ignorance denies them knowledge of the probabilities of being at any particular economic/social level in the society. To choose average utility is to take a risk on whether or not one's position is a good one; it is the logical choice if the principle of 'insufficient reason' is followed, and the probabilities for each position are regarded as equal. Rawls says that the POP would reject such risk-taking and would, as we shall see below, adopt a 'maximin' strategy.

Rawls states that utilitarianism suffers from two major defects:

– *Utilitarianism ignores the distinctness of persons.* The utilitarians assume that just as rationality requires making small sacrifices for larger gains so it also requires a trade-off of the welfare of some against the welfare of others. This idea of trading off the welfare of some against the welfare of others conflicts with our moral intuition. In Simmonds' book on *Law, Justice and Rights* the author uses the analogy of having a toothache and going to the dentist and suffering great pain for a few moments in order to have the toothache cured. This is a utilitarian calculation and it is submitted it is a legitimate utilitarian calculation because one is talking about sacrifices for oneself. One is undergoing the pain in order to gain the pleasure for oneself. As indicated in the previous chapter the problem with utilitarianism is that it speaks of sacrificing the pain of others for the pleasure of oneself.

Furthermore utilitarianism merely regards people as mechanisms to measure pain and pleasure and as receptacles in which welfare is to be maximised with the greatest possible efficiency.

– *Utilitarianism seeks to define the right in terms of the good.* Utilitarianism begins with an account of good and defines as right that which brings about the good. Herein is the anomaly, because utilitarianism takes account of unjustly obtained happiness. According to Rawls,

'... Justice is the first virtue of social institutions in the same way as truth is the first virtue of thought. And like truth, justice is uncompromising ...'

ii) *Characteristics of a theory of justice*

Having rejected utilitarianism, Rawls goes on to consider the conditions which any theory of justice must satisfy before it is a useful theory of justice. These are:

– The theory must be general

– The theory must be universal in application

– The theory is public in the sense that the population must know about it, there being no point in having a secret theory of justice

– The theory must impose an ordering on competing claims

– The theory must have finality.

b) *Content*

According to Rawls, justice is prior to happiness. It is only when we know that happiness is just that we regard happiness as having any positive value. Is Rawls then affording us a neutral conception of justice? Rawls believes that justice represents the framework within which different individuals have a fair opportunity to pursue their own goals and values. His theory seeks to meet the criticisms that he levelled against utilitarianism and attempts to employ the criteria of rational prudence in a manner consistent with both the distinctness of persons and the priority of the right over the good.

In his book, Rawls uses a complex mixture of two forms of reasoning – deductive and inductive – and of two bases for argument – the contract and reflective equilibrium. We will look at the two bases in turn.

i) *Contract*

As we have said, Rawls envisages an original position (OP) in which, in conditions of equality (discussed below), the parties (POP) agree to the principles to judge society. A contract model is used for two reasons:

– *Exposition*

As a nice framework within which to explain the various conditions which can reasonably be imposed on such an agreement – the conditions we accept as 'fair' – and to show how the principles can be reached from these conditions.

– *Justification*

The contract is not supposed to have been made *in fact*, but the device is used to show – to emphasise – that the principles chosen are 'fair', ones we would accept given a fair starting point. Anybody at any time can enter the original position and if they did and were rational they would arrive at the same conclusion, the same principles of justice, that Rawls arrives at. For this reason these principles are said to be objective and would be binding on the members of the society. He has thus, it is submitted, overcome the difficulty with the earlier social contractarian theories that could not account for how the contract was binding on those not party thereto. The contract model is thus justificatory, in support of the principles and giving them some degree of legitimacy, as well as expository.

Having established the conditions of the contract, the argument is both deductive and inductive. Rawls attempts to show deductively that the principles would in fact be chosen by the POP, and why they would be chosen. They would value liberty very highly, as the first principle chosen shows: they would then adopt maximin as in the second principle. The two principles result from the conditions of the OP and that deduction.

The main argument, as Rawls calls it, is of another kind. It involves looking at a list of other conceptions of justice, particularly variants of utilitarianism, and seeing why the two principles should be preferred. This argument is not deductive. Nor is it a complete argument: there may be further conceptions of justice not yet disclosed which would win, and anyway Rawls' list is not complete re present conceptions.

In our discussion of Rawls, we concentrate on the deductive argument from the OP.

ii) *Reflective equilibrium*

How are the conditions in the OP decided upon? Basically, they are conditions we accept as reasonable to impose on (people choosing our) standards of justice; for example the veil of ignorance encourages impartiality. There is, however, another important aspect, that of trying to reach reflective equilibrium (RE).

Rawls outlines the derivation of principles, following a process whereby reasonable conditions are used, and the principles that result are discovered. These principles are tested against our considered judgments in particular situations. If they run counter we must either, after thought, reject our considered judgments, or alter the conditions of the OP. The results of those altered conditions emerge, are checked against our considered judgments, and so on. Eventually, by modifications at both ends, RE emerges between the principles emerging and our considered judgments. We have then reached the best version of the OP, which expresses reasonable conditions and yields principles matching our considered judgments. The starting point, the conditions of the OP, is tinkered with until correct principles emerge.

This argument is clearly not deductive. It also makes the OP itself redundant, if one is being harsh. Why not just put up possible principles and modify them with regard to our considered judgments, without referring to the contract idea at all? We must refer to the earlier points (contract as exposition and justification) to see why Rawls uses a contract even though it is not strictly a necessary part of the argument.

c) *The original position*

i) *The parties*

Rawls does tell us who the POP will be; they are various representatives, all of the same generation. We will not consider who they are in detail: it is pointless since one or all come to the same conclusion. The conditions are meant to be such that the two principles are the 'correct answer', to which everyone will agree.

ii) *What choice?*

The POP are to choose general principles by which society should be organised – principles of justice for that society. It is interesting throughout to consider how various other possible theories are eliminated by Rawls. We discuss this below.

As pointed out above, the choice is made primarily by arguing against other conceptions, but also by a positive deductive argument for the various facets of the two principles.

iii) *What motivation?*

The POP agree to principles that we term 'principles of justice', but it is important to note that from the point of view of POP the principles are not principles of justice, but the terms of the contract/agreement made on the basis of self-interest in an OP. As we've seen, the conditions of the OP put everyone in the same situation, and 'self-interest' is therefore non-specific; but given the conditions of ignorance, etc in the OP, the POP are trying to get the 'best deal' for themselves.

How can they do this, bearing in mind that they knew nothing about themselves? The answer is that they will try to get the highest possible total of primary basic goods. One thing that is removed from the POP is an awareness of their own, particular, plan of life – their conception of what is a 'good life', and what specifically, they need to live it (time, money, power, responsibility, etc). They do, however, know general facts; one of these general facts is that to fulfil a plan of life everyone wants more and not less of the 'primary basic goods'. These goods – rights, powers, health, etc – fall into two categories, social and natural; the POPs will try to arrange liberties, opportunities, powers, self-respect, income and wealth. Everybody's plan of life will be enhanced by these.

iv) *The conditions*

What conditions are the POP under?

– Veil of ignorance: the most obviously necessary condition is one to ensure impartiality, ie that one's own position and views shouldn't influence the choice. This is a traditional feature of justice theories; a similar device to Rawls' is the impartial spectator.

Rawls' device is a veil of ignorance, behind which the POP are working. The POP do not know their place in society, their status or class, their fortune, level of natural ability, intelligence and so on. All are in a condition of equality: hence 'justice as fairness', and hence unanimity of result (important, according to Rawls, because it shows a genuine reconciliation of interests). POP would be rational, free and have knowledge of the general situation but no specific knowledge of the particular. They would know that there is a society; they would know there is intelligence; they would know that there are sexes but they would not know where they as individuals would fit in society. Behind this veil of ignorance any knowledge of all those features which distinguish one person from another will be excluded. Rawls argues that it would be just to impose these conditions and that any decision reached in this condition would become binding. The veil would then be lifted to the extent of the proposition and there would be no possibility of repeal of the principle. I propose to show how this works by an example at the end of this section.

– Non-altruism: the POP must look to their own self-interest and not to the interests of others, or incoherence will result.

– Non-envy: In any non-equal situation, the problem of envy will arise. If the POP thought they would be envious of anyone who did better than they did, strict equality would be the only choice, and that might mean that increases in wealth for all are missed. To avoid this, Rawls says the POP will not be envious: they will want the best possible result for themselves, but it will not be a factor against an arrangement that someone else might do better.

Great inequalities could be sanctioned in this way: but Rawls' two principles escape this inequality. The first principle gives liberty to all equally. The second principle does allow the unequal distribution of primary social goods, but within strict limits. In any case, one of these goods being distributed is self-respect, and one's self-respect would clearly be harmed by any massive inequality resulting in a small share of the other goods.

– The just savings principle/family feeling: the POP are all from the same generation. What is to stop them from deciding as follows: we cannot alter how previous generations have acted? Motivated by self-interest (non-altruism) we care not for future generations. Therefore we will use up as many of the resources of the earth as we wish, and we will not, individually or as a society, be concerned about what investment we make for future generations.

Logical, yes; just, no. To avoid this conclusion, Rawls added a condition that the POP were concerned about their families including other generations thereof. (This, of course, results in the just savings principle in the second principle.)

– Risk aversion: the POP will choose the least worst alternative and not the best possible alternative because of their self interest that dictates that they avert risk of a worst possible scenario.

Let us look at a worked example of how this process is meant to occur. We have entered the OP. The proposition that is put to us is that there should be accorded more rights to men than to women, in other words that there should be discrimination against women in the allocation of benefits in the society. This is one of the questions a society has to address. This is the question. POP do not know whether they are men or women. Acting in their own self interest (non altruism) and seeking to avert risk, the POP will apply the maximin principle seeking to maximise benefit while minimising burden. Let us say that POP opt for sex discrimination; the consequences are as follows:

1) If they are men then that will be the best possible scenario.

2) If they are women then that will be the worst possible scenario.

3) If the POP act according to the maximin principle they will choose that there should be no sex discrimination in which case whether they are men or women will make no difference. True, they will lose the chance to have all the benefits that accrue to men if there was discrimination, but they will also avert the risk of all the loss were they women.

Hence it is clear, I think, that the use of this OP together with the conditions stipulated by Rawls will lead to a denial of all arbitrary discrimination in accordance with established liberal thought.

c) *The principles of justice*

From the OP, we arrive at the two principles of justice:

'1st: Each person is to have an equal right to the most extensive total system of equal basic liberties compatible with a similar system for all.

2nd: Social and economic inequalities are to be arranged so that they are both:

A) to the greatest benefit of the least advantaged consistent with the just savings principle, and

B) attached to offices open to all in conditions of fair equality of opportunity.'

Generally, the first principle is totally prior to the second.

We will look at the two principles in three stages. First, the deductive argument for the two principles. Second, the 'main argument', rejecting other conceptions. Third, the argument for priority of the first principle over the second, the priority of liberty.

d) *Deductive argument for the two principles*

i) *Assumptions*

The conditions of the OP are above, but we should mention at this stage that there are two more assumptions, which shape the form and content of the two principles. The first of these is *social co-operation*. No-one can succeed in the plan of life without society, therefore everyone will be willing to enter into social co-operation. Talents are pooled to the benefit of all; the major question is how the results of that pooling should be distributed: what distribution should be decided upon?

It is this assumption that knocks out natural rights theories like those of Nozick's. Is social co-operation a successful argument against the millionaire who argues against re-distributed taxation? Rawls would say that without society that million would not be made or increased. Is the millionaire right to say that he gives more (jobs, investment) than he takes out?

The second assumption is *risk aversion*. The veil of ignorance hides from the POPs both the position they will occupy in society and the probabilities relating to the various positions. If there are five million poor people out of 500 million, the odds are one in a hundred that any given individual will be a poor person: but the POP don't know this. In this situation the logicians would suggest the acceptance of an 'insufficient reason' standpoint whereby all possibilities are taken as equally likely. Rawls rejects this, and says the POP would instead choose a maximin position, arranging society so that the position of the least well off class is maximised. The POPs are then risk averse: rather than chancing a possibly very poor position by going for an arrangement which produces very good results at the top end, they will choose that situation where the bottom end is as high as possible.

Do you think the POP would be risk averse? Might they decide to gamble?

ii) *The argument*

The POPs set out, then, to derive principles upon which they can agree to arrange society. They wish these principles to result in the best possible arrangement of primary social goods, and they will decide to adopt a maximin outlook.

The starting point is equality: the parties would start by thinking what the principle to be chosen should be, simply that everyone gets equal shares of everything. They would then realise that some inequalities will benefit everyone: incentives to high-flyers, for example, would motivate them to achieve a greater degree of productive enterprise, and thus to produce more for everyone. The yardstick for this is a maximin calculation, looking to see whether the inequalities result in the best possible result for the least advantaged.

This calculation is made for several different areas, as follows:

– *Liberty*: The claims of liberty have, for Rawls, an absolute priority after a certain level of economic well-being has been reached. This priority is a major keynote of the theory. For this reason it is treated separately below.

Above the level of priority, inequality is not allowed: trade-offs for increased economic well-being would not be accepted. Thus, the first principle – the right to the most extensive total system of equal basic liberties compatible with a similar system for all. This is reflected for example in Article 17 of the European Convention on Human Rights and Fundamental Freedoms 1950, which provides that the rights granted in the Convention cannot be used to deprive others of the rights in the convention. This has been the topic of case law, see *The Federal German Communist Party* case (1957) concerning the ban on that party whose objects were held to be incompatible with the freedom of association for others, and more recently the case of *Glimmerveen & Hagenbeck* v *The Netherlands* which concerned the outlawing of the expression of racist sentiments being held to be consistent with the freedom of speech.

It should be noted that Rawls is not here referring to the liberty of the individual but rather to certain liberties.

– *Fair equality of opportunity:* Economic and social advantages are attached to offices and positions open to all in fair equality and opportunity. This is despite the fact that fair equality and opportunity might be contrary to the difference principle (see 'the difference principle' below, the maximin position on social and economic advantages). In some circumstances, one can envisage a 'closed shop' appointment system which might work better than an open system. Rawls argues that those who lost out in a system because fair equality of opportunity was not in operation would feel unjustly treated, and lose self-respect. (In fact that argument seems inconsistent with some other things Rawls says: such feelings and considerations of dessert wouldn't convince the self-interested POP. Also, the choice of fair equality of opportunity over available alternatives is not convincing, since criticisms against those alternatives, particularly that they are morally arbitrary, also apply.)

– *Just savings principle*: We have seen the OP presumption that leads to this: the POP are taken to have inter-generational family ties. They are therefore concerned to save for future generations. This is the clearest example of a condition of the OP introduced, as a result of our considered judgments, in the RE process.

– *The difference principle*: With the qualifications in the previous two paragraphs the POP will accept such economic and social inequalities as benefit the position of the least advantaged. In contrast with average utility, the least well-off do not sacrifice themselves for the better off; rather, they are put in the best position available. The difference principle, of course, follows logically from the adoption of a maximin strategy.

e) *The main argument: why prefer the two principles to other possibilities?*

The two principles are preferred to each of a list of possible alternatives found on page 124 of *A Theory of Justice*. Rawls admits the argument is highly intuitionistic, and that there might be other possibilities he hasn't thought of.

It would here be necessary to outline briefly his reasons for rejecting various other conceptions, only some of which appear in his list. *Egoism* as we have seen, is knocked out by formal constraints (requiring a choice of general principles).

Non-tolerant conceptions are knocked out by the veil of ignorance, because it hides the person's own conception of the good. By a non-tolerant conception, I mean one that would not be prepared to allow (certain) other conceptions to be pursued. For example, an extreme religious fanatic might have a conception of the good life that included a prohibition of other forms of worship: his conception of justice would include this provision. In the OP no one would choose that conception of justice, because there is a chance that they would be the holders of a prohibited religious viewpoint – an intolerable situation.

Non-tolerance will sometimes be linked with *perfectionism,* a conception under which society is organised in such a way that it furthers a particular ideal state of affairs. An extreme religious viewpoint might again provide an example. Such a conception would not be chosen, and this is another argument against non-tolerant conceptions being chosen, because the POP (not knowing their own conception of the good) have no reason to choose principles according with only one theory of the good. Instead they will choose one which allows freedom to differing conceptions in order that they, whatever their own 'good life' turns out to be, can pursue their own chosen course.

Rawls explicitly places *intuitionism* as a last resort. If any acceptable principles can be found by which society's affairs can be arranged, the intuitionist's suggestion that at each point the decision maker should follow his discretion can be rejected. Only if no such principles exist does the intuitionist 'win'.

On the list of other conceptions, there are some *mixed conceptions*. These include the first principle with a different second principle. A particularly important alternative second principle is average utility plus a social minimum condition. Such a condition could resolve the problems average utility has in relation to sacrificing the least well-off. The two principles are to be preferred to this mixed conception, because of the difficulties of deciding the social minimum and the fact that it could be the two principles in disguise! The two principles would match its results, and should be chosen for their greater clarity and precision.

Apart from these various points aimed at showing why the POP would choose the two principles and not any other possibility, Rawls gives at this stage the considerations working in favour of the two principles. The first is that they do not involve sacrificing oneself for the sake of others, and therefore there are not the strains of commitment imposed by other theories. This is true of the least well-off, who are at their best possible position, unless of course, they are envious (perhaps they will prefer to be poorer but equal?). High-level producers might not be so enthusiastic about a system which takes away their hard-earned profit to improve the position of the less well-off. Isn't the high-flyer being sacrificed for the bottom rung?

Second, the two principles have the advantage of psychological stability. Since no one is being sacrificed for others, and everyone's self-respect is enhanced, the two principles will receive public recognition and lead to a sense of justice. This 'advantage' is akin to the first; it is subject to the same sort of criticism.

f) *The priority of liberty*

The first principle is generally 'lexicographically prior' to the second; this means that its demands must be met in full before the considerations of the second principle are taken into account. (The exception is when the society has not yet reached a sufficiently developed economic position: this point is not explicitly decided by Rawls.) Liberty can only be sacrificed for liberty's sake in two circumstances.

   i)   Less extensive liberty must strengthen the whole system shared by all; an example is the rules of order in a debate.

   ii) Unequal liberty must be acceptable to those with less. For example, equality of opportunity might be sacrificed to lead to greater political liberty.

Rawls is not discussing all possible liberties, but a set list – political liberty, freedom of thought and conscience, freedom of the person and the right to hold personal property, and freedom from arbitrary arrest and seizure. The POP would not allow these freedoms to be limited for the sake of an improvement in economic or social well-being. Why not?

Rawls principally used the example of freedom of religious belief. Such belief is so central and important that the POP would realise that its sacrifice would be intolerable, and therefore is prohibited. This can be seen as a maximin point, that a poor economic situation and freedom to worship as you choose is always better than no freedom of worship.

A further argument utilises the fact that a certain level of well-being is required before the priority is absolute. Once that point is reached, survival and economic goods become less important, and cultural and intellectual pursuits (and therefore the freedom to pursue them) become increasingly so. Remember here the Aristotelian principle, that people desire to engage in more complex activities if possible.

I am not convinced that Rawls establishes the priority of liberty beyond doubt. First, he does not discuss sexual freedom (although at one point he says he has proved his point re 'religious and sexual freedom'); nor is it totally clear why the liberties on his list are chosen. Second, he only argues from religious freedom. It seems intuitively possible to distinguish between this and the other liberties. Religious liberty is central to the existence of most people (even if it is the liberty to have no religion) in a unique and most important way; the same is not true of the other liberties. Is owning a house as important as faith? And haven't people often given up their personal freedom for religion? The conclusion here might be that while priority is logical for POP to choose, re religious liberty, it is not necessarily so re the other liberties.

For these other liberties, the absolute priority of liberty over economic and social development is hard to accept, even given the fact that civilisation must have reached a level where economic needs are not desperate. Assume that by sacrificing five years' political liberty to a totalitarian regime, massive increases in wealth would result, including a great boost to the maximin position. Is it logical for the POP to rule out choosing this sacrifice? Wouldn't the resultant economic gain in fact greatly enhance the value of the restored liberty? In fact, Rawls does not find a proper place for the idea of the value of liberty: but what is the use of freedom of thought if the economic necessity to work proves too exhausting to allow it? And what use the freedom to attend plays/concerts if they cannot be afforded?

Finally, giving liberty this priority seems to me to be allowing into the theory Rawls' own conception of the good life. This point will be discussed more fully in the next section.

18.3 Evaluation of Rawls

There are many criticisms of Rawls' work. I shall consider some of the main ones that appear in the literature.

a) One criticism is that, through many avenues, his own conception of a proper plan for life, the proper way for someone to live, encroaches on the theory. The POP are denied knowledge of their own plan of life, their own conception of the good: as a result, society will inevitably be tolerant, even though the majority of people within it are in fact non-tolerant. The POP are motivated by a desire to maximise achievement on an Aristotelian scale of complexity, but it is not true for all. A monk, for example, would want no income, wealth, etc; many of the primary social goods would be useless for him. Rawls' OP fits only a certain category of person.

Further, an element is missed in the OP. The POP would logically be interested not only in how many primary social goods they got, but also how many everybody else got. This is not envy but a directly personal concern relating to quality of life. For example, imagine the POP deciding whether they should have cars. They would put into account not only the convenience of an individual having a car, but also the inconvenience and discomfort of living in a society where everyone had a car. This consideration is not mentioned by Rawls: surely it would affect the POP's determination to achieve maximum primary social good level?

Rawls is perceived as adjusting the conditions in the OP to ensure the principles that he wants are arrived at; behind a supposed veil of objectivity his subjectivity emerges. This is regarded as an intellectual sleight of hand trick, as he started from the two principles and their arrangement in lexicographical order and worked backwards. Simmonds takes a less cynical approach to this. He maintains that perhaps Rawls is 'attempting to elucidate the deep philosophical presuppositions that underlie his two principles'.

b) One of the most important criticisms of Rawls emanates from one of his former students – Robert Nozick. Much of the following chapter is devoted to an elucidation of Nozick's theory of justice, so it will suffice, I imagine, to demonstrate here some of his main criticisms of Rawls which will be further elaborated upon in the following chapter. Nozick maintains that if one is interested in justice then one cannot deny the importance of Rawls' theory. One has either to work with Rawls' theory or explain why one is not working with it. Very flattering!

Nozick continues by attacking the notion of what he calls 'the patterned distribution of social good'. Any patterned distribution would really require one to consider the following problems:

i) If one is prepared to allow for the coercive redistribution of wealth then why not also allow the coercive redistribution of bodily organs? For example, if one has two healthy kidneys then why not give one healthy one to a person without any healthy kidneys? – the point being that to regard ability or organs as common resources appears to give persons rights in other persons, so that the least advantaged have got a right to the best advantaged, raising the standard of living of the least advantaged. The example of taxation can be cited here. Where one person has to pay tax so that the money can be redistributed to the least advantaged then this is in effect a form of forced labour or slavery, because that proportion of one's time is spent working solely for others and not for oneself. It should be noted that Nozick is not talking about the need to raise tax in order to fund roads, hospitals or missiles, but about the tax that is used to pay for the poor such as supplementary benefits.

ii) Nozick also rejects the difference principle as being unjust. He cites examples. Let us assume that everyone starts off with the same – an equal distribution. People will then freely enter into contracts and be prepared to pay in order to get what they want. In his Wilt Chamberlain example, to which we will return later, Nozick shows that the spectators will become materially worse off while the player will become much better off. According to Rawls, that distribution is unjust because the least well off become poorer. Of course this concentrates on the financial position of the parties and that may not be the entire picture. As we shall see, Nozick replaces this patterned distribution with his 'historical entitlement theory'.

c) Hart, from a socialist perspective, raises some criticisms of Rawls. He questions whether the POP would opt for the two principles and necessarily prefer liberty to equality of opportunity. Why not prefer equality to liberty?

According to Hart, Rawls also underestimated the difficulty of balancing conflicting interests. It is the ideal that underlies his treatment of the allocation of resources. Rawls is interpreted by Hart as saying that a public-spirited person imbued with the notion of service to the community will decide never to give up any political freedom for material gain. Essentially this is because Rawls does not have any concept of the state in his theory. He pays too little attention to the institutional arrangements by means of which the distribution is to be carried out, in that those who in effect carry out the distribution will be the most powerful group in society. Can we really expect those people to act in a public spirited way?

Although not specifically a Hartian criticism, Rawls has assumed a consensus model of his society. We have already addressed the question as to whether such a picture is accurate (see chapter 8). Is this what a state is there to do?

d) Dworkin, a fellow liberal whose theory we shall consider in more detail in the following chapter, maintains that the right to equal concern and respect is not a consequence of the social contract but a presupposition of Rawls' use of the contract.

e) Lloyd argues that there would be a conflict between the two principles themselves. The rich have a different type of liberty from the poor in that they can choose whether to work. Inequality in wealth and power always produces inequality in basic liberties. Lloyd does, however, acknowledge that this is a question of empirical social theory. Rawls' response is to draw a distinction between liberty as a concept on the one hand and the worth or value of liberty on the other, and this, he admits, is affected by unequal wealth.

f) Daniels, as editor of an important book on Rawls (*Reading Rawls*), pursues the socialist perspective. He maintains that Rawls is arbitrarily excluding economic factors from his category of constraints which defines liberty. Daniels' criticism is not confined to Rawls specifically but addressed to all liberal theorists whom he says uniformly assume that political equality can exist with social and economic inequality.

g) A Marxist criticism would maintain that Rawls' assumptions are the product of ideology. Thus Fisk in *History and Reason in Rawls' Moral Theory* argues that it is impossible to extract man from his material circumstances. A Marxist would subscribe to a conflict model of society and would also criticise Rawls for assuming consensus. Furthermore, it could be argued that Rawls' difference principle is all about the distribution of resources but it fails to deal with the structure of the production process and, as such, ignores what for a Marxist would be the real rules of distribution.

h) With further regard to the difference principle, if justice is, as Aristotle maintained, all about deserts, then one should get what one deserves. What one deserves has got nothing to do with the least advantaged in society.

i) Dahrendorf, a fellow liberal, points out that it is not clear whether Rawls is speaking about liberty or liberties. If he is speaking about liberty then he ought to know that liberty is indivisible.

j) Fisk focuses on the idea that Rawls is engaging in an intellectual sleight of hand in constructing his model in order to lead to the results that he wants. MacCormick replies that this is of no consequence if one is not in a position to suggest anything better. Furthermore Fisk argues that the OP is highly artificial. People cannot be stripped of their values in this way.

k) Lloyd and Freeman conclude that when Rawls hunts out the mutually acceptable ground rules 'he is of course looking for an ideal ...'

A final question you ought to ask yourself: is Rawls' argument convincing? Does he persuade us that the OP should be used, that the POP would conclude with the two principles, and that the two principles are the best possible principles by which to govern society? From a liberal point of view his theory does produce a fair concept of justice, but not from other points of view.

18.4   Nozick's theory

I do not, you will be relieved to hear, intend to say as much about Nozick as I did about Rawls. Robert Nozick's *Anarchy, State and Utopia* is a fascinating book, containing a new natural rights theory as well as criticisms of utilitarianism and Rawls, a plea for vegetarianism, and much more. It is recommended as a stimulating 'read' on justice and some related topics – though only if you have time and the inclination.

In brief, Nozick's theory is as follows. Man has certain natural rights, including the right to acquire property. These rights must not be violated by anyone, without the consent of the right-holder: they act as moral 'side-constraints' on action. To be justified, a state must be such that it would arise from a no-state position (the state of nature) without infringing the rights of anyone who did not consent; only a minimal state offering protection against violence, theft and breach of agreement would emerge in this way. Any further state is not justified; particularly, a state redistributing wealth is not justified, and taxation to bring this about is the equivalent of forced labour. The only legitimate way of coming to hold property is by just acquisition, just transfer, or rectification of a past injustice.

Nozick, in the words of Lloyd, extols the virtues of 18th century individualism and 19th century laissez faire capitalism. It has certainly represented a profound shock to legal theory. The book is a provocative essay and one which in my view has had a very considerable impact on political reality. After reading Nozick one may ascertain where many of the ideas of Thatcherism have derived their origin, although they have undergone some modification in the process. Nozick's views, to the extent that classification is at all legitimate, may be referred to as libertarian. He questions whether liberty and equality are compatible and concludes that they are not. His central thesis rests on the proposition that the individual is inviolable. This point is crucial to an understanding of his theory.

I will attempt to explain his theory in more detail. In his critique of Rawls, as we have seen, Nozick rejects any 'patterned' conception of justice. A patterned conception is one that views justice as a matter of the pattern of distribution of benefits and burdens that is achieved eg the Marxist idea of the distribution according to need. As stated he prefers his 'historical entitlement theory', the content of which it would be appropriate to outline as follows:

a) *Natural rights*

Rather than examine the pattern of distribution, Nozick seeks to concentrate on the question of how the distribution came about in the first place. If that distribution is brought about entirely as a result of freely entered into transactions then it is just. He put it thus, '... If each person's holdings are just then the total set of holdings is just ... '

The individual has certain natural rights, including the freedom from violence against his person, the freedom to hold property, and the freedom to enforce his other rights. Concentrating on the right to hold individual property, a person can legitimately acquire property in three ways:

i) *By just initial acquisition*

This details the circumstances under which a person may acquire ownership of formerly unowned resources. This right of appropriation follows Locke. Locke, you will remember, had the proviso that 'as much and as good be left for others'; Nozick has a more limited proviso, merely that the remainder be left for others, and not necessarily as much/as good. (In any case, MacPherson says that the Lockean proviso ceases to be relevant once money is invented, since there is always some of that property available.)

ii) *By legitimate transfer*

This details the means by which ownership of resources may be transferred from one to another. If I choose to give you some of my property, or we agree to swap bits of our property, then you receive my property legitimately by transfer.

iii) *By rectification of past injustice*

This details the action to be taken to rectify a distribution which is unjust in terms of the first two principles. If I acquire property in an unjust manner, it can be taken from me and restored to its proper owner. This principle in fact justifies a less limited state, in some circumstances, to remedy a series of past injustices. (Could it justify our present Welfare State?)

These rights cannot be violated without a person's consent; this is his meaning of the distinctness of persons. A person's separateness and individuality must be respected; he must not be treated as a means to an end. Each person has exclusive rights in himself and no rights in others. What is important is that in the pursuit of our own aims we do not violate the rights of others. As we have seen and stated above, Nozick's theory originated in a critical evaluation of Rawls. He has criticised Rawls on the grounds that individual abilities are not common assets to be exploited for the benefit of the least advantaged. For this reason, Nozick rejects goal-based principles of justice. These are principles which judge a society by reference to whether or not it matches a particular goal, a particular end-state. Such principles will require the right of the individual to be sacrificed for the goal or desired end-state, the person being treated as a means to that end. The Wilt Chamberlain example, in (c) below, is a graphic illustration of Nozick's point.

Rather than such an end-state, goal-based principle, Nozick insists that an 'historical entitlement' principle be chosen. This means that a situation is judged not with reference to whether or not it matches a given end-state, but rather with reference to whether or not it came about justly, with no infringement of anyone's rights (hence the three just processes by which property may be acquired).

Under this entitlement principle, people's rights are respected: they become moral 'side-constraints' which forbid decisions and actions which violate them. Natural rights can only be infringed with the consent of the right-holder. For example, a road can only be built across someone's property if he consents to it: if he does not, his rights may not be infringed however much some particular goal (average utility, the best position for the least advantage, or whatever) may be enhanced by such an infringement.

These rights are the right to liberty and the right to property. Their inter-relationship is interesting. The right to liberty is defined by reference to the right to property and the right to property is the result of the exercise of rights in one's own labour. The right to property is then an expression of the right to liberty. Nozick believes that private property increases freedom, an idea that has considerably influenced Conservative politicians. The idea of Nozick that, when one mixes one's labour with an object that is not owned, one acquires a right to that object which can then be transferred, does not address the question as to whether the exercise of one's labour gives a right to the whole value of the object with which it is mixed. It is questionable whether wealth is brought into existence by the efforts of individuals, is this true of natural resources? What of natural talents and abilities? These are not possessed as a result of any labour but as a result of natural and, it is submitted, morally arbitrary distributions.

b) *The minimal state*

Nozick envisages a state of nature, and asks whether any state would emerge without harming people's rights. In fact, a state will emerge, through an 'invisible hand' process, ie one which occurs without anyone intending it or aiming for it by morally permissible means and without anyone's rights (in Nozick's sense of the word) being violated. In brief, the process is as follows:

i) To protect themselves, people form protective agencies, pooling their protective resources and leaving themselves free from fear of attack.

ii) In each region, one protective agency becomes dominant, but there are still independents.

iii) The dominant agency will prohibit independents from enforcing their own rights, since they will distrust the independents' procedure for determining violations. This prohibition involves infringing the independents' rights (to enforce their other rights), and demanding compensation; this compensation is 'paid' by protecting the would-be independents as well.

The dominant agency develops into a 'night-watchman' state, carrying out a minimal range of duties – protection from theft, violence, fraud, and breach of contract. This state claims a monopoly of force. If the state engaged in a patterned distribution then it would be exercising excessive powers as it would entail constant interference with liberty. Nozick does, however, recognise the need for some state, otherwise there would be anarchy. Hence his minimal state can be seen as the way to Utopia where individuals are inviolate.

c) *Distributive justice*

Any state other than the minimal state is rejected by Nozick. He would clearly see the present UK set-up as unjust: through social security and other aspects of the Welfare State, money is taken through taxation from the wealthier people, and given to the poor. This taxation is forced labour in disguise: such proportion of one's working time as is reflected in the national insurance and income Tax contributions that are used for redistribution to the least advantaged is spent working for others. The redistribution involves violating rights to property; unless it involves setting right past injustices (many would argue that it does) it does not fit into any of the three methods of just acquisition. Thus redistribution where resources are justly obtained would not rectify an inequality but would rather produce one.

Nozick rejects the difference principle. Social co-operation is a good thing, since it probably produces better results for everyone, but especially for the weak and poor who would have nothing if they had to act on their own. The difference principle – that economic and social disadvantages should be so arranged as to benefit the least well-off – gives all the benefit of their co-operation to the poor, which is asymmetrical and unjust. (This does not mean that Rawls' argument from the OP is wrong: it might be rational for the POP to choose it. The difference between Rawls and Nozick is in their starting points: Rawls starts from a standpoint of equality, and asks for reasons why we should accept inequality; Nozick starts from the idea of rights, with a consequence that a man owns the property he has worked for and created. For Rawls, the rich man must show why his wealth should not be taken; for Nozick, it cannot be taken without his consent.) Wealth is created by individuals and they that create it have rights over it. Hence Nozick maintains that one is not entitled to regard society's total wealth as a cake to be divided up.

That this question of distributive justice is linked with that of goal-based v entitlement principles is illustrated by Nozick's Wilt Chamberlain (a basketball star) example. Assume, says Nozick, that at the start of a season your favourite end-state principle is satisfied in society: let us say, the difference principle. Chamberlain fixes a contract, giving him $1 of every spectator's entrance fee. At the end of the year, the million spectators who have watched him are each $1 worse off, and Wilt is a millionaire. Each $1 has been willingly given, a just transfer. Why should Wilt have to pay back some of his million to again satisfy the difference principle? Where is the justification for redistribution?

18.5 Evaluation of Nozick's theory

Nozick's theory is interesting and a strong challenge to Rawls. It is not, however, without its defects. What becomes clear from an evaluation of this topic is the close relationship that the authors bear to current political agenda. I think that a major evaluative point in favour of Nozick is that many of his ideas are now the topic of intense political debate both in this country and in the USA. In that light perhaps we ought now to examine some of the main criticisms that have been made of his theory.

a) He takes rights as his starting point. The rights he takes are of uncertain pedigree: how are they derived, where do they come from? There is a strong body of opinion that denies the possibility of any objective rights, such as those Nozick must contemplate. He sees his rights as inherent, as natural: the idea of such rights should be established (if it can be), not assumed. Further, the choice of rights to assume is a value-laden process; why not include a right to welfare and help from others? Or, to put it another way, why limit the 'moral landscape' to just rights? Why not have duties as well, to assist others in need?

b) The argument from rights to a minimal state is not without its problems either. Particularly, at one stage, the dominant protective association prohibits the use by independents of their own rights-enforcement procedures, at least unless those procedures have been vetted and found acceptable. Surely this involves a strong violation of the independent's rights to protect himself, which is not properly compensated for even by membership of the dominant agency? And wouldn't this compensation be free, resulting in only some people paying for the services?

In any case, it is not clear that the dominant agency idea would work out as Nozick thinks. Might not the strong people in a community think that the only opposition or problem will be from other strong people, and therefore form an organisation with them? It would be cheaper for all concerned if weak people were not allowed to join, and prohibiting their own enforcement would not be necessary, because it is not to be feared (since they are weak). Doesn't the state idea therefore include some element of compassion for the weak?

On the other hand, assume that we get to a minimal state, surely logic would require even the right and strong to accept a greater state? Assume you are rich/strong now, and tomorrow you are robbed/lose all your money on a business deal/are knocked down and paralysed. And don't most people grow old and infirm? Isn't it logical to accept and agree to pay for a state which will provide a safety net in case such things happen to you (or your family and friends)?

c) I think that Nozick's view of the free market is somewhat idealistic and unreal. The purpose of competition is not the provision of a service to the consumer but the elimination of competition. There is in a truly free market a tendency towards monopoly.

d) Lukes argues that Nozick has an unreal conception of the relationship between the individual and the society, to the extent that he has excluded what for Lukes (I think accurately) is the ever growing role of the state. Lukes further maintains that the central flaw in Nozick's arguments is 'the abstractness of the individualism they presuppose'. Lukes maintains that it is not possible to divorce an individual from his society.

e) Hart, not surprisingly, takes issue with Nozick's theory. He maintains that Nozick's assault on utilitarianism is paradoxical as it shows that he is unwilling to disturb the exisiting pattern of distribution. Hart further takes exception to Nozick's likening of taxation for the sake of redistribution of wealth to slavery, which is so rooted in Nozick's belief in the absolutely inviolable character of property rights. Hart maintains that one is talking of two different types of burden. Man is free to decide whether to work, what work and how much work to do; a slave is not so free. Hart would speculate whether rights which are derived from human interests and needs could outweigh property rights.

f) Lloyd and Freeman are unsure as to how Nozick's minimal state would emerge from the state of nature without infringing individual rights. They say that Nozick does not adequately explain this. Furthermore they maintain that Nozick leaves many questions unanswered and makes a number of assumptions which do not stand up to examination, not least the point of where do people get their rights from? Is this historical – some initial act of appropriation which then confers unlimited rights of use and disposition?

g) In an interesting comment on Nozick, O'Neill in *Nozick's Entitlements* argues that work is a way of losing one's labour and of contributing to society.

h) Nozick's rejection of welfare rights which, as Simmonds aptly points out, is essentially logical with the structure of his theory is a rejection of a right to the assistance of others. This neglects the interests of the weak. Nozick's view of the assistance to the weak is privatisation of philanthropy. The matter is essentially one of private charity, a view echoed by one British government minister following the recent cutting of the upper tax levels when it was suggested that some of the money handed back to those tax payers ought to go to private charity. I am not sure that human dignity and the receipt of charity are compatible.

19 ADJUDICATION 1: CONVENTIONALISM, PRAGMATISM AND LAW AS INTEGRITY

19.1   Introduction

We have been much concerned in the analysis in this text with the question, 'What is law?' The fruits of what has been a varied and confusing Odyssey may be found in the question, 'What is a judge doing when he makes a decision?' To a certain extent we have covered much relevant ground, positing ideas and criticising old ideas of where law comes from. However, ultimately, the student must be concerned with law as being 'what the judge pronounces'. We have already seen how, to the Imperative thinker, his words are as the commands of the sovereign, while the Realists doubt that it is very much more than his own point of view. We have investigated law as being rules and law as being norms. Ultimately, the shaker in which this cocktail of philosophies is mixed, must be the judicial mind. If the judiciary do not simply 'make it all up', how much is a legal decision a matter of pragmatic discretion, and how much is a commitment to rules and norms of the legal system?

A debate that has overshadowed this area of juristic battle has been that between Hart and Dworkin. It is, however, now widely held, as has been persuasively argued by Phang in *Judicial Oaks from Mythical Acorns*, that the appellation 'debate' is not a proper one. As with the 'Hart-Fuller debate' and, in Kelsen's view, the 'Hart-Kelsen debate', the 'Dworkin-Hart debate' seems to be based on mutual 'comprehensive misunderstandings'. In the fascination of lawyers, who seek the truth as a result of the adversarial system, many have become committed to joining the battle against one side or the other. In this chapter, the present task is to draw out some of Dworkin's insights into the critical question of what judges are doing when they come to a final legal decision.

19.2   The potential judicial considerations

a) *Legal sources*

The question of what to treat as an authoritative legal source brings us back to the debates of earlier chapters. However, it seems clear that the judicial function presupposes the existence of 'raw material' in the form of rules, commands, principles, standards and permissions that are considered to be authoritative. However, what an authoritative source is, depends on what concept of validity a judge adopts. The judge is only under a legal duty to apply what is valid law. Any other considerations might thus be seen to be his own. Thus, the criterion of validity of legal sources is critical to the understanding to what extent the judge is 'ad-libbing' when he delivers a judgment.

There is a duality of approach to conceptions of validity that might be illustrated by comparing Kelsen's 'normative validity' with Hart's 'normatised validity'. Kelsen sees legal sources as being identified by higher legal norms, while Hart considers that ultimately if the courts display a 'normally concordant practice' we can derive an understanding of what they think is valid law. Thus, there is a fundamental difference between their positions. To Kelsen a court may display a normatised practice, with Hart's characteristic 'critical reflexive attitude', but unless this relates to a higher legal norm that authorises it, Kelsen would deny it is a legal rule. He would not assert that it could not be a 'norm of judicial politics/morality', but a valid legal norm cannot derive its force from mere legal behaviour, only another legal norm. On the other hand, Hart's reliance on a 'critical reflexive attitude' has its own flaws. As Raz points out, the *practice theory* does not, inter alia, distinguish between rules and widely accepted reasons; and deprives rules of their normative force. As such Hart's theory cannot explain normative behaviour that is not accompanied by a critical reflexive attitude. I would submit that the differences between Hart and Kelsen have a similarity between the differences between Hart and Dworkin that we shall consider a little later.

However, it must be pointed out here that anything that falls outside the definition of authoritative legal sources, if used as the basis of a decision, will be treated as an extraneous consideration or as deciding a case on discretion.

b) *Ignoring legal sources*

The Realists emphasised the role of judicial discretion. Indeed more extreme support for discretion comes from Gray who states that 'all law is judge-made law'. As Lloyd and Freeman point out, this is to mistake power for authority. It is clear that there is a level of normatised behaviour within a legal system, particularly a hierarchical one, such as the English court system. Thus, although a court may overstep the boundaries of its authority by flagrantly ignoring relevant law, a superior court will normally overrule its decision.

c) *Open rules and practical reasoning*

To insist that judges have no discretion at all, is to ignore the existence of numerous rules of common law and statute. Frequently, legal rules are formulated in an open way, that is not in the normal all-or-nothing form. Thus, judicial discretion to exclude evidence in a criminal case is exercisable where the 'probative value' of the evidence is outweighed by the 'prejudicial effect' on the defendant. This requires the judge to evaluate and weigh two principles or standards. Other discretions require even broader evaluations, such as considering 'all the circumstances' or the 'interests of justice'. These explicit rules, however, require a bona fide consideration and usually prescribe that if the judge finds one factor to outweigh another, he must follow a given course of action. Thus, open rules are, essentially conferring 'weak' discretions, in that the evaluation is expected to be impartial, or at least made in good faith. Moreover, the consequences of his evaluation return him to the confines of the relevant rule – if he finds, in all the circumstances, such and such, then he must do such and such. A 'weak' discretion of this kind requires more than a mere comparison of the law to the facts of the case, since a judge is required to *evaluate* these facts before he can return to his consideration of their relevance to the law.

Apart from the Realists, who are sceptical towards any kind of rule, there seems to be little problem with these explicit discretion-conferring rules. Whether judges act impartially and in good faith is a question of fact, rather like the question of whether they are guided by rules. The question of whether they have a discretion is a normative question, to which there can be a normative legal answer – eg the statute confers a discretion.

19.3 The different battlegrounds of the Hart-Dworkin debate

Perhaps the most fascinating element about the Hart-Dworkin debate is that it seems to exist on several different planes, rather like a game of three-dimensional chess. Sometimes, it seems that Dworkin is arguing on a level (where Hart has no pieces deployed) that Hart's account of discretion is a pragmatic compromise between predictability, as embodied in rules, and flexibility, which entails giving the correct remedy. On this account the first level of the Dworkinian argument is that a theory of law, based on rules, is logically inferior to pure discretion and must therefore collapse into pure pragmatism, as exemplified by the Realist conception. This is the first level of debate: *Conventionalism collapses into Pragmatism*. The second level of argument is one on which Dworkin seems to have conceded defeat. Simply, his assertion was once that judges have *no discretion*, now he concedes that they do 'interpret' material. However, the argument has moved to level three with the assertion that there is *one right answer* to a legal case. This logically entails that there is *no strong discretion*.

A further confusion is whether Dworkin is talking in normative terms or descriptive terms. In my discussion of Kelsen, I mentioned that a legal norm exists on a duality of levels. Law exists as both a social practice and as a system of normative reasoning. Hart, it may be remembered, looks for a critical reflexive attitude, rather than seeking after elusive 'rules of law in the descriptive sense'. Dworkin seems to regard non-rule based institutional material as having a normative force. Hart seems to be asking, 'Do judges have a discretion?' in the sense that he is seeking to explain in descriptive sociological terms judicial behaviour. Dworkin, on the other hand, asks the same question, but asks whether the judge is constrained by legal reasoning when making decisions. This view envisages the *law as integrity*.

We shall consider these aspects of the debate individually, so as not to be constrained by the confusion of the arguments.

a) *Does Conventionalism collapse into Pragmatism?*

N E Simmonds considers this aspect of Dworkin's critique of rule-based theories in *Why Conventionalism Does Not Collapse Into Pragmatism* (CLJ) 49(1), March 1990, in response to Dworkin's argument in *Law's Empire*. Simmonds detects several misconceptions in Dworkin's argument. It is not greatly interesting to recount these misconceptions in the context of the Hart-Dworkin debate. However, they are relevant to other views of law and therefore are worth explaining.

It will be remembered that, amongst others, Bentham saw an aspect of law as being the prediction of circumstances when a sanction would be visited. This aspect of conventionalism, ie the adherence to preset standards, might be termed the 'fair warning' view. Rules (imperatives in Bentham's case) give warning to those as to when the government might resort to force. Bentham's account fits neatly into what Dworkin terms unilateral conventionalism. If there is a clear rule in the favour of a party, then he wins, if not he loses, if neither have a clear rule in their favour, then the burden of proof would determine it. (This is a brief and deficient synopsis of the view, but is adequate for our purposes). Bentham was very scathing of 'judge-made law' since he viewed the job of legislation as the duty of the legislator alone.

However, even Austin was critical of this, advocating something more along the lines of 'bilateral conventionalism', by which new rules of law may be created so long as they do not interfere with existing expectations and interests, in order that 'hard cases' might be resolved and the content of the law may be expanded upon and improved in the interests of legal flexibility. Dworkin's argument is as follows, (per Simmonds):

> 'Bilateral conventionalism seems to fit the facts [of the way in which judges do behave] ... Dworkin argues, even if it satisfies ... [this] ... descriptive test, it fails prescriptively. The strategy of decision proposed by bilateral conventionalism is rationally inferior to the pragmatist approach. Bilateral conventionalism proposes a trade-off between flexibility and predictability, but only in one particular way; where a case falls within a clear rule, one must respect the value of predictability, allowing considerations of flexibility to have force only in cases not covered by a clear rule. This imposes an arbitrary constraint on the process of trading off two values against each other ...'

Dworkin suggests that it would be more logical if, in each individual case, the arguments in favour of enforcement of rules were weighed against arguments for non-enforcement. He suggests that both judge and justice would be better off if rules could be judiciously ignored when necessary if the only justification for adhering to rules was to ensure 'fair warning'. This is essentially the pragmatist approach. Dworkin's conclusion is that adherence to rules under the bilateral conventionalist view, is either:

   i)   not a correct description of the way in which cases are decided;

ii) an irrational practice on the part of judges;

iii) collapses into pragmatism.

Thus, at least the Austinian view of conventionalism is severely limited. However, as Simmonds points out, this does not really address itself to Hart's concept of the role of rules. The rest of the article is an interesting one, although I remain unconvinced that Simmonds fully refutes the criticism. In a simplified form, Dworkin's argument against 'fair warning' conventionalism is that either a person's claim is judged on the legal rule that applies, or the court is simply moving the goal-posts in an arbitrary way, depending on whether other people have expectations under the rule. To illustrate this, imagine that you have a claim, justified by a little-known, but nonetheless valid precedent. You pay a generous fee to your legal advisers, only to find that the court has decided to change the law on the grounds that the law should be changed and such a change would not upset the expectations of too many others.

However, neither am I convinced that Dworkin's account (below) would in descriptive terms, avoid such a situation, although, theoretically this would not happen in Dworkin's model.

b) *Dworkin's 'no discretion' model*

The early form of Dworkin's 'no discretion' theory stems from his article, *Hard Cases*, which developed into his 'rights thesis' in *Taking Rights Seriously*. The basis of his contention that judges had no discretion was the notion of legal principles. Even if there was no rule that explicitly covered a case, there would be principles to which the judge must adhere. In earlier writings Dworkin seemed to suggest that these principles could even override rules. He discussed *Riggs* v *Palmer* 115 NY 506 (1889) 22 NE 188, a US case where the rules of succession were not followed because that would have resulted in the murderer of the deceased taking the estate, contrary to the equitable principle that no one can benefit from his own wrong. He now seems to have withdrawn from this position, although principles still feature in his model.

Principles differ from rules in the following two respects:

i) Principles, unlike rules, cannot be 'torpedoed'. A rule either applies or it does not, whereas a principle can be one of several factors that apply.

ii) Different principles have different weight and are of varying importance when applied to a legal problem.

These principles, Dworkin suggests, might be ascertainable in total, by a superhuman judge, who could derive all of the implicit and explicit principles that lie in ratios, statutes and constitutional law. This process is elaborated on in *How Law is Like Literature* as an interpretative one. The process has two stages: the determination of what the application of legal principles would suggest as the answer to a hard case; if there is more than one interpretation possible, then 'substantive political theory' comes into play, to decide which result would 'fit' best.

One aspect of the argument to be found in *Taking Rights Seriously* is an attempt to differentiate policies from principles. The two arguments that Dworkin has not abandoned in this distinction are of interest:

i) The first has been developed into what I term the liberalised 'no strong discretion' thesis.

ii) The second relates to the coherence of the legal system and its 'chain-novel' quality.

However, before we go on to consider these evolutionary forms found in *Law's Empire*, we might cynically consider why Dworkin was so keen to advocate the 'no discretion' thesis. There are, it is suggested, two motivations:

i) Dworkin seems concerned to marry together two conceptions of justice that may be rather familiar. On the one side, in common with Bentham, Dworkin does not see it as fitting that the judge should make new law. This is manifestly 'anti-democratic'. The concept of justice being done, in the procedural sense, is that the relevant rules and principles of law have been strictly complied with (procedural justice). However, Dworkin is also concerned to marry into this the sense of common sense and objective moral standards that were traditionally association with law. The judge is therefore 'like any other reflective member of the community willing to debate about what fairness or equality or liberty requires on some occasion ...' However, the judge looks with objectivity at the moral implications of past legal decisions, rather than relying on his own personal preferences.

This has proven problematic for readers of Dworkin who subscribe to a view of law as a ramshackle system of haphazard norms. What Dworkin seems to be doing is not 'resurrecting Blackstone's Declaratory Theory' nor advocating that there is an Aladdin's cave (per Lord Reid) of absolute legal truths, but instead suggesting that judges should and often do have a commitment to seeking legal institutional reasons, explicit or implicit, that give a continuity to the tradition of legal judgments. Dworkin does not see the judge as simply saying 'Neither rule applies, so it is up to me to decide what I think I should do.' Nor, indeed does Hart, who describes what Dworkin terms as considering principles as being the 'classic juridical virtues' of impartiality, deploying principles of law, weighing and balancing these principles and having due respect for the interests and rights of persons involved.

ii) Dworkin is concerned that, by 'making up' new rules, present expectations are thwarted retrospectively in the same way as they might be thwarted by an Act of Parliament. As such, rules and principles taken together at least make things a little easier. However, Dworkin's 'one right answer' thesis means that theoretically the problem is overcome entirely.

It might therefore be prudent to analyse this contention, which surely has to be one of the most bizarre of all Dworkin's assertions.

c) *One right answer*

We observed that Hart does subscribe, after a fashion, to the concept of principles. However, he expressly states that for this reason, there is 'no clear answer' because the judge has to decide on the basis of these various competing principles. Dworkin, as we shall see in a moment now accepts that judges have a weak discretion. How then can Dworkin assert that there can only be one right answer?

Moreover, if different judges come to different conclusions in more or less the same case, then how can this be so? The cases of *Johannsen* and *Novac* cited in *R v Scarrot* [1978] QB 1016 is a striking example. In both cases the accused had been charged with gross indecency with young boys, picking them up at amusement arcades, offering them money etc. The facts of both cases were remarkably similar, however, the decision to apply a particular rule of evidence – the similar fact rule – differed in both cases. In *Scarrot* Scarman LJ referred to, 'I hesitate to say a striking similarity, but certainly a remarkable similarity between the salient facts ... it is very difficult to determine why and how the court reached the decision that it did in these cases.' The application of the similar fact doctrine is based on an evaluation of the probative value of evidence, rather than a rule of law. Two points might be noted:

i) Scarman LJ seemed to expect that on the same facts, despite the absence of a clear rule, the same legal conclusion would be arrived at in both cases, since the absence of factual differences made both cases seem to address one question.

ii) There obviously was not one right answer for the two differently constituted courts.

Thus, one might argue, Dworkin's 'one right answer' thesis is still-born on the basis that it fails to accord descriptively with our experience of courts. However, the American jurist does not give up so easily. He employs the notion that we attributed to Hart's concept of justice in an earlier chapter; that of 'essentially contested concepts'. If you remember, Hart sees the appeal to justice as universal. Everyone has an idea of justice yet people's conceptions of justice differ. The concept is universal, yet there are varying conceptions of it (Gallie). This is appropriate to Dworkin's approach to the 'one right answer' thesis, since he posits it on the basis of what is essentially an appeal to procedural justice.

Dworkin argues that the reason why there seems to be more than one answer to a legal problem is not because judges think there is more than one right answer, but because they have different conceptions of what that right answer is. Thus, no matter how many disagreements between courts there may be, essentially, all judges are in search of the same thing – the right answer. This is, as Phang observes, somewhat of a 'double-edged sword'. While it prevents the critic from demonstrating that Dworkin's theory is descriptively wrong, it also means that Dworkin is prevented from saying he is descriptively right, since in fact there is no 'one right answer' However, it is submitted that Dworkin makes a lot of mileage out of what looks, on the surface, to be an untenable position.

What we are left with is thus descriptively useless, since it does not actually account for what judges do. Dworkin might argue that this is the 'psychological' belief or aspiration of judges, rather than the result of their performance. However, as Lord Reid comments, this 'fairy-tale' of the legal truth as an absolute, has long been abandoned. Dworkin is left exhorting the value of judicial solidarity in seeking the 'one right answer' as well as advocating that lawyers should keep their minds on the job, rather than harbouring secret agendas of courtroom legislation. Such a prescription amounts to a plea for democratic justice.

One factor that some critics have overlooked is that this approach is also a method of justice. If the judiciary were committed to finding one right answer, to finding the just resolution of a case, according to institutional materials, they may or may not succeed in their enterprise, but will at least be *seen* to be doing so. If they simply say, 'There are no absolute truths in law,' while being philosophically tenable, this means that they are unlikely to bother looking for any. If a man genuinely seeks justice and fails to prove that what he has found is justice, he is at least a just man. However, if he does not embark on that search, he is not even that. I think that Dworkin would accept this comment.

In a footnote to this discussion, Lord Devlin, in a recent interview on television, stated that he felt he had never made an unjust decision. It seemed clear that this did not mean he always made the decision he thought was right as an individual, but that his decisions were right as a judge. Dworkin seems to have been similarly informed by this distinction in ethical philosophy. Nowell-Smith, in his book *Ethics*, notes that there are two possible ways in which the word 'right' might be used:

i) 'Right' might mean 'fitting', in the sense that I might use the 'right' key to open a door. Dworkin certainly means more than this, since he sees only the first stage of interpretation of institutional material as finding the answer that has an 'institutional fit'. I would submit that Hart and other positivists have misconstrued Dworkin as saying that there can only be one institutionally fitting answer. However, Dworkin does concede that there may be more than one institutional fit, requiring a second stage.

ii) 'Right' might also mean morally correct, in a subjective or objective sense. Dworkin talks of the second stage being the weighing up of institutionally fitting answers in the light of substantive political morality. It may be that Dworkin means that the judge should go further to seek the 'right' answer in terms of substantive political morality, ie the values that a political society is formally committed to, such as liberty, democracy, moral and political autonomy etc. This is as opposed to 'right' in terms of the subjective views of the judge.

What Dworkin seems to be saying is that judges have and should have a duty to not only find an institutional 'fit' (right answer in Hart's sense), but have a duty qua judge to decide according to objective values in the form of 'substantive political morality', including considerations of any limitations of how far a judge should go in departing from existing institutional material. For one judge, in one case, can there be any more than one 'just' or 'right' answer? I submit that in these terms Dworkin might succeed in his assertion that there can be only one right decision. Dworkin, perhaps like Hart, sees the appeal to justice as universal, although conceptions vary. Dworkin seems to be emphasising an aspect of the judicial process that is frequently overlooked. A judge has a duty to society, based on an ideal of justice.

d) *No strong discretion*

It may be considered that the two stages of interpretation involve a discretion. This has been conceded by Dworkin in his later works. He states that judges have a 'weak' discretion, as opposed to a strong one. Some, like Phang, find it difficult to understand that there is a real difference between 'strong' and 'weak' discretions. The student might resort to the brief account of statutory and common law rule-based discretions early on in this chapter (open rules). The discretion is weak because it is constrained by the requirements of the empowering statute/common law. A judge cannot do what he pleases, but may evaluate facts in the light of given variables, such as probative value and prejudice to the defendant, in the example given earlier. Dworkin seems to suggest that where the law is less clear, the judge has a finite but overlapping amount of considerations that he must objectively consider in the light of the facts. One might simplify this approach by considering a 'stop-list' of variables that the judge must follow:

METHOD: If case can be clearly decided on a given level, then do not proceed. If not, then proceed to next level.

LEVEL 1: Statutory rules and explicit statutory discretions.

LEVEL 2: Common law rules and explicit common law discretions.

LEVEL 3: Clear analogies with relevant common law rules.

LEVEL 4: Institutional principles such as, 'A man should not profit from his own wrongdoing.'

LEVEL 5: Remote institutional principles such as considering the expectations of persons not party to the immediate dispute.

LEVEL 6: Substantive political morality, up to and including the requirement that a judge, not being elected, should not legislate, but should base his decisions on institutional materials and values.

NOTE: Levels 3-5 involve balancing of considerations in an objective manner, so that the judge is bound to decide the case, according to the predominant weight of relevant principles. If there is more than one possible answer that has an institutional fit, then the judge may decide between them on Level 6 considerations.

This is not intended as a representation of Dworkin's own views, but to illustrate what I think he is proposing. What must be noticed is that although there is a strong element of judgment involved, this is a judgment as to the comparative relevance of principles in the light of the facts. Thus, the judge's discretion is limited to considering objective principles in an objective manner, rather than any subjective considerations. I would suggest in summary that Dworkin's concept of a weak discretion is one that is constrained by objective legal and meta-legal (eg substantive political morality) conceptions, rather than the open reasoning of expedience and pragmatism and moral and political autonomy that characterises the legislator's role.

e) *Law as integrity*

It will seem fairly clear to the reader, by now, that Dworkin does not see law as a system of rules that hold together like a frayed string-vest. If there is always one right answer and there is no room for anything but institutional judgment, then it is rather a gapless universe or 'seamless web' as Dworkin terms it. Dworkin seems law as being rather like a 'chain-novel', where one novel is written by successive writers, whilst retaining the themes and continuity of the story. Statutes and new rules might be introduced or evolve out of the background, like new characters in a 'soap-opera' and may die with equal suddenness. Time might roll by and atmospheres change, but for Dworkin it has a unity and consistency that stems from the unity of purpose of judges.

As well as being a powerful metaphor, it does conform with the way judges in England seem to act. When we see Denning twisting and wrestling with precedent and principle in *High Trees*, it is almost like an author who seeks to bring out an incredibly bizarre coincidence in order for the plot to continue. However, Dworkin is advocating more than a 'suspension of disbelief' when looking at judicial decision-making, but that the authors (judges) maintain that belief. He criticises sceptics in that they destroy the platform of judicial argumentation.

19.4 Evaluation

The reader will probably have noticed that I have considerable sympathy with Dworkin's point of view. The standard criticism is that Dworkin is a dreamer and judges simply consider what they think the right answer ought to be and then superimpose justifications. I think there may be some truth in this. Dworkin does not rule out internal scepticism in the interpretative stage, but insists that judges do try to make judicial rulings look consistent with legal history. He does not deny that lawyers are creative – creativity is the life of a judicial process – but he denies that law can ever have the arbitrary justification of a judge making a bare assertion that he has run out of rules and will now start to 'make things up'. Certainly Hart would not contest this. Dworkin seeks to explain the reason why judges do not wish to give this impression as well as the reason why they should not. He has described the expressions of judicial reasoning and, having found a coherence in their behaviour, sought to explain it in normative terms. As such the theory is both semantically descriptive and normatively descriptive (the latter in the sense that Kelsen uses when talking of rules of law in the descriptive sense).

It may be remembered that positivist sociologists of law denied that legal behaviour could be described by including the normative ideas that gave coherence to their practice. Hart's view has a little in common with this, in that his approach is an empirical one; there cannot be one right answer, unless the question has been asked before. Therefore while Dworkin's judge Hercules is superhuman and achieves the ideal of justice, Hart's judge is human and is satisfied with a compromise of earlier decisions. Compare Dworkin's 'every hard decision is a vote for law's dreams' with Hart's view that the sensible lawyer simply wants a good night's sleep, somewhere in between the fulfilment of legal 'dreams' and the nightmare of there being 'no right answer' (see *American Jurisprudence through English Eyes: The Nightmare or the Noble Dream*). I leave the choice to the student, but would make the following metaphorical allusion. If Beethoven had conceded that short of basic harmonic conventions, there were no single right notes, would his symphonies have been as good as they are? Dworkin views the legal enterprise as a creative one and the judge's duty as the obligation to strive for achievement of the ideal of justice, ie the objective evaluation of existing legal information and values in order to give the best decision. I feel Dworkin is quite right that judges should aspire to some coherent ideal, since the alternative must logically be the mediocrity and inconsistency promised by pure pragmatism. Why adhere to rules if there is no reason other than convention? Whether in the post-realist and post-positivist world judges do so aspire, or whether they merely follow the motions of a now redundant tradition, is a more open question. The following of rules might now have no more significance than the wearing of wigs in court. In such a case Dworkin's resurrection of the ideal that gave reason to the coherence of decisions serves as a reminder that the law is not a profession for idealists, but for sceptical pragmatists. If this is the case, then the common law should (morally) throw off its pretensions to consistency.

19.5 Sartorius and a footnote on Hart

A defect that Raz has observed (see Chapter 6) is that Hart's emphasis on rules, to the exclusion of principles, is a little unsatisfactory. Sartorius suggests that the Rule of Recognition can accommodate principles as valid law by 'loosing up a bit Hart's concept of a rule of recognition, which must include the rule of stare decisis, so as to take account of the fact that the doctrine of precedent gives authoritative status directly only to particular decisions, rather than to general results. As so modified, it will identify constitutional provision, legislative enactment, and judicial decision as authoritative sources of law.'

(per Lloyd and Freeman). However, Sartorius does not go as far as Dworkin. Without considering the theory in depth, it entails what is largely an acceptance of statutory, rather than common law principles that are adopted on the basis of a test of 'coherence'. It might be submitted that Sartorius attempts to do what Raz has already more convincingly achieved, by abandoning the Hartian concept of rules, in favour of 'norms' that can embrace principles.

Once again there is a gradual convergence of the views of the positivists with the idealists (such as Dworkin). The ultimate synthesis will be interesting to see!

In *The Logic of Choice* Gottlieb seems to predict what this synthesis might look like. He disputes the distinction between discretion and rule, since courts are not really (logically) bound by rules, but merely use them as the sources of evaluative reasons and exclusive reasons. Similarly, discretion is not exercised by lawyers with a free hand, but with consideration of interests, constitutional criteria and other objective factors that do not stem from subjective, arbitrary preference. If Dworkin could maintain that such objective considerations are part of law, then his seamless web would be sustainable. Legal decision-making would simply be objective reasoning that is guided by a peculiarly different weight attributable to certain principles, guided by tools to enable that felicitate choices. As such law could be reducible to basic normative principles: eg the wrongdoer should be punished; society should be protected; individual rights should be protected. These would be hedged in by institutionalised aids to decision-making, such as more precise rules and principles, beyond which the judge should be wary to stray, lest he should end up serving another principle, such as 'law should be interesting'.

20 ADJUDICATION 2: JURISPRUDENCE OF THE COMMON LAW TRADITION

20.1   Introduction to precedent

The judge has two tasks. He must resolve the dispute before him and he must reach his decision by reference to some impartial rule of law. One of the most obvious aspects of formal justice is that all cases should be treated alike; one of the commonest and most noteworthy features of many human institutions (clubs, societies, companies, etc, as well as states) is the tendency to repeat earlier practice and follow earlier patterns. For these and other reasons, most legal systems have developed a system of precedent, including the use of past decisions as a guide to present decision. A moment's thought by any student of English law should bring scores of decisions based on precedents to mind.

As we shall see, though, the English system – the common law system – in fact uses precedent in a slightly different way from civil law systems. In England, precedents of an appropriate authority not only guide decisions in later cases, but bind the judges in those later cases: within the given hierarchical structure, a judge in an inferior court may obey the decision of a higher court on the same point. This is the doctrine of stare decisis.

Any system using precedents will require a method of keeping them in an acceptable and accessible form; this need for law reports is obviously greater where precedents are law (since they bind later decisions, they are actual law, and not just guides to what the law is). In the stare decisis based system there will also need to be a defined hierarchy, and an established way of working out what part of an earlier case is binding: we call this the ratio decidendi (reason for deciding.)

In the following sections, we look at the doctrine of stare decisis and how, if at all, it differs from the civil law use of precedent; the flexibility introduced into stare decisis in various ways (including an analysis of the problems involved in identifying the meaning of ratio decidendi); and the present English rules on precedent and stare decisis.

20.2   Stare decisis in theory

From the Latin stare decisis et non quieta marere: the doctrine of stare decisis lays down that decisions of superior courts bind the lower courts in later cases. The exact details will be discussed in 20.4 below. The courts fall into an hierarchy, House of Lords (HL), Court of Appeal (CA), Divisional Court (DC), judges of the High Court (HC) and so on, with the European Court of Justice (ECJ) thrown in for good measure.

This doctrine is the result of a combination of historical factors, really beyond our scope. One necessary factor, as was noted in the introduction, is a satisfactory system of law reporting. From the Year Books onwards, law reporting in England has been a developing and now integral part of our court system. The private collections of law reports (eg Coke's) gave way in the nineteenth century to the reports of the Incorporated Council of Law Reporting whose reports remain the most authoritative (since they are checked by the judges), although still unofficial. There are many other series: reports in *The Times* each day, the weekly *All England Law Reports* and the *Weekly Law Reports* (published by the council in addition to their main series), and many others. The computer revolution has made possible the storage of details of many more cases; the HL has recently disapproved some of the consequences in terms of increasing citations of cases from computer records.

Past cases – once the ratio is determined above – bind. This distinguishes the English doctrine of stare decisis from the treatment of precedent in civil law countries, and even in some common law countries. In civil law countries, past decisions are not binding, but merely persuasive, with the strength of persuasion depending on the authority of court and judge; in some common law countries, eg USA, the stare decisis doctrine is not applied as rigidly as in England. Several factors play a part in this distinction. In both the USA and France, for instance, the court structure is not as strictly hierarchical as in England, with many, particularly state and district courts, of concurrent jurisdiction with no authority over one another. Further, the basis of French and other civil law is a code: past decisions must always be justified on the basis of the code, and its wording can always provide a justification for not following past cases. Similarly, with US Supreme Court decisions on the Constitution; the Supreme Court's role as the arbiter of that document mitigates against strict stare decisis, and many of its landmark decisions (eg *Brown* v *Board of Education* (1954) 347 US 483, outlawing segregation in schools) are in fact reversals of earlier rulings.

The mode of reporting and of giving judgments in France also works against the English model. Judgments tend to be pithy statements, frequently just on the facts; they are often accompanied in the reports by influential commentary on the case and its effects by jurists. This tends to decrease the role of the judgments, and increase the importance of the learned writings, in discovering what the law is.

In any case, the differences between France, for example, and England in this respect can be over-estimated. While the code is the last word, it is – just as English statutes are – often uncertain or vague, and it is the decisions of the courts which make the detailed law. A set of decisions pointing the way will, in France, be quite settled; in England, one decision on a particular point may be 'binding' on lower courts, but certainly not on upper courts. Also, the authority of the French Cour de Cassation is such that its decisions are almost always final.

In marginal cases, there is a difference: even a long series of cases does not fully bind a French judge, and particular precedents considered incorrect or out of date or unjust can be overruled or not followed without fear of criticism by higher courts, and without some of the devices (such as distinguishing) we discuss in relation to our own system in 20.3 below.

Does the doctrine of stare decisis have a value over and above the ordinary precedent system? The advantages held by the latter are certainty (to enable people's affairs to be arranged and conducted within a known legal framework), uniformity (like cases treated alike) and logic (fields of law developing harmoniously), mixed with a degree of flexibility to prevent injustice. The ordinary system sacrifices a degree of the certainty, uniformity and logic of the stare decisis system for the benefit of slightly increased flexibility and, hopefully, decreased injustice.

Think about the two options, bearing in mind the various tones of flexibility introduced into the stare decisis system. Is either option clearly the better one?

20.3 Stare decisis in practice – flexibility

The bald statement of the stare decisis doctrine makes it appear rigid and inflexible. In fact, in practice, judges do have a wide measure of flexibility and movement. If a judge does not want to follow a particular precedent, there are several techniques or devices he can use to avoid it: such avoidance is not always possible, but it frequently is.

One factor a judge always has to weigh up is the authority of the report itself and of the court. Present sets of reports are generally considered accurate (although the council's reports are most acceptable, as they have been checked by the judge), but earlier private sets of reports were not complete, and are of varying quality: Coke's, for example, are thought to be of high quality. Since the hierarchy is so important, a judge must always decide if he is bound by the cited decision or if it is just persuasive. If it is just persuasive (Privy Council, lower courts, other judges of the High Court perhaps, foreign judgments), the judge must weigh how much persuasive authority it has (Privy Council judgments, for instance since they are normally given by House of Lords members, are very persuasive).

A judge must then decide which parts of the earlier case actually bind him. He must distinguish the ratio decidendi of the earlier case from the obiter dicta in it (which do not bind him); and this distinction is one of the major sources of flexibility. While any student will quite happily expound on the ratio of a past case, and be prepared to inform a judge of exactly the extent to which he is bound, in fact the actual definition of a ratio decidendi is uncertain: and frequently it is difficult for a judge to identify the correct *ratio*. Is there any definition of ratio decidendi that adequately captures judicial practice?

a) *Definition of ratio decidendi*

The *traditional view of ratio* is that it is the rule of law enunciated by the judge to the extent that it is necessary for the decision of the case. Even if we do think that the judge's expressions of relevant law are the ratio, this definition is not practically very useful: the important question is, what part of the judgment is relevant? In *Donoghue* v *Stevenson* [1932] AC 562 was Lord Atkin's 'neighbour principle' relevant and necessary, or just the narrower principle relating to manufacturers' liability? Also, what if the judge does not state the law, but just decides the case before him? In any case, the statements of the judge are not always considered to be correct statements of the ratio when considered in later cases: it is not thought doctrinally incorrect to say 'the case really decided X, even if the judge said Y'.

If we reject the traditional view, we find no shortage of suggested alternatives to take its place. Wallbaugh proposes a reversal test: if the reverse of the proposition would have led to a different decision in the case, that is the ratio. However, that does not help us distinguish between the two statements of principle in *Donoghue* (since it is not clear for which of them the Wallbaugh test is true), nor between them and general statements like 'there is a tort of negligence', 'manufacturers can be liable for negligence', and so on. The reversal test can tell us what is *not* the *ratio,* but cannot help us work out what *is*.

Others will argue that one should try to find the underlying principles. At what level of generality? Also, it is acceptable to reject the underlying principle of a case like *Donoghue* (the neighbour principle, perhaps?) while considering the case to be correct on a narrower ground (the manufacturers' liability). The 'underlying principles' test is too vague. Two other tests, which we can quickly reject as being contrary to our experience of how judges work, are those of Lord Halsbury in *Quinn* v *Leatham* [1901] AC 495, that a case is only authority for the order made on those facts (this seems far too narrow to capture the 'width' given to the rationes of past cases), and of Lord Devlin, that the ratio is the reason for the decision which the judge wishes to be the source of precedent. (Is it then incorrect to say that a case is a precedent and binding in a way the judge never intended?)

A definition which has carried much persuasive weight was that of Professor Goodhart, for whom the ratio is the decision based on the facts treated as material by the judge (he was particularly concerned to move away from treatment of the ratio as the judge's statements of law). A judge views certain facts, explicitly and implicitly, as material: his decision on those facts is the binding ratio. This view is interesting, and expounded at length by Goodhart (see Lloyd and Freeman's *Introduction to Jurisprudence;* but some problems do arise. It is often difficult to tell which facts the judge implicitly takes into account, and ex post facto any interpretations thereof may well be wrong; while there is always the problem of being tied to the facts the judge found as material.

The approach of Professor Stone is illuminating. He maintains that there is not a unique ratio of a case, but rather a choice of rationes available for later judges to choose from. Stone identifies two possible rationes, the descriptive and the prescriptive. This, it is submitted, is a good explanation of the nature of the common law system. The descriptive ratio is ascertainable from the decision once given but the prescriptive ratio is how a subsequent court treats the earlier decision. In *Evans* v *Triplex Safety Glass Co Ltd* (1936) where a windscreen smashed and caused injury to the driver of the vehicle, the court – bound by *Donoghue* – held that the ratio of *Donoghue* was that a duty of care arose only when there was no possibility of interference in the product between the time it left the manufacturer and the time the loss was caused. The court held that there was such a possibility in *Evans* and so the plaintiff would not recover. The view of *Donoghue* stated in *Evans* was the prescriptive ratio of *Donoghue*. Dias goes slightly further, and suggests that the ratio should be viewed in a continuing time framework, as the interpretation of the case given by later judges. These views help us to understand a central feature of the stare decisis precedent system, that it is important to see how cases are treated in later cases to discover for what they are taken as authority: in *Donoghue*, the example we have been citing, it is clear that it is authority in 1988 for the neighbour principle.

However, the Stone, or Dias, view does not provide us with a definition which explains how the judge decides what the ratio of a previous case is: in the case of negligence immediately following *Donoghue* a judge had to decide what its ratio was. Knowing that there were several for him to pick from (Stone) and that the full import of the case would not be known until after the series of decisions (Dias) doesn't make it easier for us to understand the use of *Donoghue* made by that next case judge.

Montrose has stated that the argument is essentially one of a terminological nature. His purpose was to reassert the strength of the common law tradition. He seeks the meaning of the ratio and identifies three possibilities:

i)   the rule of law to be found in the actual opinion of the judge forming the basis of his decision – this is the meaning that Montrose preferred;

ii) the rule of law for which the case is binding authority;

iii) any reason which ultimately brings about the decision – essentially this relates to the reasons for the ratio.

Does this really take us much further?

b) *No definition of ratio decidendi*

We must in fact admit failure: no-one has yet adequately defined ratio decidendi. A judge looks for the principle of law as applied to facts that appears to him to be appropriate, and takes that as the ratio, and we can be no more precise than that. We can close our discussion of ratio by looking briefly at why it might be difficult to identify that principle in particular cases; several obvious reasons spring to mind. Judges do not always explain themselves properly; they often give several different reasons for a decision. Sometimes the actual decision may follow as an exception to a field or rule expressly considered in detail (eg *Hedley Byrne* v *Heller* [1964] AC 465, where the House of Lords laid down a new rule on negligent mis-statements but decided the case on an exception to the rule, viz the bank's disclaimer), and even sometimes the decision may not seem to follow from the reasoning. In cases with more than one judge, all saying different things, working out the ratio can be impossible. (In a case from the USA Supreme Court, *University of California Medical School* v *Bakke*, the ratio is said to be the decision of one of nine judges. This justice, Powell, agreed with four justices on one point, and the other four justices on another. The accepted ratio is thus one which eight of the nine justices would not agree with!) When you add to these uncertainties the problems of later decisions, choosing one possible ratio (as per Stone), and later courts having to decide on a series of cases in this way, the complexities of discovering ratio decidendi become apparent!

It is possible that a case will have no ascertainable ratio at all. This, according to de Smith, *Constitutional Law,* is the case with *Nissan* v *Attorney-General* (1970) concerning a claim for damages caused by British troops billeted in a Cyprus hotel where the judges in the House of Lords all gave separate reasons for their decision. The case of *Harper* v *National Coal Board* (1974) shows a further difficulty. This was a decision of the House of Lords in which by a majority the decision went one way and the reasons went the other way!

Those parts of a judgment which are not the ratio are called obiter dicta. These parts – of however high a court or respected a judge – are like the decisions of lower courts, Privy Council (PC), foreign courts, etc: merely persuasive. Some, especially House of Lords, dicta are treated as near binding – the statement of principle in *Hedley Byrne* for example, and the CA discussion of precedent rules in *Young* v *Bristol Aeroplane* [1944] KB 718. Many dicta are ignored or expressly contradicted (just as many non-binding cases are not followed).

Flexibility, so far, has entered the stare decisis doctrine via authority of court or report, via choice of what is the ratio – because it is much in doubt, of course, it almost goes without saying that later judges have flexibility in choosing what it is – and in disregarding or accepting dicta. Judges can even avoid a case that is binding on them by a device known as 'distinguishing'; ie taking it as not covering the facts of the present case. Obviously the choice of ratio is important to this process: choosing the relevant facts for the ratio at a different level of generality, or suggesting that facts in the previous case which do not appear in the present case were material to the decision. All law students can remember instances of this: and also instances of cases where earlier decisions have been treated as authority only on their own particular facts. In these ways, judges can 'distinguish' past cases, and limit their precedent effect.

The doctrine of stare decisis appears fixed and settled; in practice it is a flexible weapon in the hands of a judge. A core area of fixed law is surrounded by a fringe area in which judges, by distinguishing, approving and following past cases, steadily develop the law.

20.4 The rules of precedent

It would be appropriate for general background information to include here a summary of the rules of precedent as they apply in each of the main courts in this jurisdiction. It is not expected that this is examinable (that was more part of your English Legal System course in your intermediate year).

a) *The House of Lords*

The Practice Statement (PS) adopted by the House in 1966 changed the previous practice of the HL, laid down in *London Tramways Co* v *London County Council* [1898] AC 375. The previous rule was that the HL would not depart from its previous decisions under any circumstances; the 1966 PS stated that they would do in future if it was 'right to do so'. Their Lordships remained aware of the importance of certainty in the law (particularly in relation to contractual etc arrangements and criminal law), but strict obedience to past decisions could cause injustice and restrict development of the law.

Some surprise has been voiced that this change was made in a Practice Direction. However, rules of precedent do not form part of the ratio (nor do rules of statutory interpretation, see below) of cases, and are just judicial practice.

A more interesting question is whether the HL should have changed the rules. It seems to me that the PS was a good thing, allowing the HL to be honest in their treatment of past authorities now felt to be unsatisfactory. Rather than distinguishing, they can now overrule. Certainty is a virtue, but one that can be over-indulged in.

The PS has been directly used less than a dozen times in the last twenty-two years: *Miliangos* v *Frank* [1976] AC 443, overruling *Re United Railways of Havana and Regla Warehouses* [1961] AC 1007; and *ex parte Khera and Khawaja* [1984] AC 74, overruling *ex parte Zamir* [1980] 2 All ER 768, are two of the examples.

b) *Is the Court of Appeal bound by the House of Lords?*

Recently the CA has attempted to free itself of HL dominance in relation to HL cases it finds unacceptable. In *Cassell* v *Broome* [1972] AC 1027, the CA said that the HL decision in *Rookes* v *Barnard* [1964] AC 1129 was arrived at per incuriam (ie without citation of relevant binding authority, in this case two previous HL decisions). The decision was inspired by Lord Denning and was the subject of almost unjudicial condemnation in the House of Lords when the matter went on appeal.

In *Schorsch-Meier* v *Hennin* [1975] QB 416 the CA refused to follow the HL decision in *Havana Railways* that currency judgments must be expressed in sterling, on the basis that the reason for the rule had gone: cessante ratione legis: cessat ipsa lex (if the reason for the rule ceases, so does the law). In *Miliangos* v *Frank* the HL deplored the CA action in *Schorsch*. Strict adherence to the hierarchy was required for the precedent system to work.

The CA is bound, then, to follow the HL loyally. The problems when it does not, as in *Shorsch*, can be seen from the dilemma of the first instance judge, Bristow J, in *Miliangos*. Should he follow the HL decision, or the later (but heretical) CA? In fact he followed the HL (the CA followed itself in *Schorsch*). Opinion is divided on whether Bristow took the right side; but united on the difficulty of his position!

c) *Is the Court of Appeal bound by past decisions of itself?*

In *Young* v *Bristol Aeroplane Co Ltd* [1944] KB 718, Lord Greene MR laid down the still applicable position for the CA. It is bound by a past CA decision, unless:

i) There are two conflicting decisions – one must be overruled.

ii) Whilst not expressly overruled by, it is nonetheless inconsistent with, a subsequent HL decision.

iii) It was arrived at *per incuriam* (relevant binding authority not cited)

We should note two other exceptions: the CA is free to follow a later PC decision inconsistent with a previous CA decision: and in a criminal case, the CA is not bound if it would cause injustice in the instant case. (Remember CA (Criminal Division) cases do not bind CA (Civil Division) and vice versa.)

In recent years, the CA led by Lord Denning has shown an anxiety to throw off these shackles. Lord Denning has said that the CA is not bound by previous decisions (*Barrington* v *Lee* [1972] 1 QB 326 for instance) and that the CA could issue a PS similar to the HL's (*Gallie* v *Lee* (1971)). He did not always carry the CA with him, but he did lead a five man CA in *Davis* v *Johnson* [1979] AC 264 which purported to overrule two CA cases (*B* v *B* [1978] Fam 26 and *Cantliff* v *Jenkins* [1978] Fam 47) on the Domestic Violence and Matrimonial Proceedings Act 1976.

In *Davis* Lord Denning said the CA should either follow the direction of the HL PS, or add exceptions to *Young* where appropriate. Both come to the same thing: he was claiming that the CA could overrule its own previous rulings. The other two in the majority, Baker and Shaw LJ, drew up new exceptions to add to *Young*. The HL roundly condemned the CA, reaffirming *Young*. (They did however overrule *B* v *B* and *Cantliff*.)

Should the CA be bound by its previous decisions? Bearing in mind that the HL changed the 'no overruling ourselves' rule by a Practice Direction, and that the CA can arrange its own procedure, can issue a PS on the same lines as Lord Gardiner's in 1966?

d) *An alternative: prospective overruling*

The main argument for stare decisis is certainty. Certainty is a value in a legal system because it allows people to arrange their affairs in accordance with the law, both not breaking it (crime) and taking advantage of its facilities (contract, wills, etc). If judges departed from their decisions at will, these arrangements would be upset; further, the individual case would be in effect a retrospective law, changing the law as it was and applying the new law to the present case.

In the case of *Great Northern Railway Co* v *Sunburst Oil* (1932), a decision of the United States courts, Cardozo J stated that in order to avoid this problem the court could adopt prospective overruling. This is a method of treating the present case on the old law, but announcing the new law for future cases. This only, of course, avoids the retrospective argument; could it be so arranged (eg by applying the new law to future arrangements only?) to avoid affecting settled arrangements? Also, wouldn't it be extremely unfair to the losing litigant, who would have persuaded the judge(s) to accept his legal argument but still have lost the case?

The question that is really being asked is whether certainty and development of the law go together?

20.5 An introduction to statutory construction

a) *A subjective approach*

More perhaps than most of the chapters in this manual, the selection of topics and contents for this chapter, and the arrangement of them, is a very subjective one. A quick glance through any of the major textbooks on either Jurisprudence or English Legal System will show that each approaches this area differently, emphasising different points and using different case illustrations. Most of these textbooks would agree, though, in recommending Professor Cross's *Statutory Interpretation* (1976) to any student of the area.

b) *Interpretation*

As our law becomes increasingly statutory, with upwards of sixty public Acts of Parliament each year (as well as innumerable S.1s), the interpretation of those statutes becomes increasingly the judge's central role. There will always be a need for such interpretation and construction. Words are ambiguous, phrases and paragraphs are more so; and no legislator can cover every possible future case clearly. Since under our constitution matters of law are decided by the judges, the task of working out the meaning of the unclear statutory provision, and seeing if it applies to the (frequently unforeseen) case before them, falls to the judges.

c) *Ambiguous*

Various sorts of problems can arise. A distinction is often attempted between interpretation (deciding the meaning of the words) and construction (seeing if the words apply to a particular case): the definitions in brackets are only one variant. I will not use this distinction, but will instead bear in mind that, apart from those cases where the meaning is obvious and straightforward (enabling both the judge and the layman organising his affairs to see what the statute means immediately), there are cases where a particular word or phrase is ambiguous, cases where it is unclear whether a particular fact-situation was meant to be included, cases where the particular punishment intended is not clear, cases where the legislature appears to have left out an obvious case, and cases where the result on the straightforward meaning of the words is absurd.

d) *Intention*

Note how often I have used the word 'meant'. Judges often say that they seek 'the intention of Parliament': the 'great debate' between the literal meaning and the mischief-purpose approach is said to hinge on whether Parliament's intention is to be gleaned merely from its exact words ('he meant what he said') or also from a consideration of why the statute was passed (its purpose) and what Parliament would have done if it had had the particular case in mind. Any search for 'intention', purpose, etc, is to an extent a fiction. A body like Parliament is made up of many people, who may not vote at all on a measure, or may vote for the measure for tactical reasons without considering its consequences, or may vote for it for tactical reasons apart from the actual content. Often votes are on general principles, and yet the matters that come before the courts will be detailed and perhaps highly technical.

To that extent, then, one cannot say that Parliament 'intended'. However, the judges are looking at Parliament's words and must (under the Parliamentary supremacy doctrine) follow and attempt to apply those words. While guidance may not be available on a particular matter, it is clearly the case that, on general principles at least, it does not seem so absurd to search for a Parliamentary 'intention'. Surely the Sex Discrimination Act was *intended* to remedy some aspects of discrimination against women, the Unfair Contract Terms Act was *intended* to control exemption clauses and the Supplementary Benefits Acts are *intended* to set up a scheme providing those with no income with a state safety-net? And more specific provisions can be seen to be *intended* – a provision repealing an earlier provision or overturning an earlier case; a provision following a Law Commission recommendation where no-one in Parliament argued with the Commission's reasons. Whether it be intention of the draftsman, or intention of the proposer, or intention of the majority, there is some sense in the concept 'Parliament's intention'.

Having said that, again I emphasise that most often in difficult cases Parliament's intention is not clear. On a disputed provision, did Parliament intend to protect from that specific type of exemption clause? It is precisely because the words do not make clear what the intention is that the problem arises in that case, and in general – if the words are not clear, how are the courts to decide what 'Parliament's intention' was? To put it another way, what do the words as enacted by Parliament legally mean?

e) *Statutory interpretation*

The final introductory part concerns the status of decisions on the question of statutory interpretation. Assume that the House of Lords has to deal with statutory provision X1; the plaintiff claims it means X2 and the defendant X3. The House uses the literal method, and finds for the plaintiff. What is binding on lower courts? Clearly, it would seen, not the literal approach; the rules of statutory construction do not appear to be part of the ratio of any case; surely it is only the decision that, in this statute, X1 = X2. If the same words occur in a different statute, the different context and purpose might justify a different result; but on the same statute, lower courts would be bound to follow the House of Lords.

20.6 Canons and presumptions

Apart from the major rules considered herein, in cases where statutory words are obscure or unclear judges may use one or other of the following canons of construction and presumptions.

a) *Canons*

   i) *The statute must be read as a whole*

   The words of the particular sub-section in question must not be read in isolation, but must be read with the other sections (particularly any interpretation section) and with the schedules. As we shall see below, this canon is now subsumed by Professor Cross's reformulation of the major rules, where he emphasises that the context of the words is in account.

   ii) *Eiusdem generis*

   If a general word follows two or more specific words, the general word must be restricted in meaning to a meaning of the same kind (eiusdem generis). For example, *Powell* v *Kempton*

Park Racecourse Co [1899] AC 143 turned on whether in relation to places of betting the words 'house, office, room or other place' included the racecourse itself: no, said the House of Lords, since the general words 'other place' were restricted to a meaning of the same kind as the specific words, ie an indoor place of betting.

iii) *Narrow construction of penal provisions*

The individual gets the benefit of any doubt if a criminal or tax liability is imposed by statute, in particular against the imposition of liability without fault.

iv) *1978 Interpretation Act*

This Act gives presumptive interpretations to common words and phrases in statutes: so 'men' includes 'women' (and vice versa), singular includes the plural, distances are to be measured in a straight line on the horizontal plain, time refers to Greenwich Mean Time and so on: all subject to contrary intention (which must sometimes be expressly stated, but most often must just 'appear').

b) *Presumptions*

i) *Against alteration of the law*

This presumption does not work against a change in the general (common) law which appears clearly from the literal meaning of the words; but if there is a doubt, Parliament will be presumed to have left the law unaltered.

ii) *Against imposition of without-fault liability*

Mentioned above; to create a strict liability offence, Parliament must use clear words.

iii) *Against ousting the jurisdiction of the courts*

The courts are very protective of their own jurisdiction; although Parliament may alter the courts' jurisdiction even fundamentally, it must do so clearly. In administrative law, for example, in several cases the courts have evaded statutory attempts to forestall judicial review (*Anisminic v FCC* [1969] 2 AC 47, *Padfield v Minister of Agriculture* [1968] AC 997, *Pyx Granite Ltd v MHLG* [1960] AC 260).

iv) *Against the Crown being bound by a statute*

The Crown must be expressly named, or it is not bound by a statute.

c) *Against depriving a person of a vested right*

The above are just examples. It may be quite possible to find canons and presumptions to support quite conflicting contentions.

20.7   The three rules of statutory construction

It is often said that there are three rules of statutory interpretation, these being the literal, golden and mischief rules. As we shall seem they are to an extent contradictory; all can claim judicial support.

a) *Mischief rule*

This rule was prevalent in the sixteenth century. The courts have regard to the purpose of the Act, and interpret it in such a way that the purpose is fulfilled or enhanced. The classic statement of the rule is contained in *Heydon's Case* where the barons laid down four things to be considered when interpreting statutes: the common law before the Act, the mischief that the law did not provide for, the remedy appointed for that mischief, and the true reason of the remedy. Of course, not all statutes are altering the common law today, and the exact formulation therefore needs changing. The approach, while not now as prevalent as it was, still commands judicial support, and has authorities following it in many areas (see the examples given in Dias's *Jurisprudence*). A recent example can be taken form the law against racial discrimination. Although there is a requirement in the mischief rule that the express words of the statute must reasonably bear the purposive meaning given to them, in *Mandla* v *Dowell Lee* (1983) the House of Lords interpreted the Race Relations Act where it is stated that it is an offence to discriminate in certain matters against a person 'on grounds of his race, colour, ethnic or national origin' in quite a different manner. The facts of the case were that a young Sikh male wanted to join a public (fee paying) school. He was granted admission but was required to conform to uniform regulations and remove his turban and cut his hair. For reasons of faith he was unwilling to do this. There were other Sikhs in the school who had conformed to the uniform requirement and there was no suggestion that Dowell Lee (the headmaster) had any inclination to discriminate against Sikhs. The Court of Appeal carefully considered the history of the Sikh people and concluded that they were a group identifiable only by their common religion and that as the statute makes no mention of religion then the actions of the school were reasonable and not illegally discriminatory. The House of Lords, relying on a New Zealand case concerning the position of the Jews (*King Ansell* v *The Police* (1974)), held that the purpose of the section was to cover situations such as the present and that by a stretch the Sikhs could be regarded as a group identifiable by a common ethnic origin. The reason for so holding was to extend the protection afforded by the Act to Sikh people.

Had the court been minded to find otherwise then it might have followed the case of *RRB* v *London Borough of Ealing* (1972) which held to the literal approach (see below) in holding that discrimination against a Polish citizen in the granting of public housing was lawful because it was not on grounds of his national origin but on grounds of his citizenship or nationality. Perhaps this comparison between these two cases reinforces the view that in their choice of which rule of statutory construction to apply the judges in effect determine the outcome of the case. Bishop Hoadley put it thus centuries ago '... Whoever hath an absolute authority to interpret any written or spoken laws, it is he who is truly the lawgiver to all intents and purposes, and not the person who wrote or spoke them ...'. Lord Devlin perhaps has it better and in more modern language when in his *Samples of Lawmaking* he states that '... the law is what the judges say it is ...'.

The mischief or purposive rule is the one favoured by Fuller as elaborated upon in his *Case of the Speluncean Explorers* which I discussed in the first chapter of this book. Perhaps the reader would return to that article at the end of our course and extract more from it. Before you do that let us now examine the other rules:

b) *Literal rule*

Various factors, including the declining influence of the judges on legislation and the development of Parliamentary supremacy, led to a retreat from the mischief type approach to the literal approach. Here, the intention of Parliament is considered as contained in the words passed: the literal meaning of those words must be taken, even if the result appears to be one which Parliament did not intend. Lord Esher in *R* v *City of London Court Judge* (1892) stated that '... the court has nothing to do with the question whether the legislature has committed an absurdity ...'. This follows on the constitutional provision that it is the role of the legislature to make law and the role of the judiciary to interpret the law the legislature so makes.

Many cases support this 'rule' of applying the clear and unambiguous words of Parliament. For example, in *Inland Revenue* v *Hinchy* (1960) the House of Lords was construing a provision which visited upon people incorrectly completing tax returns a penalty of 'treble the tax that ought to be charged under this Act'. Presumably Parliament intended the punishment to be three times the excess owed: but those words meant three times the whole tax bill for the year, which cost poor Mr Hinchy £418 instead of £42!

Note at this stage two things. First, often words are not clear and unambiguous; two equally 'usual' meanings of a word might exist, or the application of words to particular cases might be in doubt, and so on. Second, it is not unknown for judges to consider the 'literal meaning' of the words and end up with different results (eg *Liversidge* v *Anderson* [1942] AC 206).

c) *Golden rule*

Judges have often mitigated the strict literal approach by calling into play the 'golden rule', that is that if the usual interpretation results in consequences so absurd that Parliament could not possibly have intended them, any secondary meaning may be taken. In the case of *R* v *Allen* (1872) which concerned the definition given to the offence of bigamy in the Offences Against the Person Act 1861 as '... whoever being married, marries another ...' where it was observed that such a definition if applied literally would lead to the absurd conclusion that the offence could never be committed. A person cannot legally marry if they are already married. There the court held that, as Parliament could not have intended to legislate nonsense, the words should be changed to read 'whoever being married goes through a marriage ceremony with the intention to marry etc ...'. Then the offence has meaning which would probably be consistent with the intention of the legislature.

Obviously, the three rules above cannot really be taken as strict 'rules': they contradict each other (taking the literal meaning often obscures the purpose of the statute, it might be said). At most they are approaches, with the judges choosing the most appropriate in the circumstances, generally plumping for the literal rule and taking the obvious plain meaning unless some good reason to the contrary appears.

Even this does not seem to be a good explanation of what happens if we accept that the judges generally follow the approach of looking at the literal meaning. What of those cases where two meanings are equally 'usual' and neither of the other two approaches is relevant or helpful? What of technical words?

A rather more successful attempt at formulating the courts' approach (and remember, when judges often don't advert to what they are doing and why, any such attempt can only cover some of the available case evidence) has been made by Professor Cross in *Statutory Interpretation*. He suggests that the literal and mischief rules have been mixed, and the vital element of context added: the judges look to see what the ordinary (or, if appropriate, technical) meaning of the words used is in the general context (including the objects) of the statute. It is that ordinary meaning that may be displaced by a secondary meaning if the result would otherwise be absurd: and furthermore, in cases where what seem like simple mistakes make a statute unintelligible, absurd or totally unworkable, a judge may add or delete words, to change nonsense into sense (Cross cites *Adler* v *George* [1964] 2 QB 7 and Lord Denning in *Eddis* v *Chief Constable* [1969] 2 Ch 345).

The whole problem, I think, stems from the Blackstonian fiction that statutes are intended to govern all eventualities in detail and do not merely lay down guidelines. Taken with the imprecision of words – a problem Hart has dwelt upon when he referred to the core of settled meanings and the penumbral area of doubt that surrounds words – the problem of statutory construction is manifest. This is clearly stated by Lord MacDermott thus '... the difficulty of finding unequivocal language by which to convey the will of Parliament ... [lies at the heart of the problem of statutory construction] ...'.

The Swiss, I think, have a more realistic approach. Their Civil Code in Article 1 states that a judge may decide a case on the basis of a rule which he would lay down if he had himself to act as legislator. The only limitation in this regard is contained in Article 4, to the effect that in exercising his discretion the judge must base his decision on principles of justice and equity. Lloyd and Freeman observe that although this article was initially widely used it is now subject to restrictive interpretation itself. Does this tell us something about the nature of the judicial creature?

d) *Hypothetical examples*

Much of what judges do is obvious, even when they construe difficult or ambiguous sentences or phrases: although we must consider the pros and cons of judges following a 'purposive' as against the traditional 'literal' approach, we must also emphasise that in fact it is in comparatively few cases that a straightforward 'literal v purposive' clash occurs.

The following fact situations might help to make the point.

i) A particular word or phrase has a straightforward obvious 'usual' meaning, for example 'driving a motor-car at over 70 mph is an offence'. A driver knows that once the speedometer tops 70 he is committing an offence, the judge when he is deciding applies the obvious meaning of motor-car, driving and 70 mph and convicts.

This is straightforward literal approach: in relation to this case, the words have only one meaning.

ii) A particular word or phrase has several meanings: eg the verb 'wants' ('wishes' or 'lacks'?) the noun 'will', ('volition' or the document by which a deceased person leaves his property?).

The context of the phrase in the statute makes it clear which sense is meant: eg a reference to providing what a lunatic 'wants' will refer to what he lacks; a reference to 'the will of the testator' in a statute on probate will generally mean the document (but could in context mean the volition, as 'the will of the testator was overborne by force').

The judge applies that obvious meaning. Not quite the literal approach, since there were two 'usual' meanings (and in the case of 'wants', the one chosen was, if anything, the less obvious or usual of the two). But can this really be called a purposive approach? We are looking at the in-context meaning, and purpose is relevant only as part of the context.

iii) As situation (i), except that this meaning either produces an absurd result, eg (ignoring the Interpretation Act) 'it is an offence to steal horses', and the defendant steals just one (so not guilty under literal meaning) or produces a result clearly against the intention of the Act, eg if the Race Relations Act defined 'racial group' in a technical way which excluded negroes.

As to the absurd result, holding that the statute meant something else, this clearly involves the judge in rectification, which Cross allows as his third rule; not the golden rule, as there is only one meaning the words can bear (and therefore no secondary one to fall back on).

As to the result clearly against the intention of the Act, any suggestion that the judge acts in accordance with that intention and not the words of the Act does lead to a purpose v intention conflict. Note, however, that in general the courts have not invoked the mischief rule in this sort of case: an attempt by Lord Denning to fill in the gap left in a statute in the case of *Asher* v *Seaford Court Estates* (1949) was slapped down by the House of Lords, Viscount Simmonds rejecting this 'naked usurpation' of the legislative role (*Magor & St Mellons RDC v Newport Corporation* [1951] 2 All ER 839). If the result is not absurd, the courts will follow the wording of a statute if it only allows of one construction, even if that construction does not follow the general purpose of the statute.

iv) As situation (ii), except that one meaning is clearly the more usual, but that result leads to either absurd consequences or is totally against the intention of the statute. An example of absurd consequences could be the facts of the tax case *Inland Revenue* v *Hinchy*: an example of being against the intention of the statute can be seen from the USA controversy of whether reverse or positive discrimination is against the constitutional provision; forbidding laws which deny 'equal protection of the laws': does that mean any discrimination is unlawful or could 'equal protection' be taken to include the effect of reverse discrimination in redressing the balance and hence making more equal?

If the judge takes a secondary meaning to avoid absurdity, that is the golden rule in operation; if he takes it to accord with the intention of the statute; that could be taken as using the context of the statute, if not (and in our example, the context doesn't help: the question is, how far did the constitution go?) he is using purpose to displace the literal rule.

v) As situation (ii), except the context does not assist, the purpose of the statute does not assist, and the consequences would not be (more) absurd either way. The judge uses his discretion – but none of our stated approaches/rules!

e) *Literal words v purpose*

In (iii) and (iv), then, there are possibilities for a clash between words and purpose: should the judge follow the obvious or only meaning of a phrase or sentence if that goes against the purpose of the statute?

Briefly, the arguments for the Literal approach:

i) Certainty.

ii) Avoids judicial legislation.

iii) Deference shown to Parliament.

iv) Often difficult to know 'purpose'; even if overall purpose, did Parliament intend this provision to follow the purpose or to be the limit of its extension?

v) Encourages more careful drafting.

And for the Purposive approach:

i) Often not possible to work out which is literal meaning.

ii) Not really deference to Parliament, refusing to fulfil its purpose.

iii) Judicial legislation is common, eg in common law.

Which of these sets of arguments convince you? Are there any other points to be made?

20.8 Aids to construction

Where a statute's construction is ambiguous or uncertain, various aids may be used by the judge to help him come to his decision (to minimise tedium, case references are omitted)! ...

a) *The rest of the statute*

A statute must be read as a whole, as we have said above; the judge must therefore decide in the light of the rest of the enactment (including the long title). In cases of uncertainty, those parts of the statute which are not part of it (preamble, marginal notes, punctuation) may be called in aid.

b) *Other statute in pari materia*

If construction is uncertain, a statute of the same subject may be called in aid, if it is unambiguous.

c) *International treaties*

If an Act is stated to be intended to give effect to an international treaty, uncertainties may be decided by reference to the treaty.

d) *Reports of committees*

When a committee is responsible for a Bill its report is admissible as evidence of the state of the law prior to the Act, and therefore the mischief to be remedied (eg Law Reform Committee, Law Commission).

Just as important, the judge cannot look at anything else. He cannot take the reports of committees as evidence of what meaning was intended in a draft Bill; he cannot use an explanatory memorandum attached to the Bill; and he cannot look at the reports in Hansard of Parliamentary debates.

Are these exclusions justified? The exclusion of these matters, particularly of debates in Parliament, follows from the use of the literal approach: we are looking for Parliament's intentions as expressed in the words of the statute, the argument runs, and if the words do not express the intention, extrinsic evidence can't persuade us to put it there. Further, using evidence from debates might lead to much longer submissions and much work for the lawyers (and expense for the litigants) wading through Hansard to find supporting passages, and unscrupulous MPs could say things in debate with a view to possible citation in favour of one side in a later case.

These latter arguments can be overestimated: it is submitted that the courts, by reading debates on a particular section (and the reports, perhaps, which led to the Bill), could quickly realise what the section was meant to achieve and mean, or that the legislative material was not conclusive on the point. (Surely we trust our judges to deal with legislative material appropriately?) Frequently, as our hypothetical examples show, many cases turn on the context of the words: surely, the initiating report and the Parliamentary debates will often be important in fully understanding this?

A joint report of the English and Scottish Law Commissions has suggested various reforms in this area (see Lloyd and Freeman's *Introduction to Jurisprudence* pp1154-6). Of interest here is that they agree with the present position on legislative debates, but recommend that relevant reports on which the legislation is based should be admissible. They even tentatively suggest the use of material prepared to go with the statute to explain it; in terms of a possible future code they recommend that an explanatory statement and illustrative commentary on it could be authoritative. Also they urge the courts to accept constructions promoting the general underlying legislative purpose.

A later committee, the Renton Committee on the Preparation of Legislation 1975, follows this last recommendation, and the one proposing reference to any mentioned international treaty or agreement; but they demur from the recommendation about relevant committee reports.

20.9 Effect on the draftsmen

Past and present practice of the courts on statutory interpretation clearly affect how draftsmen work on future legislation. An example from the nineteenth century Wills Act, cited by Cross *(Statutory Interpretation*, p12) shows how ridiculous were the lengths to which draftsmen then were driven to avoid the rigours of the full-blown literal approach. The courts are not quite as exacting any more, and do take at least the context into account with the words, but the enduring pre-eminence of the literal approach and the eagle-eyes of eager lawyers intent on taking every possible point for their clients do still affect the form and structure of present legislation.

a) *Procedure*

Generally, the procedure for drafting is a careful one, especially if the statute is 'lawyer's law', rather than dictated by party policy. For example, the Law Commission will issue a working paper, followed by a report with draft Bill, or the government will issue draft proposals (in Green or White Paper form) for consultation. As much time as possible is given to allow lawyers and others to look for, inter alia, drafting mistakes.

b) *Detail*

Often statutes go into great detail, to avoid unwanted interstitial interpretation: eg Employment Act 1980, sections defining the outlawed secondary action and secondary picketing.

c) *Examples*

Many statutes give examples of the instances intended to be covered as the factors to be taken into account: eg 1973 Matrimonial Causes Act, ss23-25, detailing the factors to be taken into account by a judge in deciding the financial provision on divorce as examples (because 'all the circumstances' are in account).

d) *Discretion*

When judges are intended to have discretion on a particular matter to decide in accordance with the statute's purposes, this is sometimes expressly stated in terms. Section 23 Matrimonial Causes Act is again a good example; the judge must do 'what is just and equitable in all the circumstances' in an attempt to put the parties in the position they would have been in if the marriage had not broken down.

e) *Interpretation*

Many statutes contain their own interpretation sections.

(A more direct effect of cases in legislation, obviously, is a statute to change the decision in a case, or react to judicial criticism of the law stated therein.)

And that was jurisprudence ...

BIBLIOGRAPHICAL INDEX

Stone, J (Sociology of Law) 5.1, 7.13c, 8.3c, 8.5, 17.4e, 20.3a
– *Human Law and Human Justice* (1965)
– 'Mystery and Mystique in the Basic Norm' MLR Jan 63 Vol 26
– *Law and the Social Sciences* (1966)
Stuchka (Soviet Jurist) **13.10**
– *Essays in Legal Philosophy* (1968)
    (See also Summers; *More Essays in Legal Philosophy* (1972)]

Taylor, Walton & Young (Marxist) **14.4b**, 14.5
– *The New Criminology*
Twining, W (General) 1.4, 9.3
– *Karl Llewellyn and the Realist Movement*

Von Savigny, F (Historical Jurisprudence) 8.3e, 11.1, **11.4**, **11.5**, 12.4, **15.18a**
– *Vom Beruf unserer Zut für Gezetzgebung und Rechtswissenshaft* (1814)

Weber, M (Sociological Jurisprudence) 8.2f, 8.3, **8.3e**, **8.3f**, **8.3g**
– 'Economy and Society' in ed Max Weber on Law in Economy and Society (1954)
Wilson, A (Pure Theory) 7.13a, **17.13c**
– 'The Imperative Fallacy in Kelsen's Theory' MLR Vol 44 Max 1981
– 'Material and Formal Authorisation in Kelsen's Pure Theory' CLJ 39(1) April 1980
Williams, G (Language and Law) 15.12, 16.1
– 'Language and the Law' (1945) 61 LQR 71
Wittgenstein, L (Linguistic Philosophy) 1.3a, 6.2, 7.13c, 16.3c, 16.4a
– *Philosophy Investigations* (1953)
Woozley, A (Psychology of Sanctions) **7.13b**
– (1968) 77 Mind

HLT PUBLICATIONS

All HLT Publications have two important qualities. First, they are written by specialists, all of whom have direct practical experience of teaching the syllabus. Second, all Textbooks are reviewed and updated each year to reflect new developments and changing trends. They are used widely by students at polytechnics and colleges throughout the United Kingdom and overseas.

A comprehensive range of titles is covered by the following classifications.

- **TEXTBOOKS**
- **CASEBOOKS**
- **SUGGESTED SOLUTIONS**
- **REVISION WORKBOOKS**

The books listed overleaf should be available from your local bookshop. In case of difficulty, however, they can be obtained direct from the publisher using this order form. Telephone, Fax or Telex orders will also be accepted. Quote your Access, Visa or American Express card numbers for priority orders. To order direct from publisher please enter cost of titles you require, fill in despatch details and send it with your remittance to The HLT Group Ltd. **Please complete the order form overleaf.**

DETAILS FOR DESPATCH OF PUBLICATIONS

Please insert your full name below

Please insert below the style in which you would like the correspondence from the Publisher addressed to you
TITLE Mr, Miss etc.   INITIALS   SURNAME/FAMILY NAME

Address to which study material is to be sent (please ensure someone will be present to accept delivery of your Publications).

POSTAGE & PACKING

You are welcome to purchase study material from the Publisher at 200 Greyhound Road, London W14 9RY, during normal working hours.

If you wish to order by post this may be done direct from the Publisher. Postal charges are as follows:

UK — Orders over £30: no charge. Orders below £30: £2.50. Single paper (last exam only): 50p
OVERSEAS — See table below

The Publisher cannot accept responsibility in respect of postal delays or losses in the postal systems.
DESPATCH All cheques must be cleared before material is despatched.

SUMMARY OF ORDER

Date of order:

Add postage and packing:

Cost of publications ordered:
UNITED KINGDOM:

OVERSEAS:	TEXTS		Suggested Solutions (Last exam only)	
	One	Each Extra		
Eire	£4.00	£0.60	£1.00	
European Community	£9.00	£1.00	£1.00	
East Europe & North America	£10.50	£1.00	£1.00	
South East Asia	£12.00	£2.00	£1.50	
Australia/New Zealand	£13.50	£4.00	£1.50	
Other Countries (Africa, India etc)	£13.00	£3.00	£1.50	
			Total cost of order: £	

Please ensure that you enclose a cheque or draft payable to
THE HLT GROUP LTD for the above amount, or charge to ☐ Access ☐ Visa ☐ American Express

Card Number

Expiry Date..   Signature ....

ORDER FORM

LLB PUBLICATIONS	TEXTBOOKS Cost £	£	CASEBOOKS Cost £	£	REVISION WORKBOOKS Cost £	£	SUG. SOL. 1985/90 Cost £	£	SUG. SOL. 1991 Cost £	£
Administrative Law	17.95		18.95				9.95		3.00	
Commercial Law Vol I	18.95		18.95				9.95		3.00	
Commercial Law Vol II	17.95		18.95		9.95					
Company Law	18.95		18.95		9.95		9.95		3.00	
Conflict of Laws	16.95		17.95							
Constitutional Law	14.95		16.95		9.95		9.95		3.00	
Contract Law	14.95		16.95		9.95		9.95		3.00	
Conveyancing	17.95		16.95							
Criminal Law	14.95		17.95		9.95		9.95		3.00	
Criminology	16.95						+3.00		3.00	
English Legal System	14.95		12.95				*7.95		3.00	
Equity and Trusts	14.95		16.95		9.95		9.95		3.00	
European Community Law	17.95		18.95		9.95		+3.00		3.00	
Evidence	17.95		17.95		9.95		9.95		3.00	
Family Law	17.95		18.95		9.95		9.95		3.00	
Jurisprudence	14.95				9.95		9.95		3.00	
Labour Law	15.95									
Land Law	14.95		16.95		9.95		9.95		3.00	
Public International Law	18.95		17.95		9.95		9.95		3.00	
Revenue Law	17.95		18.95		9.95		9.95		3.00	
Roman Law	14.95									
Succession	17.95		17.95		9.95		9.95		3.00	
Tort	14.95		16.95		9.95		9.95		3.00	

BAR PUBLICATIONS	TEXTBOOKS Cost £	£	CASEBOOKS Cost £	£	REVISION WORKBOOKS Cost £	£	SUG. SOL. 1985/90 Cost £	£	SUG. SOL. 1991 Cost £	£
Conflict of Laws	16.95		17.95				†7.95		3.95	
European Community Law & Human Rights	17.95		18.95				†7.95		3.95	
Evidence	17.95		17.95				14.95		3.95	
Family Law	17.95		18.95				14.95		3.95	
General Paper I	19.95		16.95				14.95		3.95	
General Paper II	19.95		16.95				14.95		3.95	
Law of International Trade	17.95		16.95				14.95		3.95	
Practical Conveyancing	17.95		16.95				14.95		3.95	
Procedure	19.95		16.95				14.95		3.95	
Revenue Law	17.95		18.95				14.95		3.95	
Sale of Goods and Credit	17.95		17.95				14.95		3.95	

LAW SOCIETY FINALS	TEXTBOOKS	REVISION WORKBOOKS	SUGGESTED SOLUTIONS PACKS (4-5 years of papers)	ALL PAPERS PACKS
Accounts	14.95	9.95	14.95	
Business Organisations & Insolvency	14.95		14.95	
Consumer Protection & Employment Law	14.95		14.95	
Conveyancing I & II	14.95		14.95	
Family Law	14.95		14.95	
Litigation	14.95		14.95	
Wills, Probate & Administration	14.95	9.95	14.95	
Final Exam Papers (Set) (All Papers) Summer 1989				9.95
Final Exam Papers (Set) (All Papers) Winter 1990				9.95
Final Exam Papers (Set) (All Papers) Summer 1990				9.95
Final Exam Papers (Set) (All Papers) Winter 1991				9.95

CPE PUBLICATIONS	TEXTBOOKS
Criminal Law	14.95
Constitutional & Administrative Law	14.95
Contract Law	14.95
Equity and Trusts	14.95
Land Law	14.95
Tort	14.95

INSTITUTE OF LEGAL EXECUTIVES	TEXTBOOKS
Company & Partnership Law	18.95
Constitutional Law	14.95
Contract Law	14.95
Criminal Law	14.95
Equity and Trusts	14.95
European Law & Practice	17.95
Evidence	17.95
Land Law	14.95
Revenue Law	17.95
Tort	14.95

* 1987–1990 papers only
† 1988–1990 papers only
+ 1990 paper only